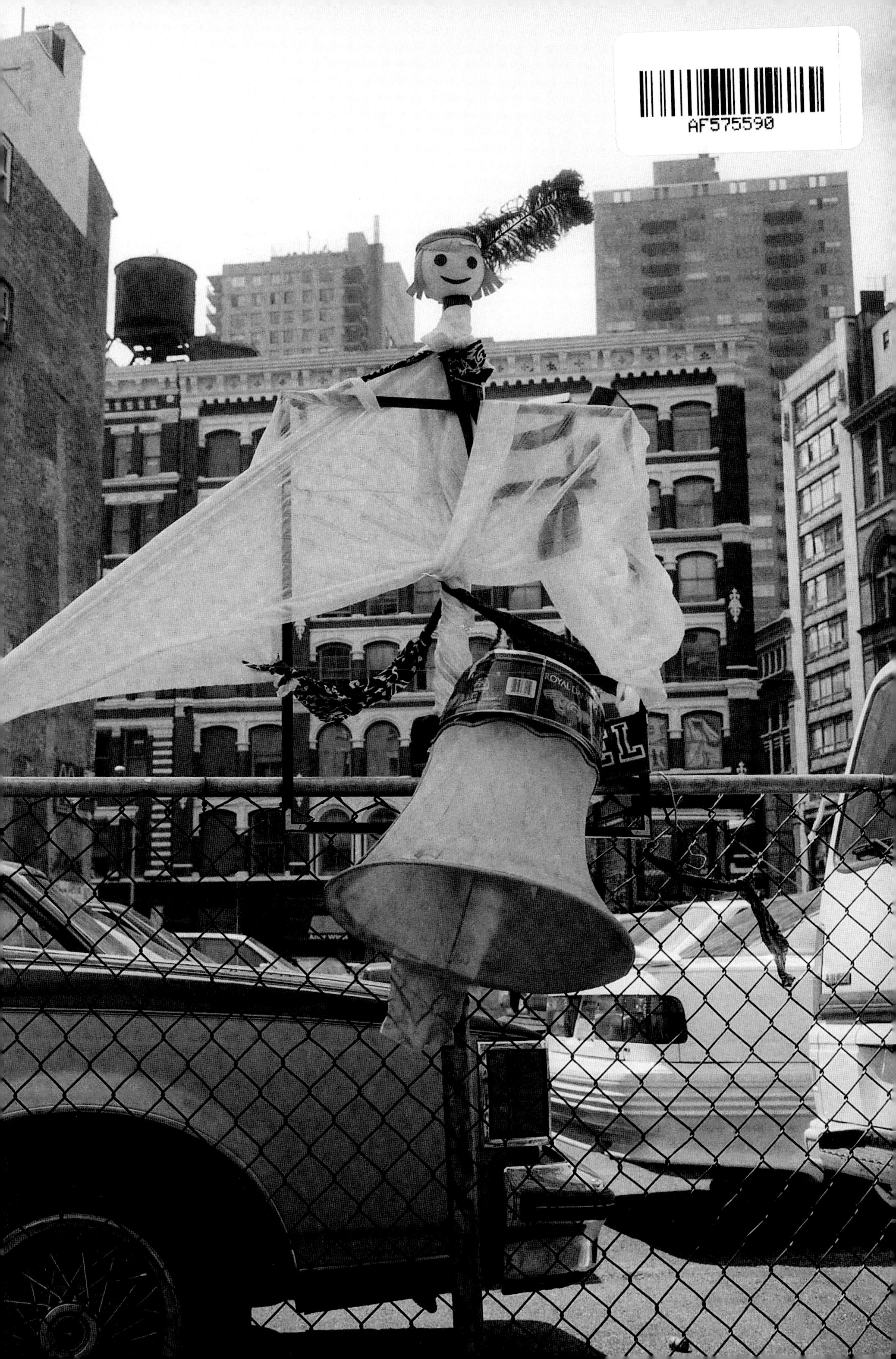

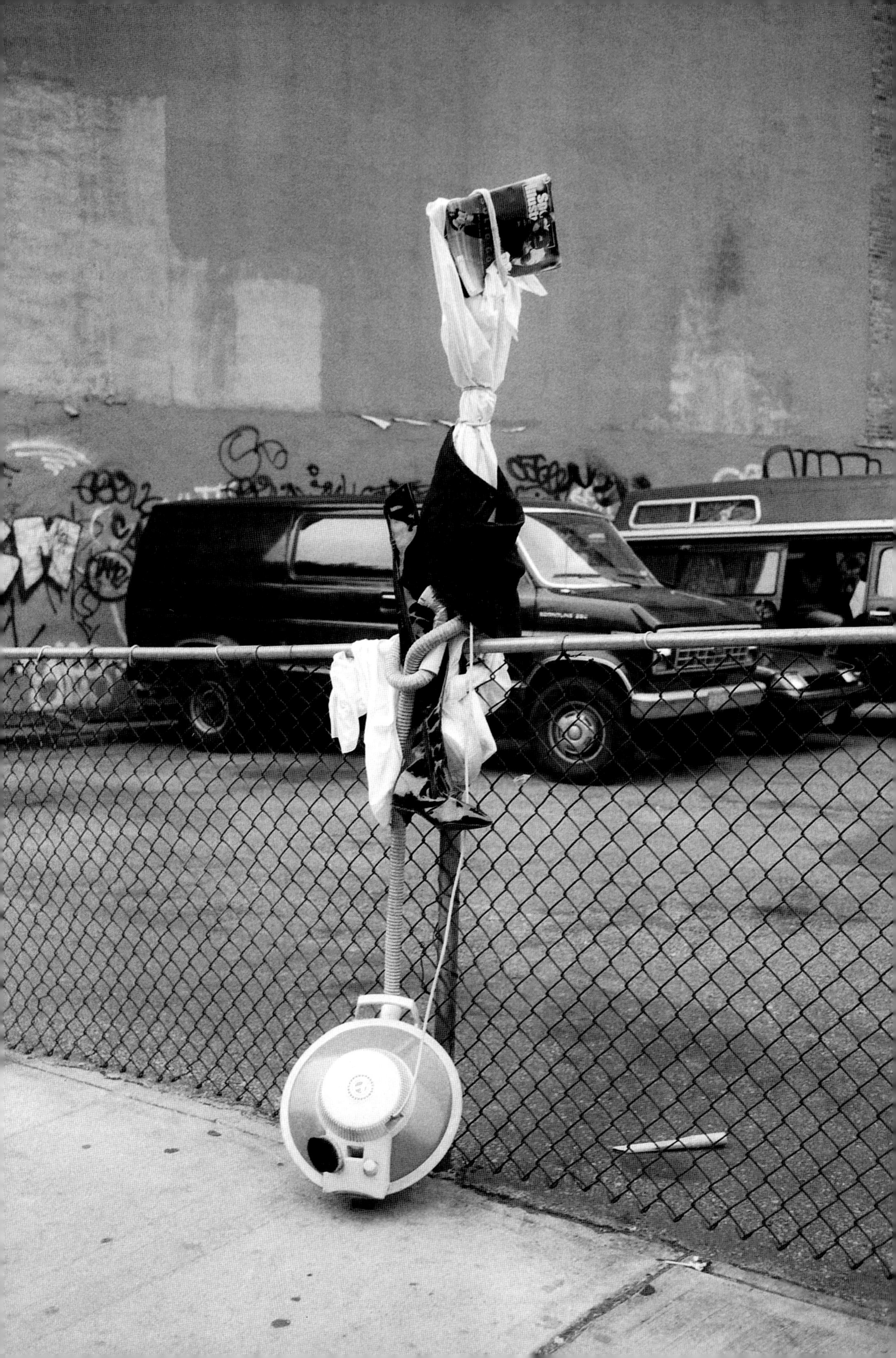

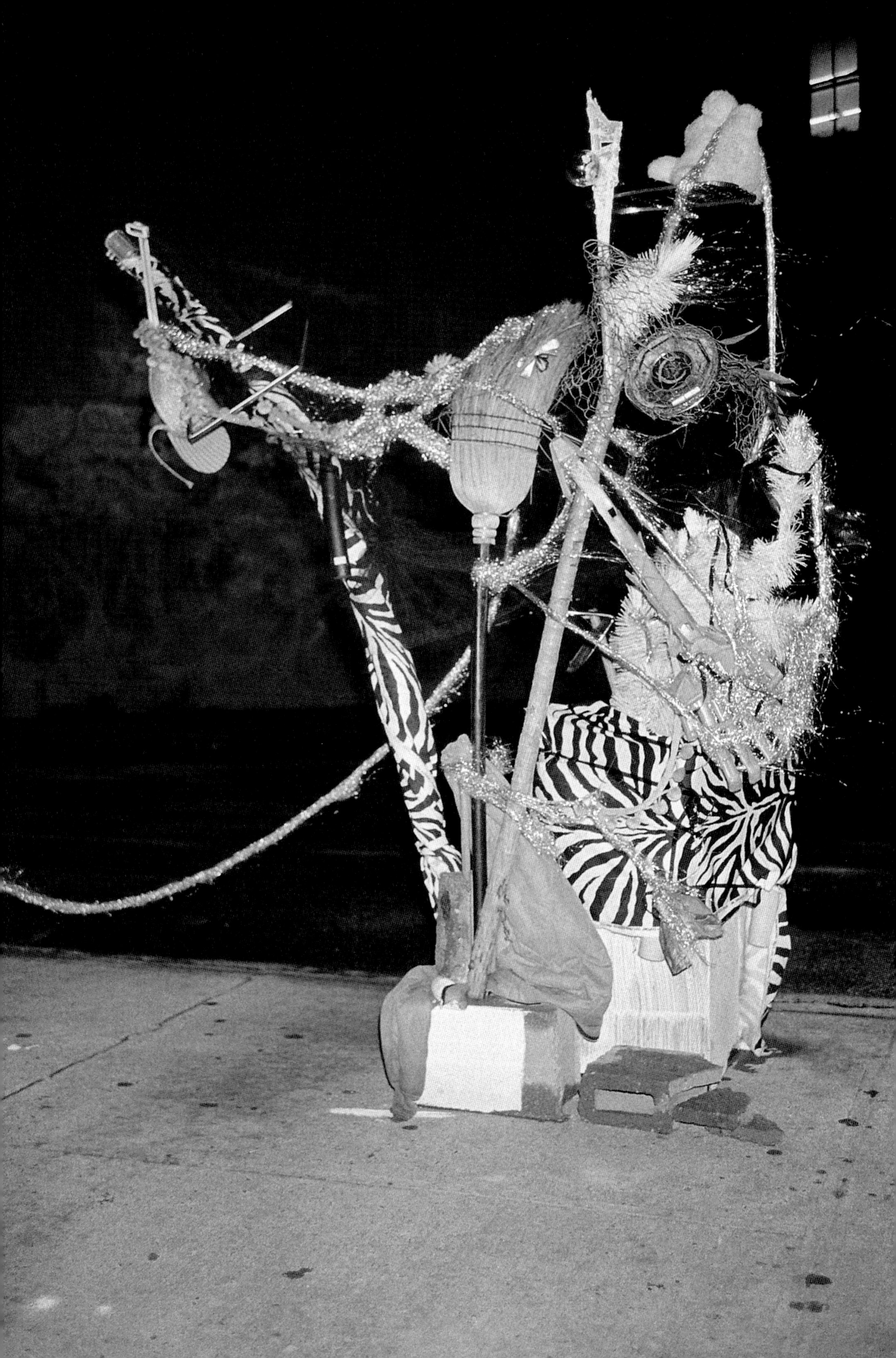

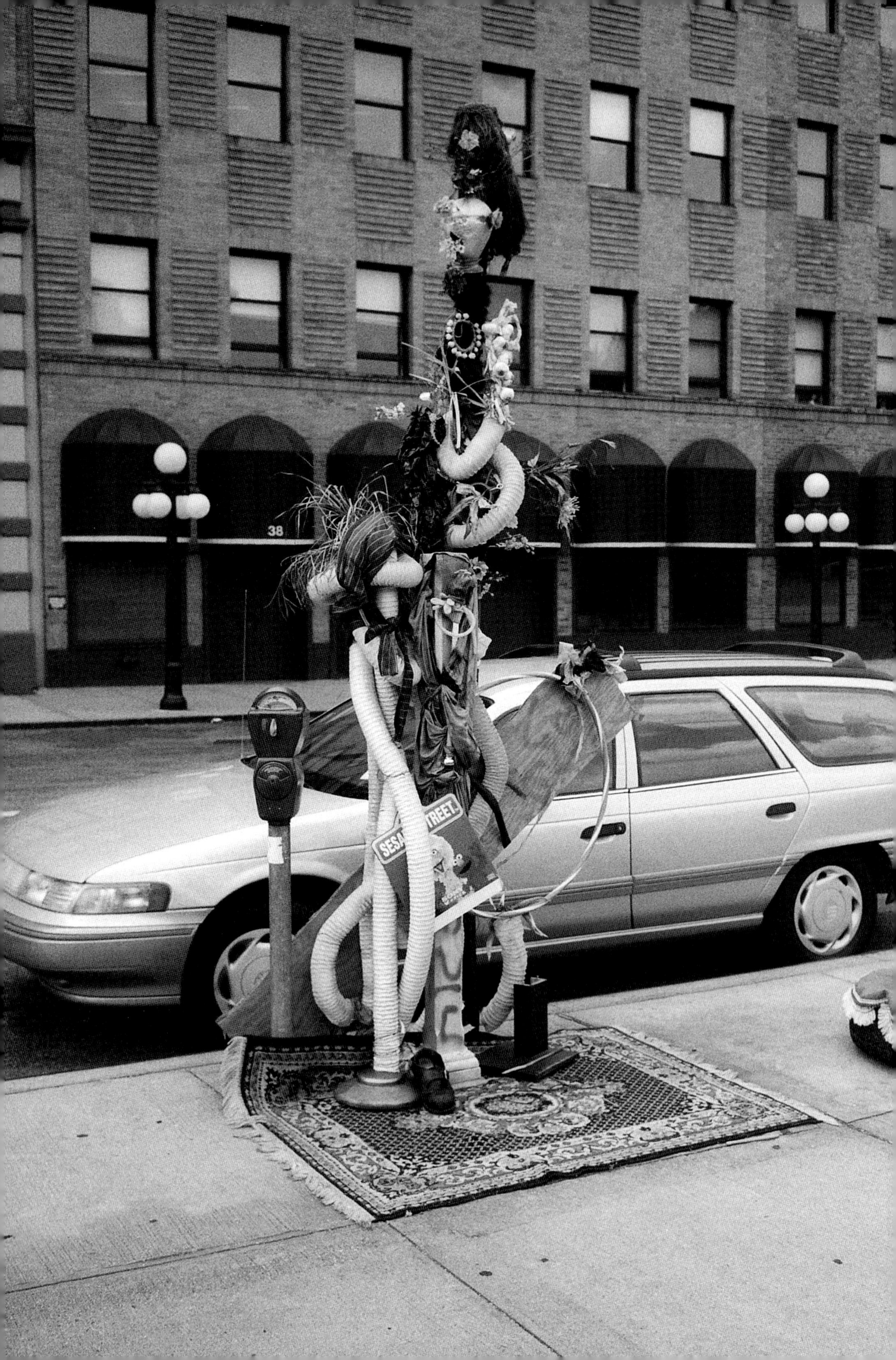
38

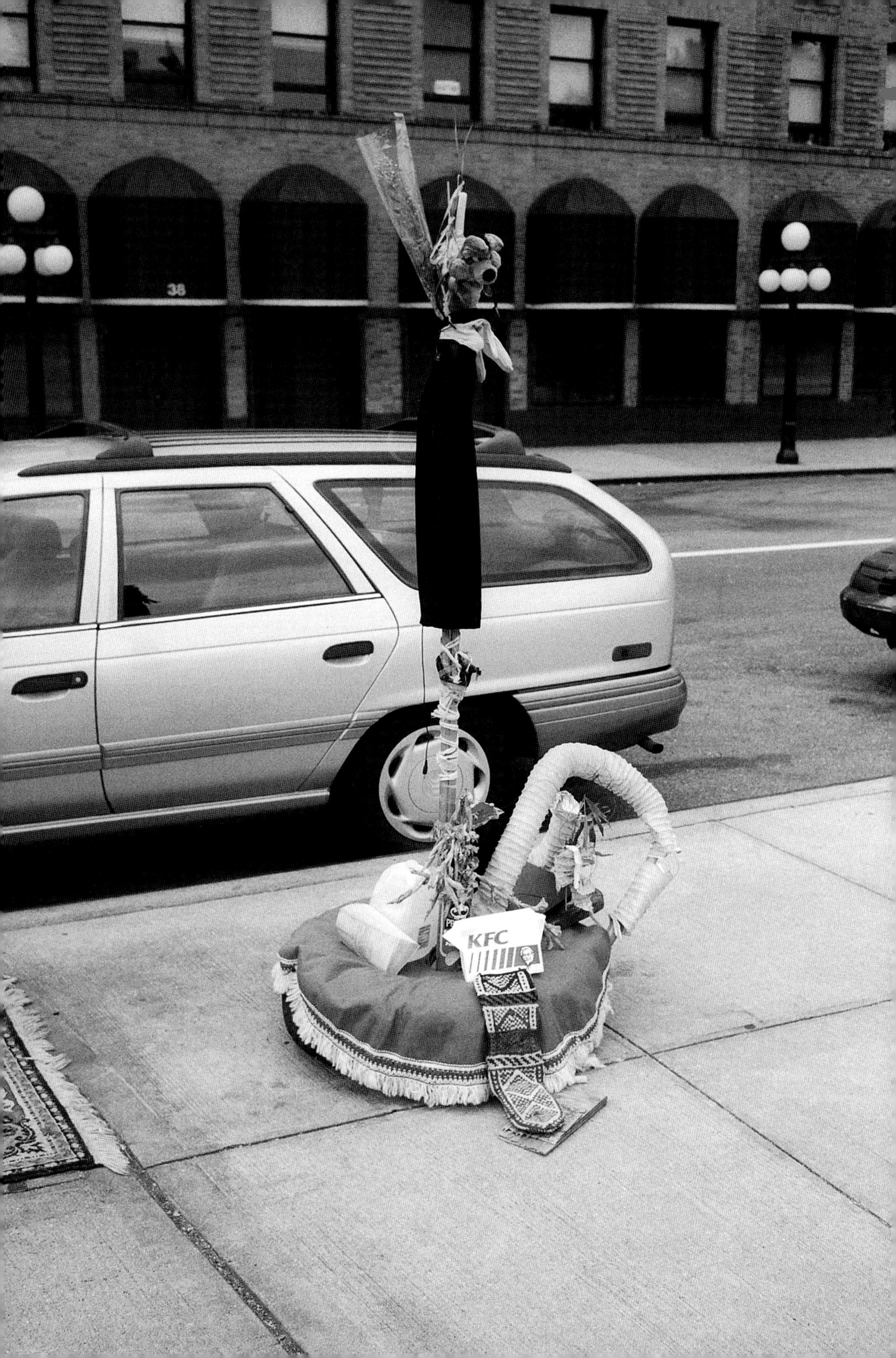
38
KFC

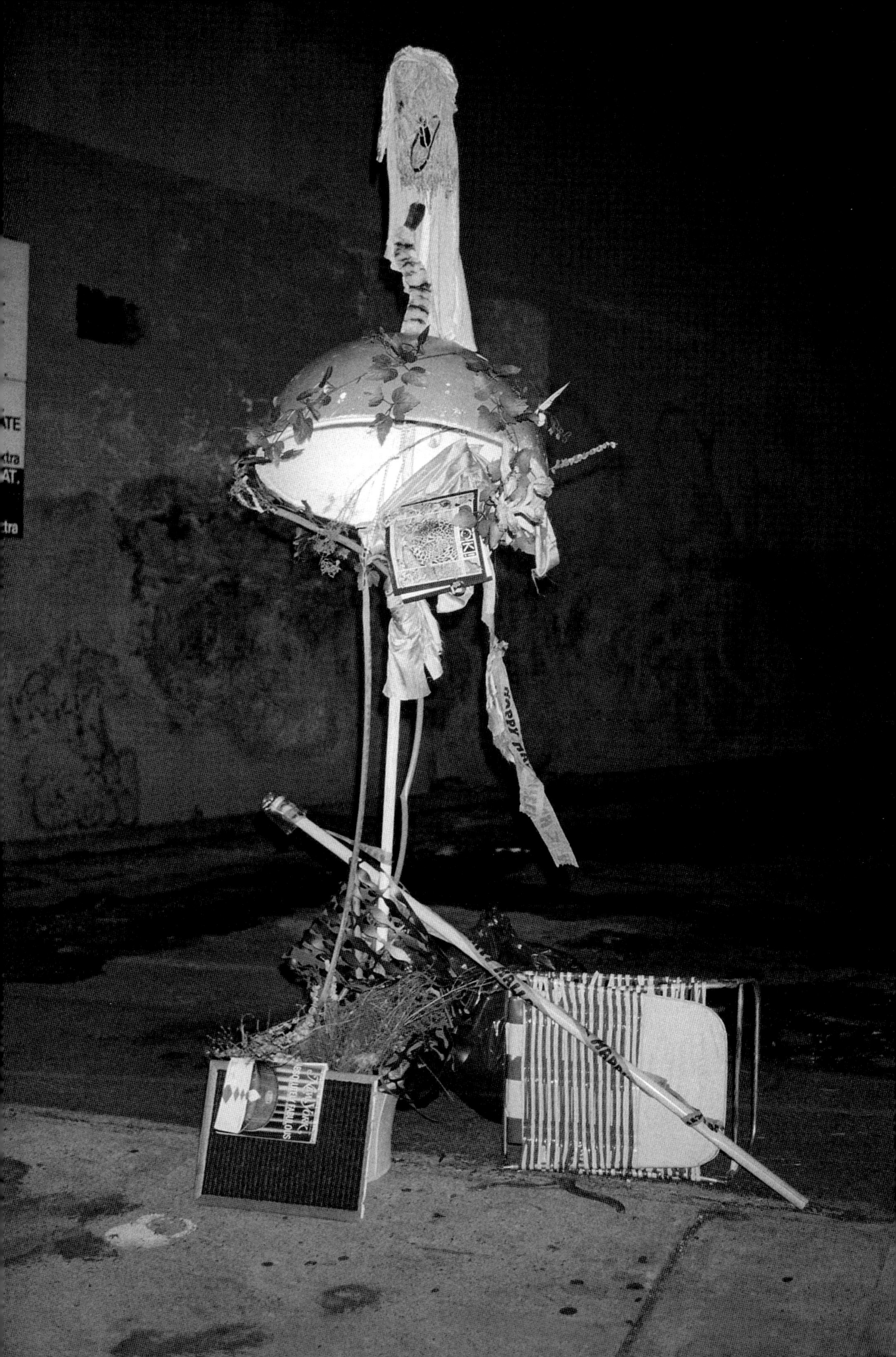
HAPPY

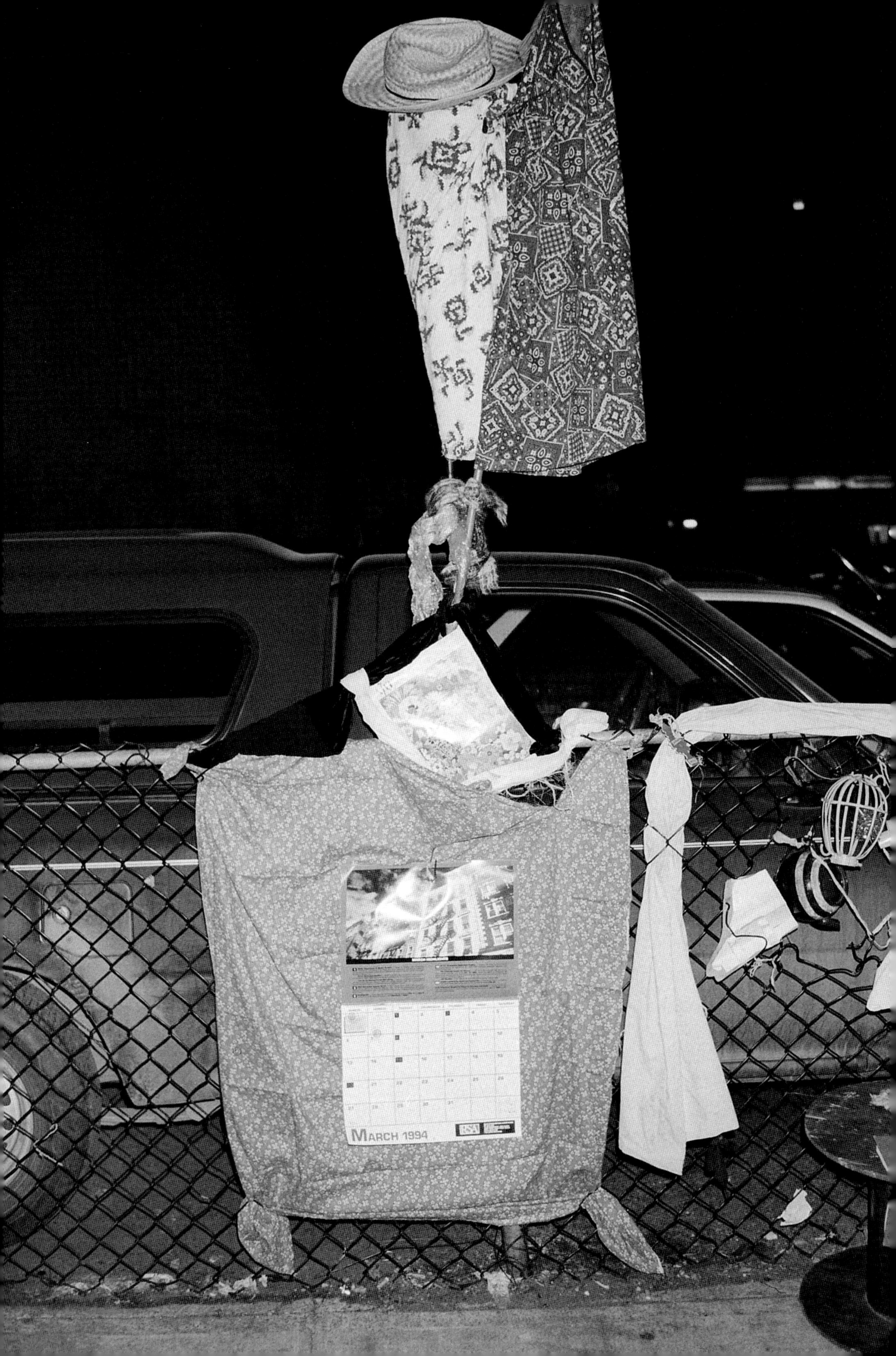
MARCH 1994

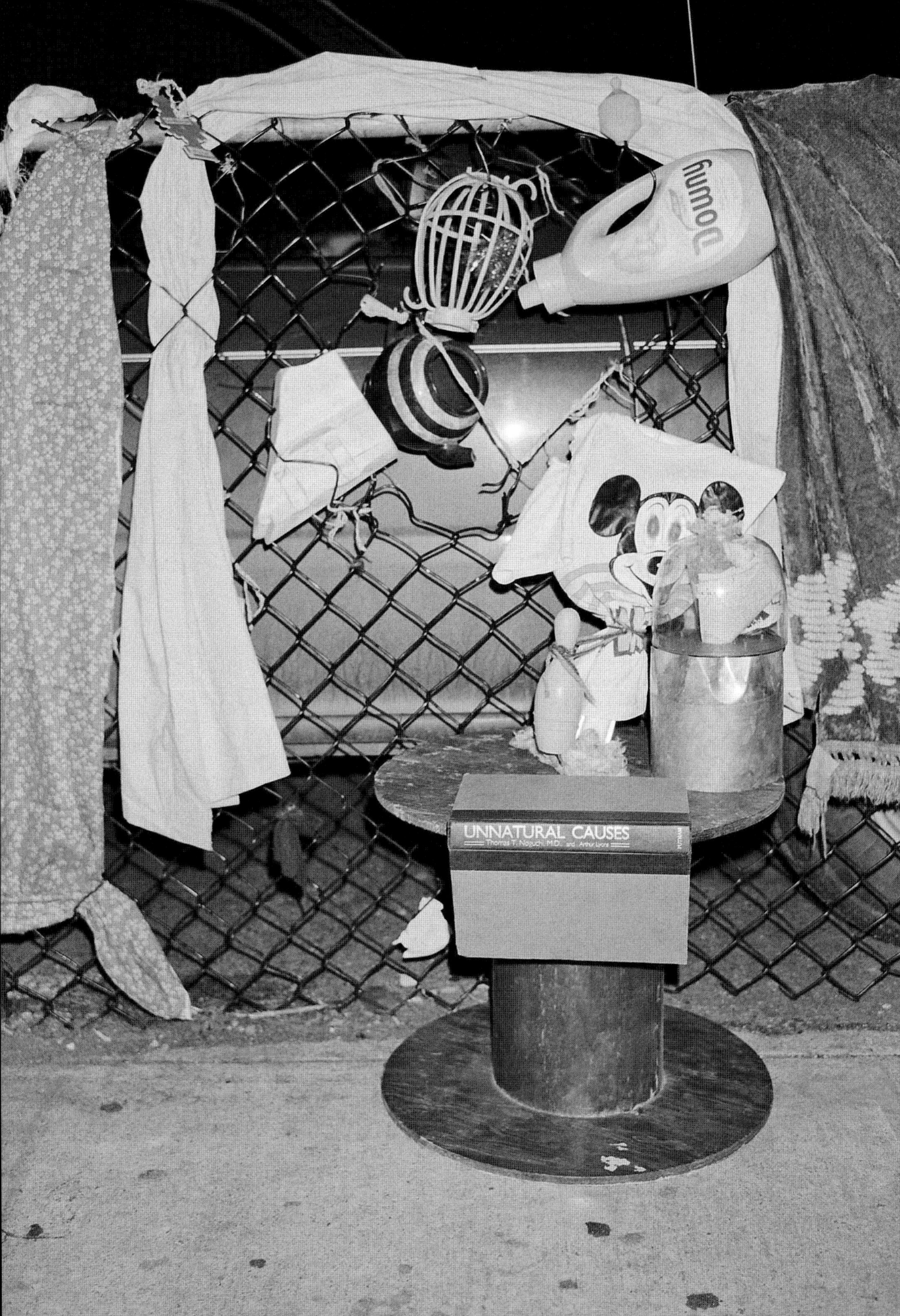
Downy
UNNATURAL CAUSES
Thomas T. Noguchi, M.D. and Arthur Lyons

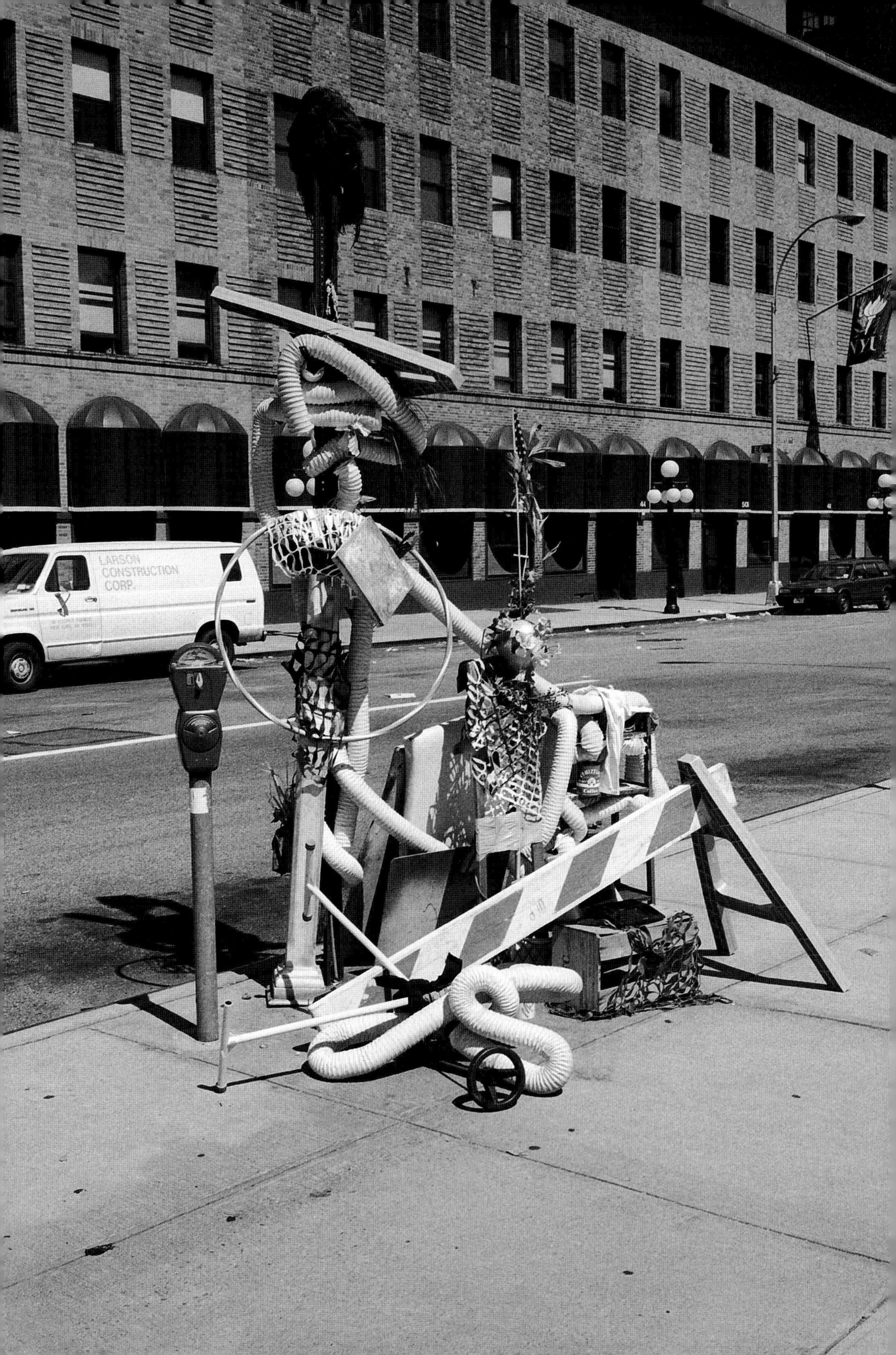
LARSON
CONSTRUCTION
CORP.
NYU

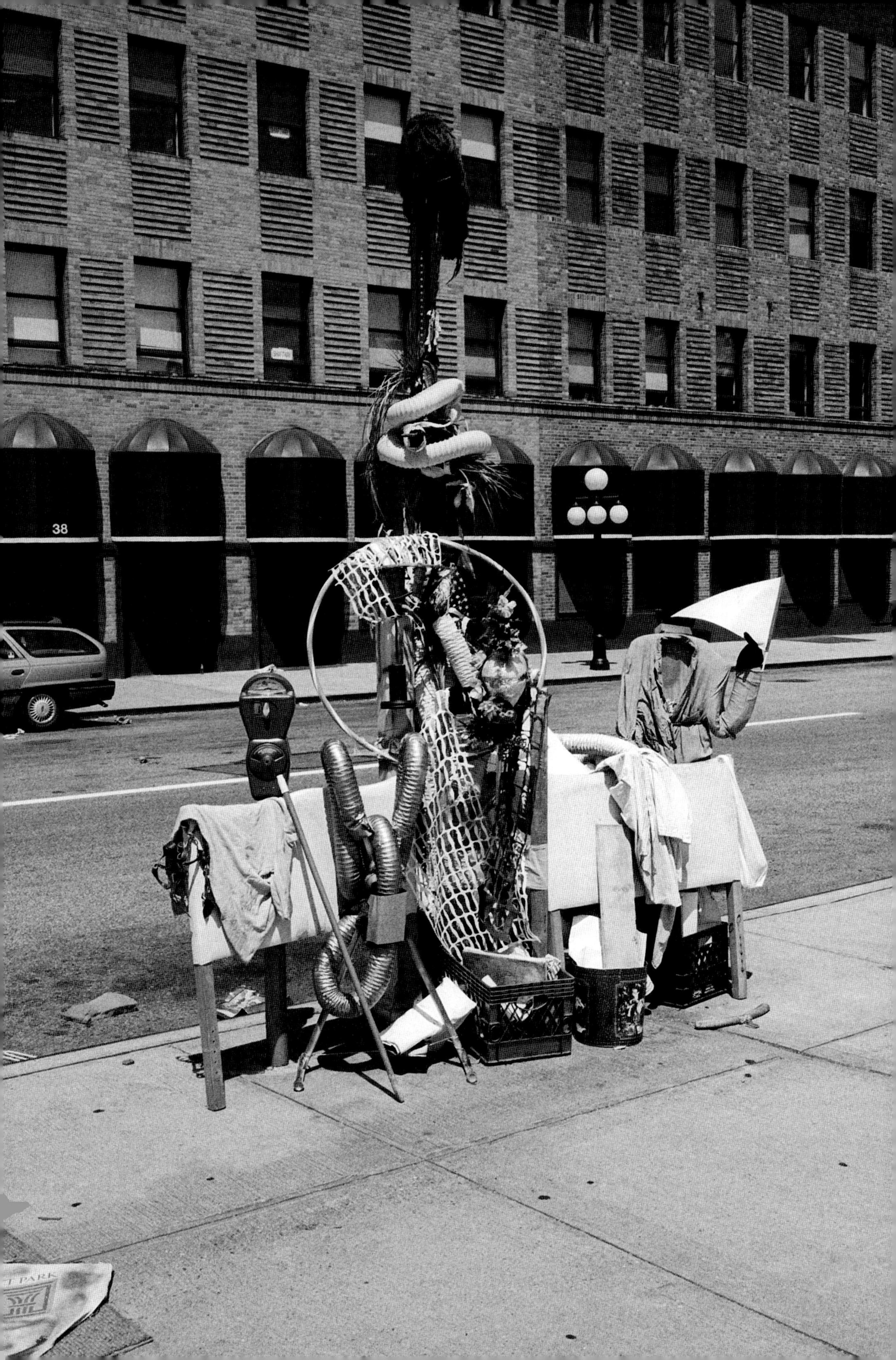
38

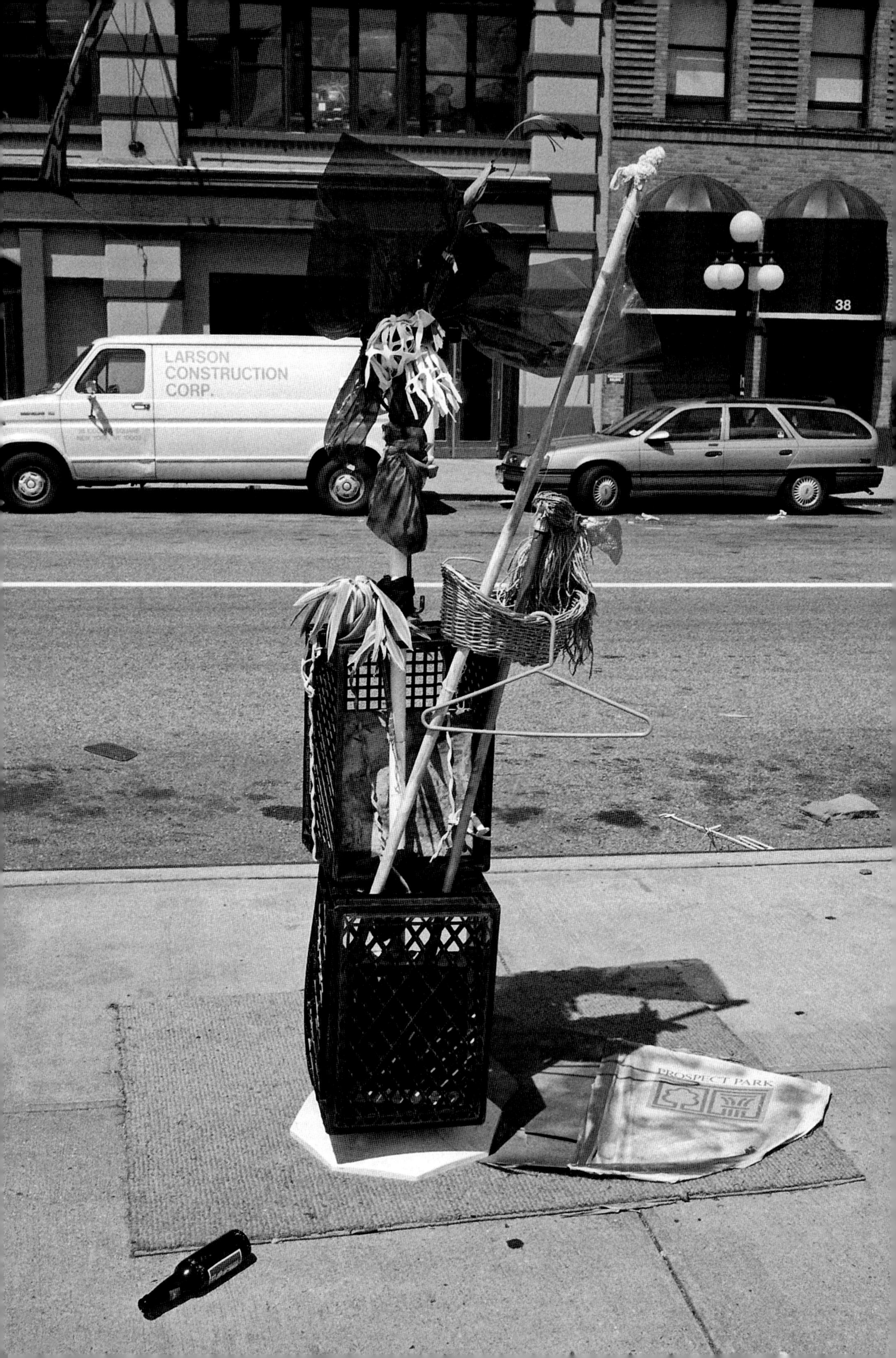
LARSON
CONSTRUCTION
CORP.
38
PROSPECT PARK

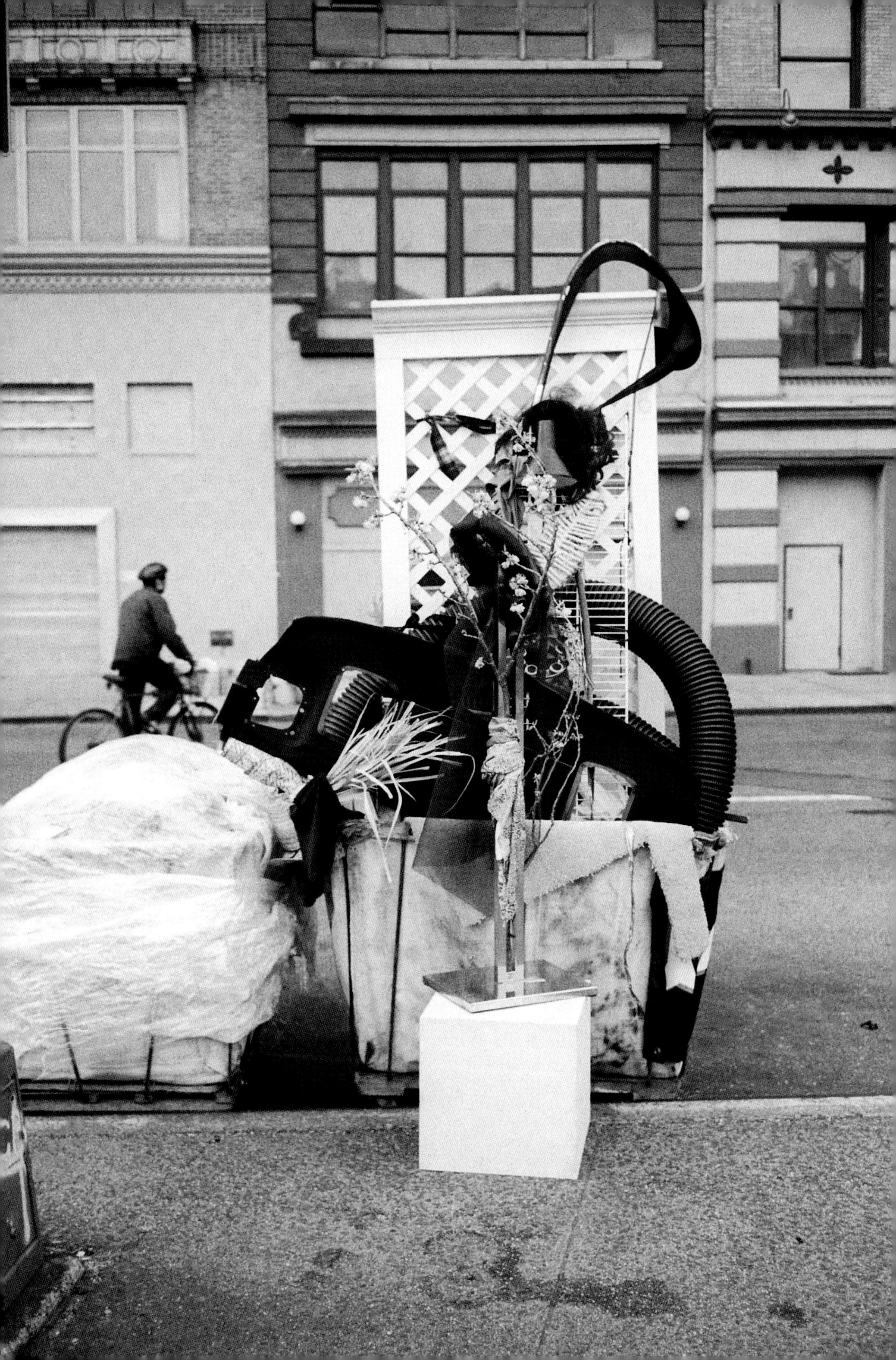

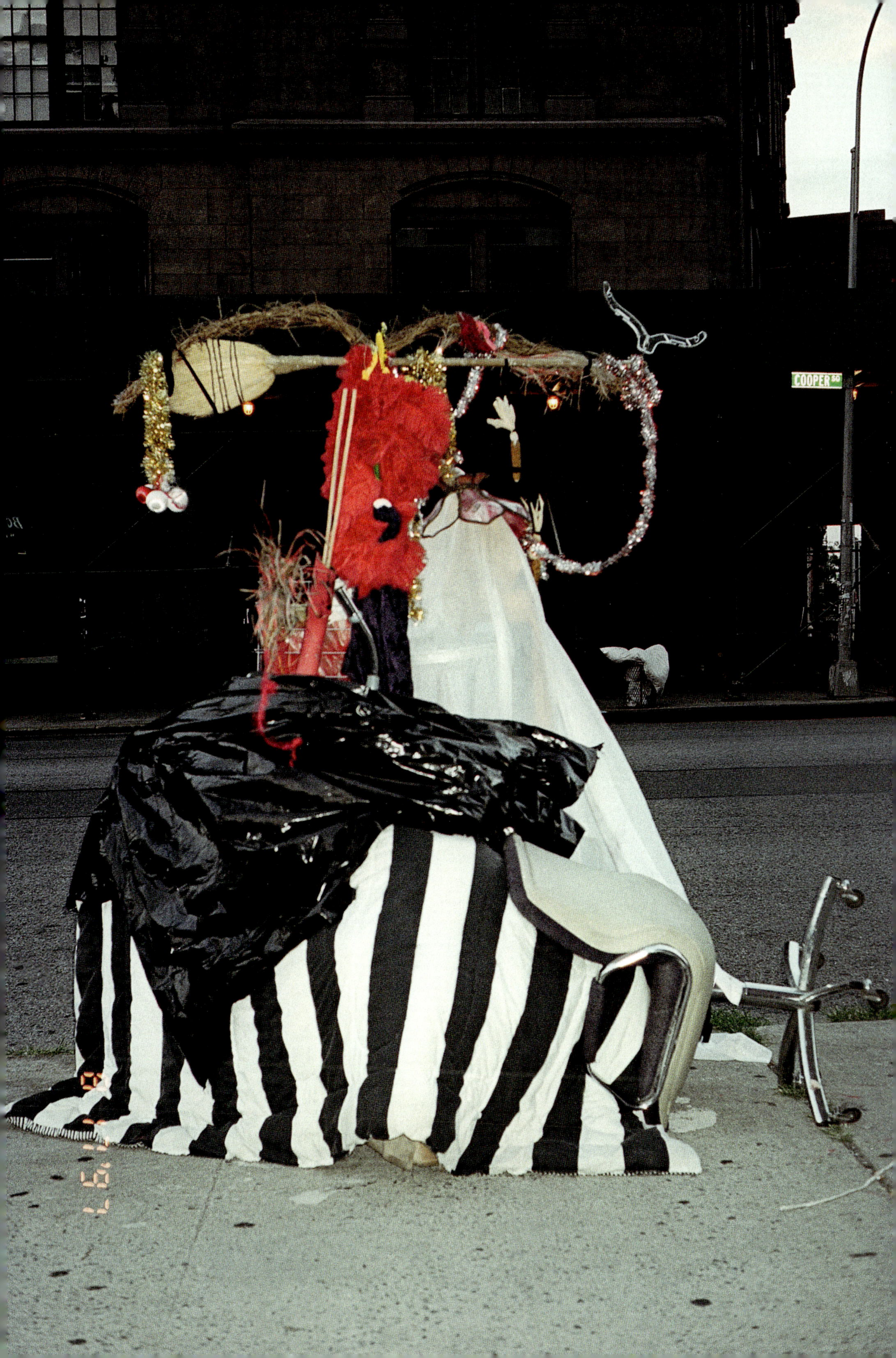
COOPER

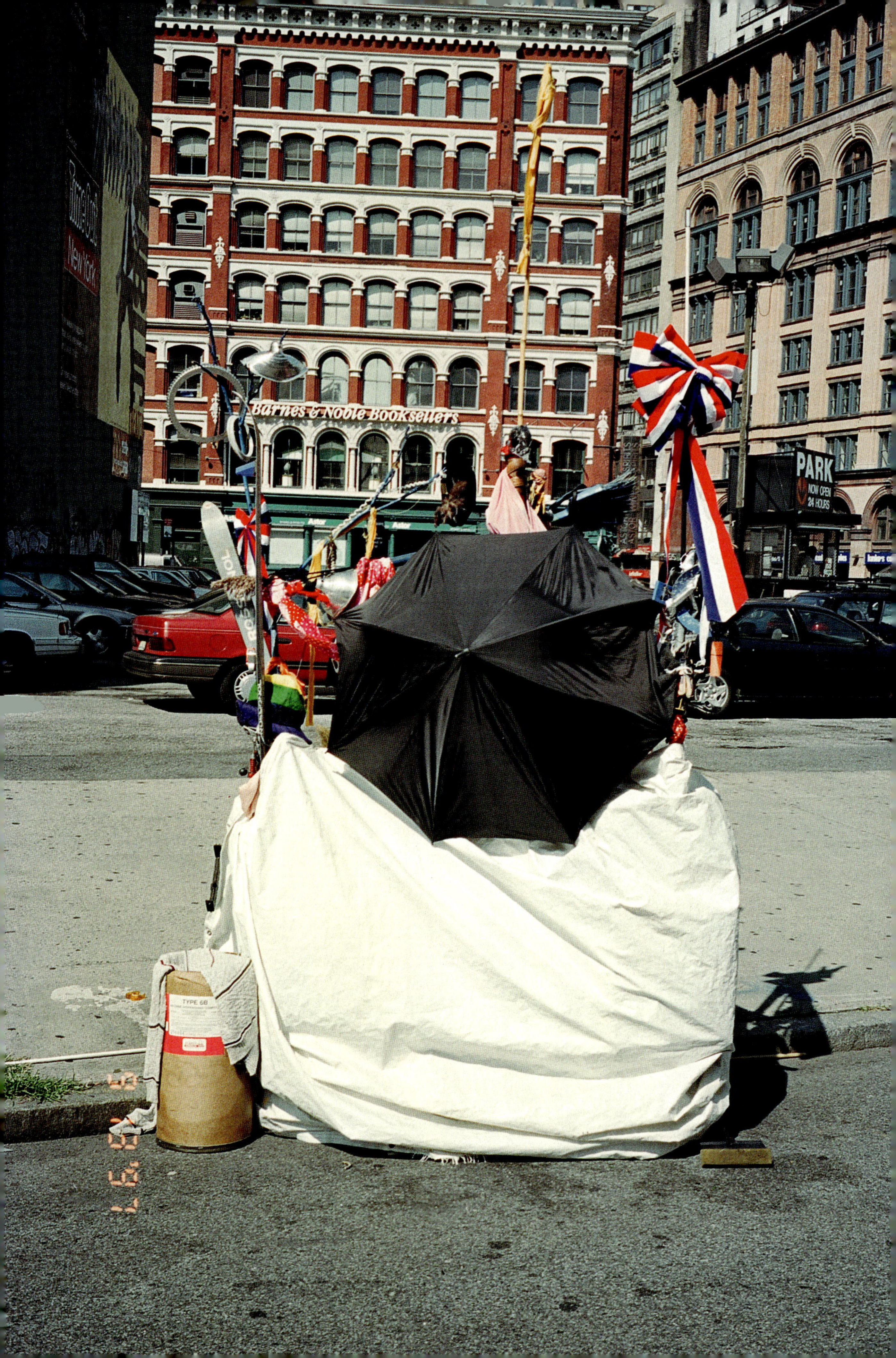
Barnes & Noble Booksellers
PARK
NOW OPEN
24 HOURS
New York
TYPE 6B

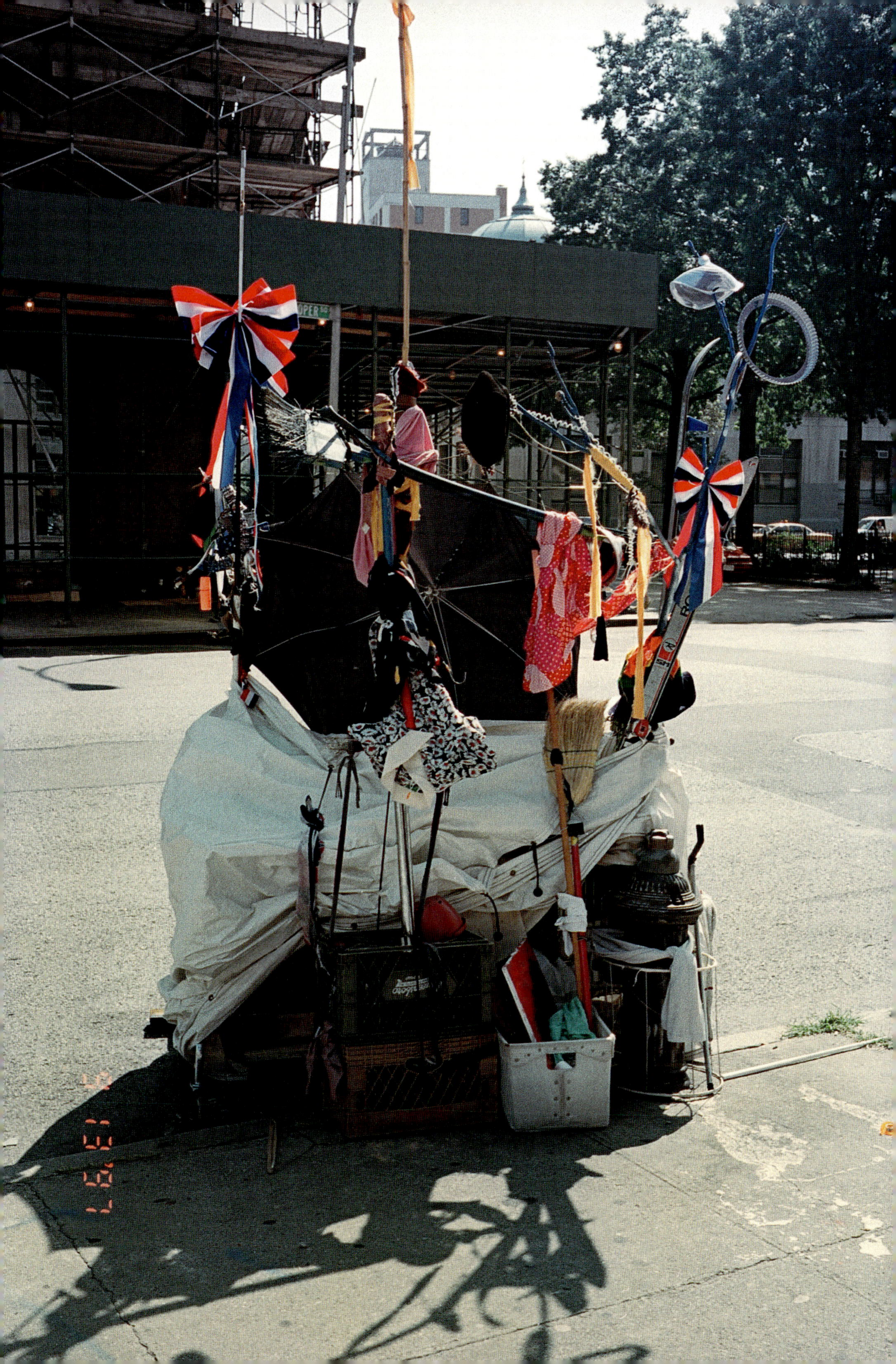

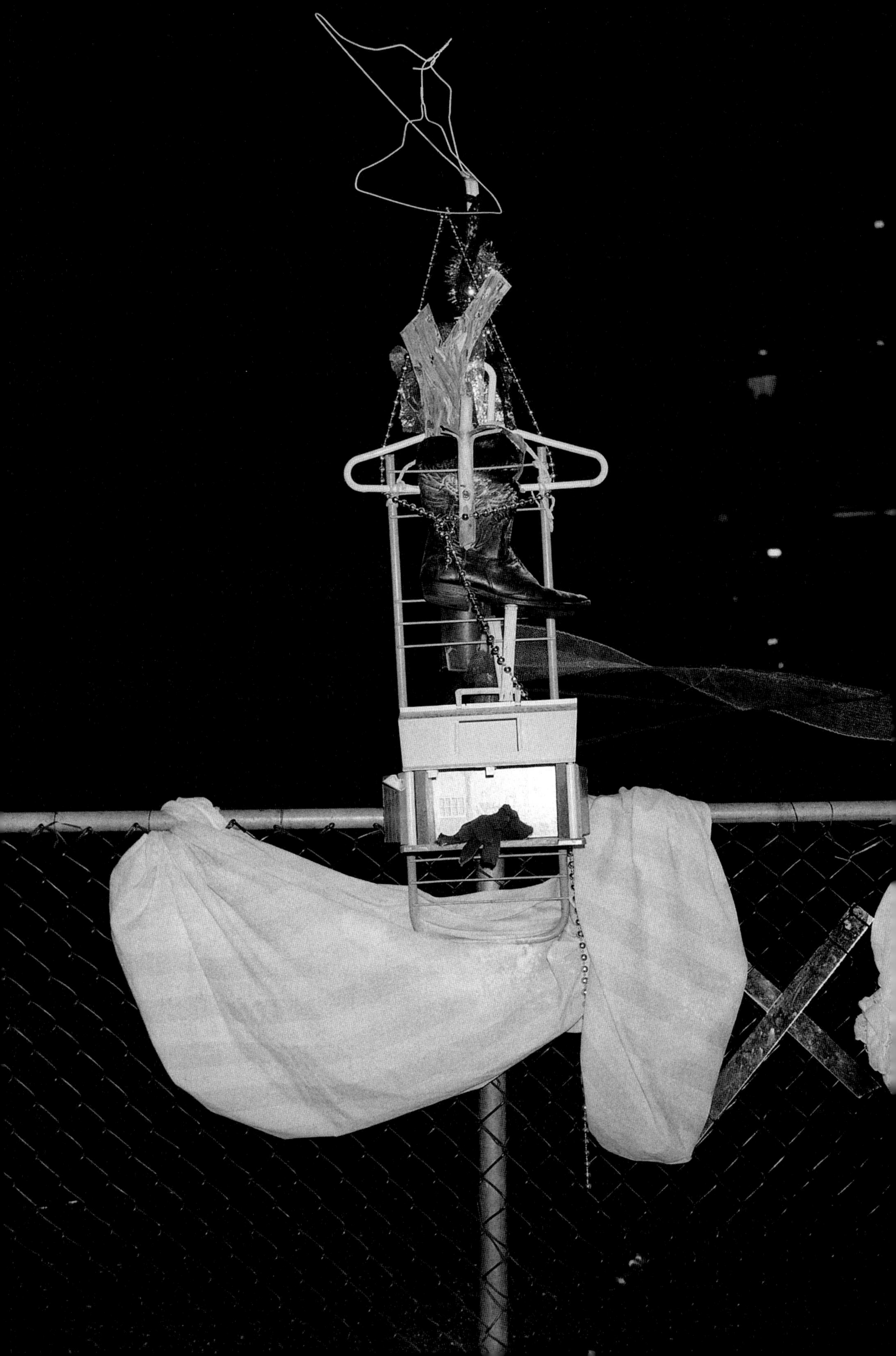

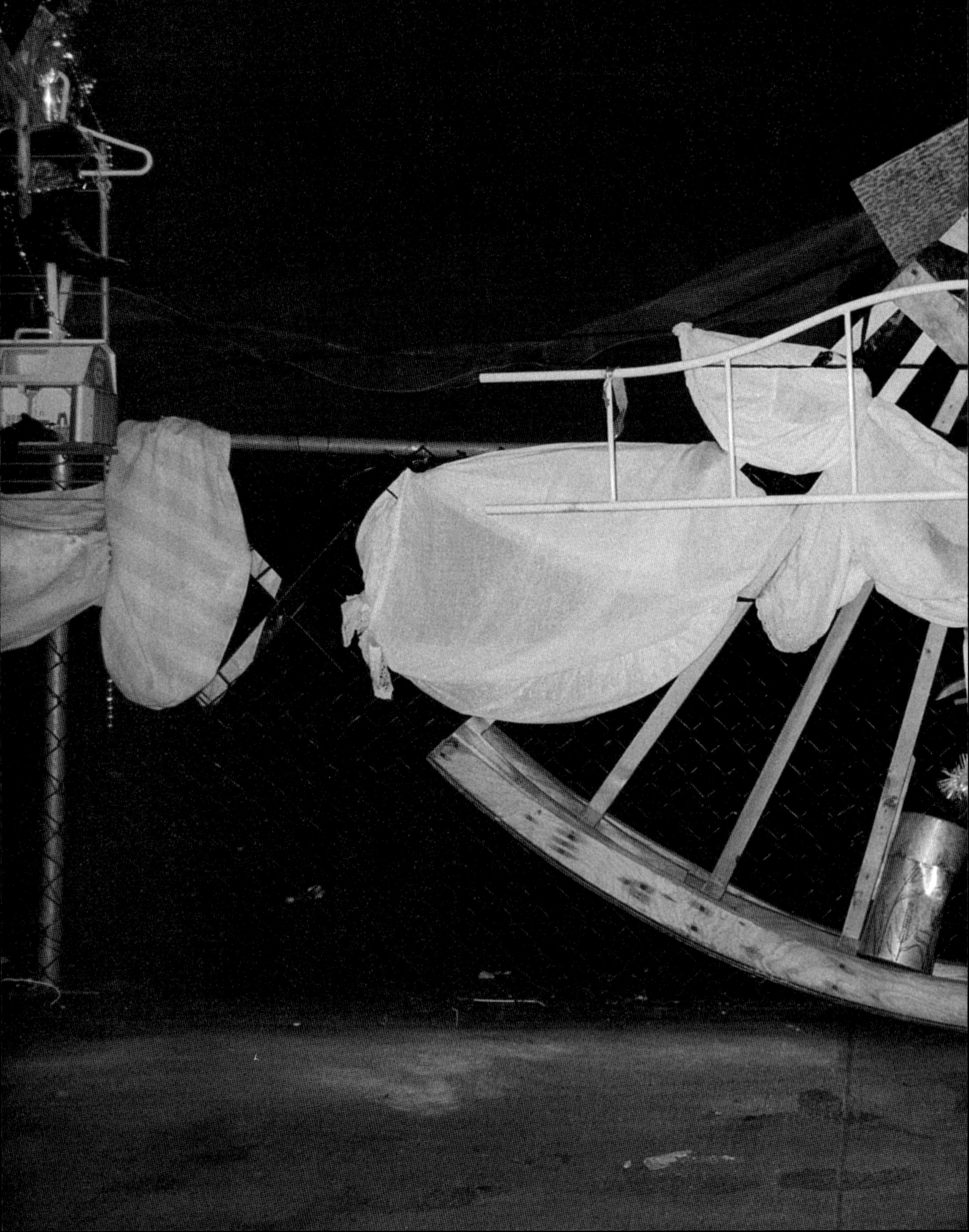

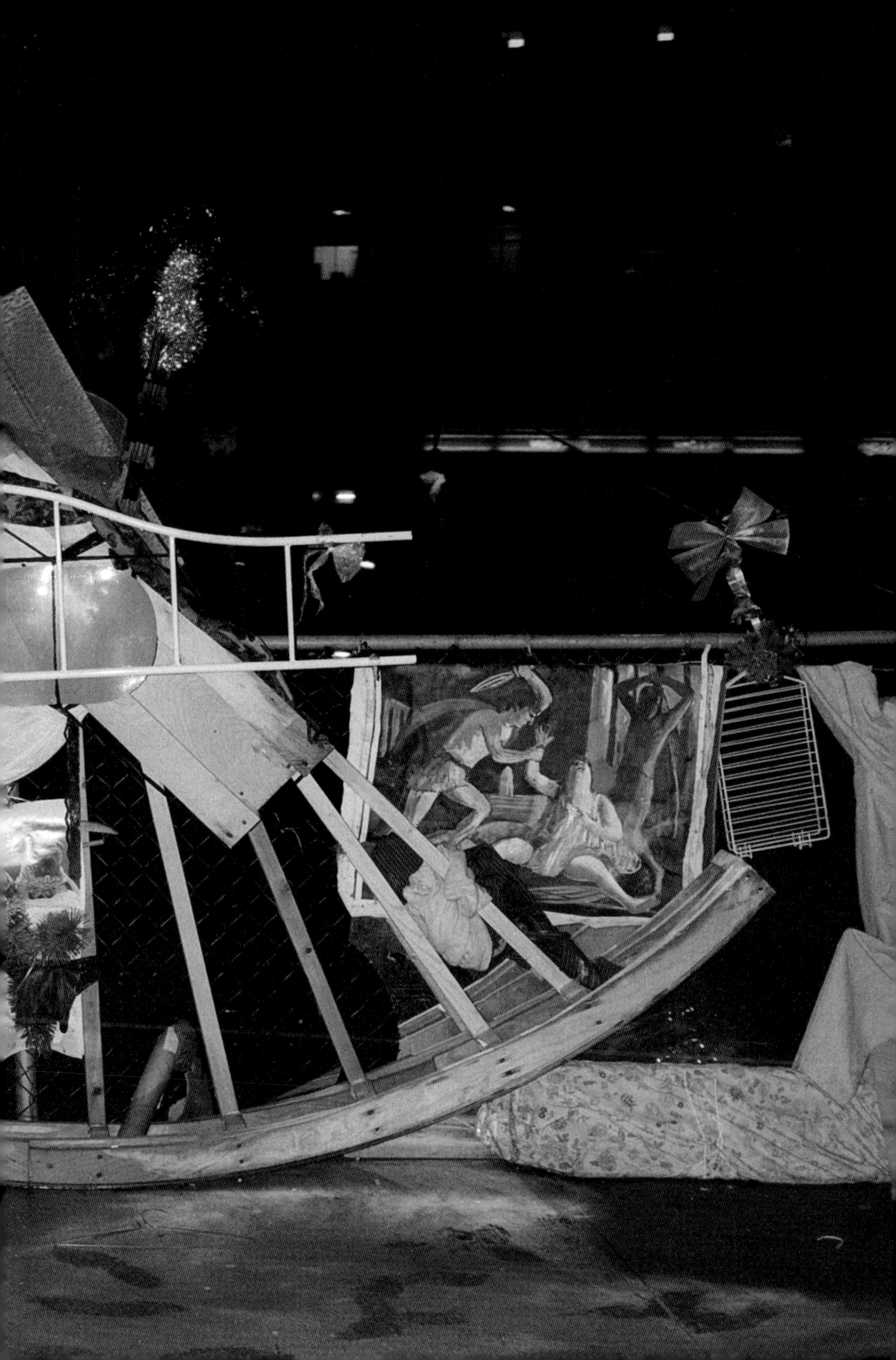

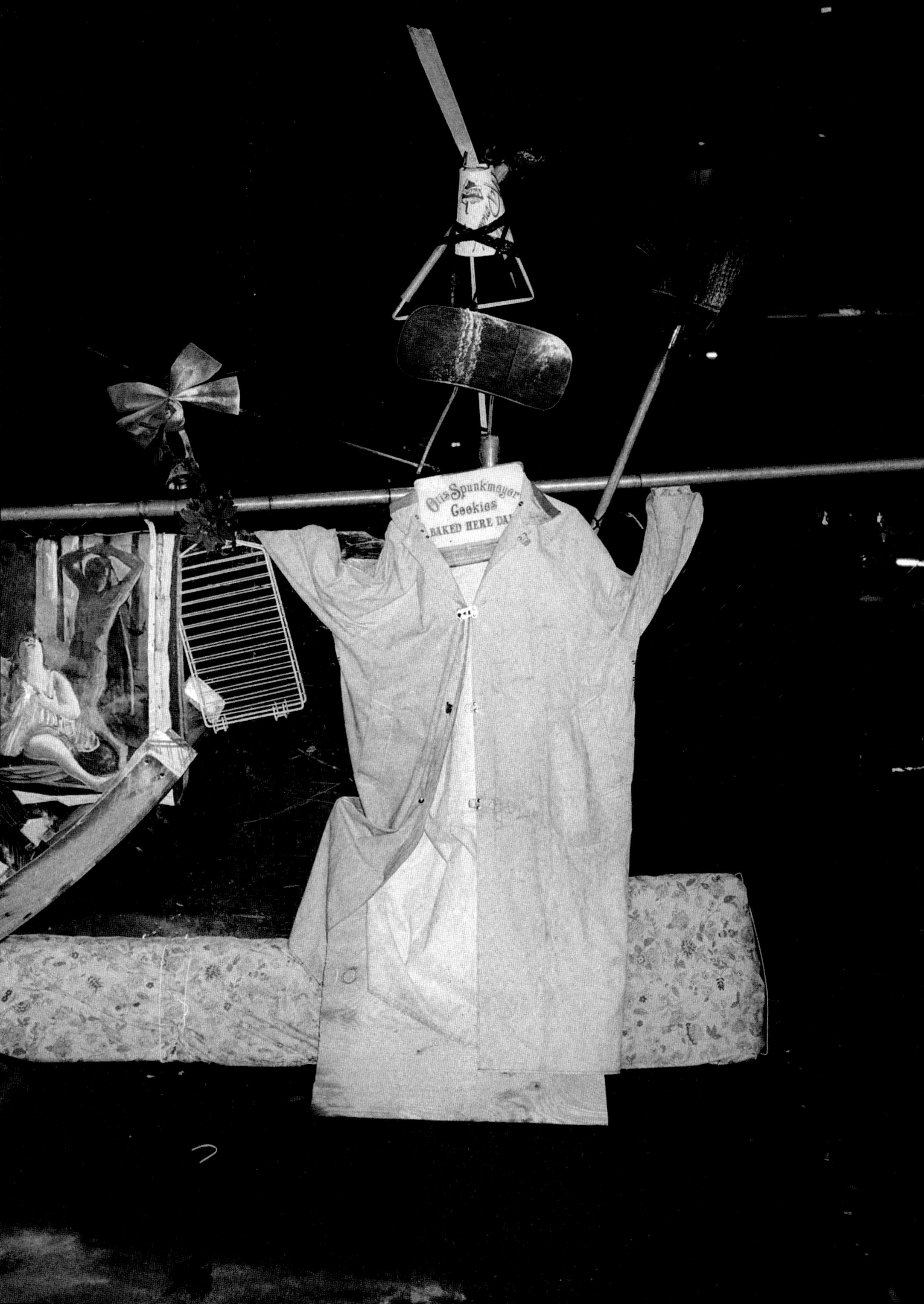
Otis Spunkmeyer
Cookies
BAKED HERE

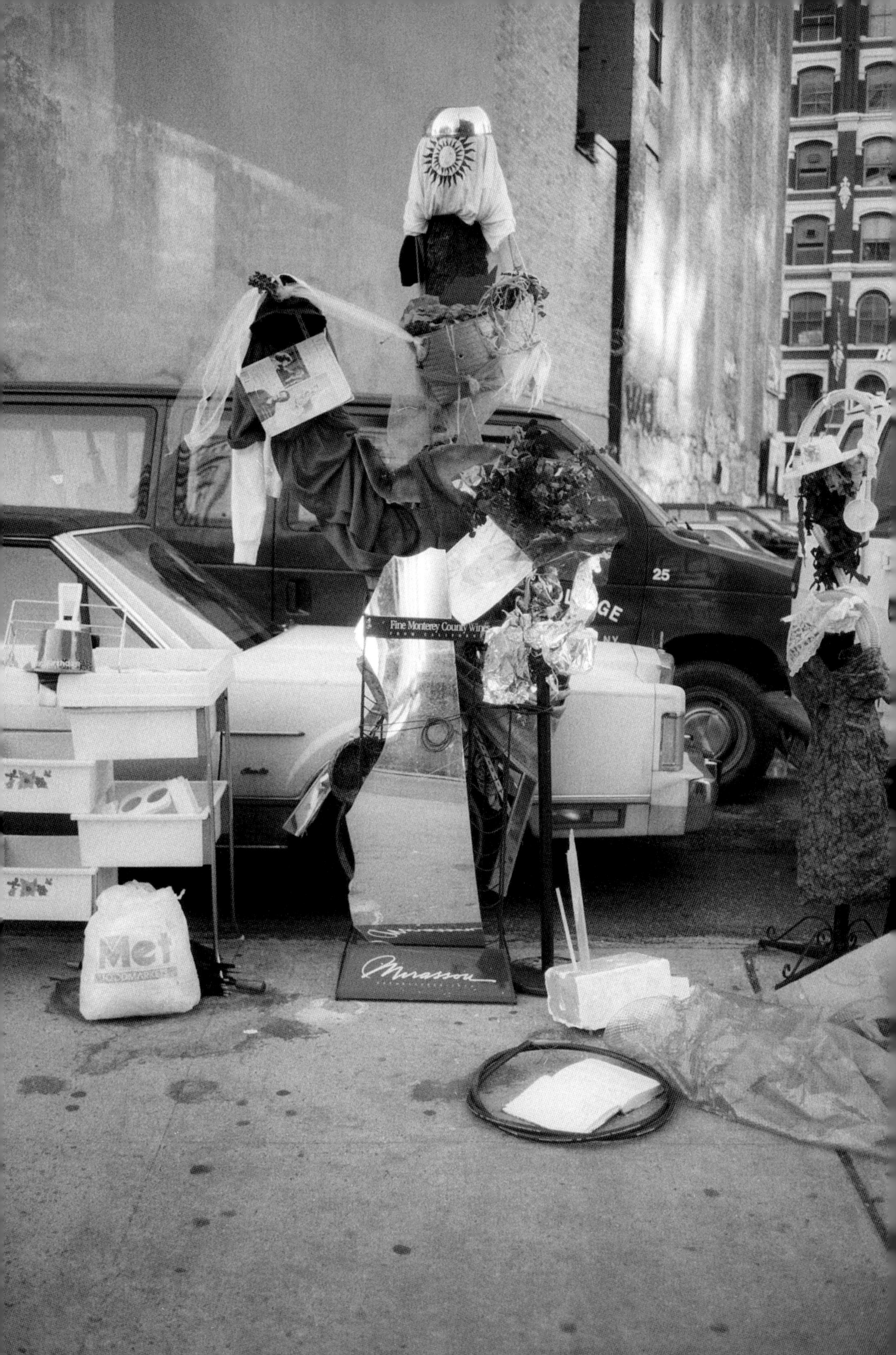
Fine Monterey County Wines
Mirassou
Met
25

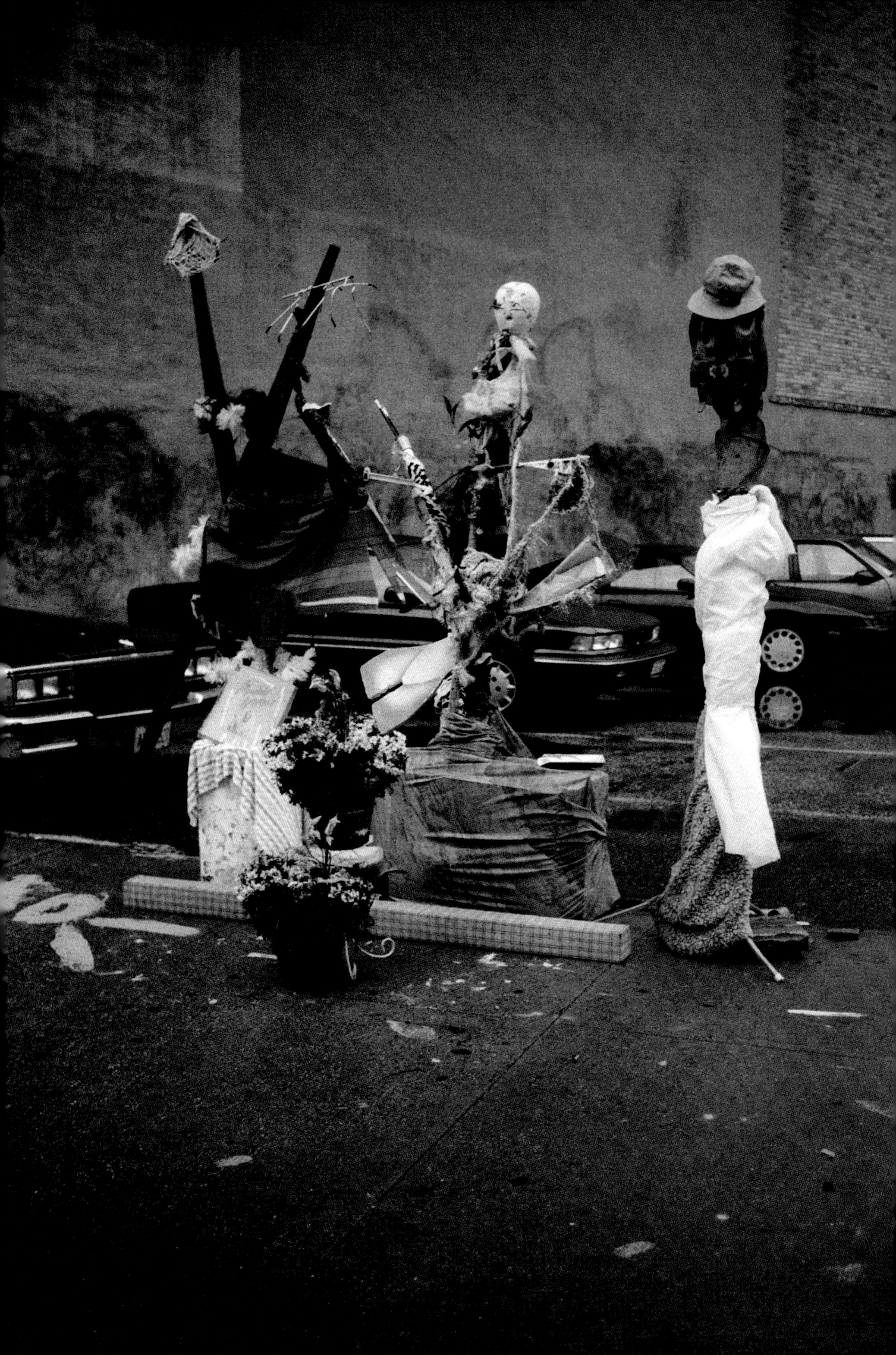

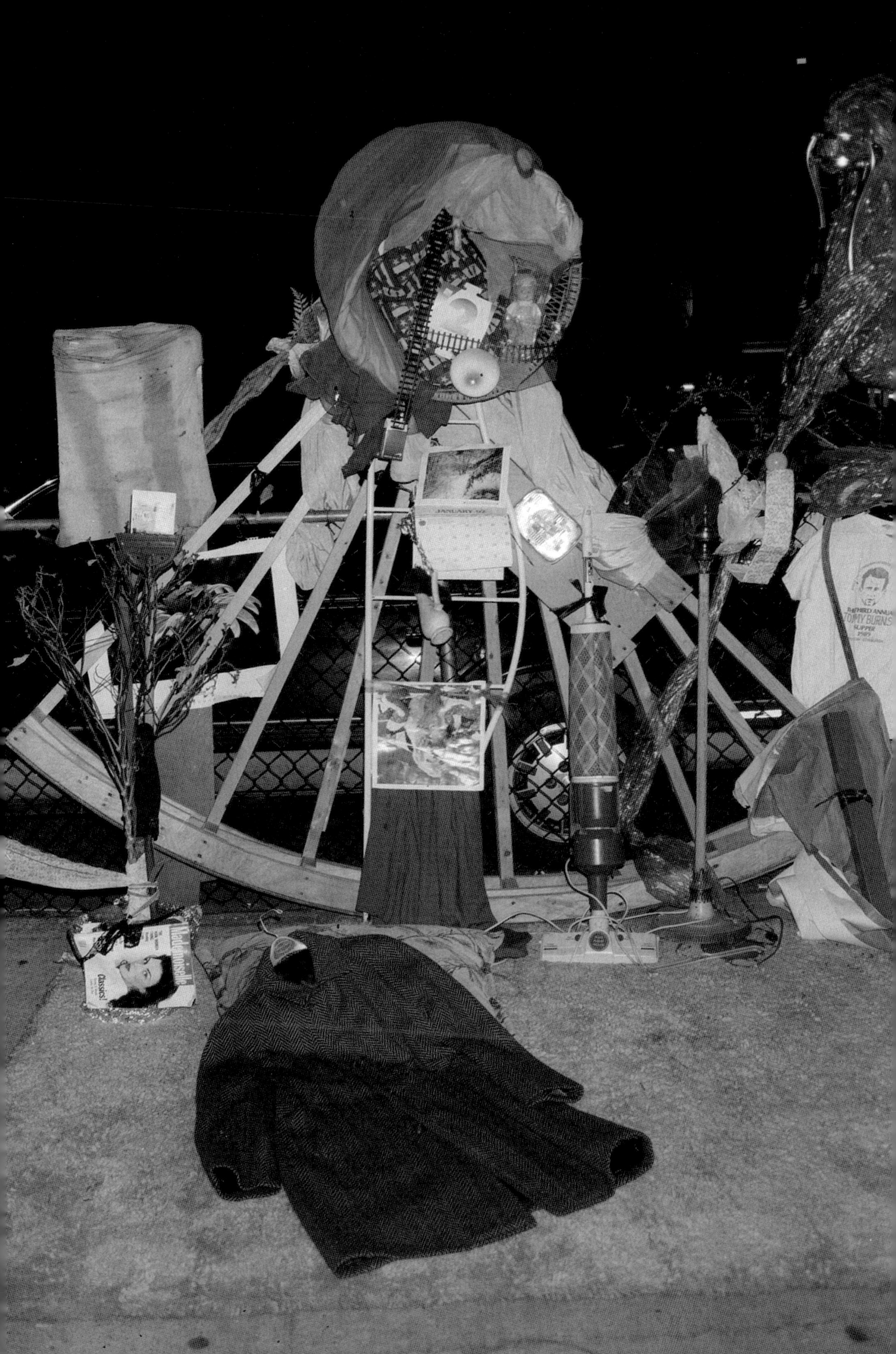

JANUARY '92
Mademoiselle
Classics!
TOMMY BURNS
SUPPER

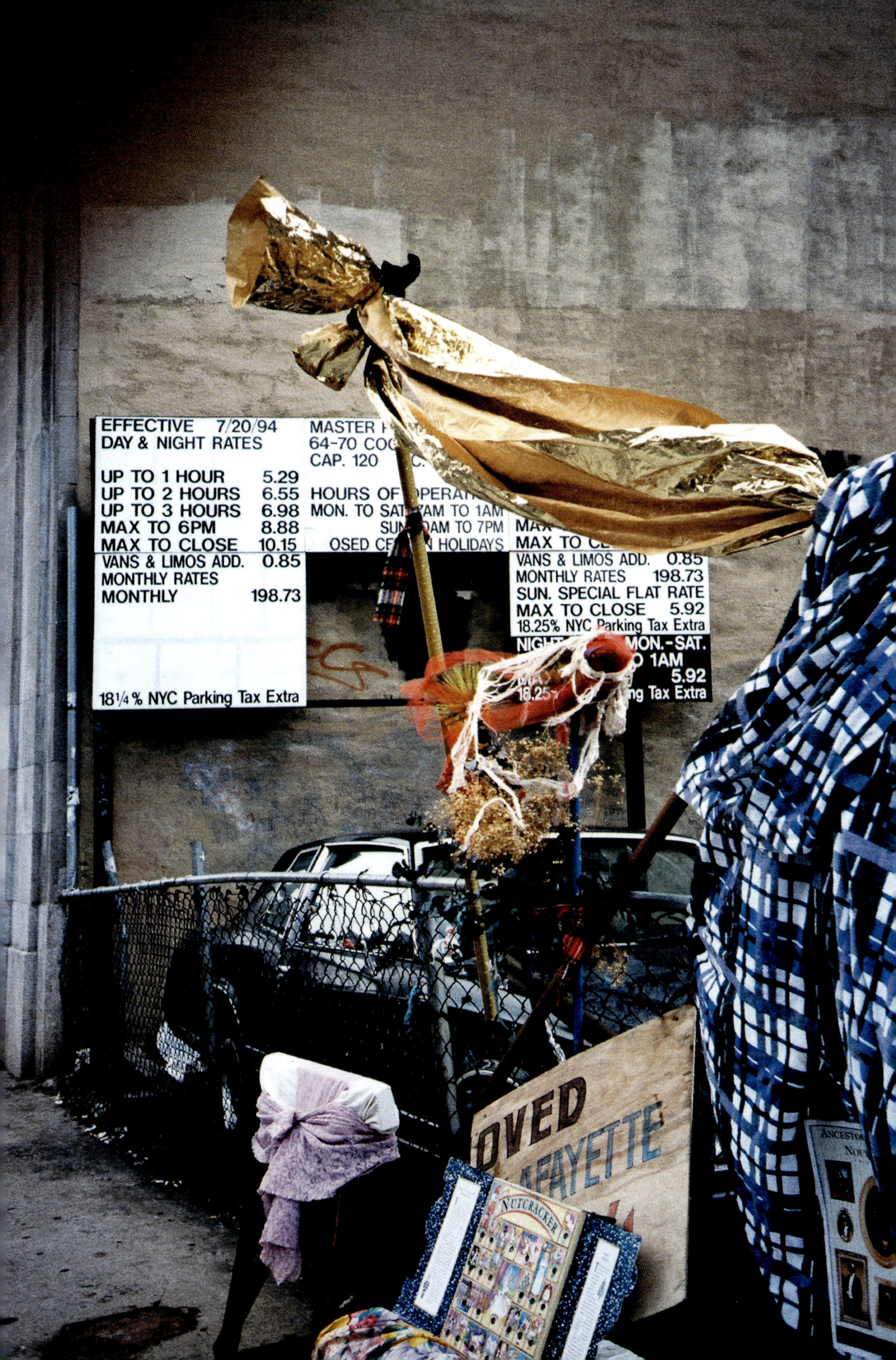
EFFECTIVE 7/20/94
DAY & NIGHT RATES
UP TO 1 HOUR 5.29
UP TO 2 HOURS 6.55
UP TO 3 HOURS 6.98
MAX TO 6PM 8.88
MAX TO CLOSE 10.15
VANS & LIMOS ADD. 0.85
MONTHLY RATES
MONTHLY 198.73
18 1/4 % NYC Parking Tax Extra
MASTER
CAP. 120
HOURS OF
VANS & LIMOS ADD. 0.85
MONTHLY RATES 198.73
SUN. SPECIAL FLAT RATE
MAX TO CLOSE 5.92
18.25% NYC Parking Tax Extra
MON.-SAT.
5.92
NUTCRACKER

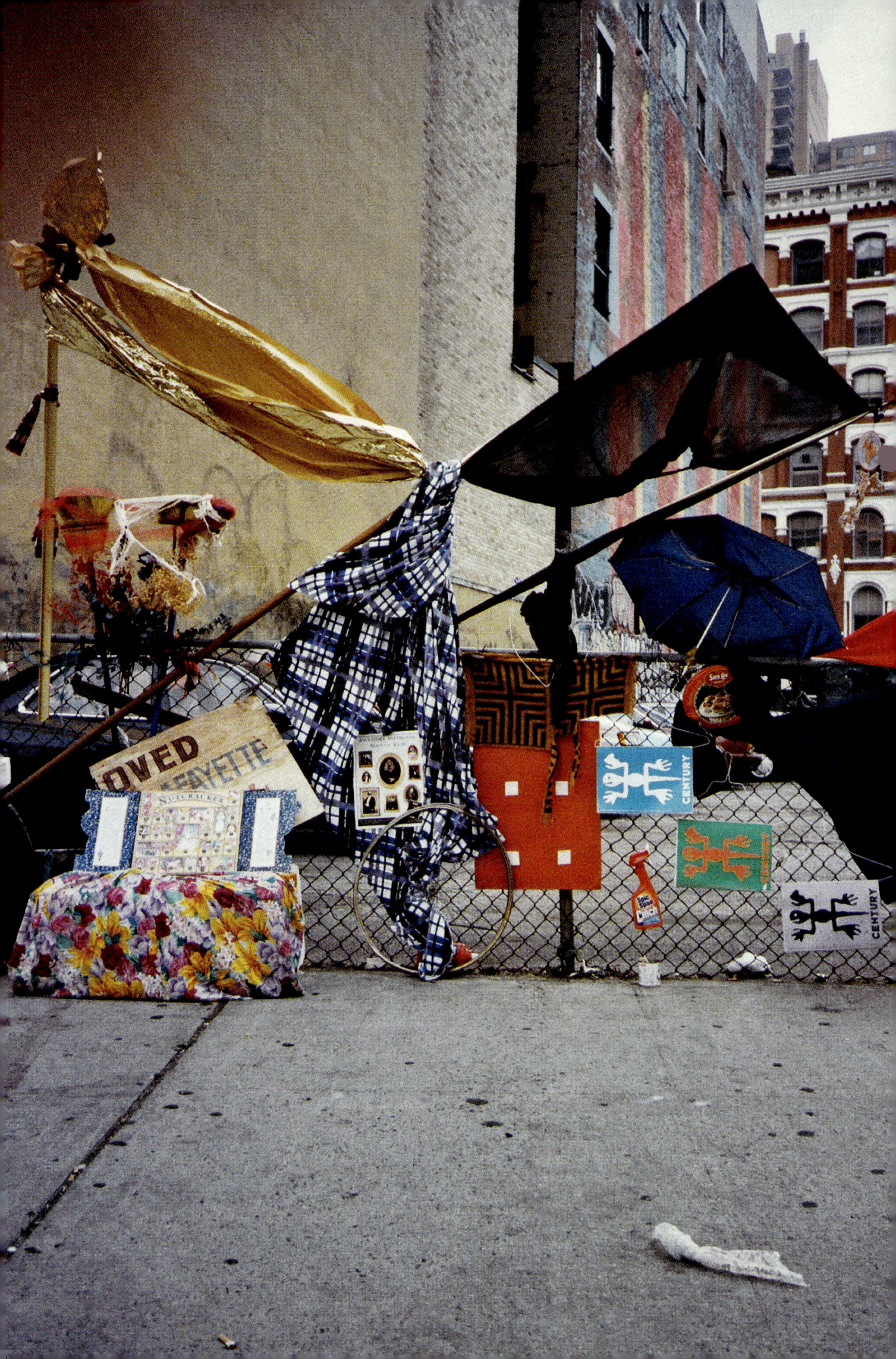
OVED
NUTCRACKER
CENTURY
CENTURY
CENTURY

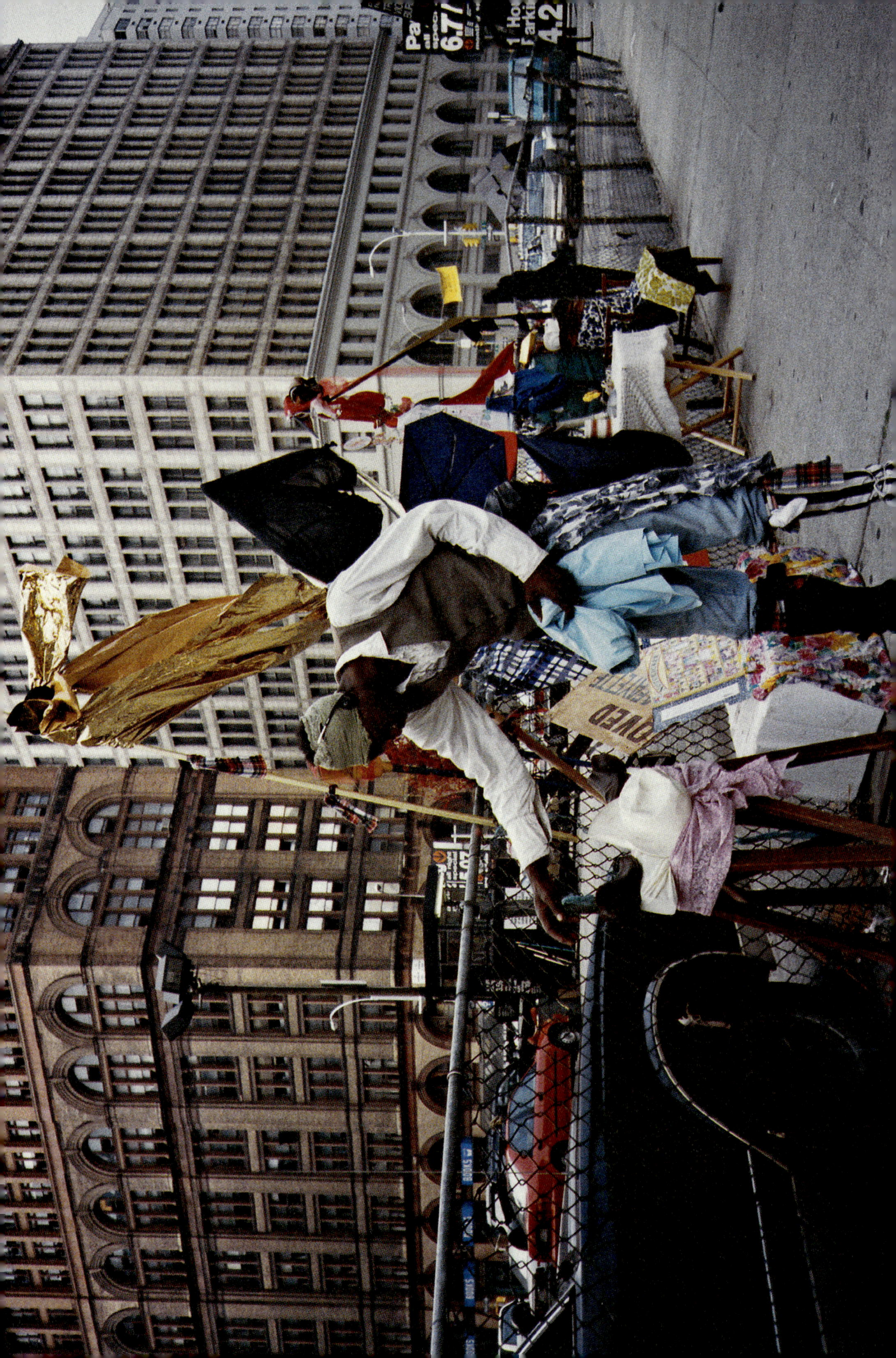

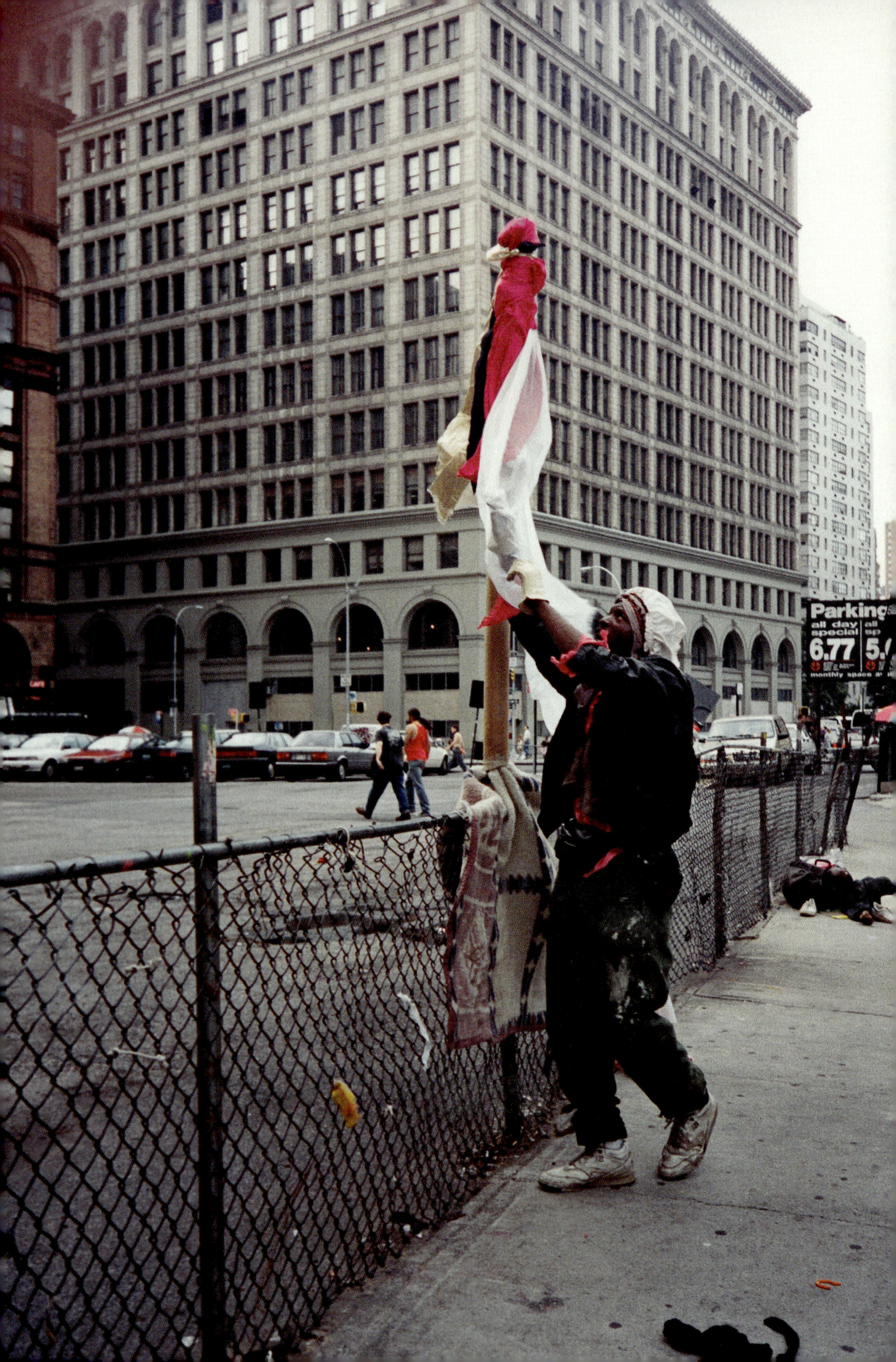
Parking
all day
special
6.77

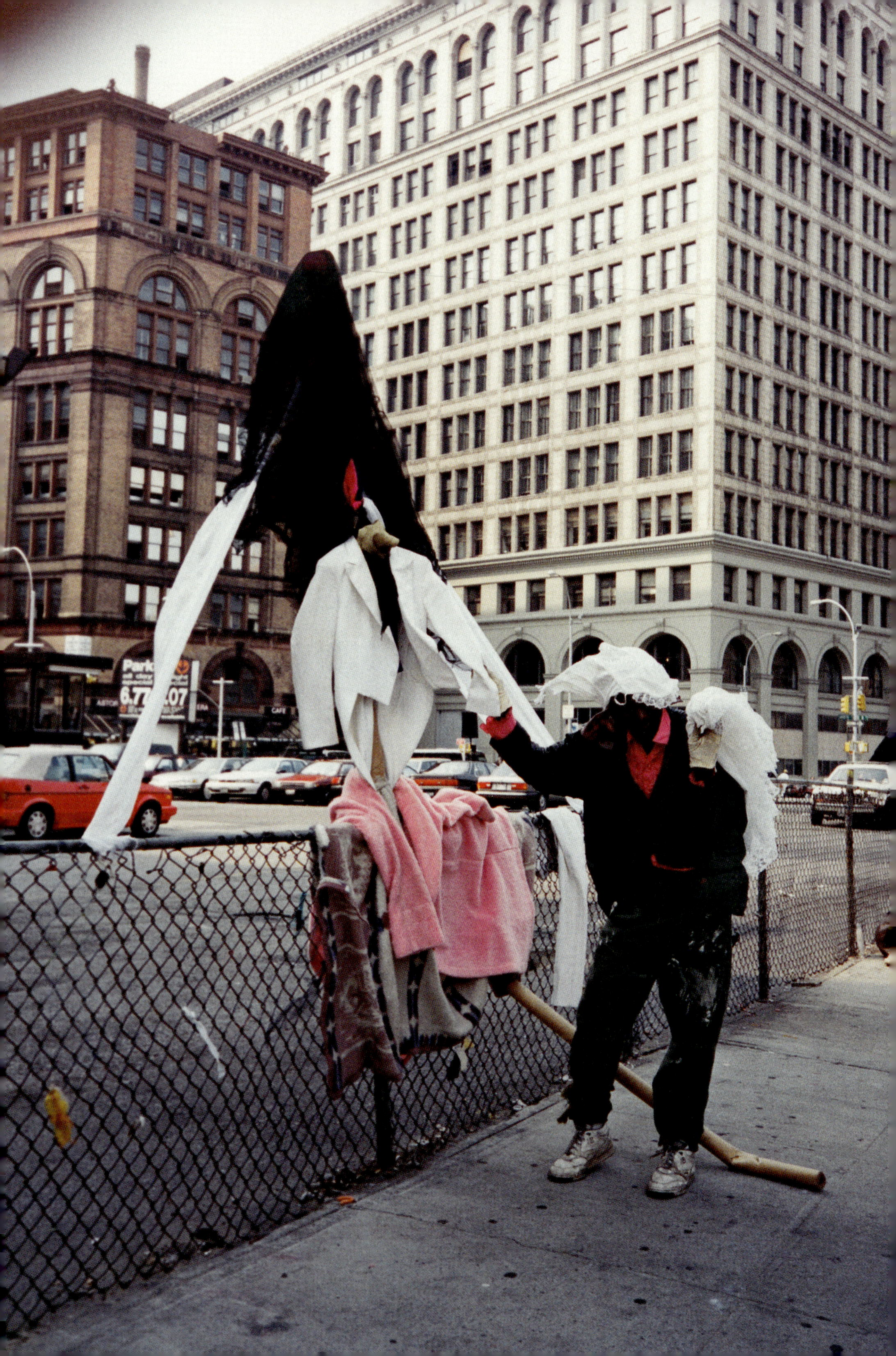
CAFE

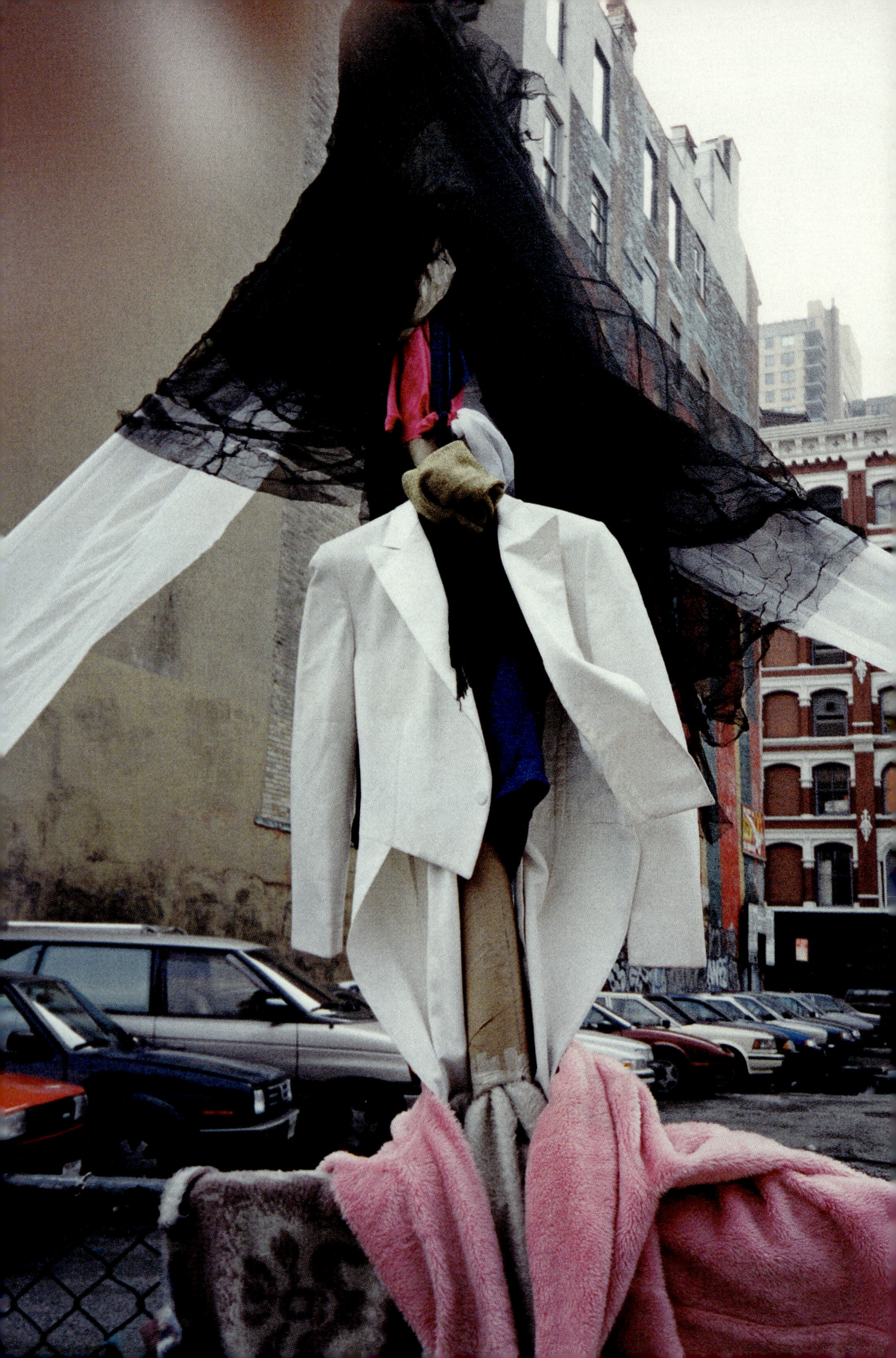

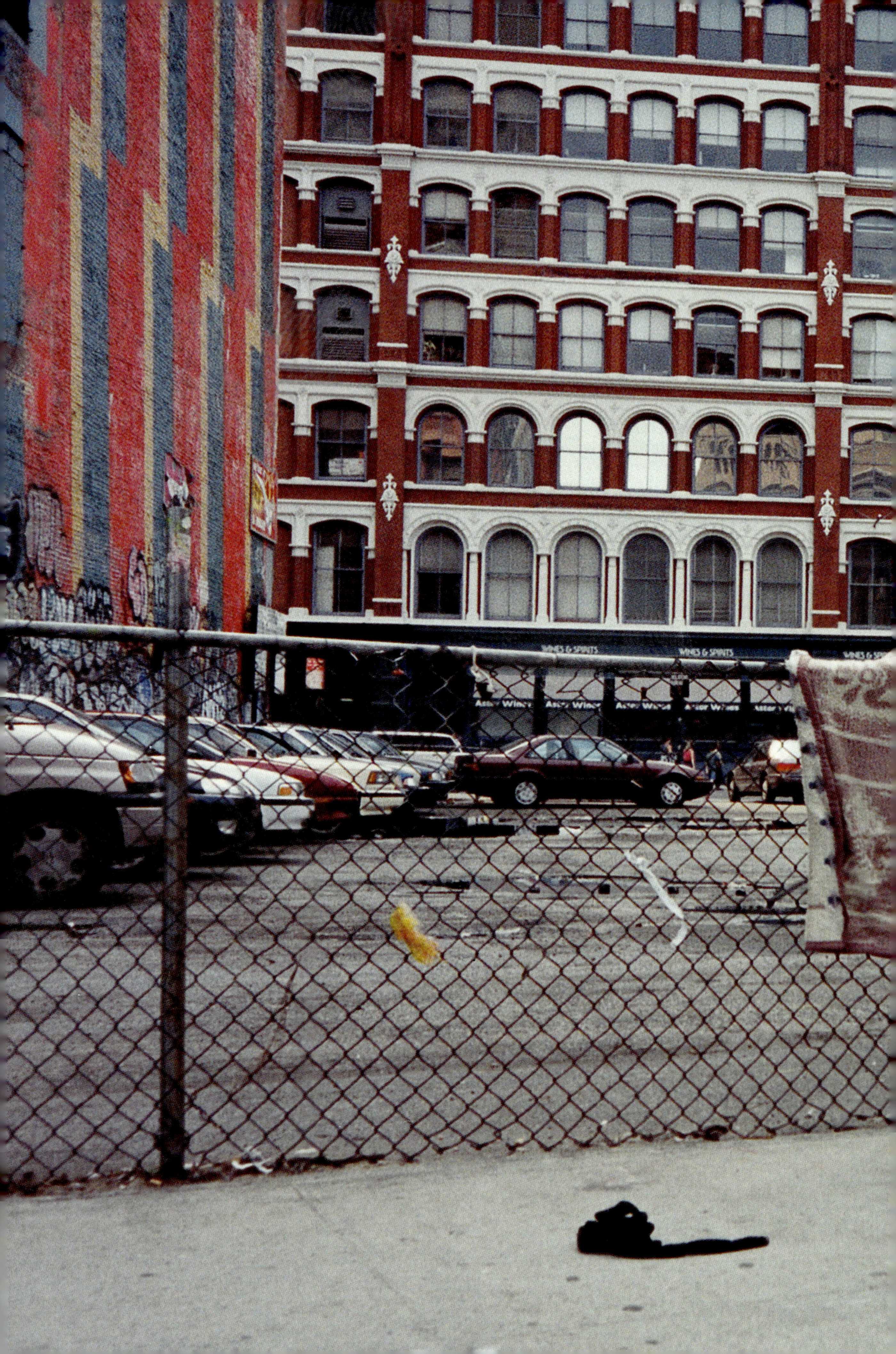
WINES & SPIRITS
WINES & SPIRITS

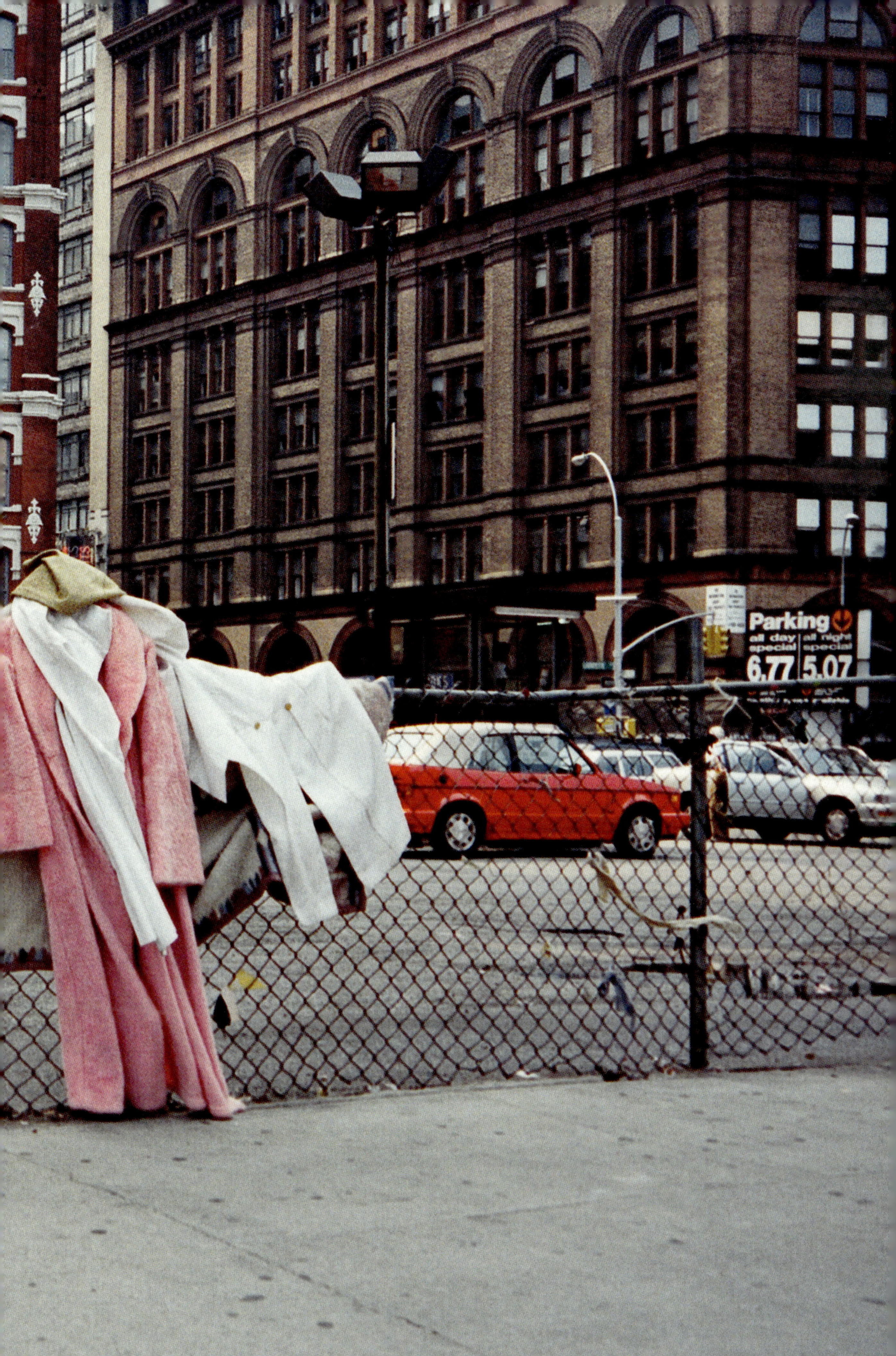
Parking
all day special
6.77
all night special
5.07

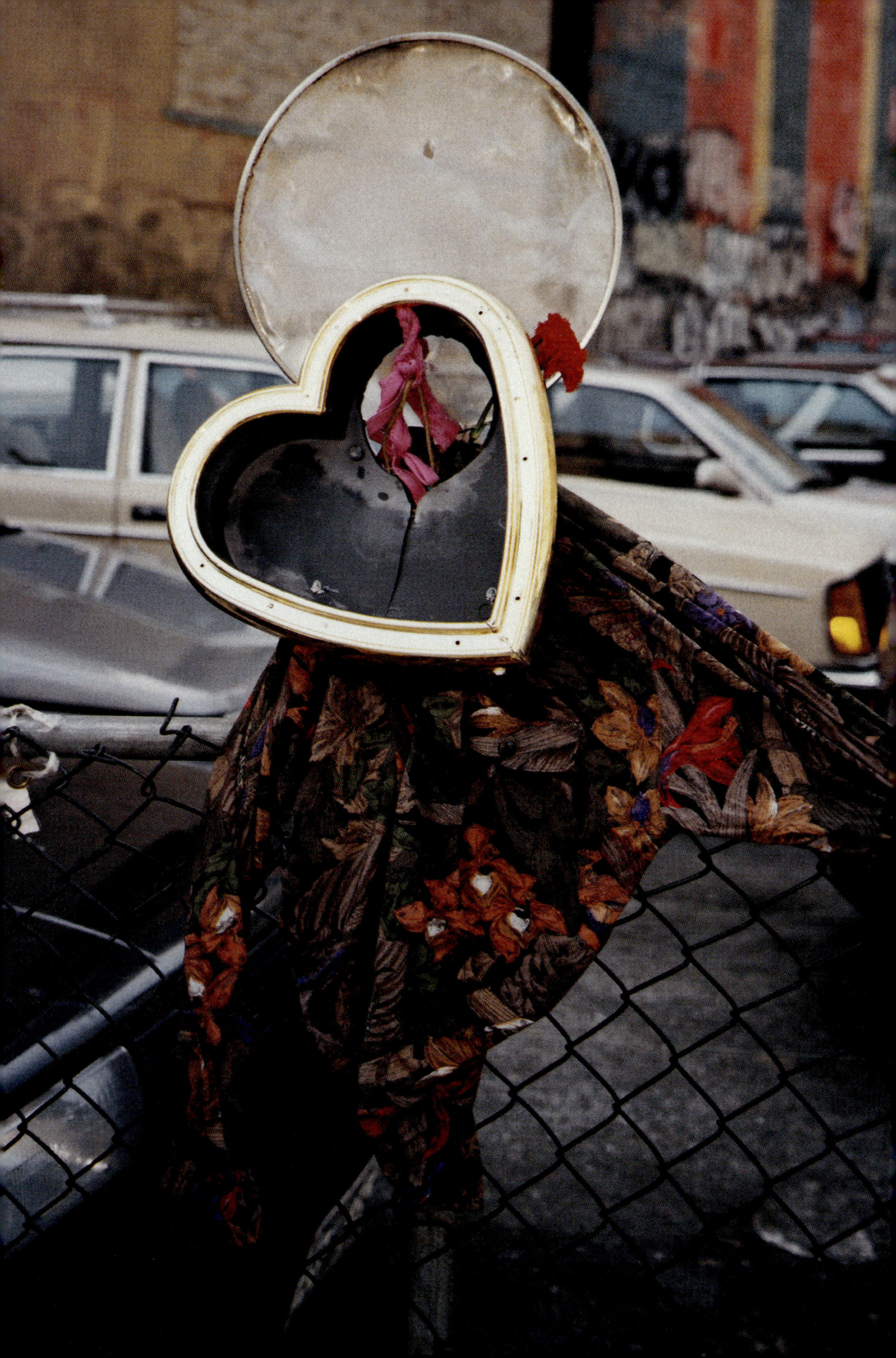

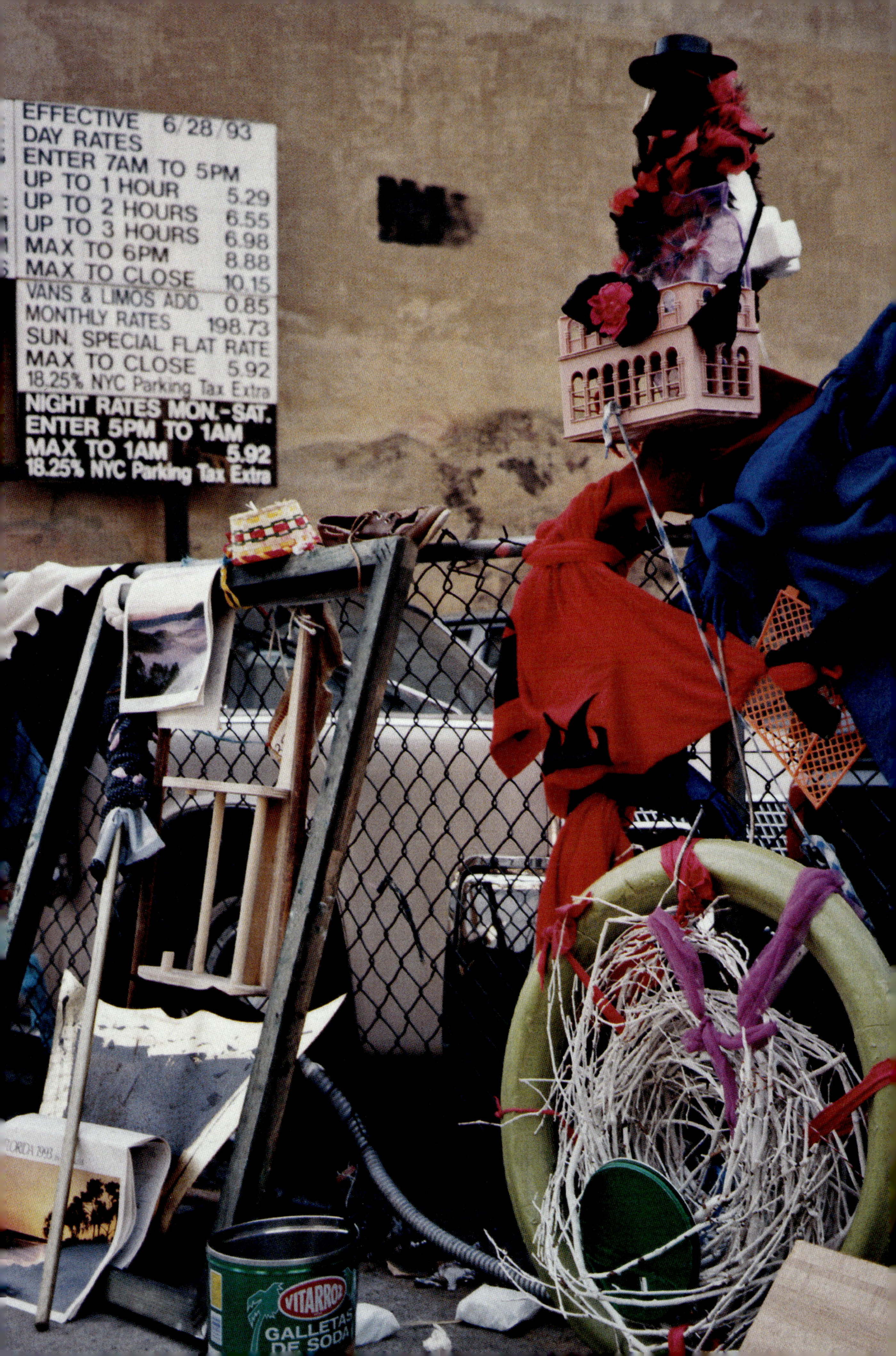
EFFECTIVE 6/28/93
DAY RATES
ENTER 7AM TO 5PM
UP TO 1 HOUR 5.29
UP TO 2 HOURS 6.55
UP TO 3 HOURS 6.98
MAX TO 6PM 8.88
MAX TO CLOSE 10.15
VANS & LIMOS ADD. 0.85
MONTHLY RATES 198.73
SUN. SPECIAL FLAT RATE
MAX TO CLOSE 5.92
18.25% NYC Parking Tax Extra
NIGHT RATES MON.-SAT.
ENTER 5PM TO 1AM
MAX TO 1AM 5.92
18.25% NYC Parking Tax Extra
VITARROZ
GALLETAS
DE SODA

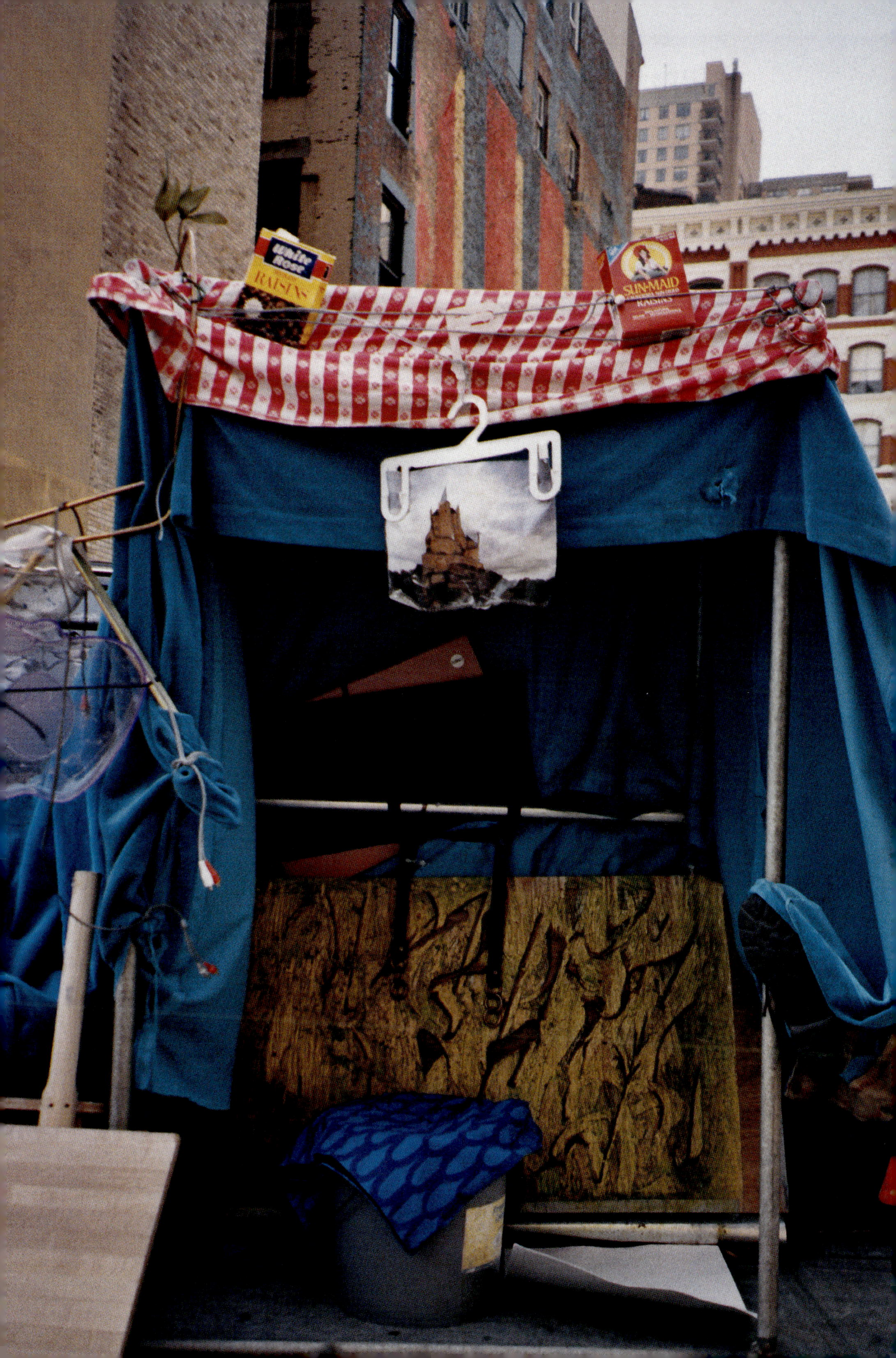
White Rose
RAISINS
SUN-MAID
RAISINS

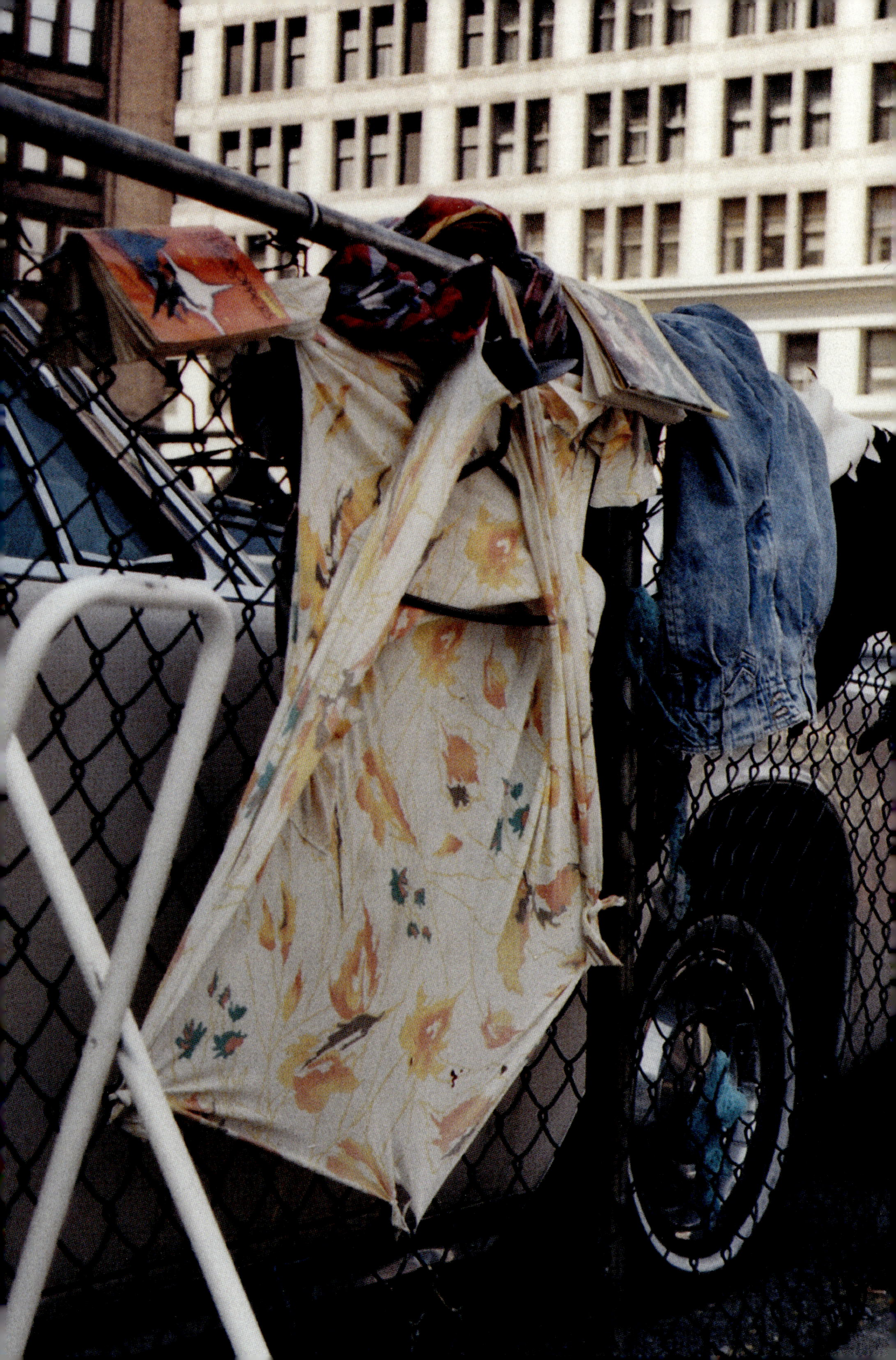

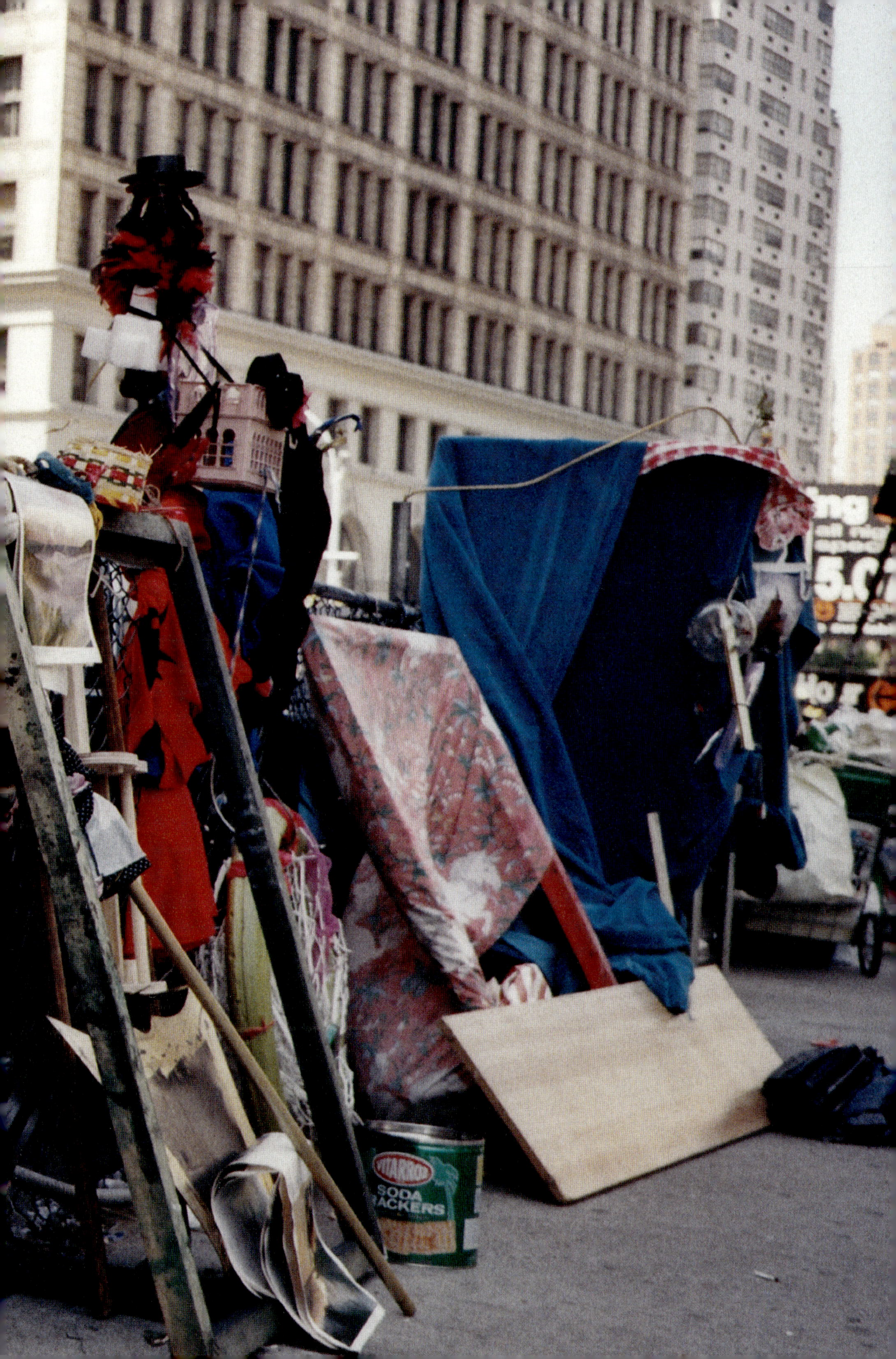
SODA
ACKERS

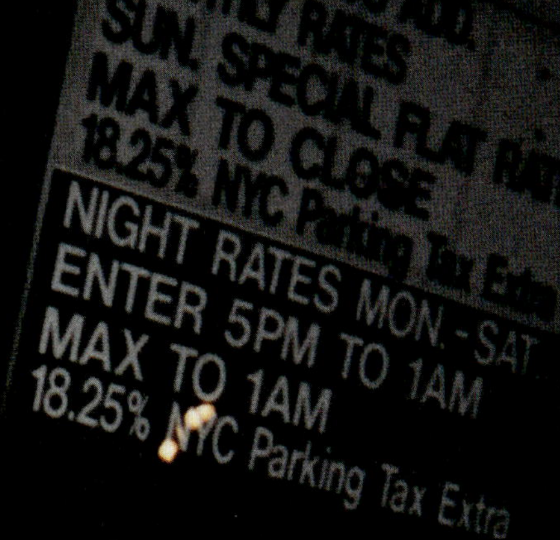
MONTHLY RATES
SUN. SPECIAL FLAT RATE
MAX TO CLOSE
NIGHT RATES MON.-SAT
ENTER 5PM TO 1AM
MAX TO 1AM
18.25% NYC Parking Tax Extra

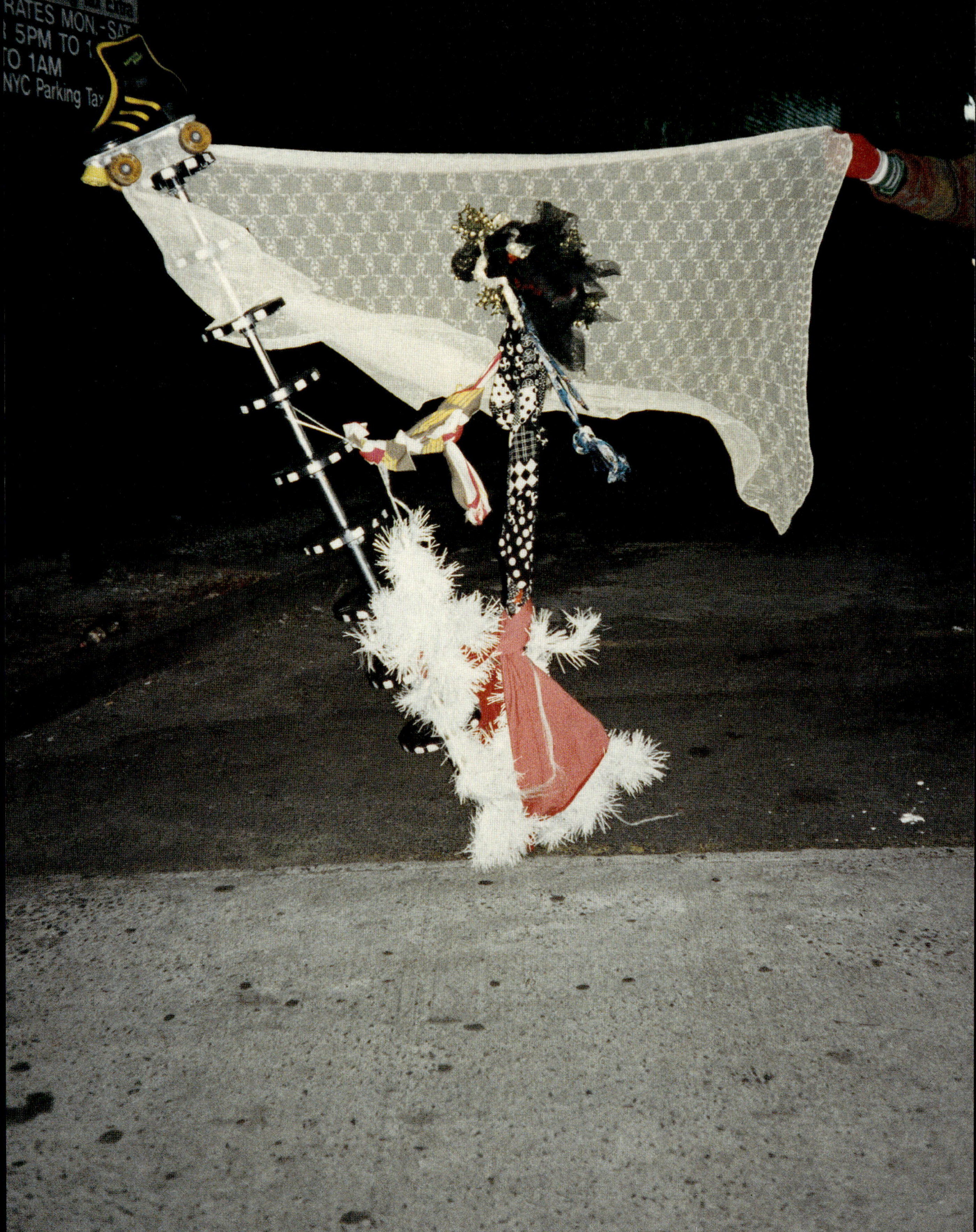
RATES MON.-SAT
5PM TO 1
TO 1AM
NYC Parking Tax

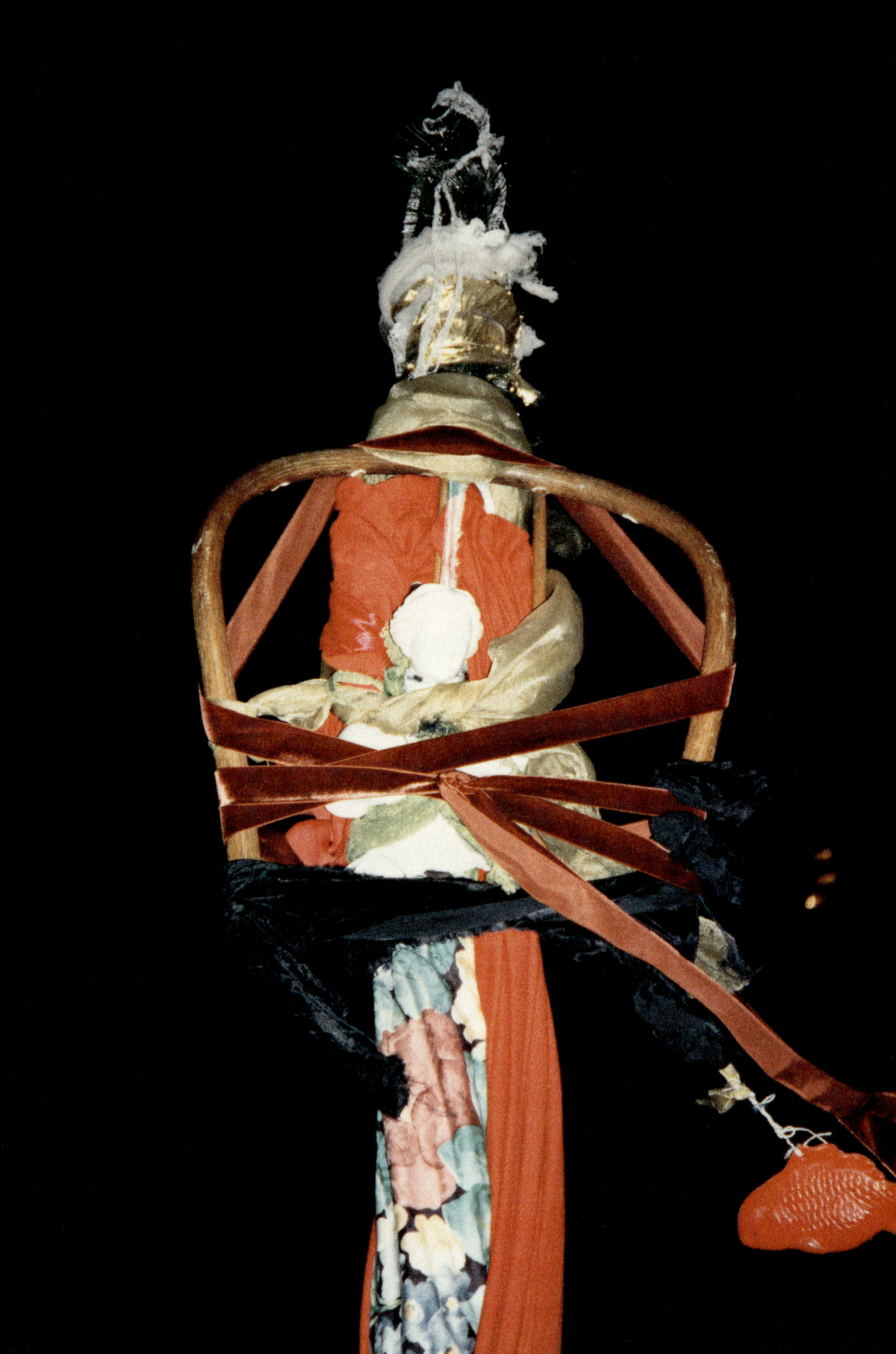

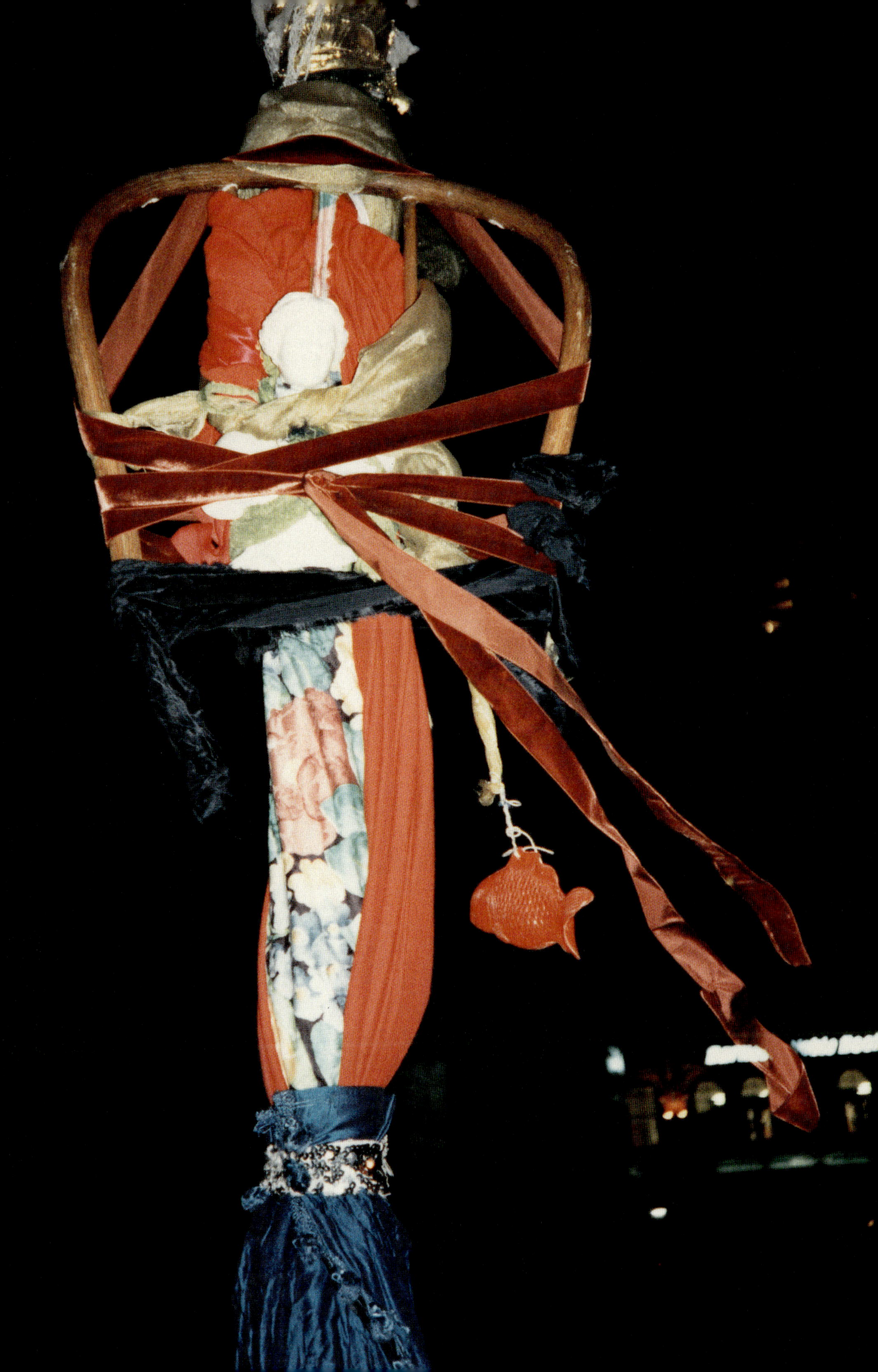

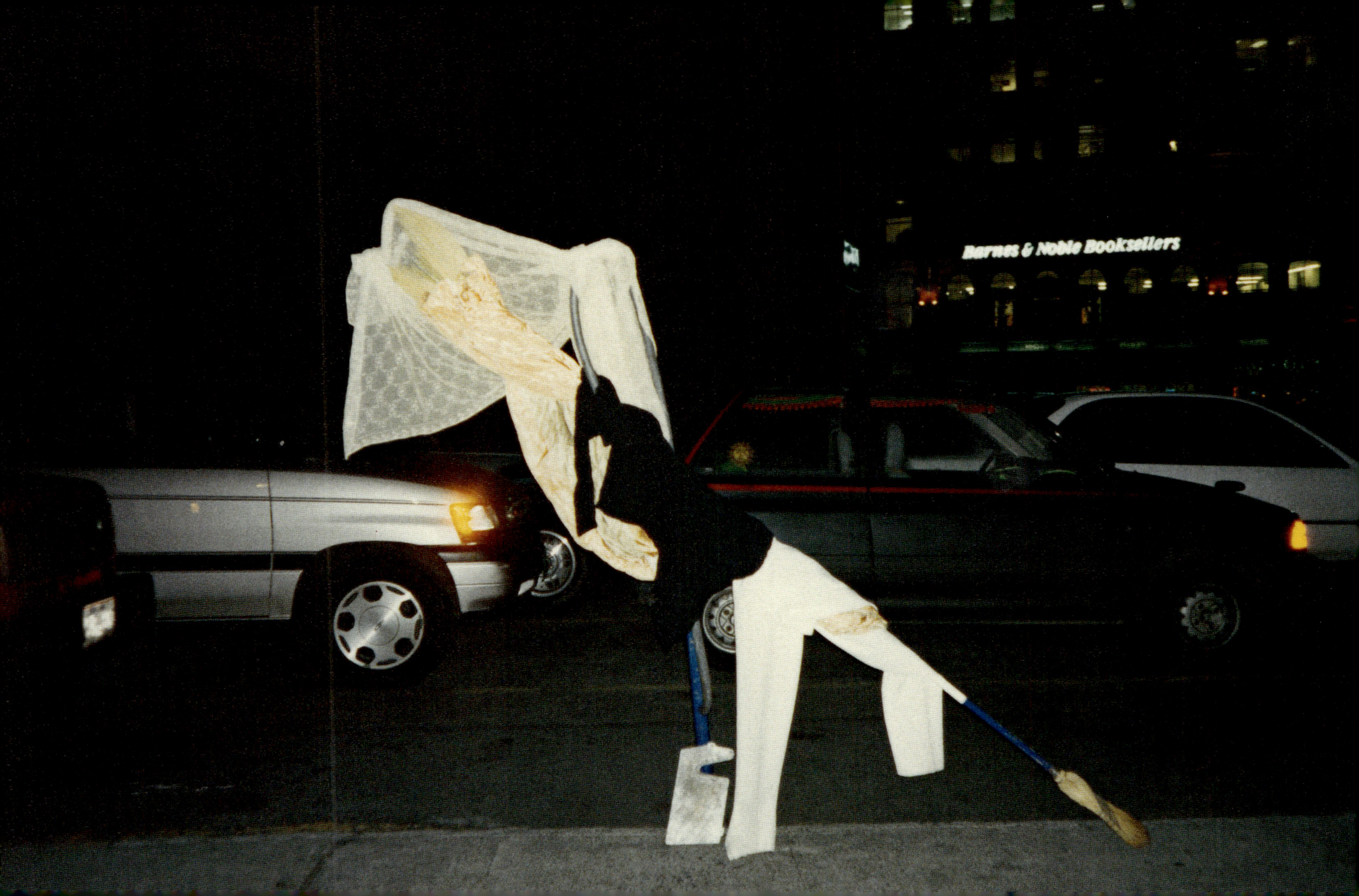
Barnes & Noble Booksellers

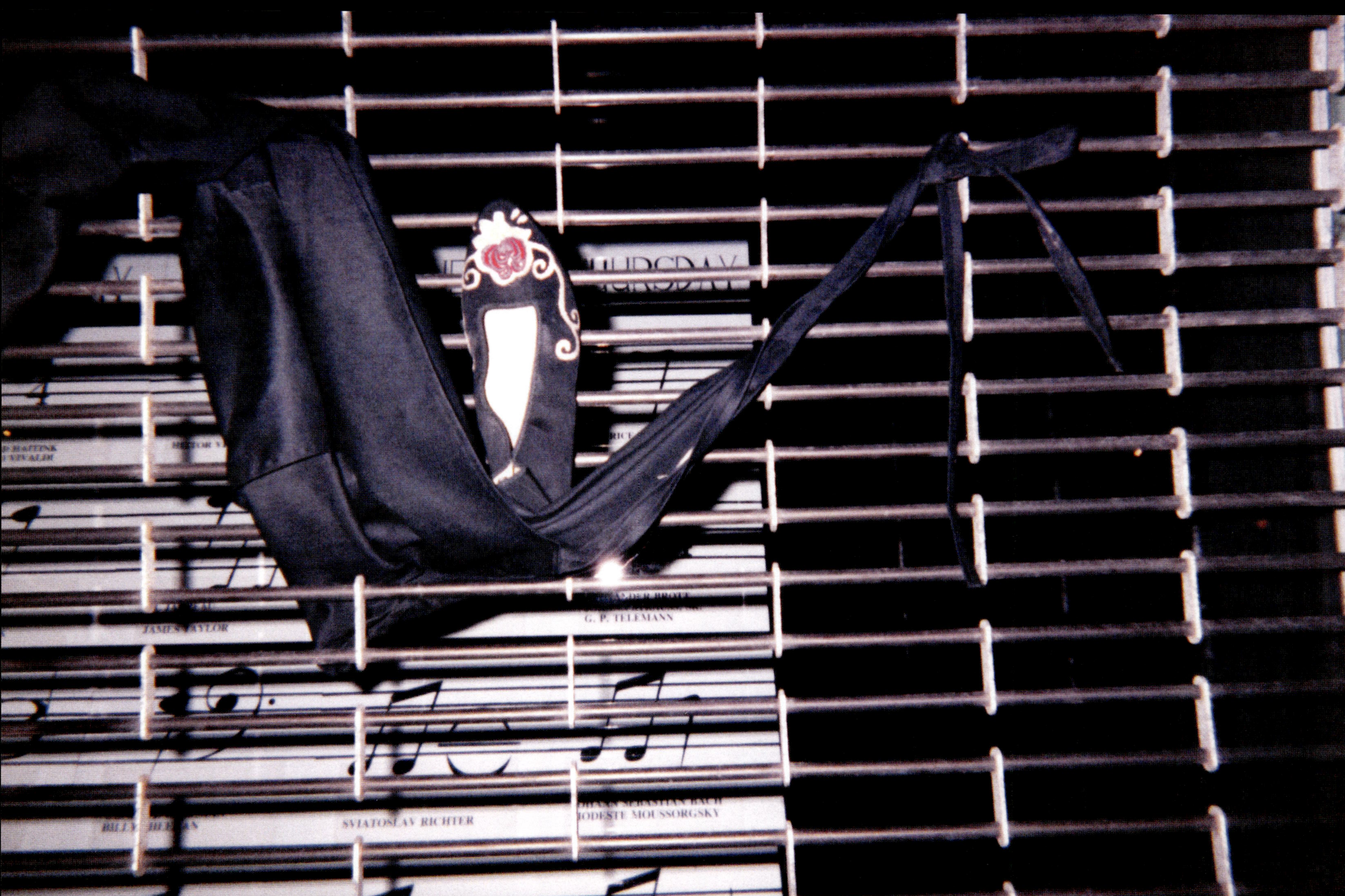
G. P. TELEMANN
SVIATOSLAV RICHTER
MODESTE MOUSSORGSKY

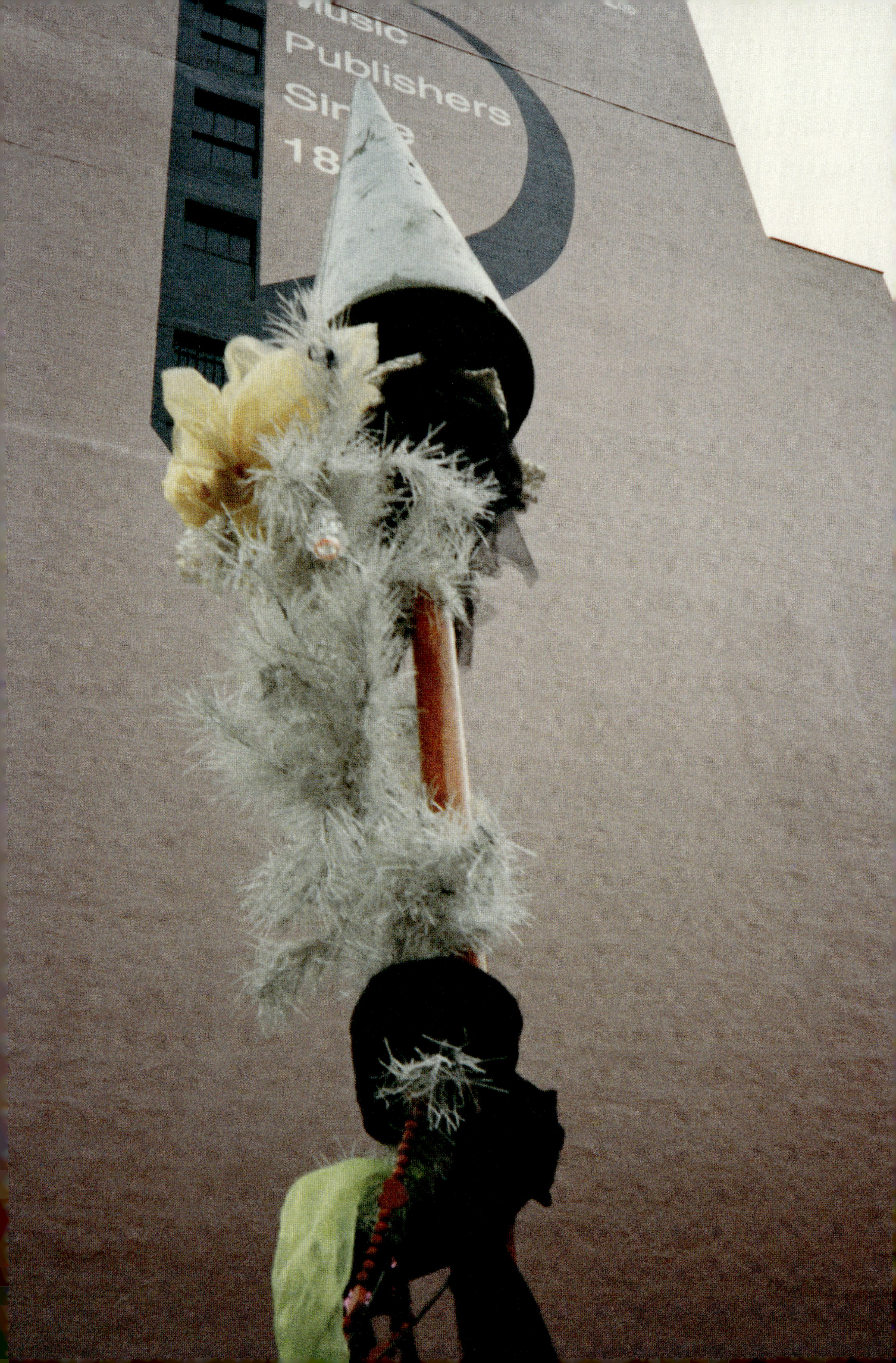
Music
Publishers

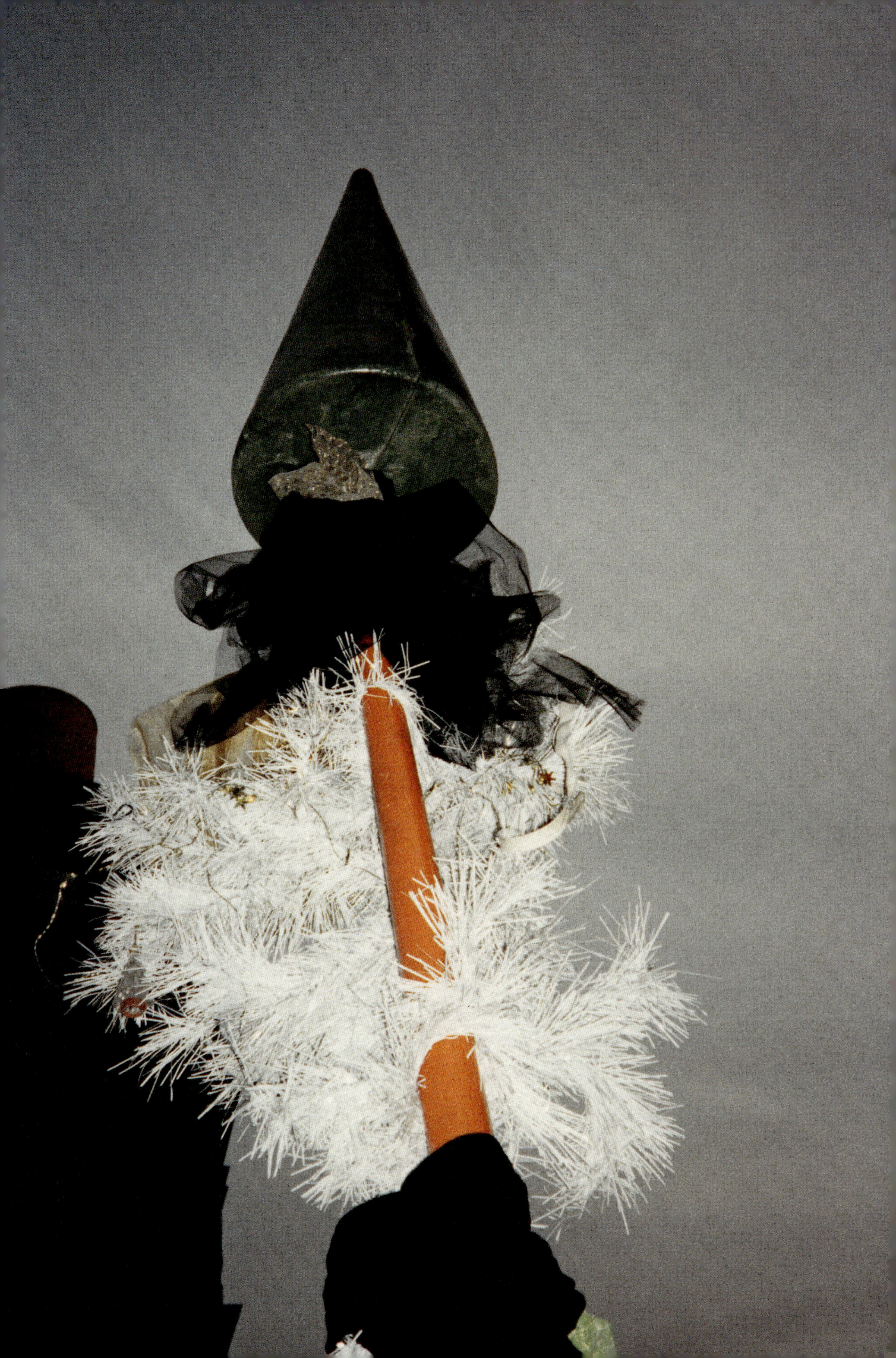

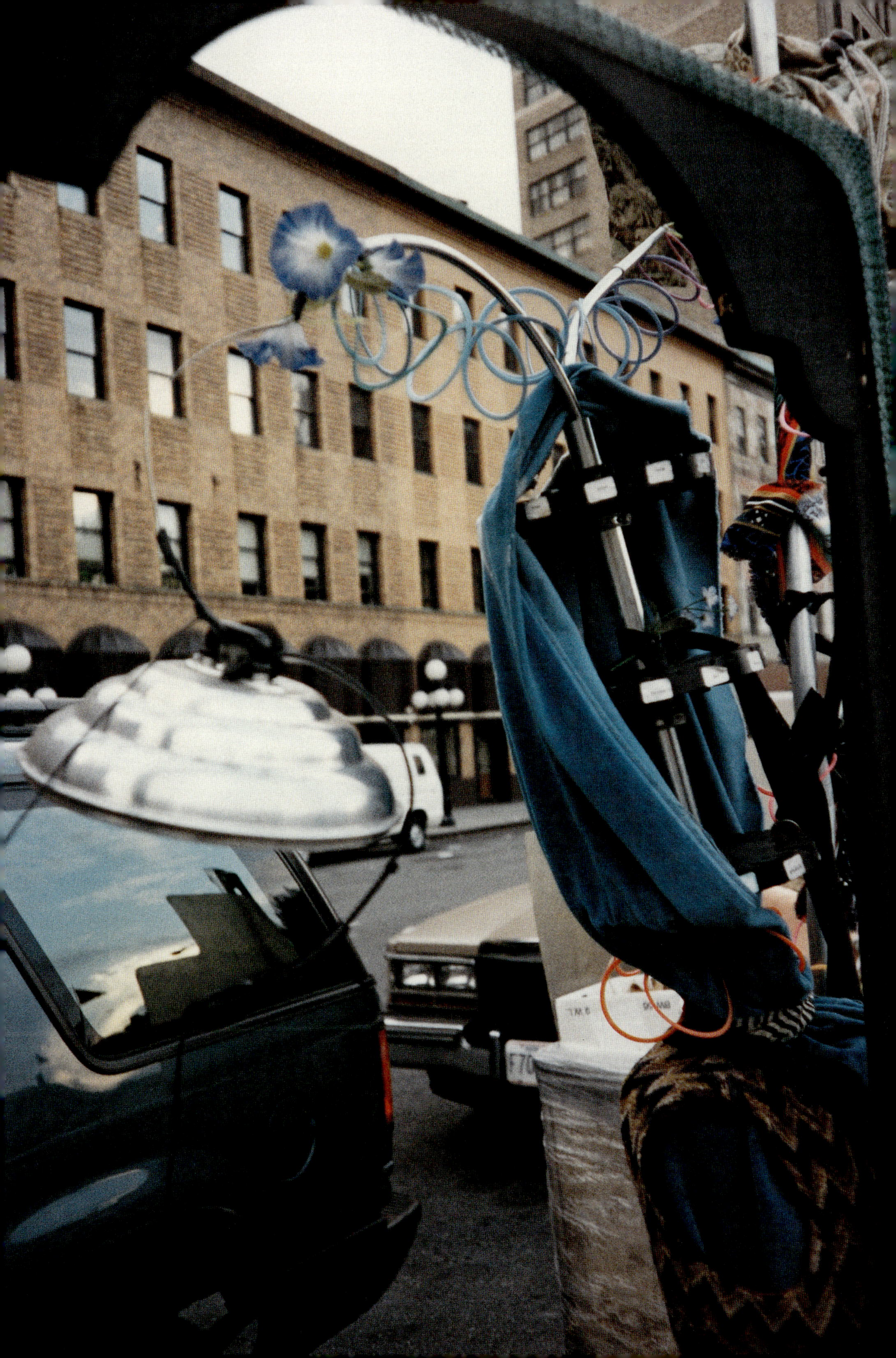

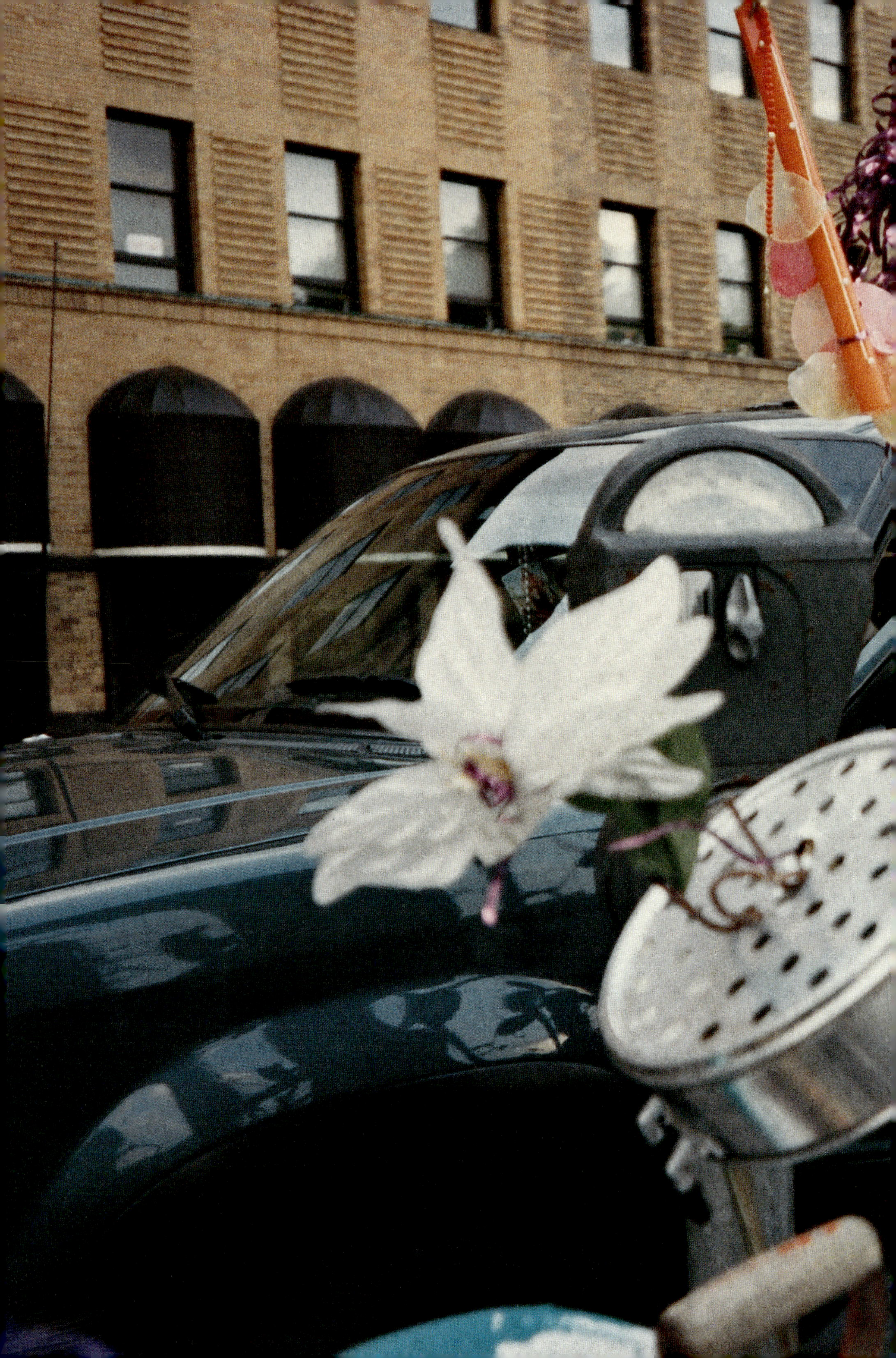

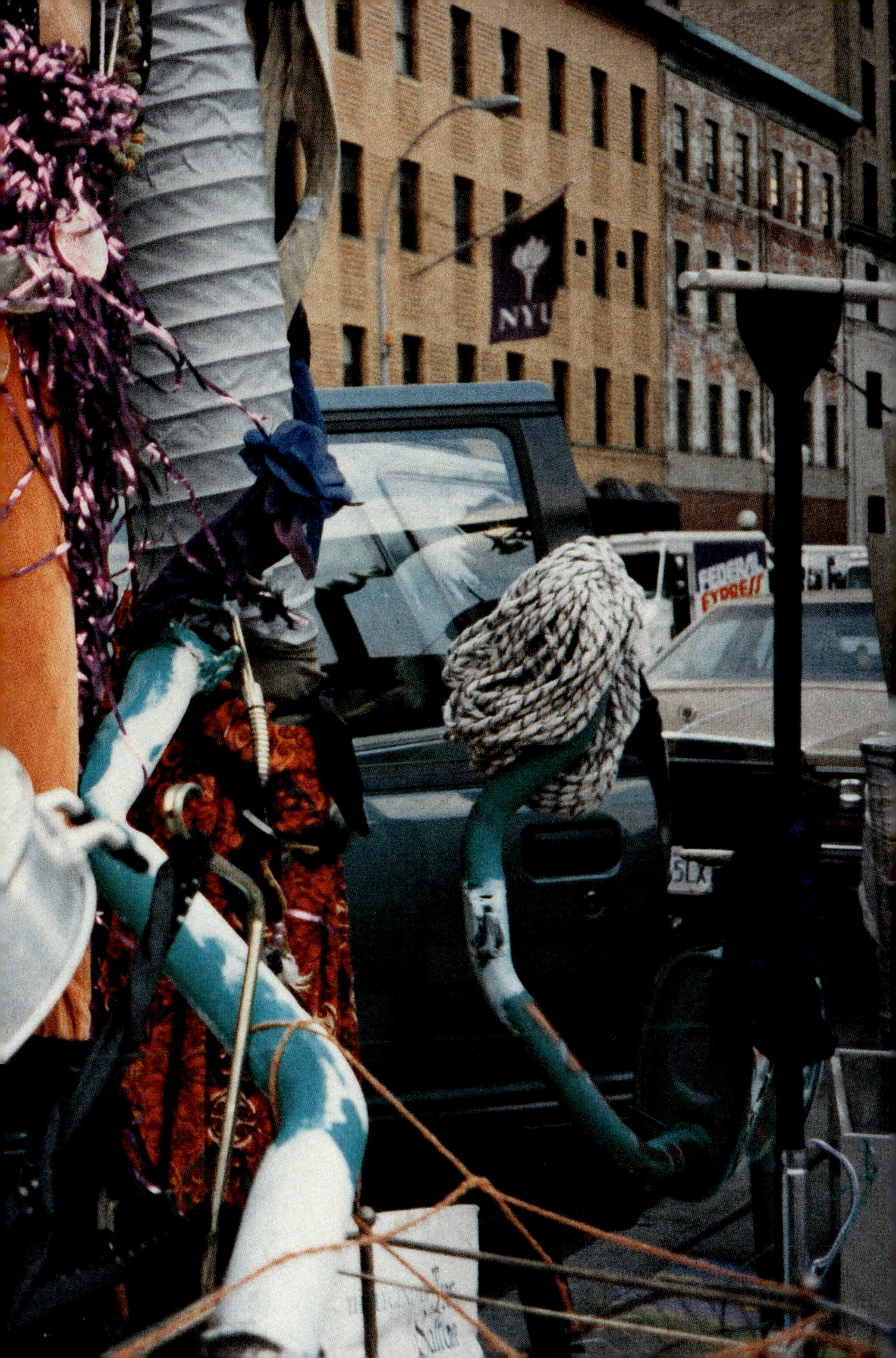
NYU
FEDERAL
EXPRESS

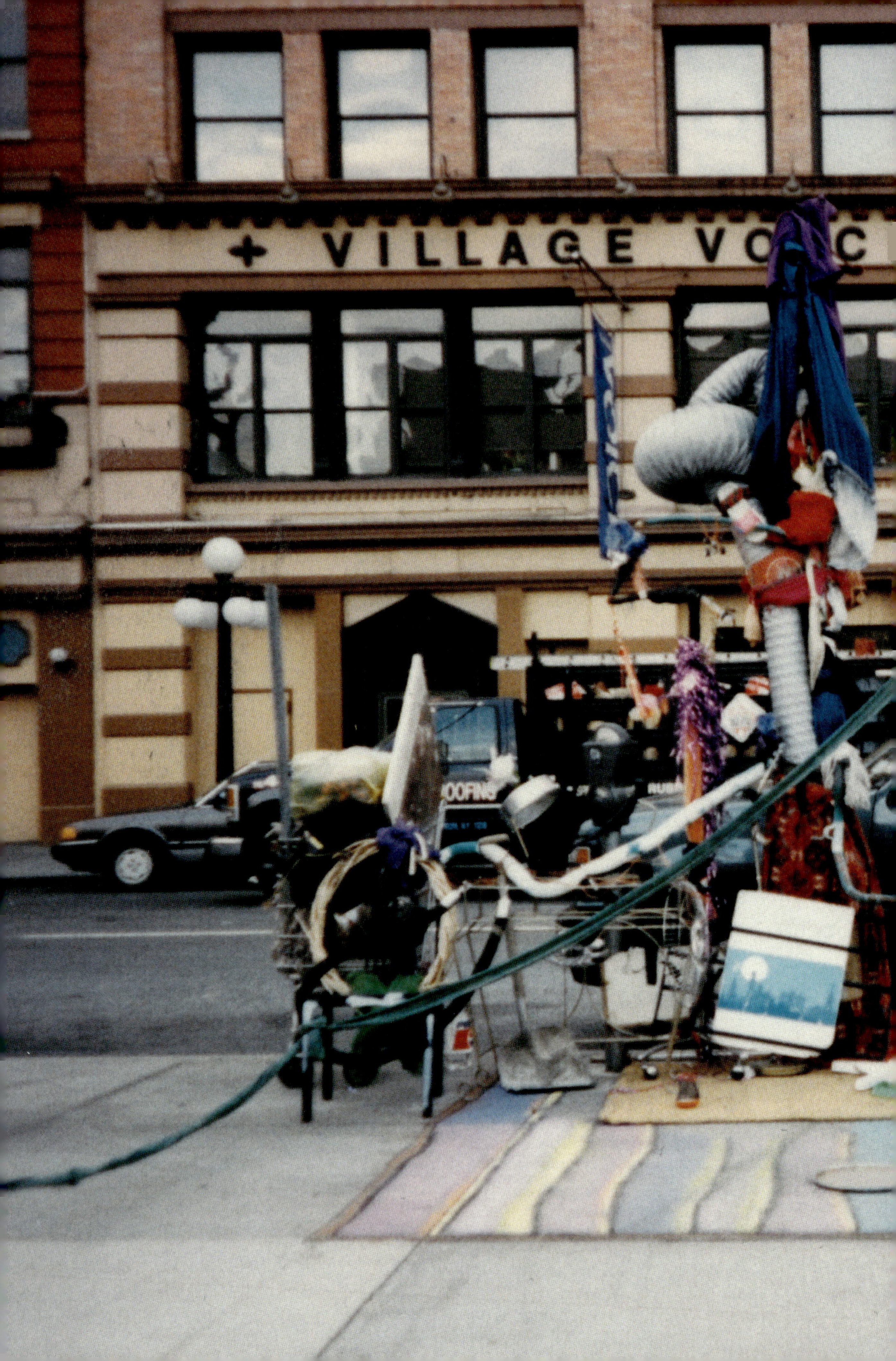
VILLAGE

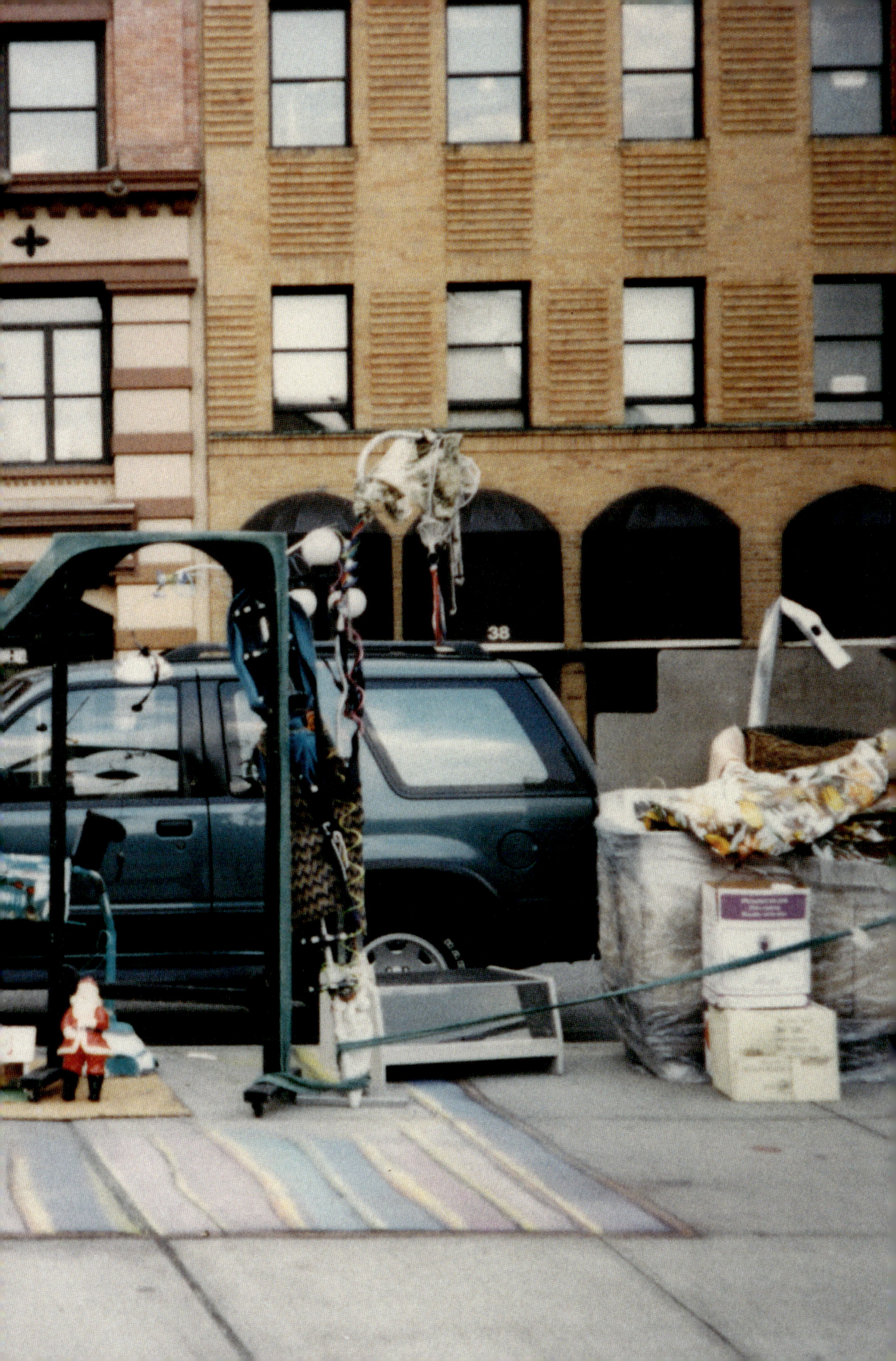
38

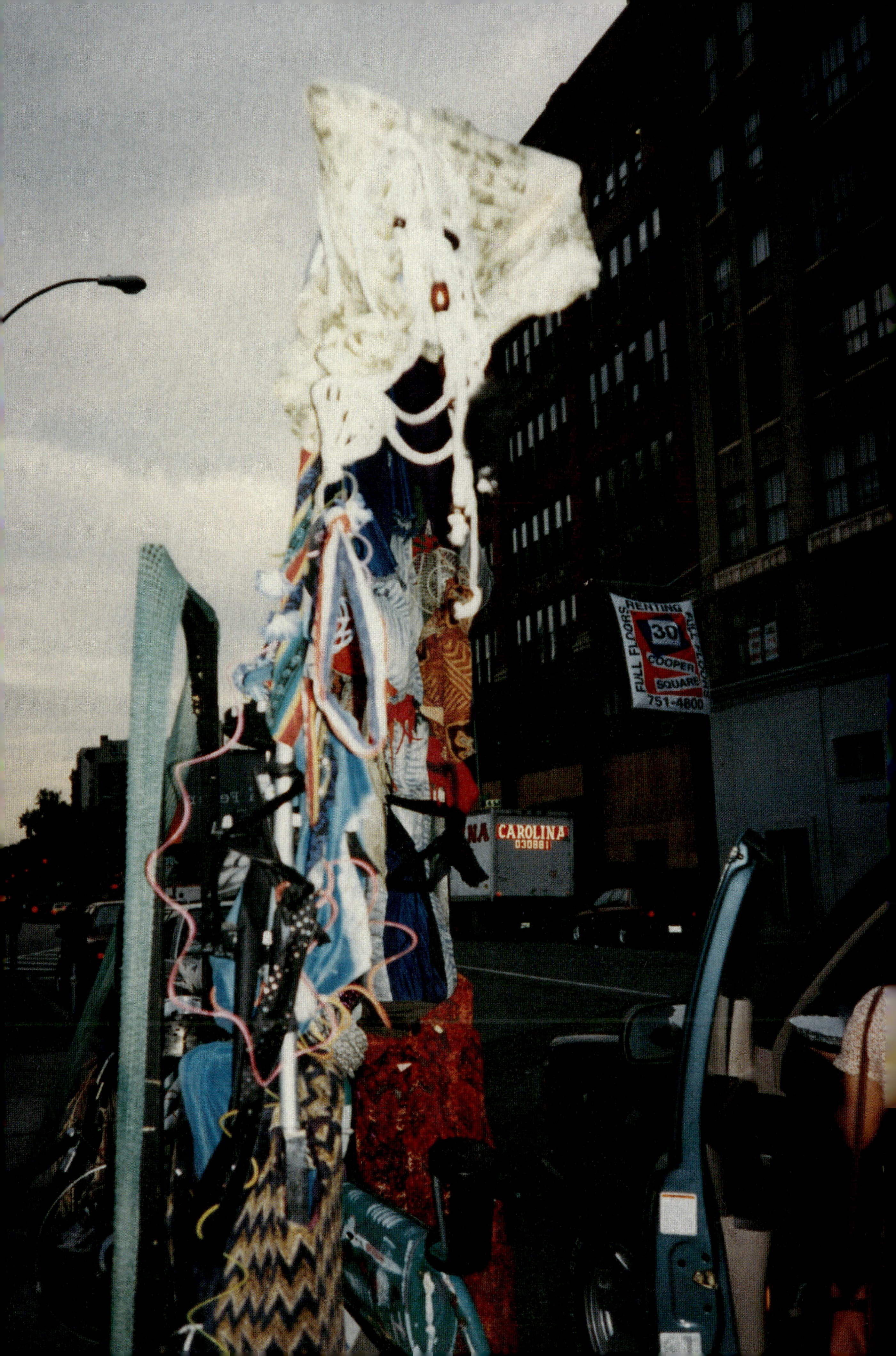
RENTING
FULL FLOORS
30
COOPER
SQUARE
FULL FLOORS
751-4800
CAROLINA
030881

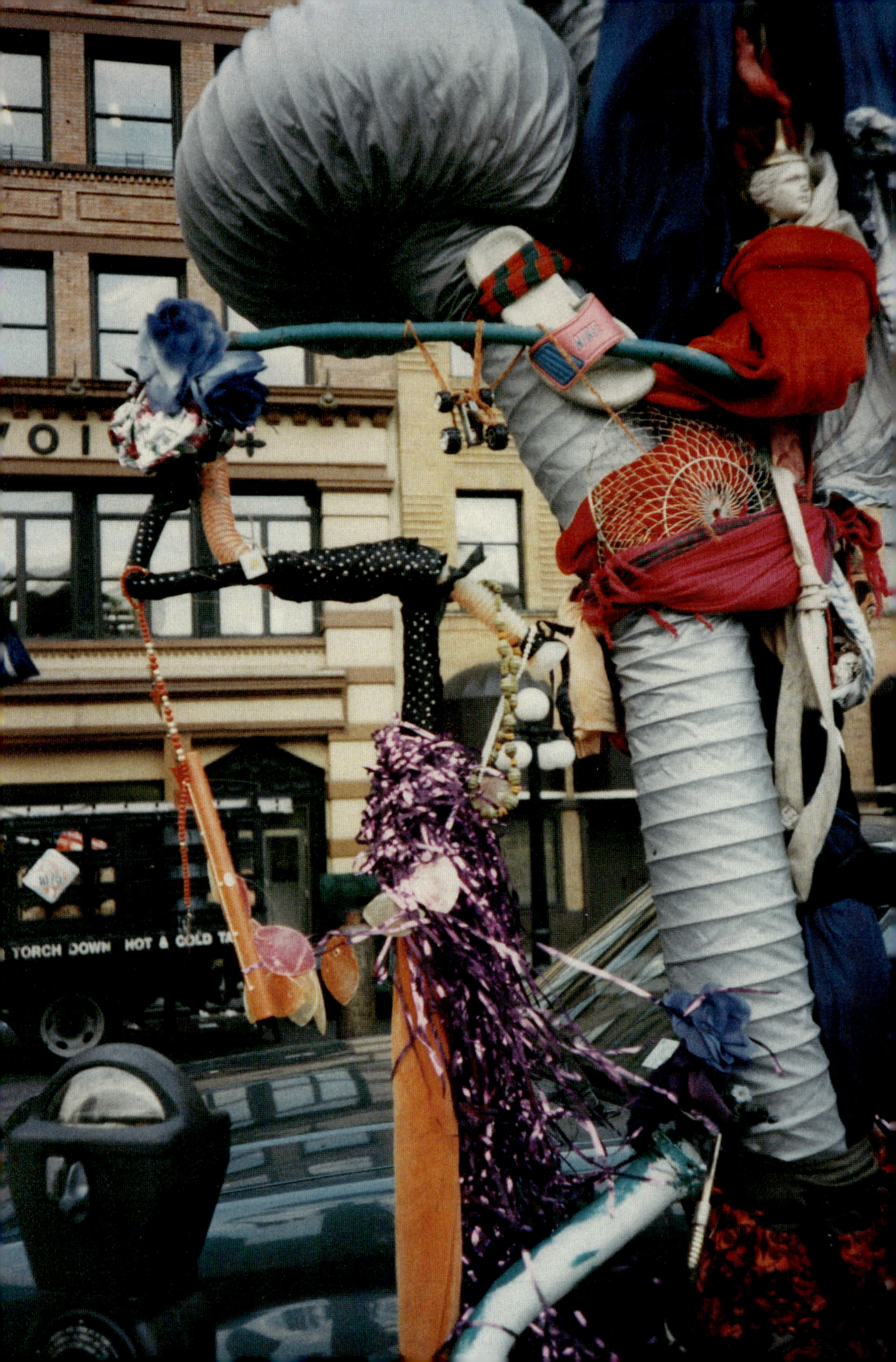
TORCH DOWN HOT & COLD

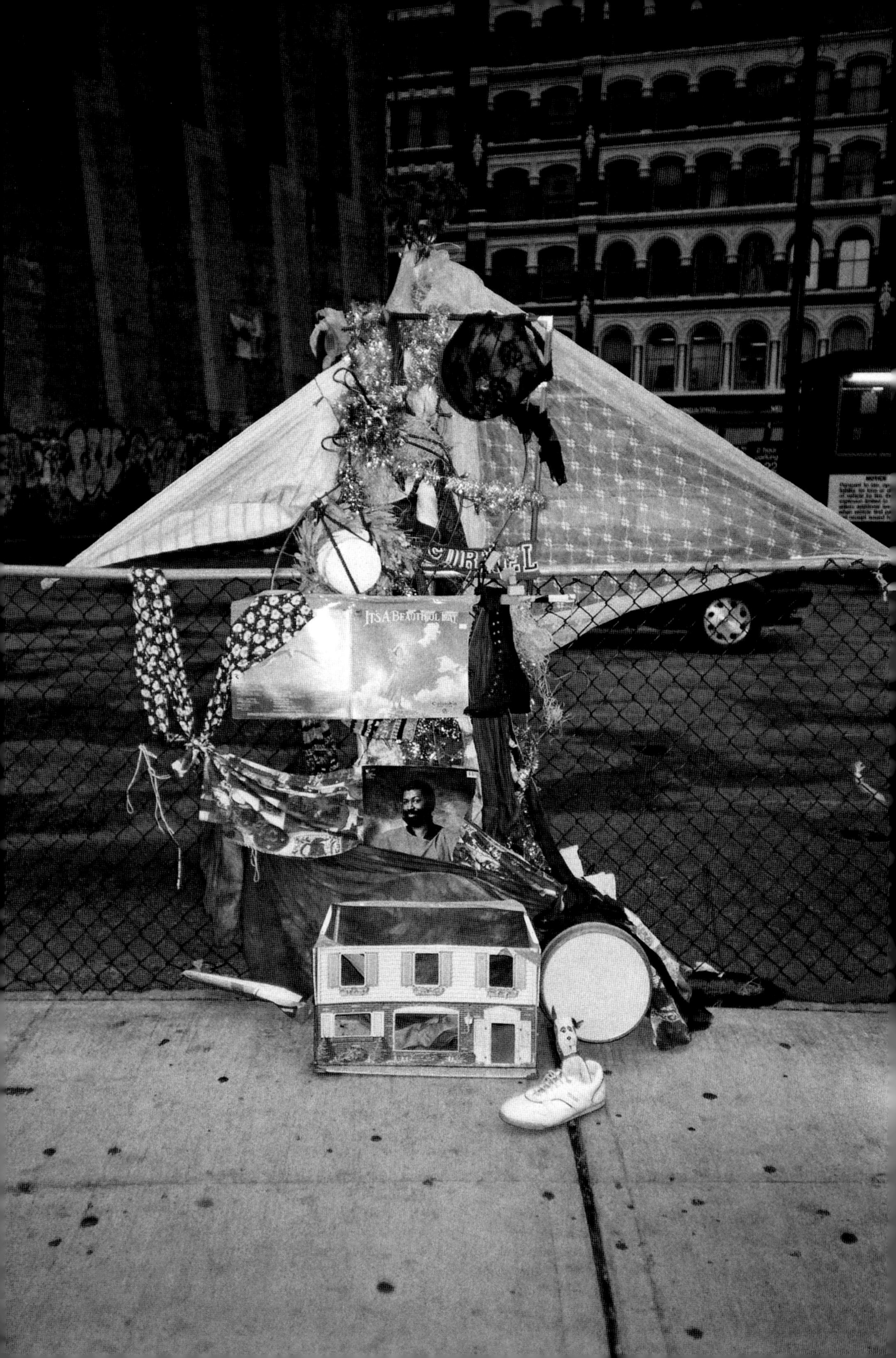

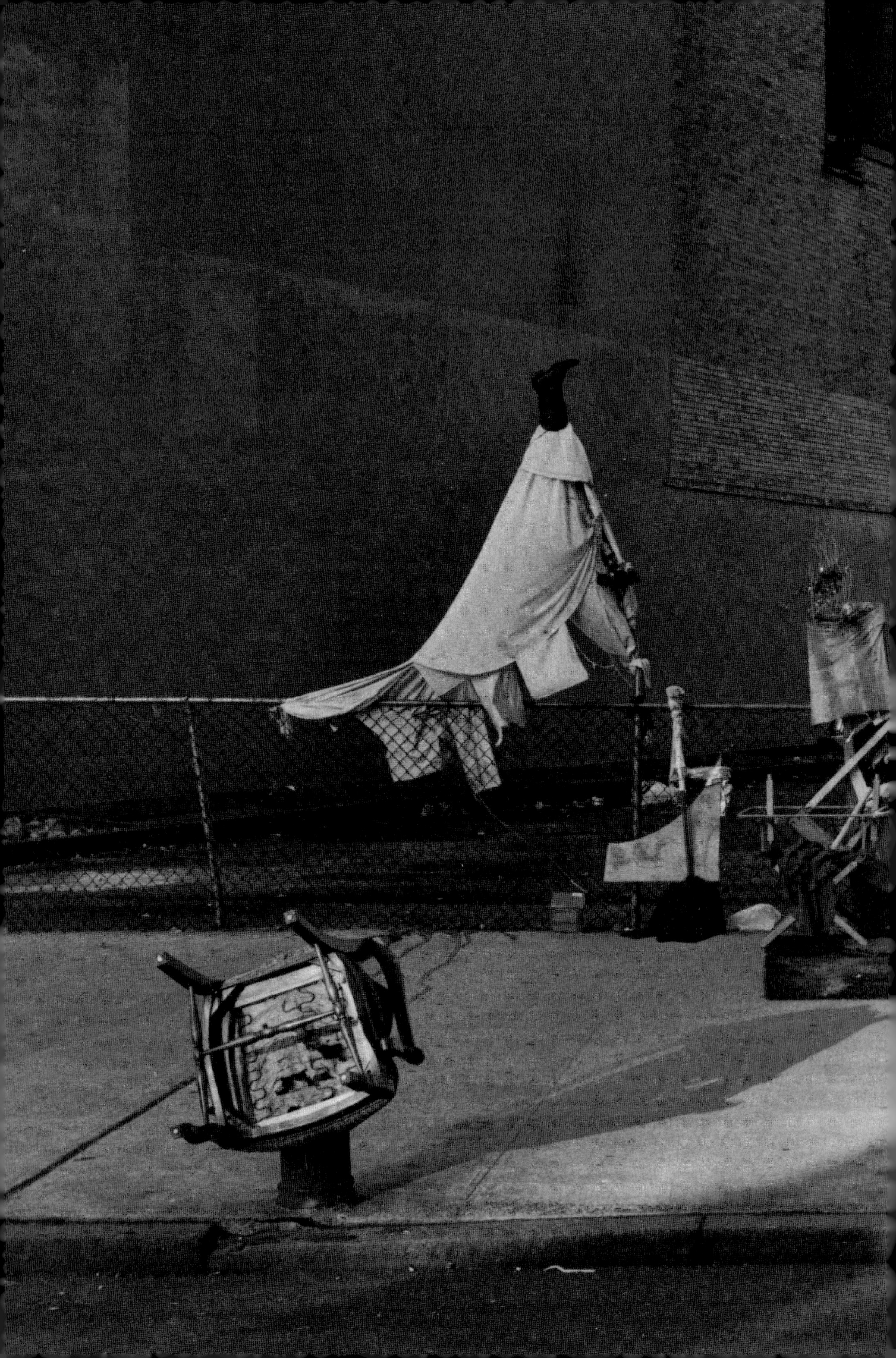

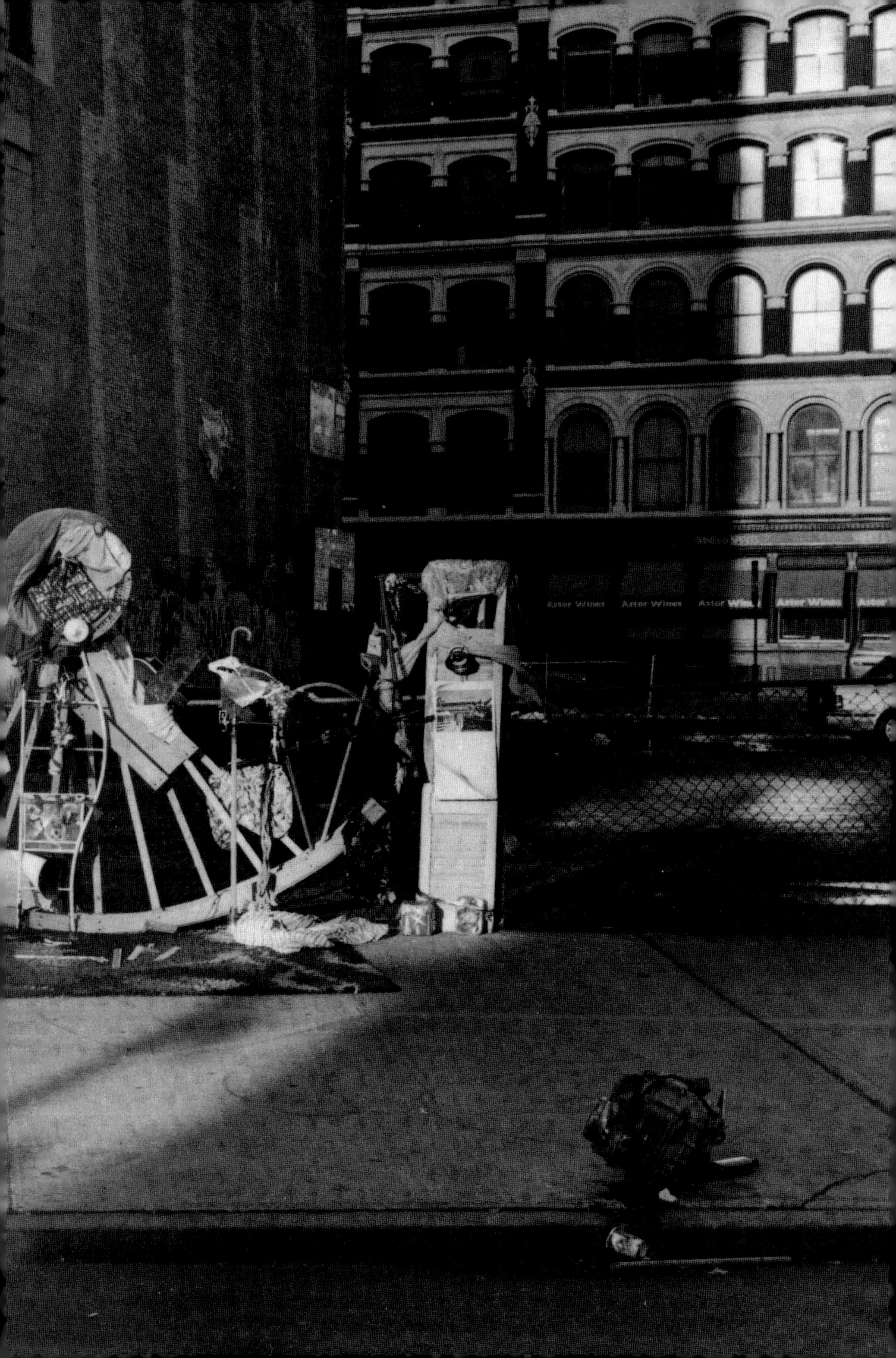
Astor Wines
Astor Wines
Astor Wines

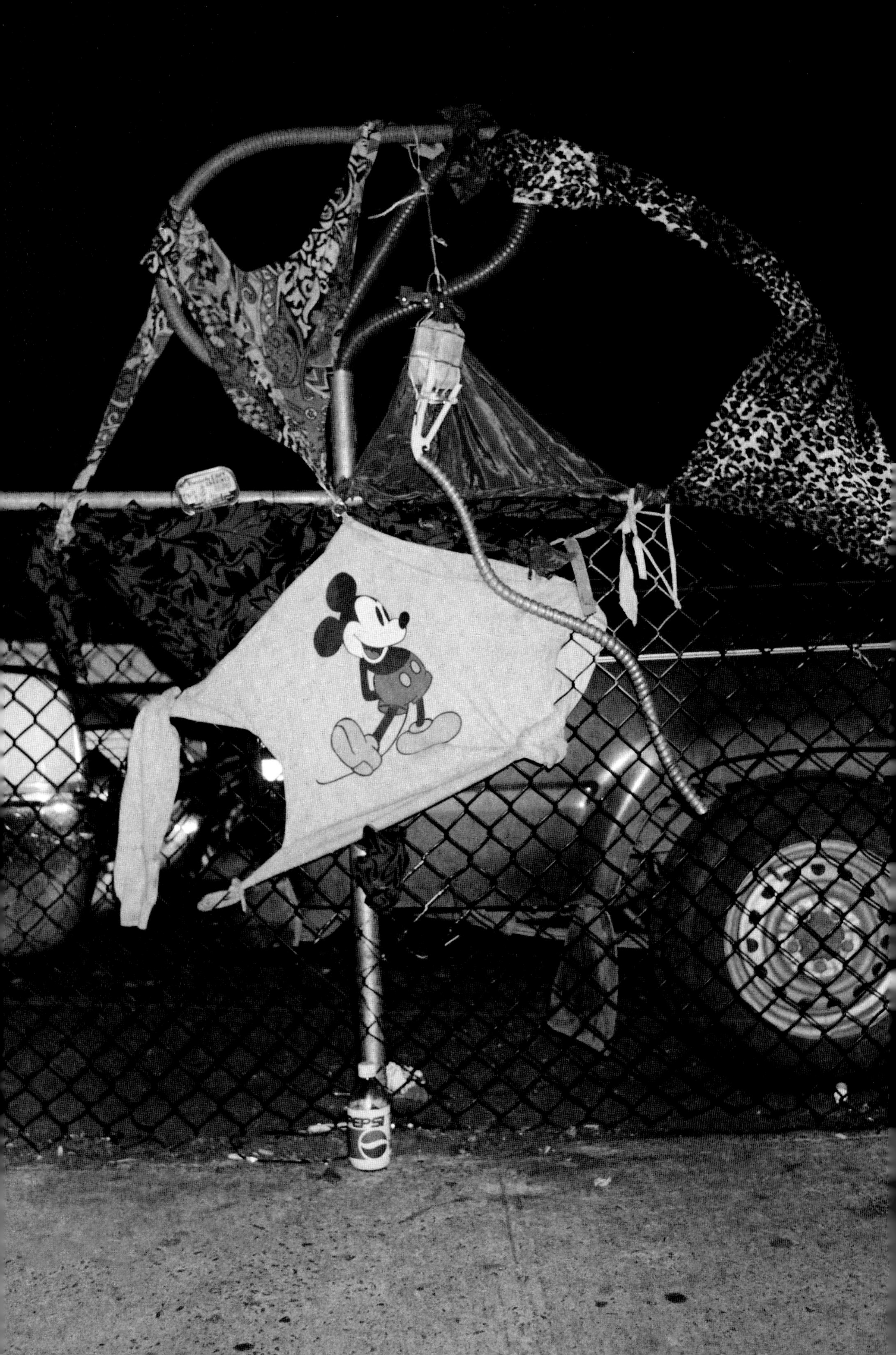
PEPSI

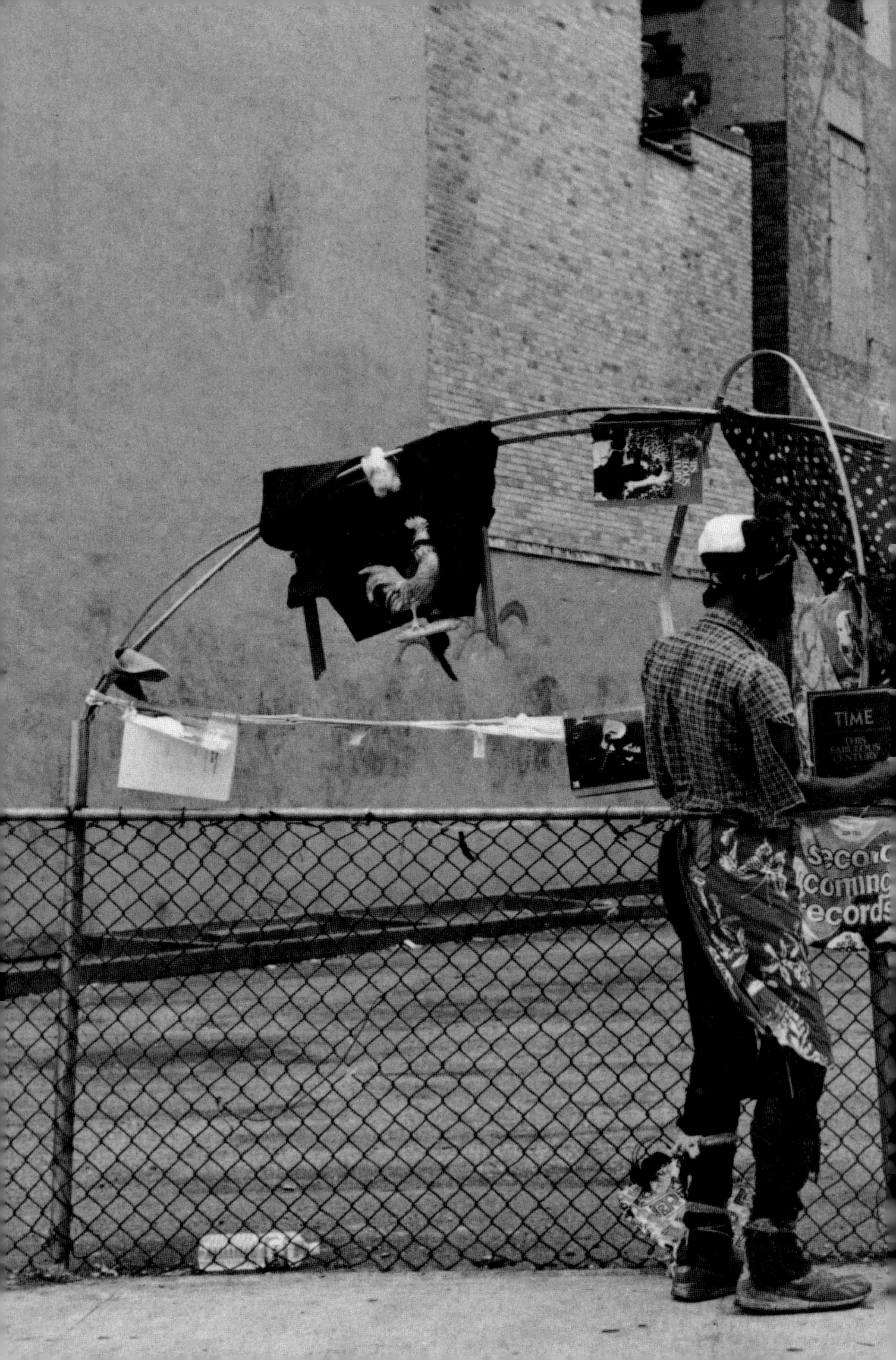
TIME
Coming

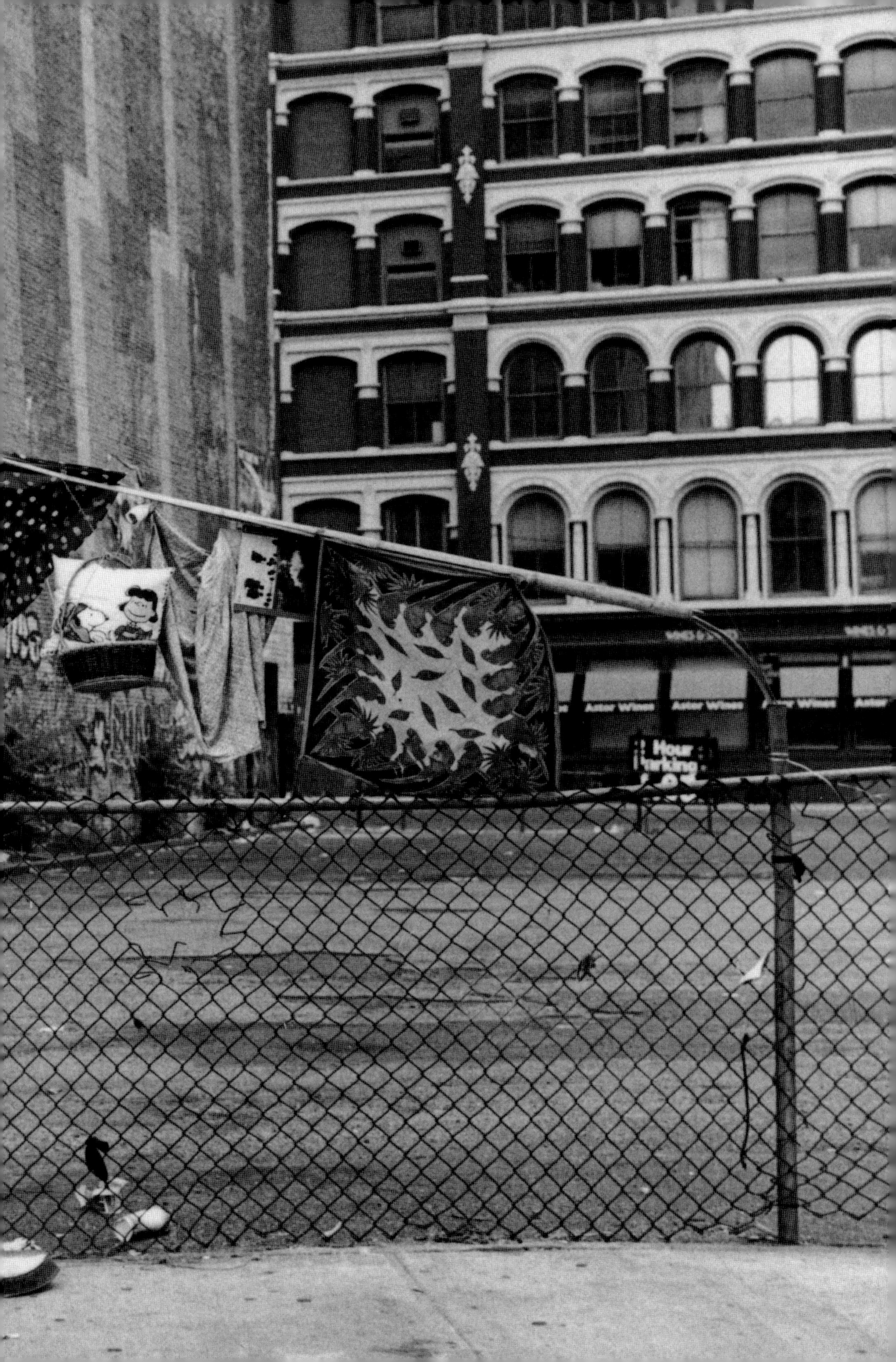
Hour

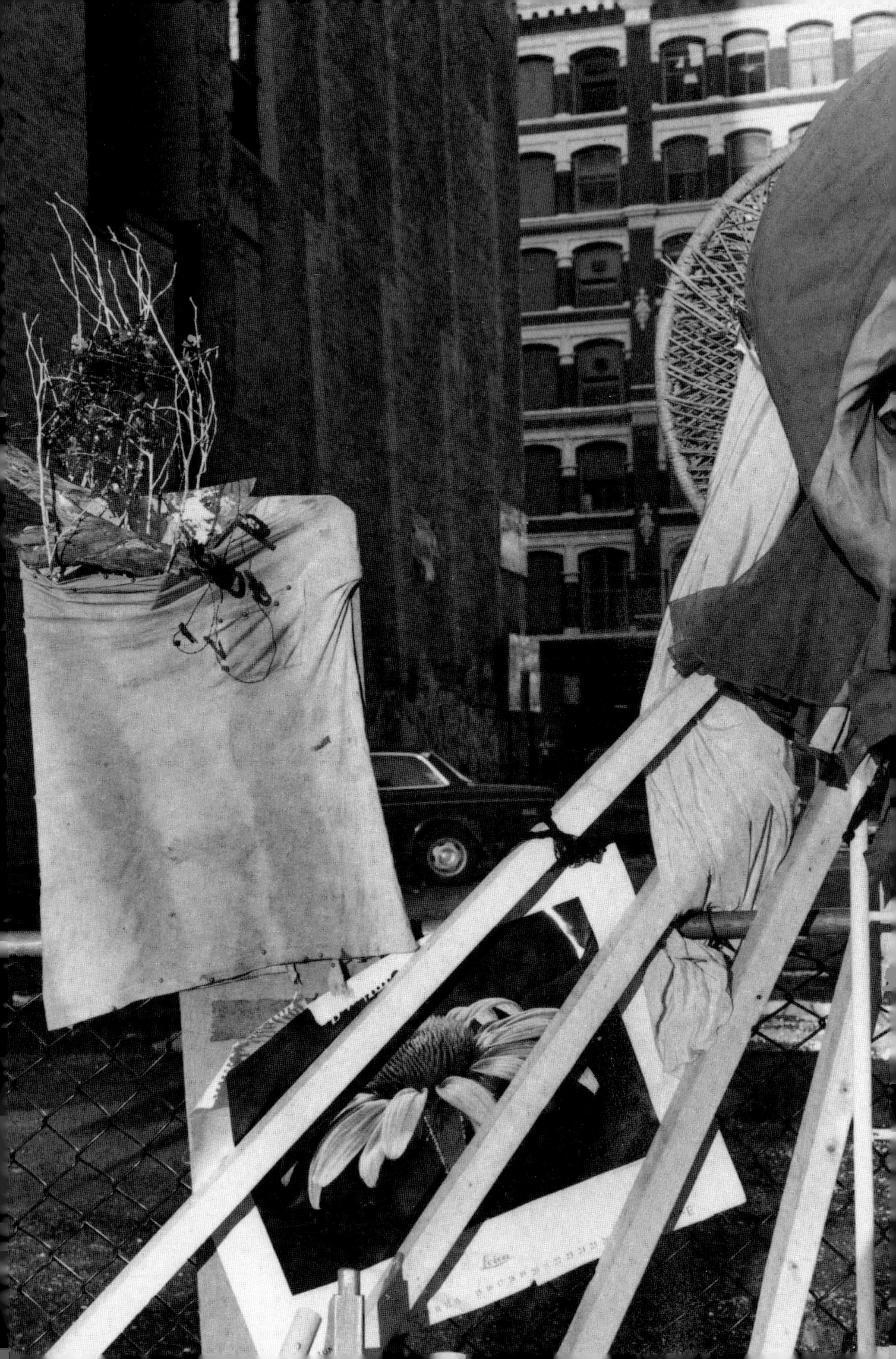

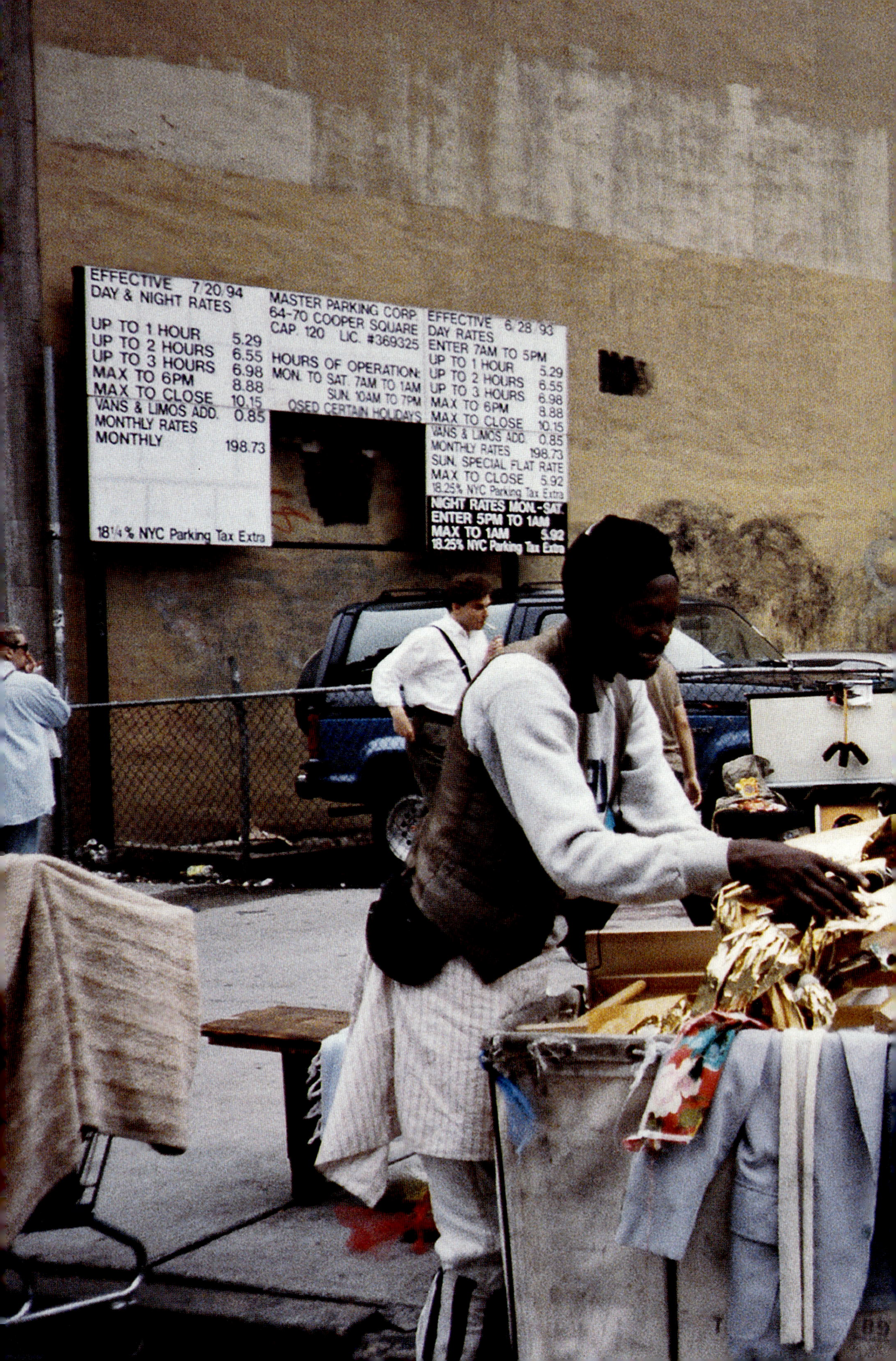
EFFECTIVE 7/20/94
DAY & NIGHT RATES
UP TO 1 HOUR 5.29
UP TO 2 HOURS 6.55
UP TO 3 HOURS 6.98
MAX TO 6PM 8.88
MAX TO CLOSE 10.15
VANS & LIMOS ADD. 0.85
MONTHLY RATES
MONTHLY 198.73
18¼ % NYC Parking Tax Extra
MASTER PARKING CORP.
64-70 COOPER SQUARE
CAP. 120 LIC. #369325
HOURS OF OPERATION:
MON. TO SAT. 7AM TO 1AM
SUN. 10AM TO 7PM
OSED CERTAIN HOLIDAYS
EFFECTIVE 6/28/93
DAY RATES
ENTER 7AM TO 5PM
UP TO 1 HOUR 5.29
UP TO 2 HOURS 6.55
UP TO 3 HOURS 6.98
MAX TO 6PM 8.88
MAX TO CLOSE 10.15
VANS & LIMOS ADD. 0.85
MONTHLY RATES 198.73
SUN. SPECIAL FLAT RATE
MAX TO CLOSE 5.92
18.25% NYC Parking Tax Extra
NIGHT RATES MON.-SAT.
ENTER 5PM TO 1AM
MAX TO 1AM 5.92
18.25% NYC Parking Tax Extra

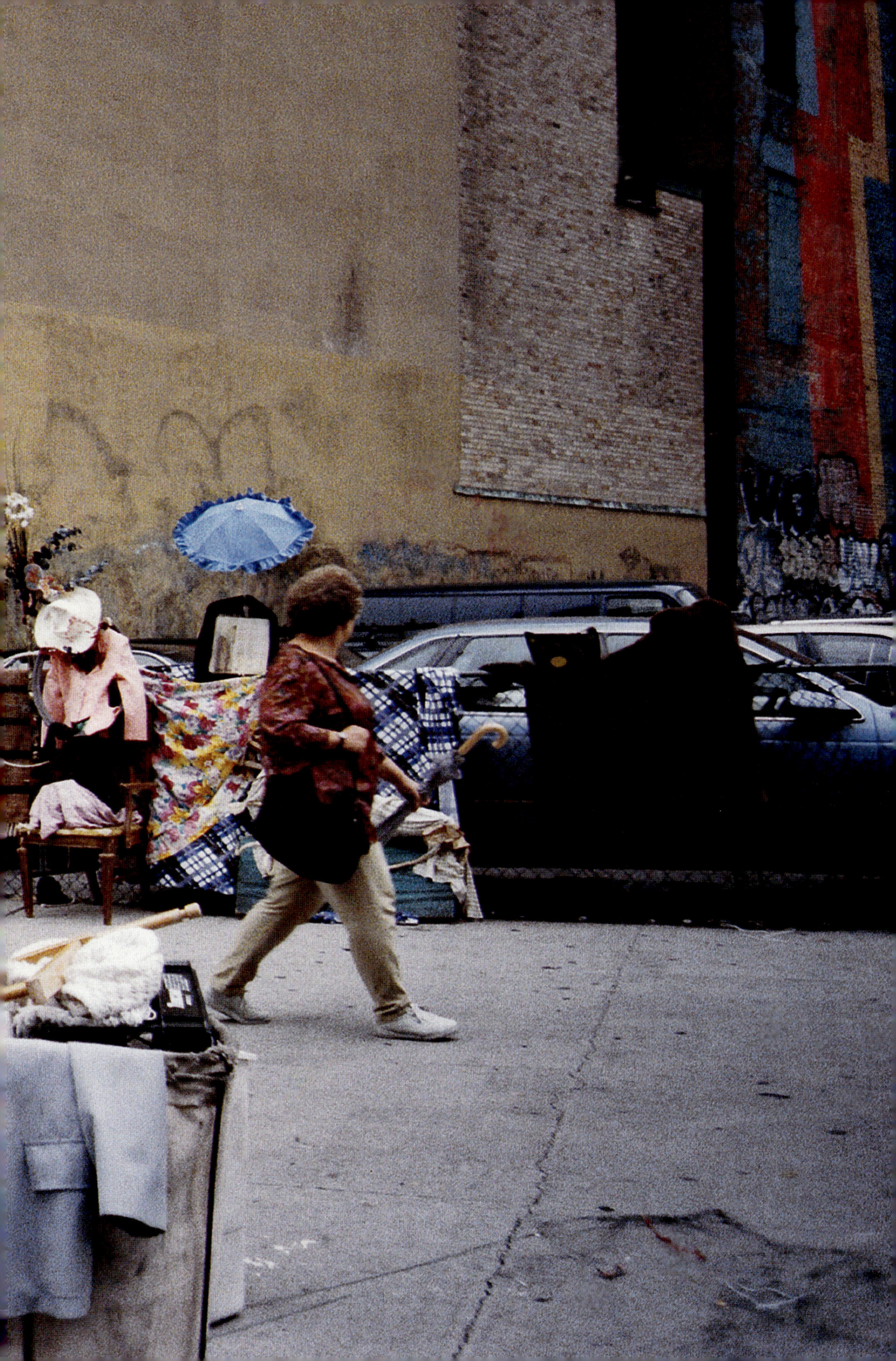

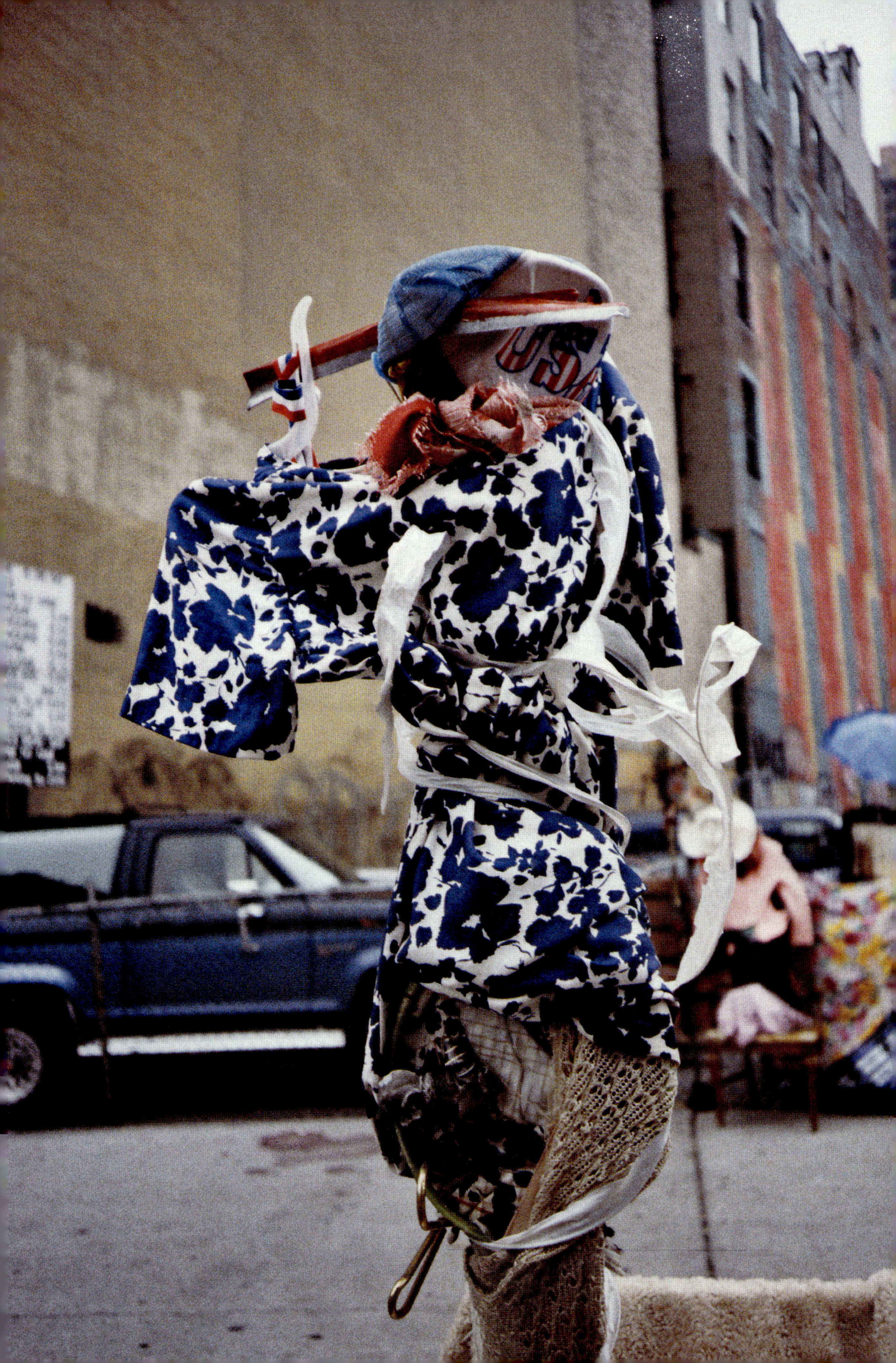

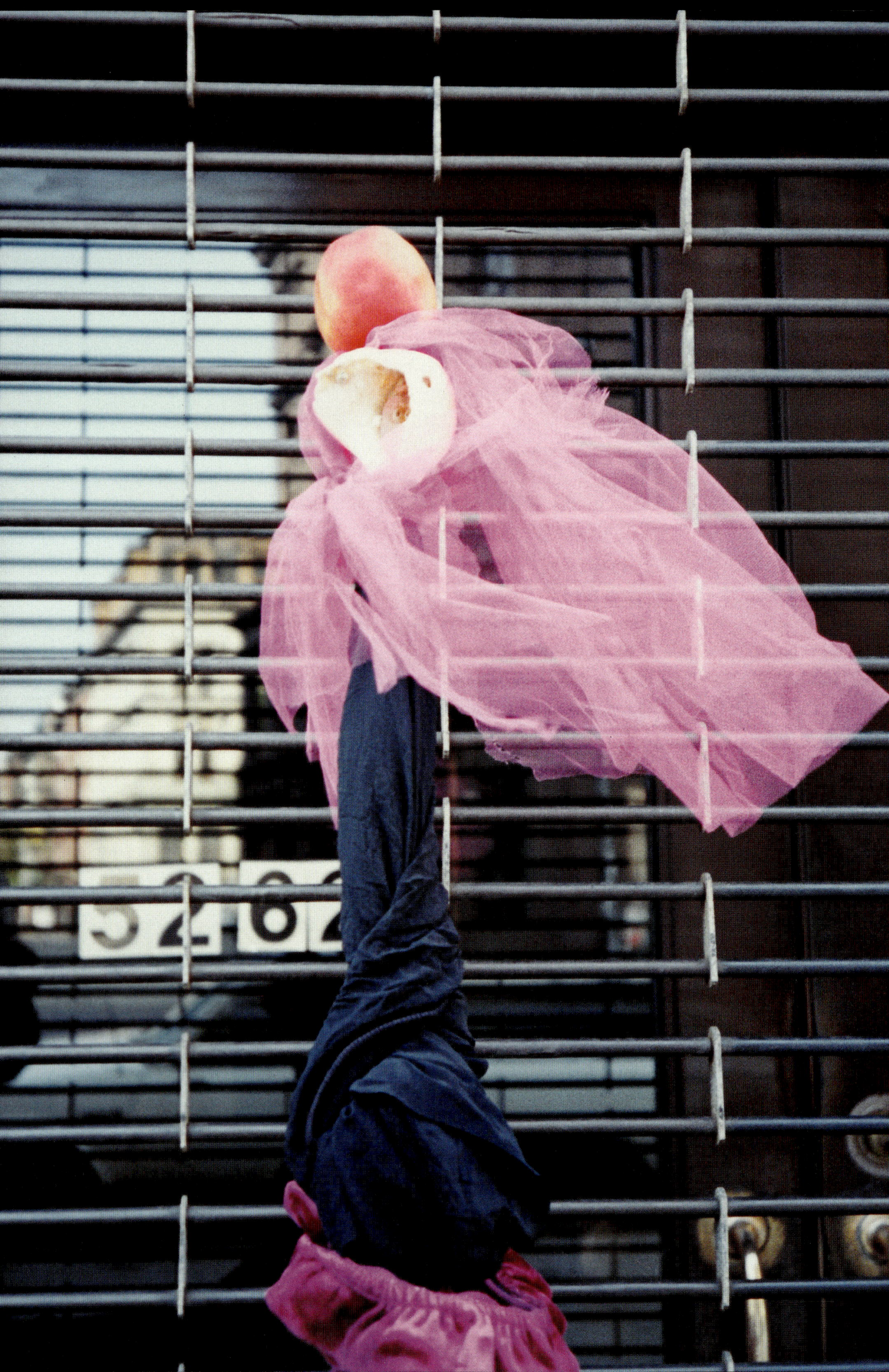

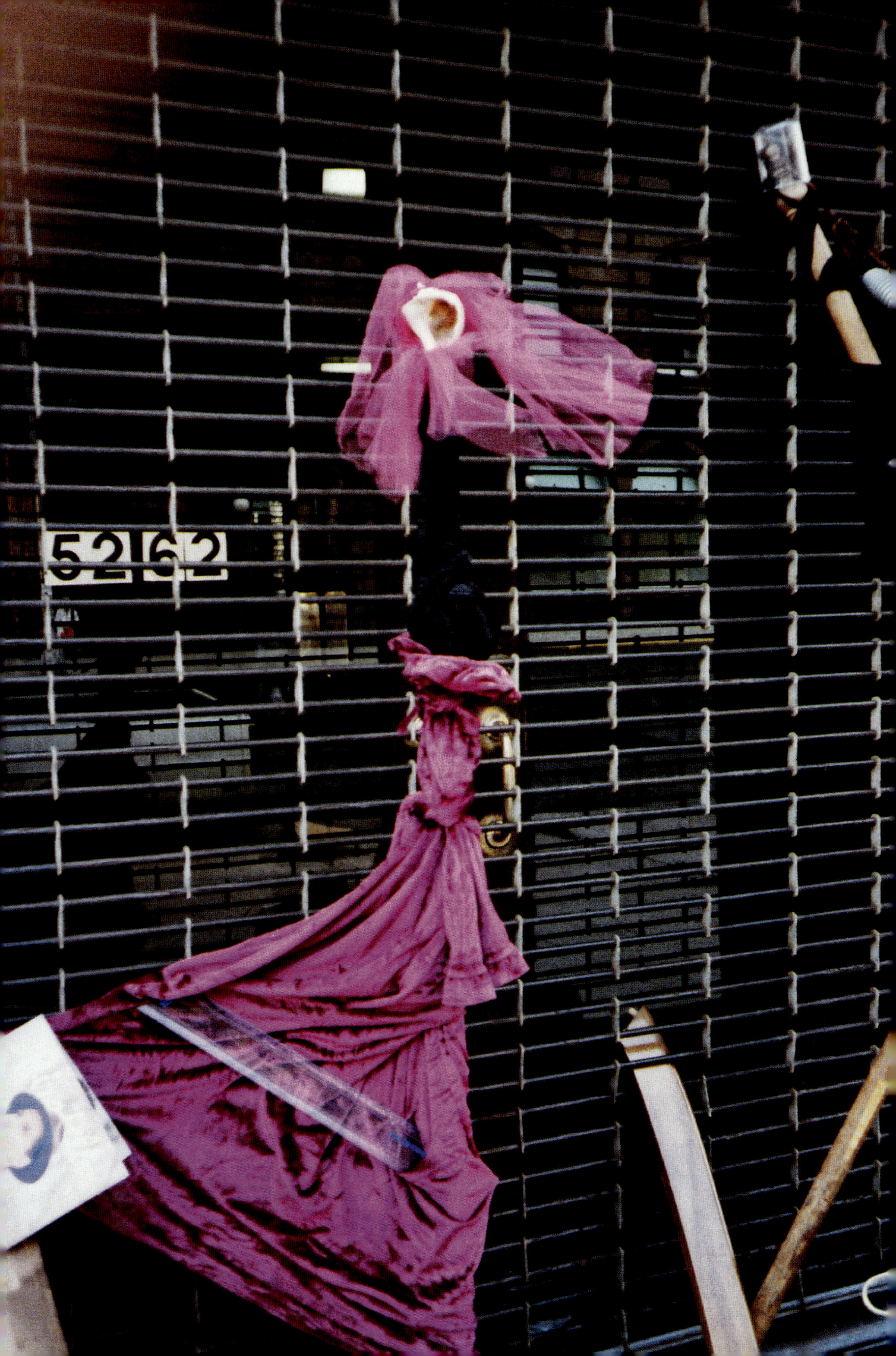
5262

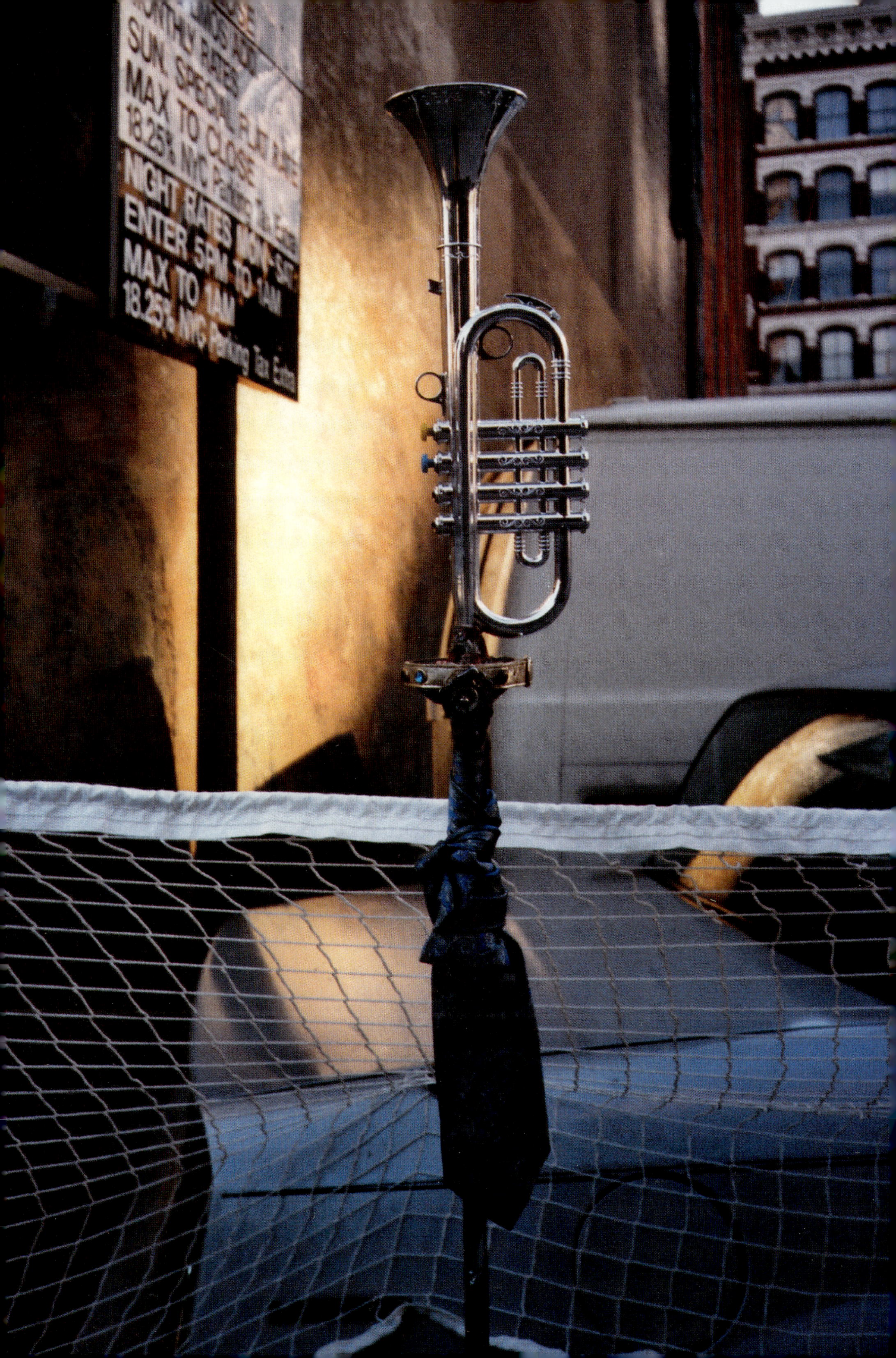
SUN. SPECIAL
MAX TO CLOSE
NIGHT RATES MON-SAT
ENTER 5PM TO 1AM
MAX TO 1AM
18.25% NYC Parking Tax Extra

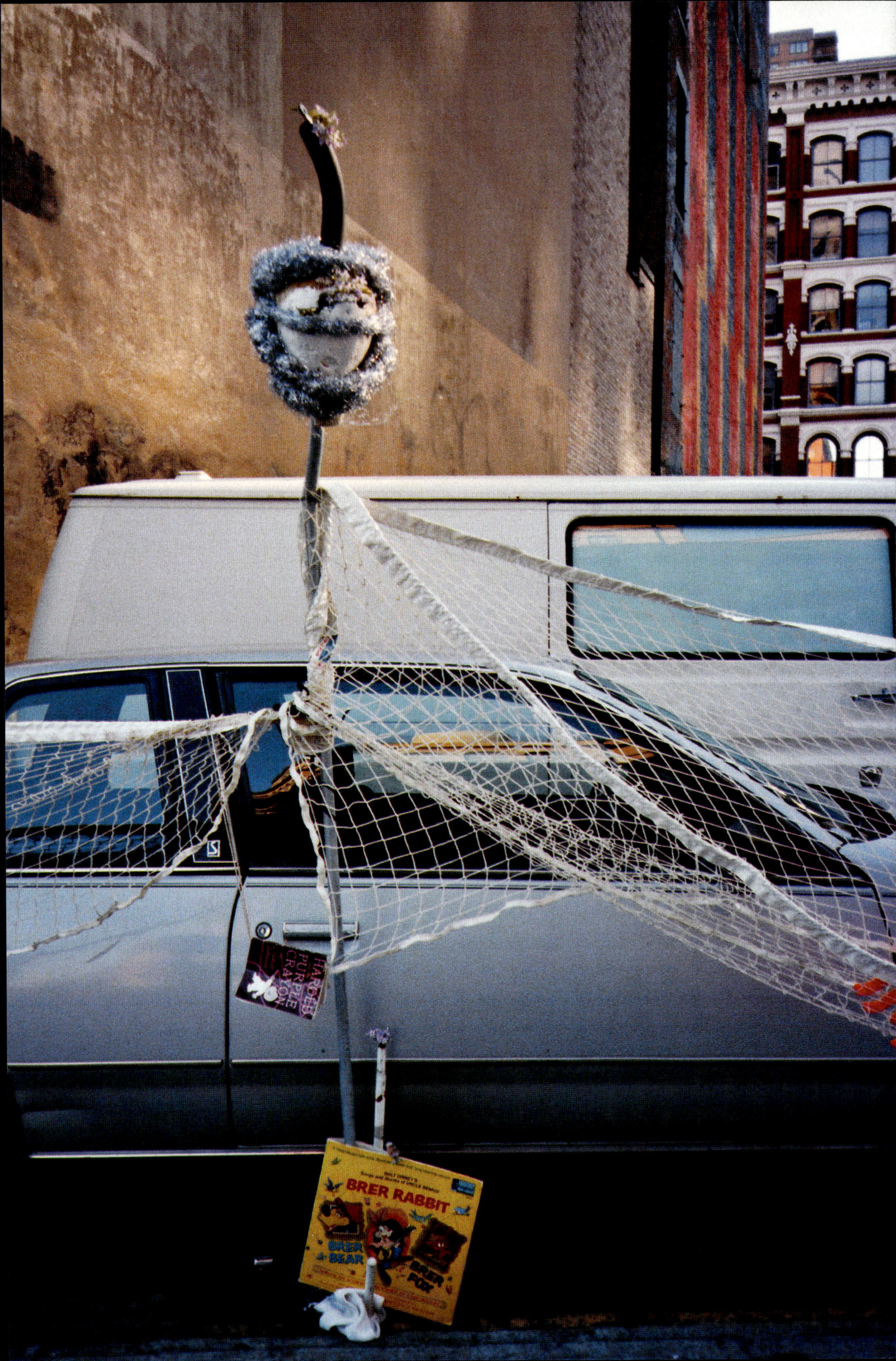
PURPLE
CRAYON
BRER RABBIT
BRER
BEAR
BRER
FOX

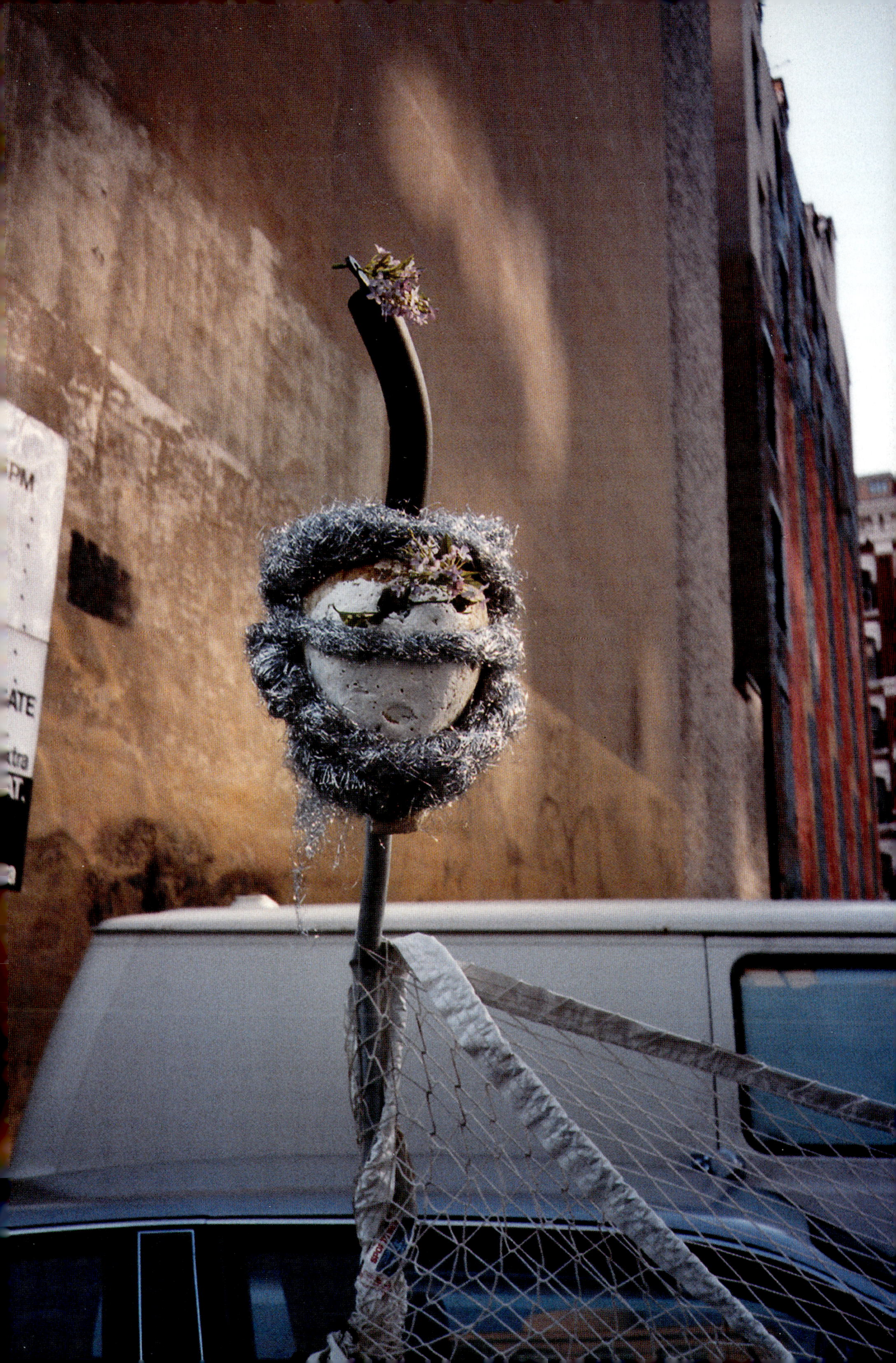
PM
ATE

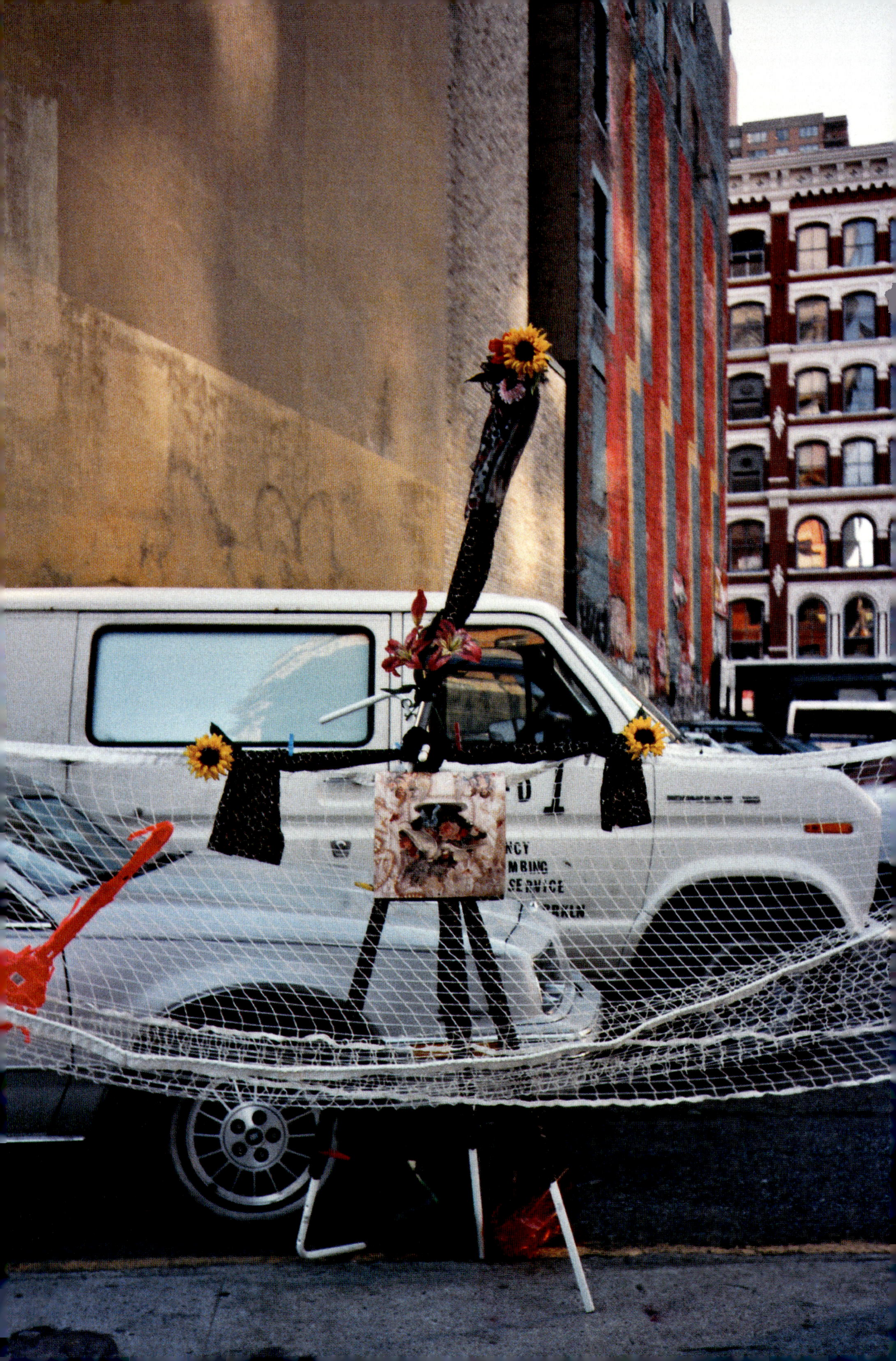

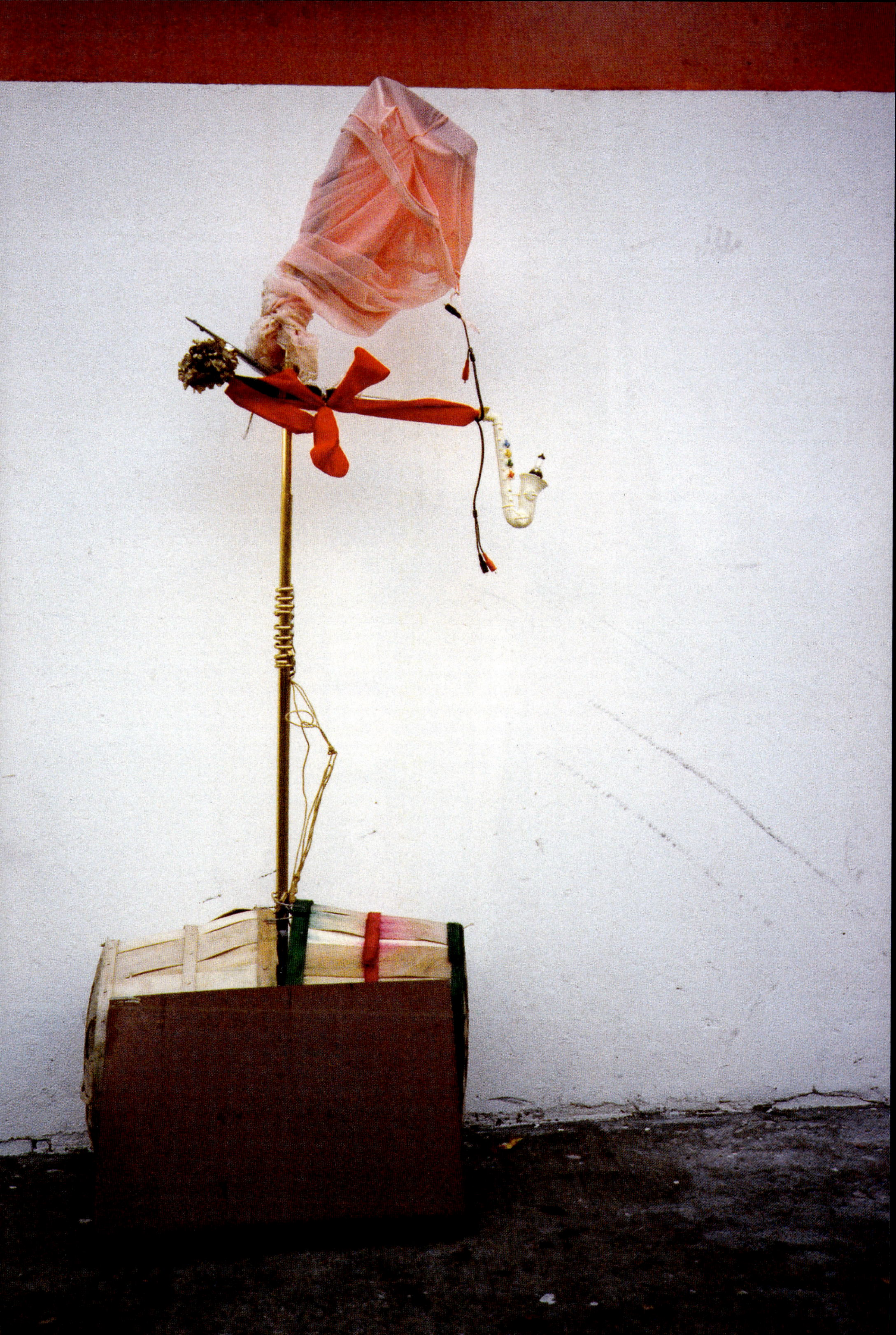

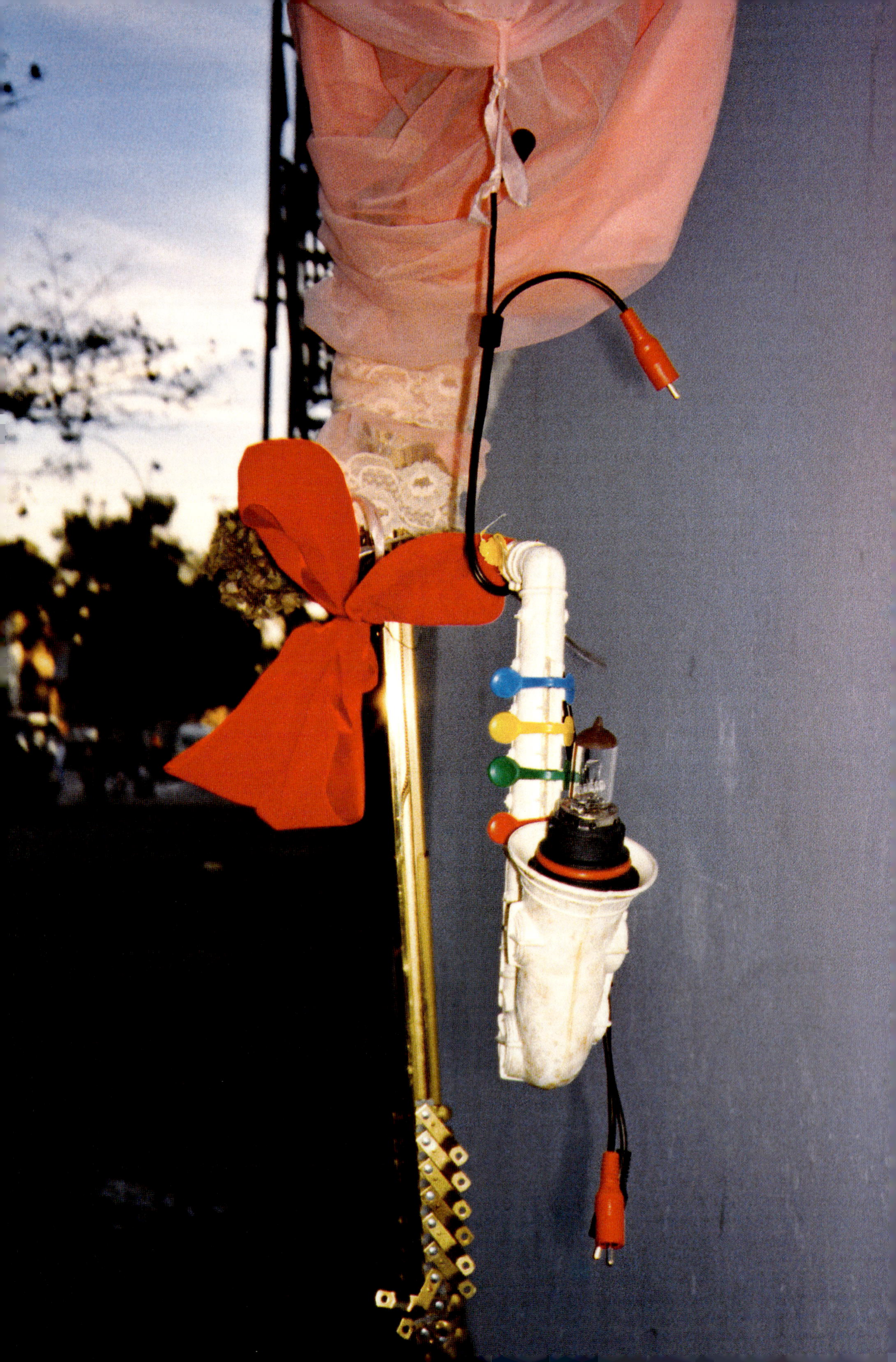

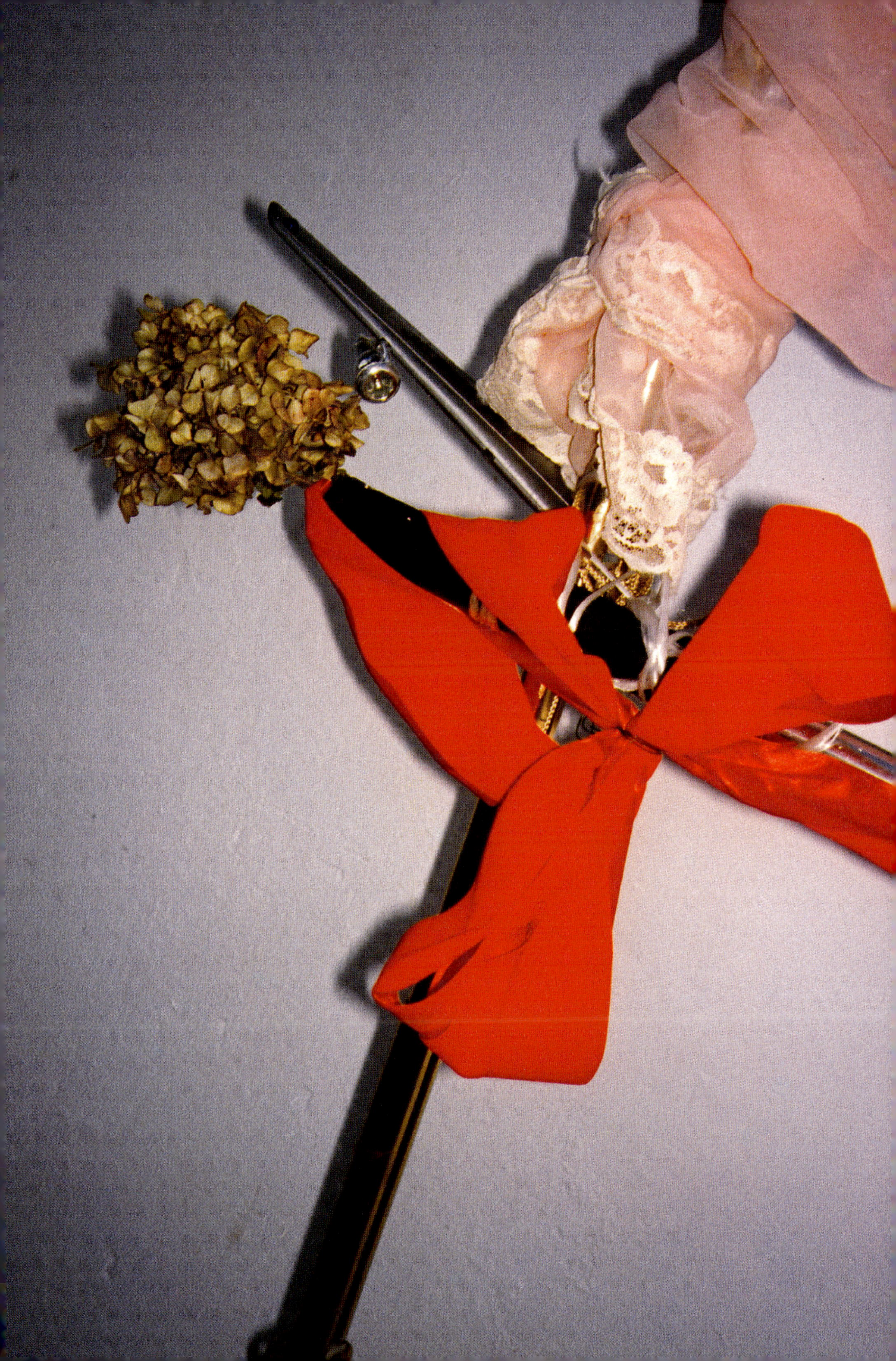

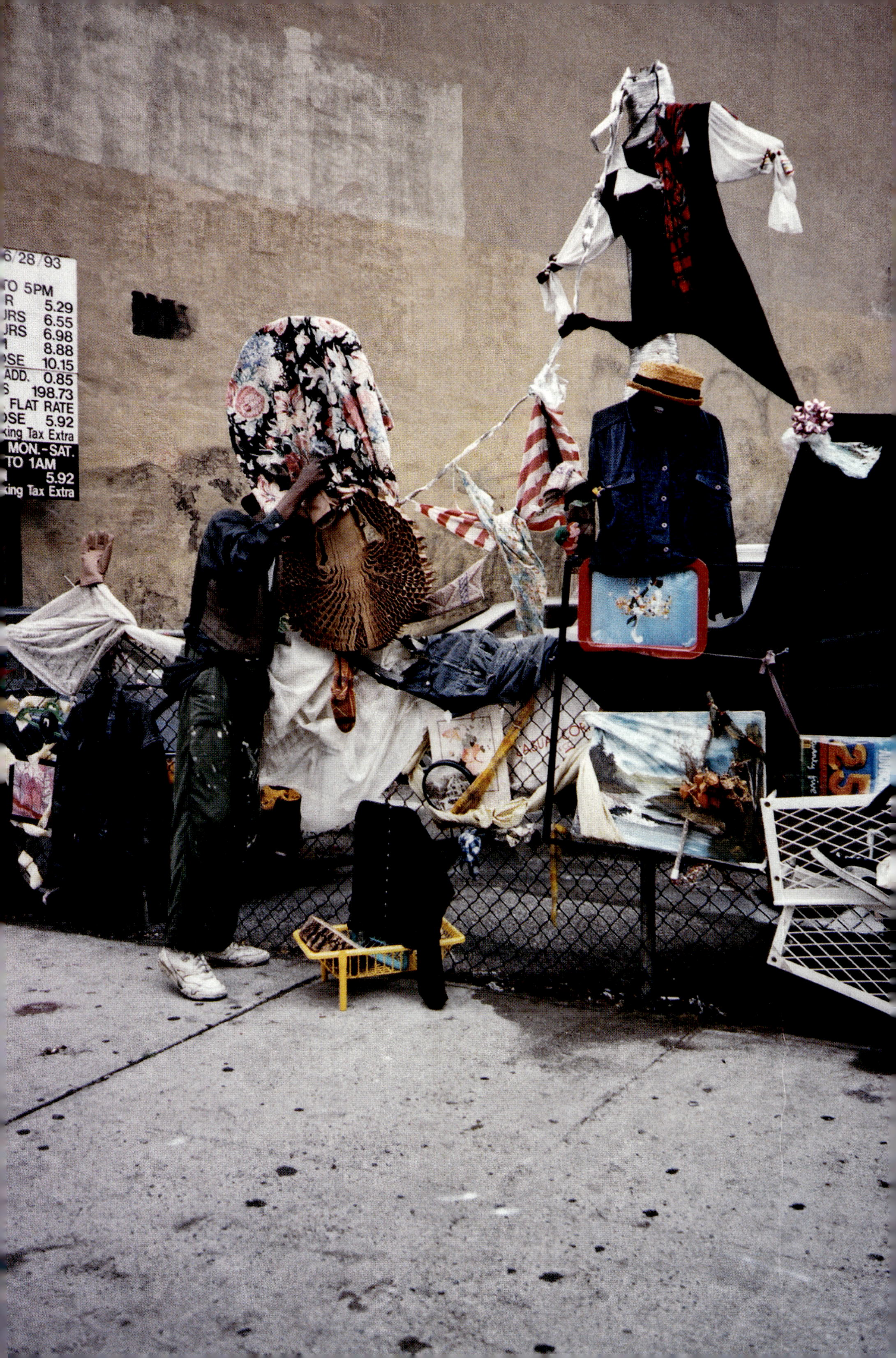

6/28/93
5.29
6.55
6.98
8.88
10.15
ADD. 0.85
198.73
FLAT RATE
5.92
MON.-SAT.
TO 1AM
5.92

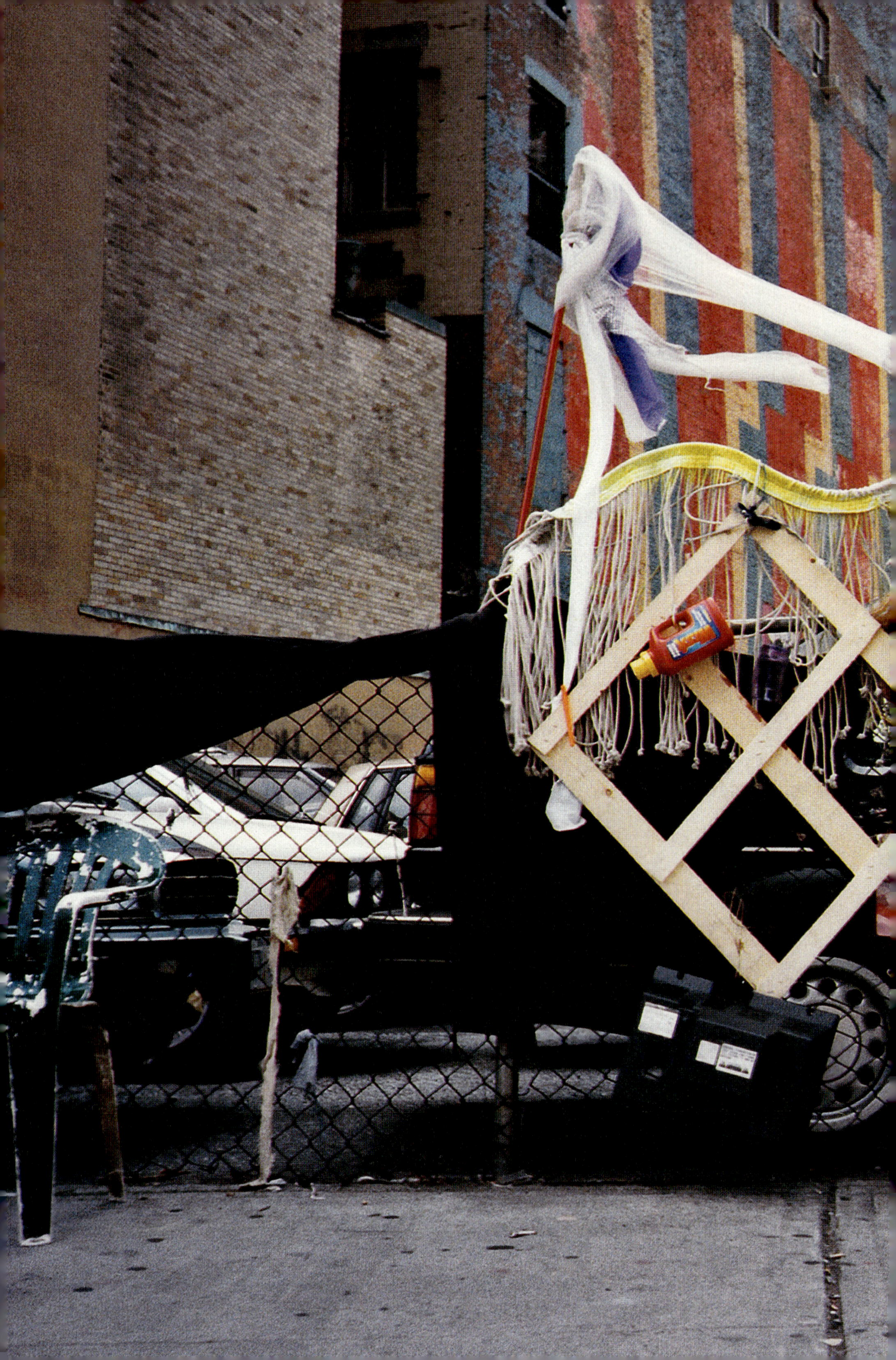

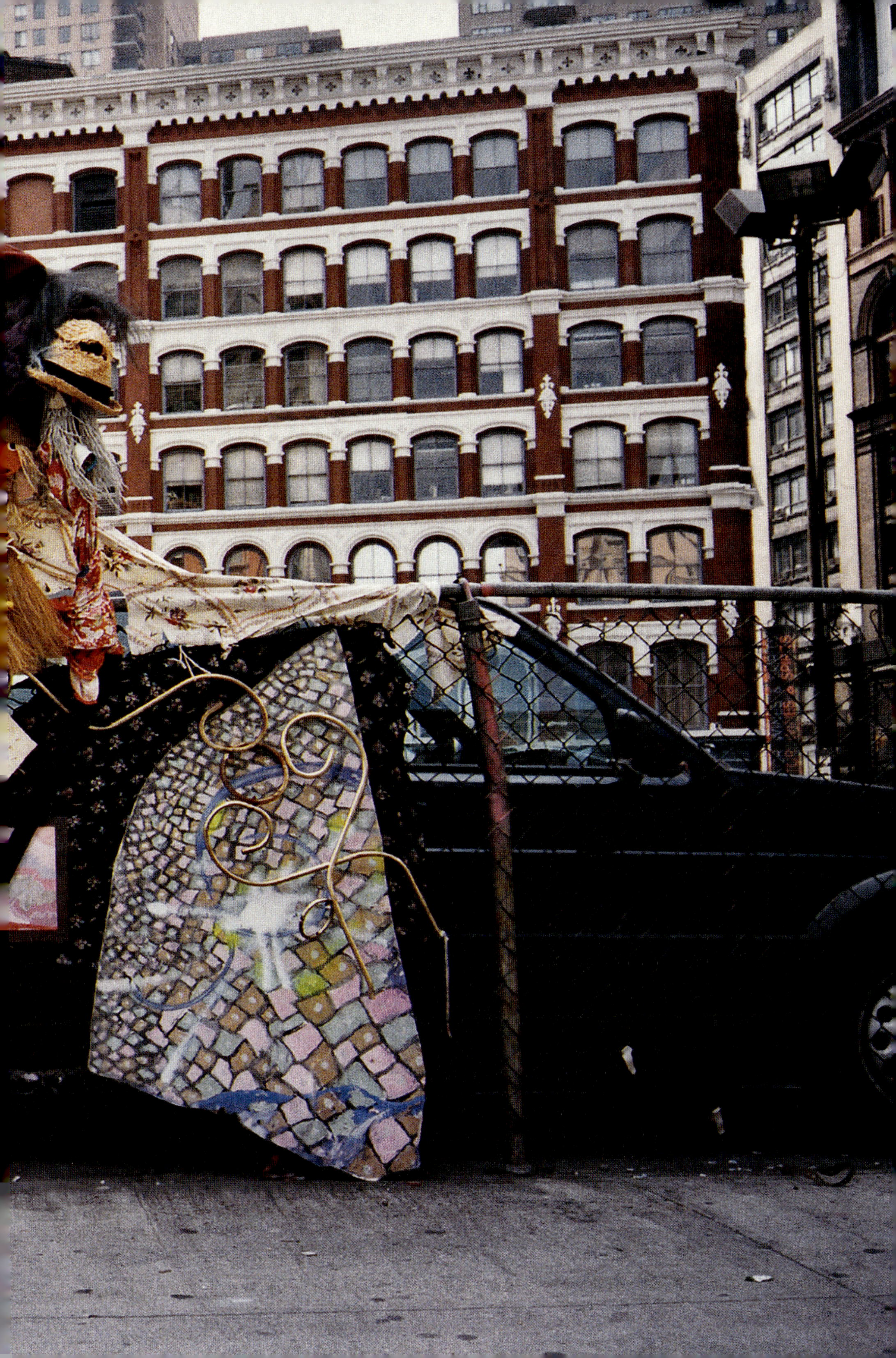

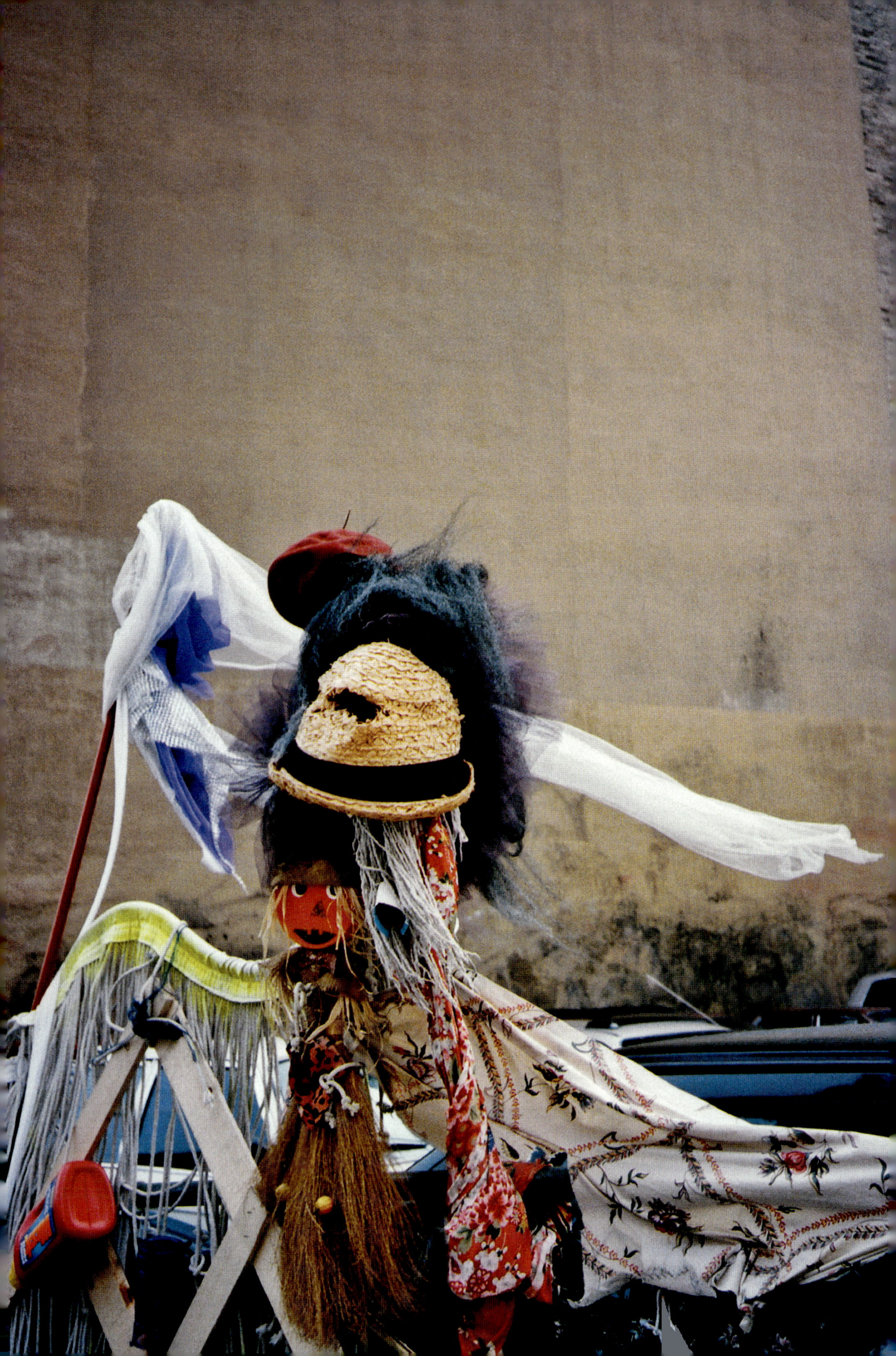

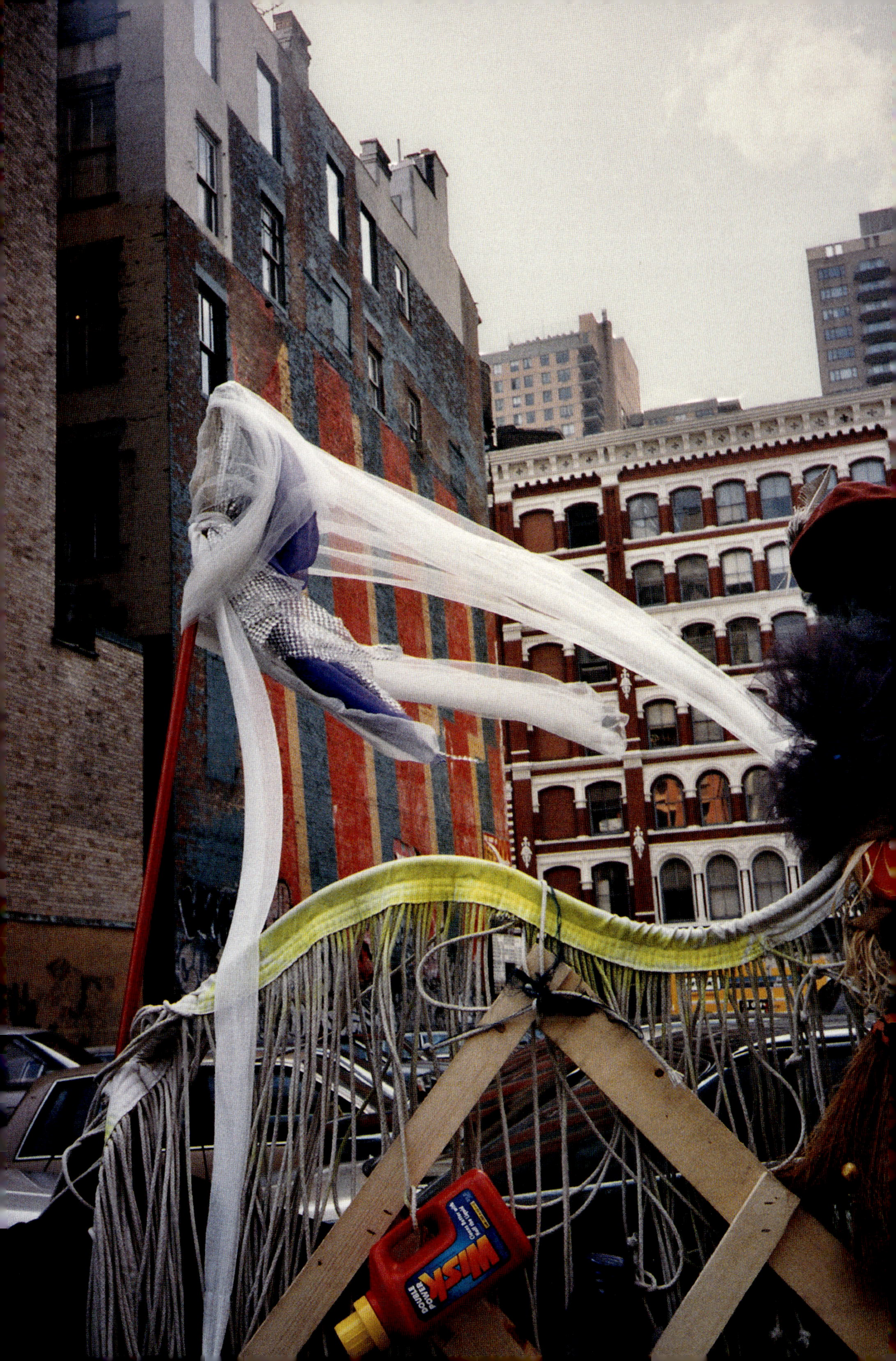
WISK
DOUBLE
POWER

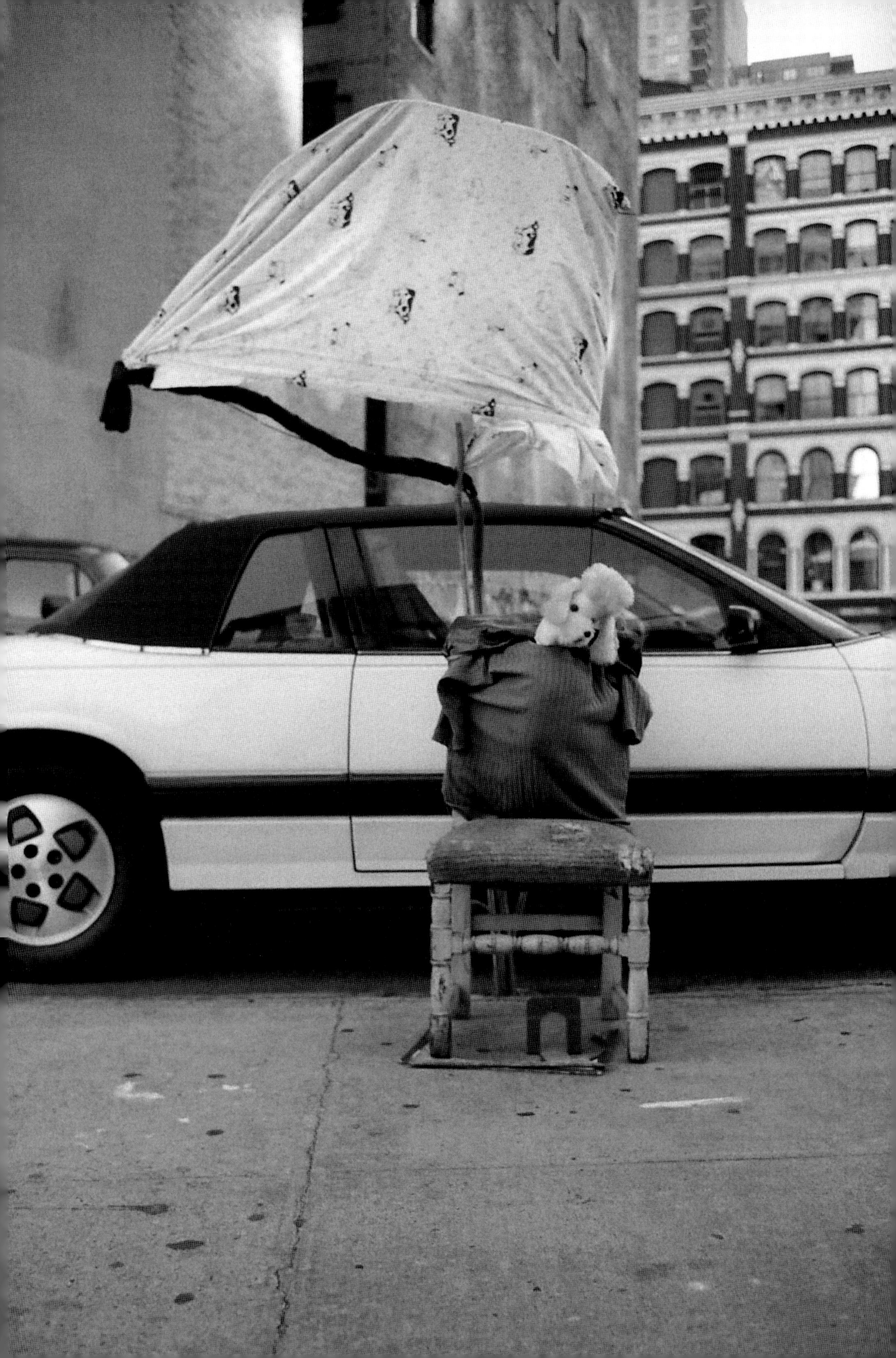

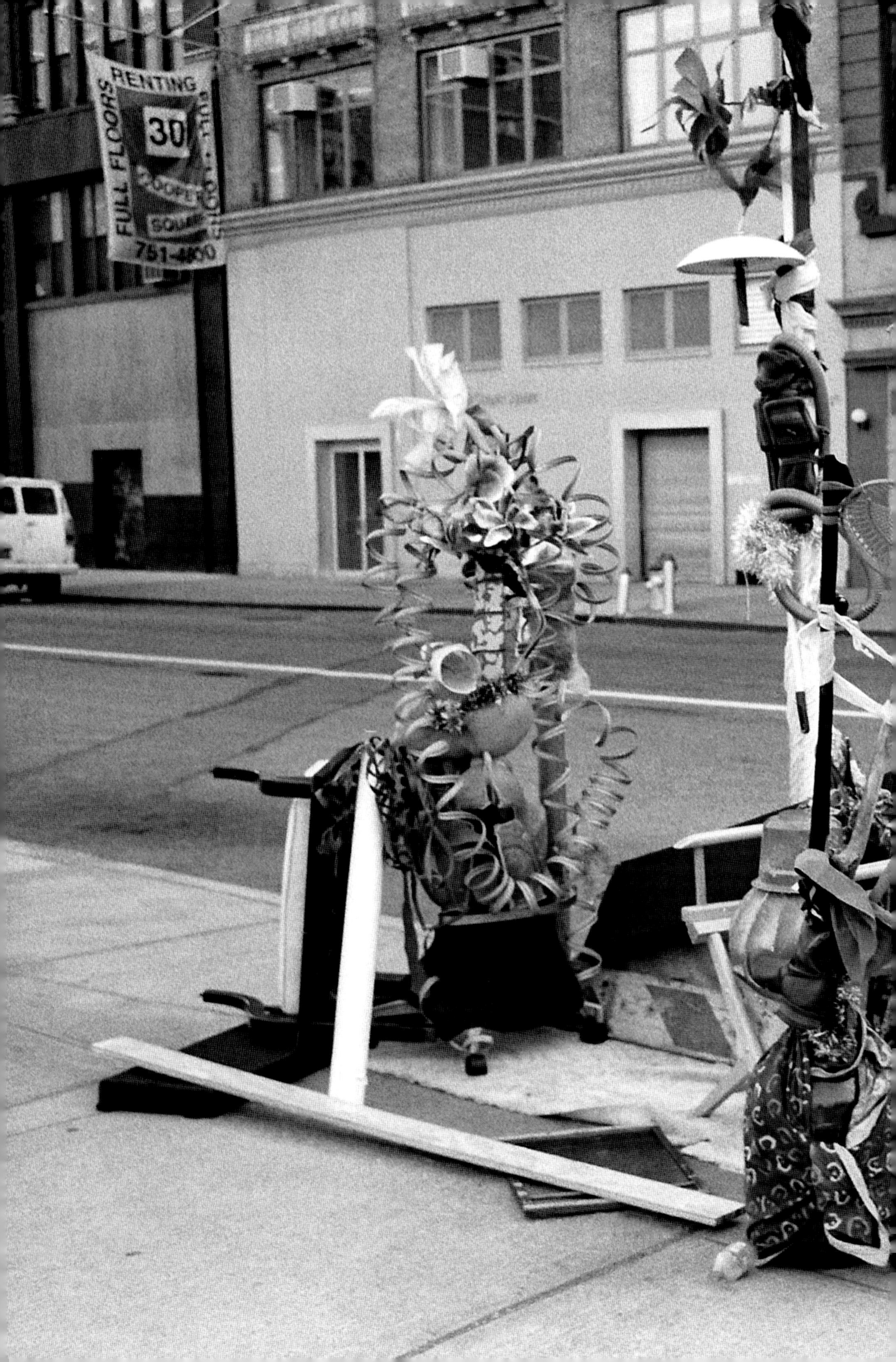
RENTING
FULL FLOORS
30

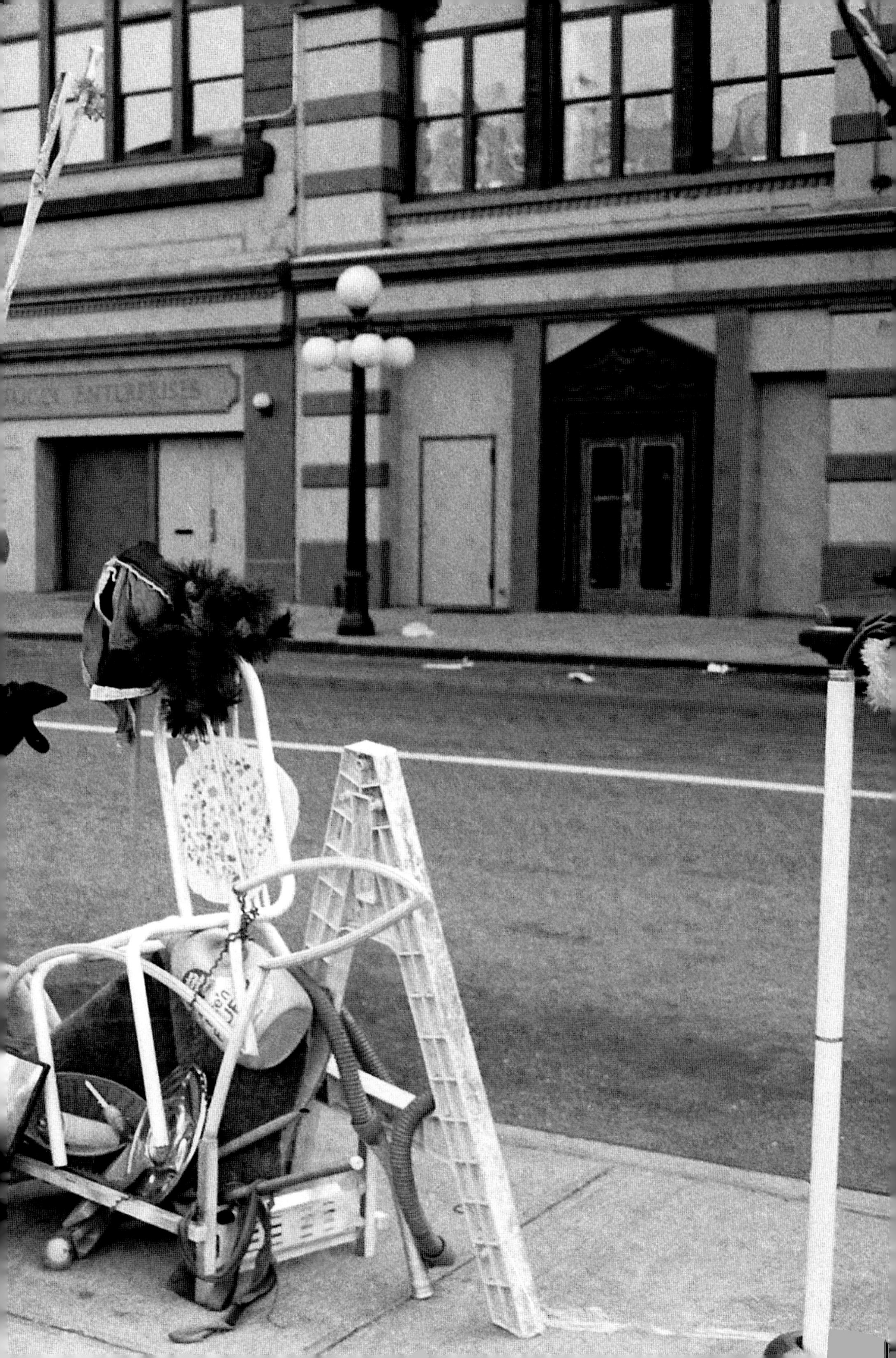
ENTERPRISES

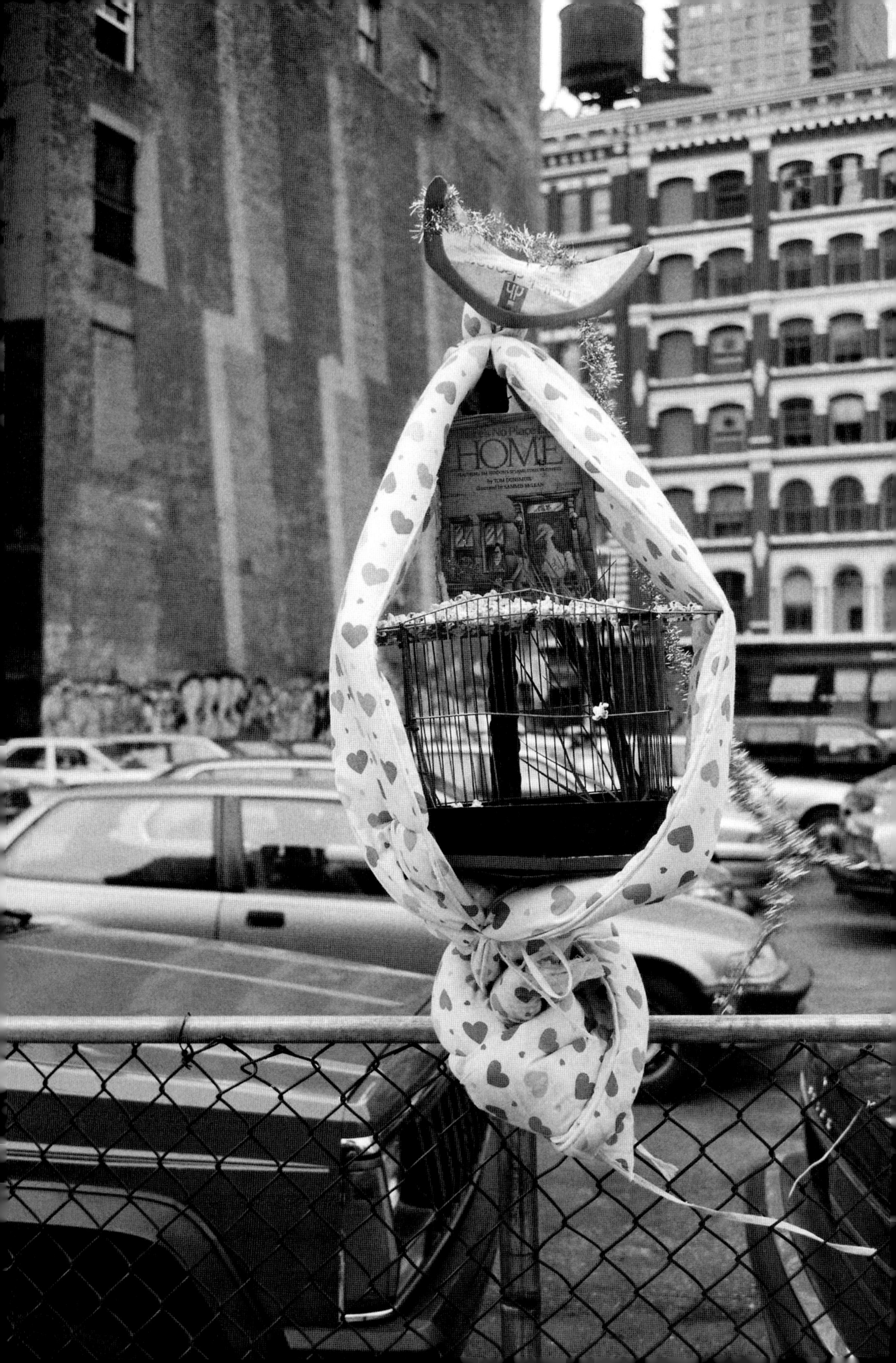
HOME

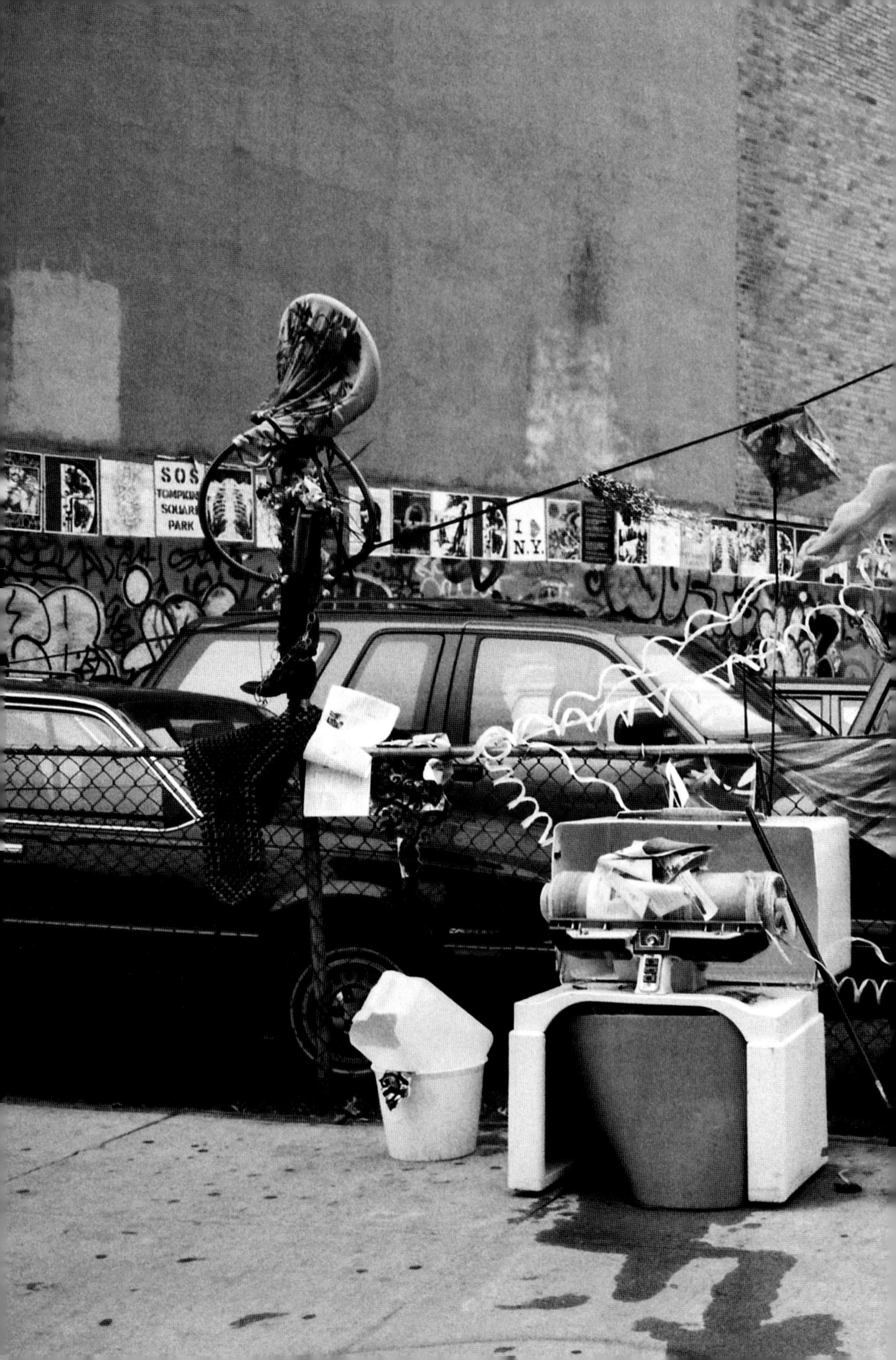
SOS
TOMPKINS
SQUARE
PARK
I
N.Y.

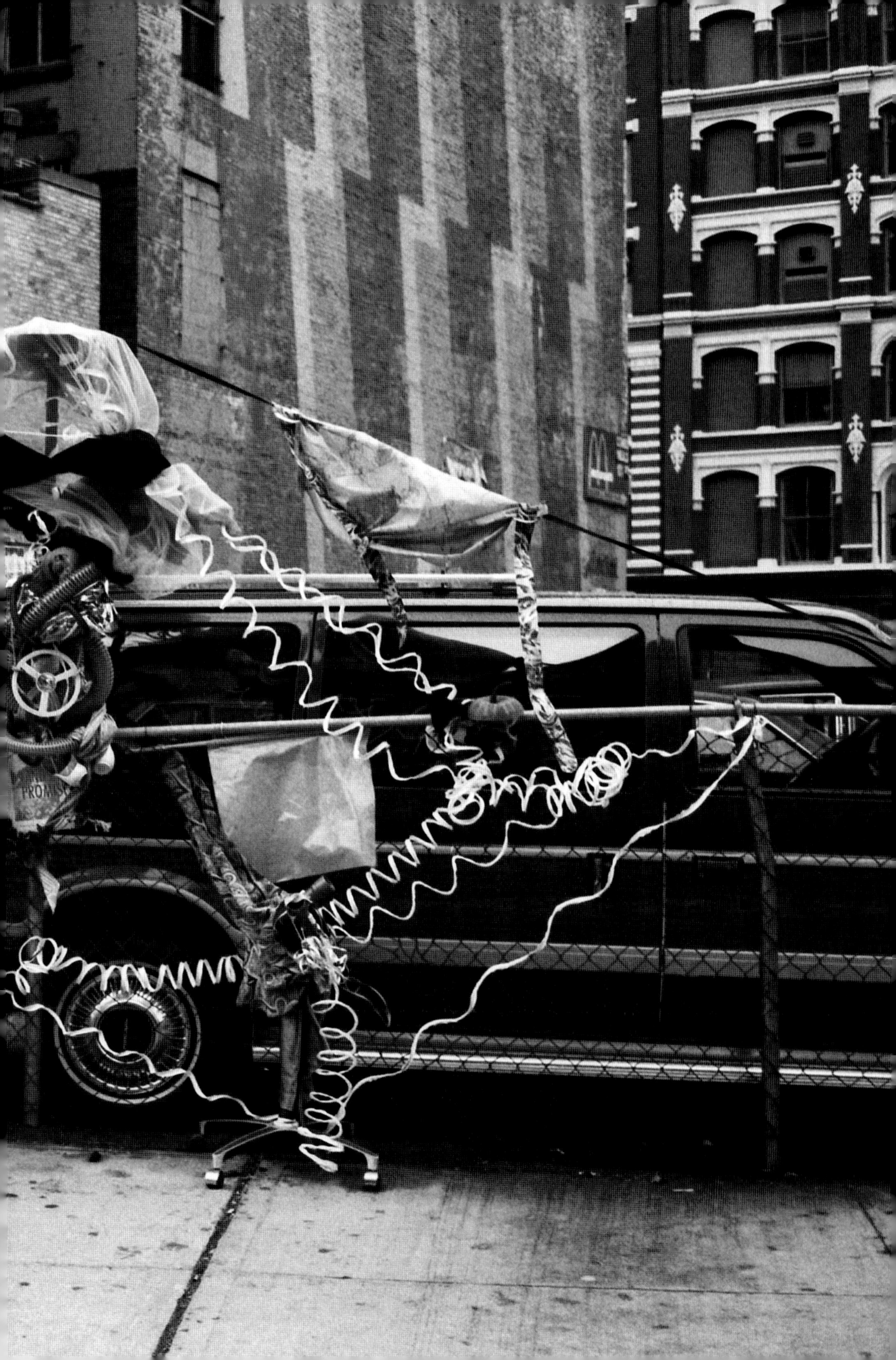

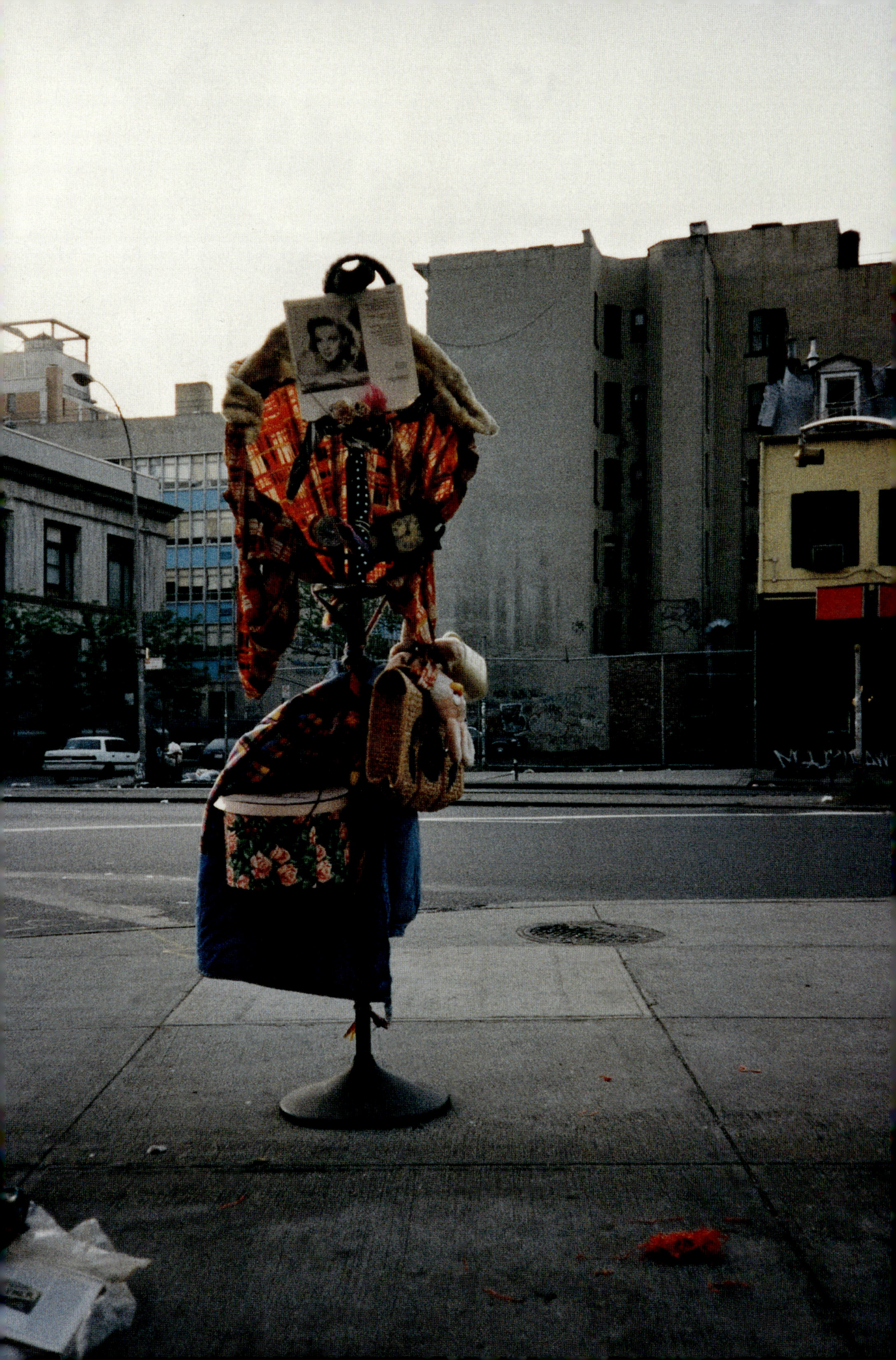

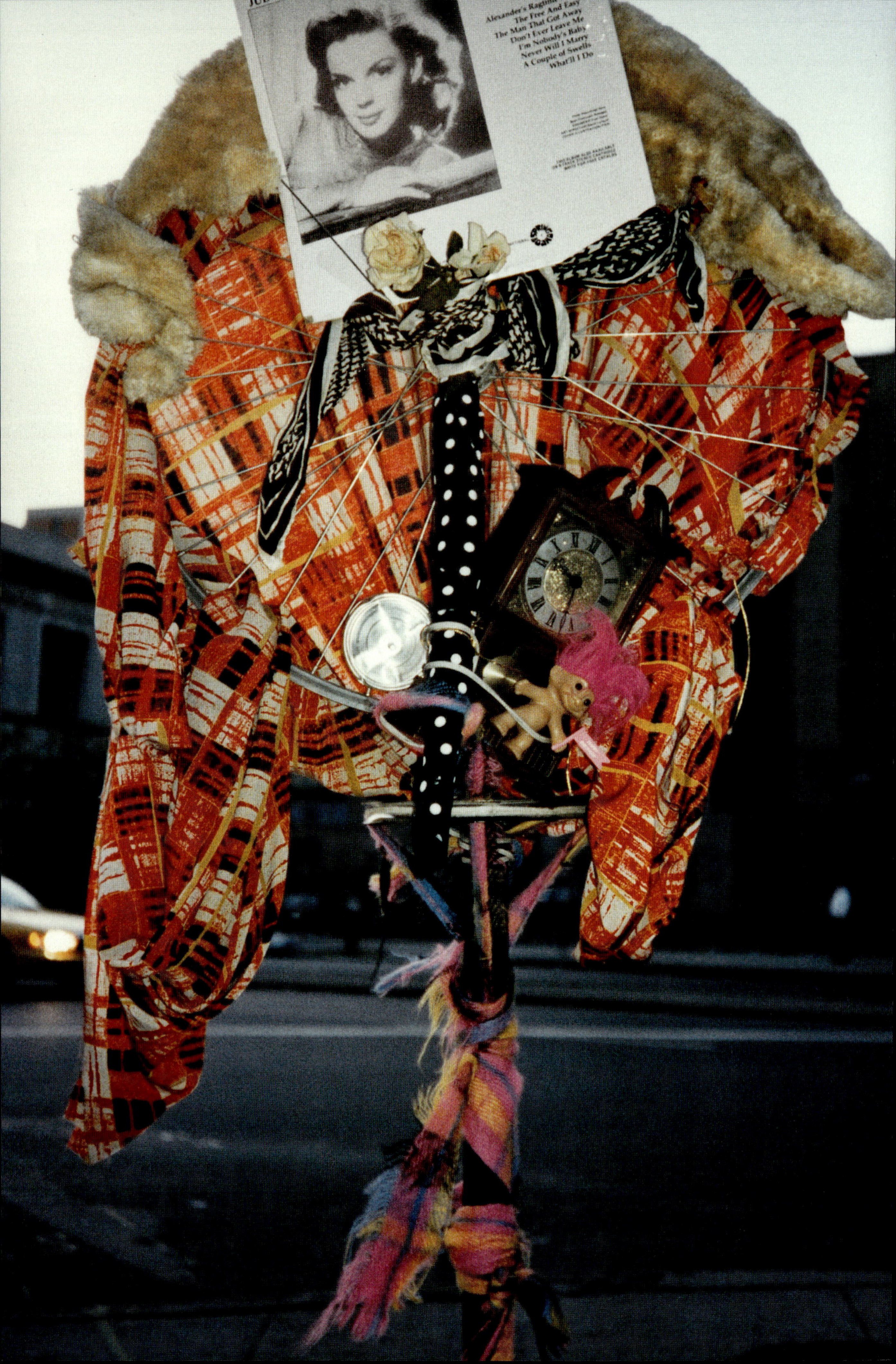

Alexander's
The Free And Easy
The Man That Got Away
Don't Ever Leave Me
I'm Nobody's Baby
Never Will I Marry
A Couple of Swells
What'll I Do

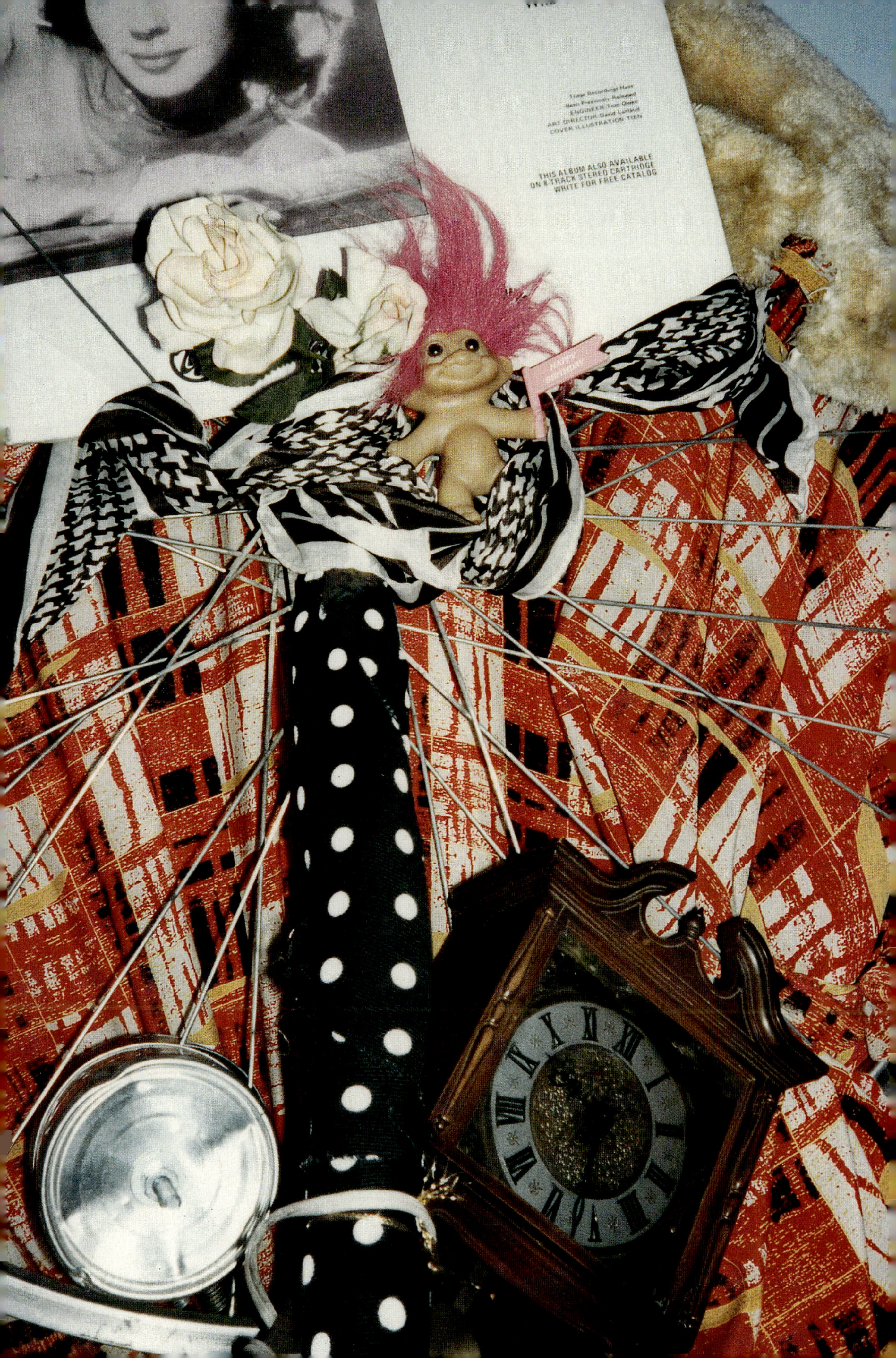
THIS ALBUM ALSO AVAILABLE
ON 8 TRACK STEREO CARTRIDGE
WRITE FOR FREE CATALOG
HAPPY BIRTHDAY

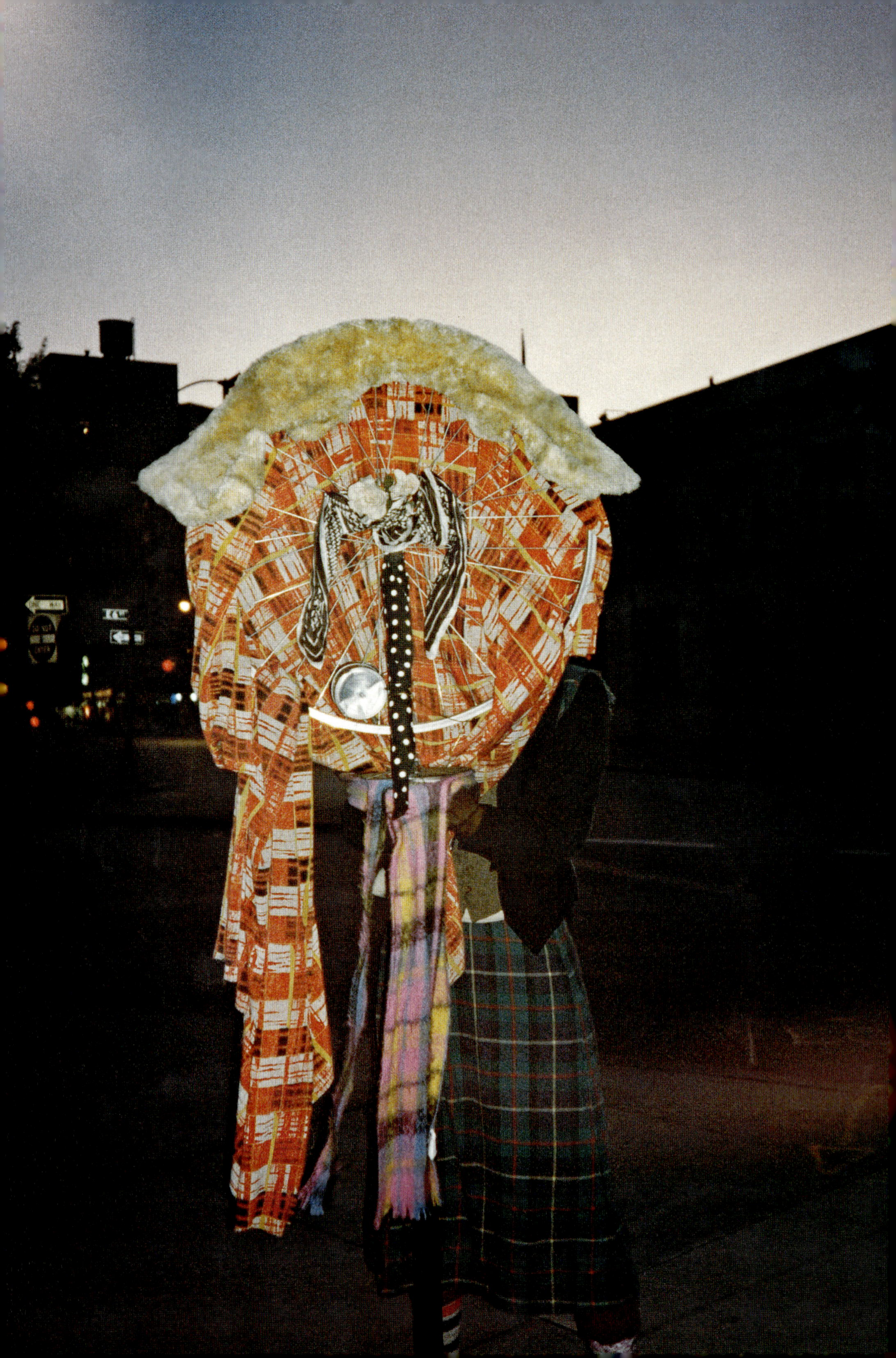

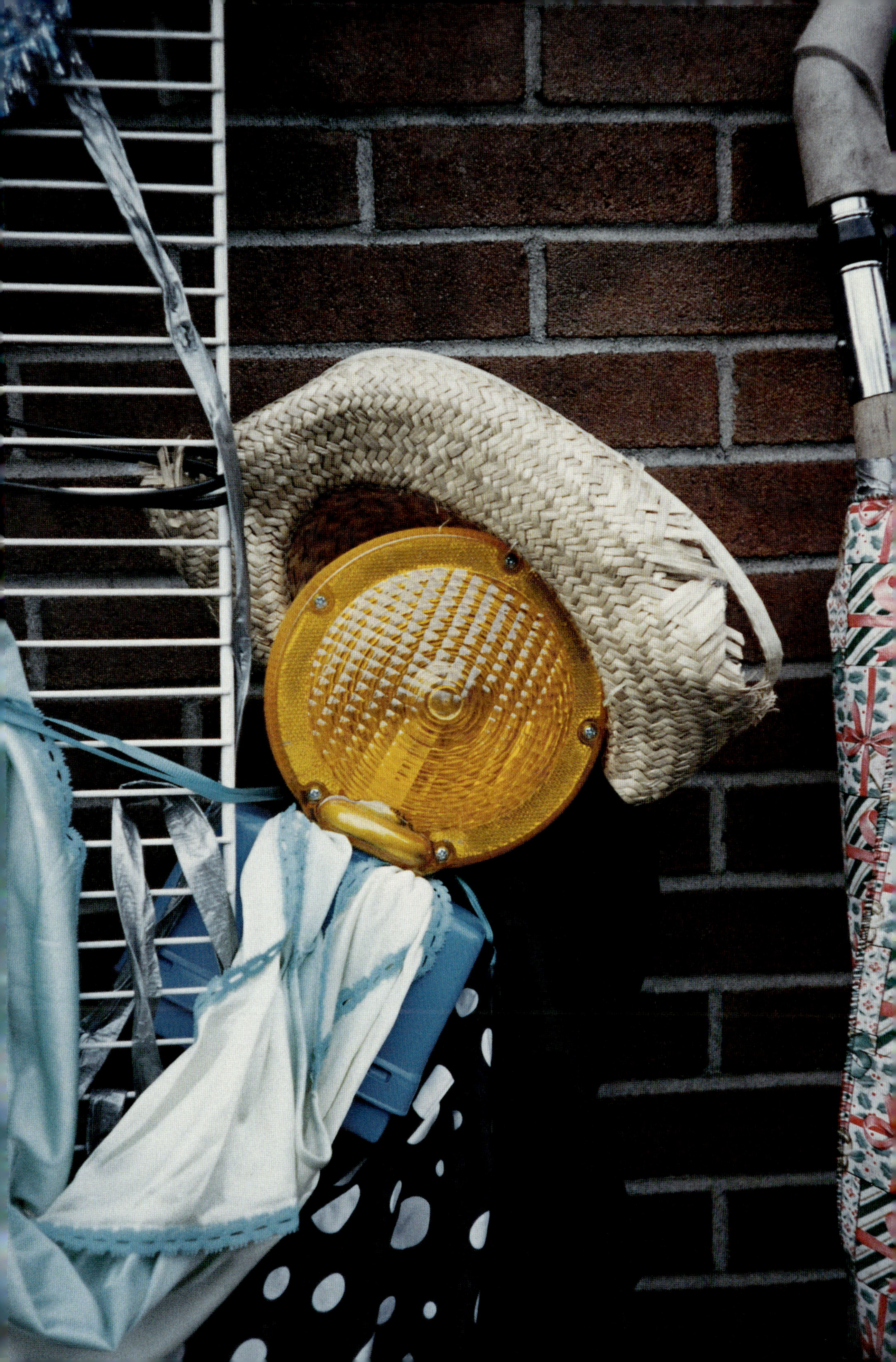

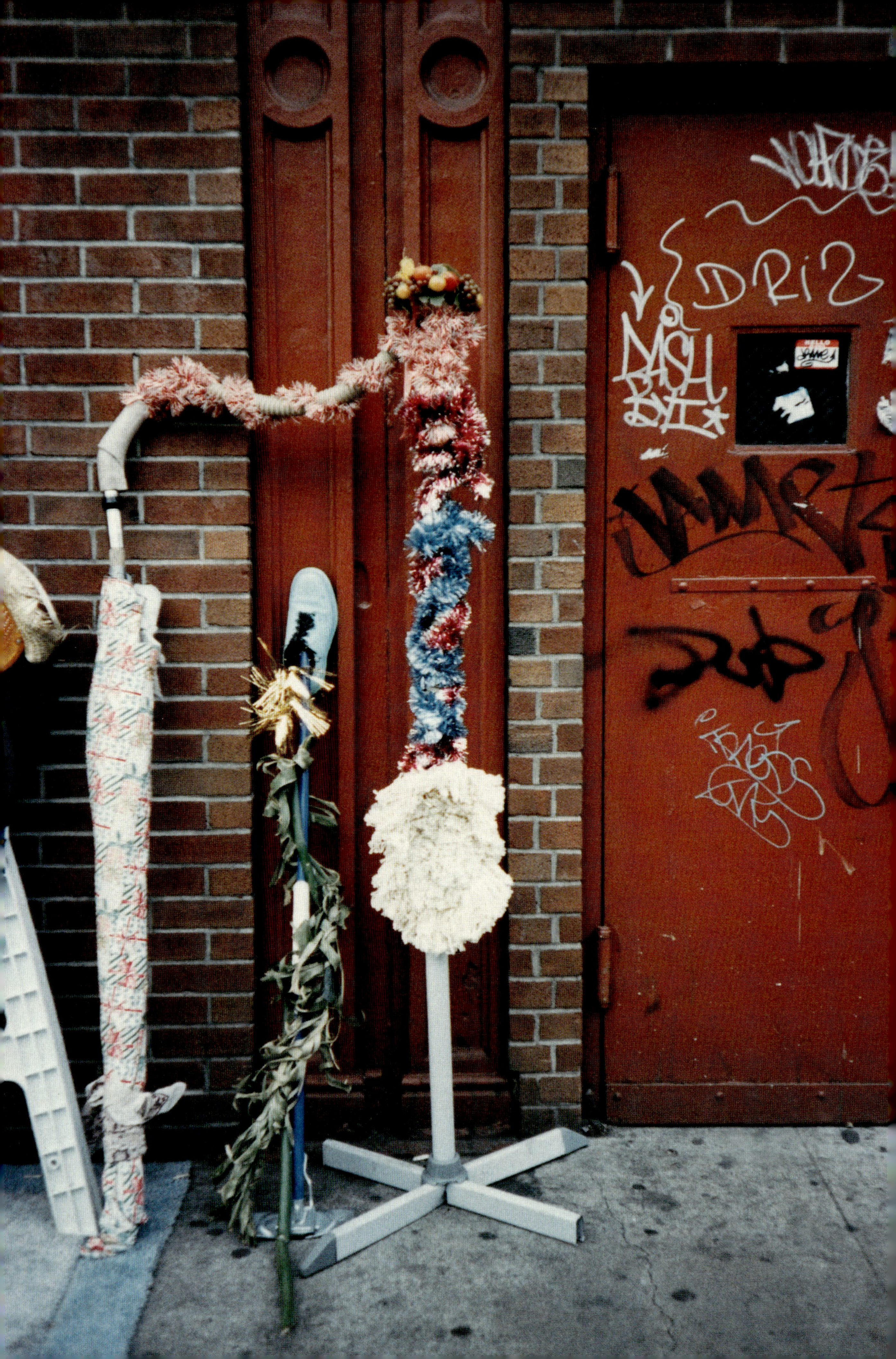
DRi2

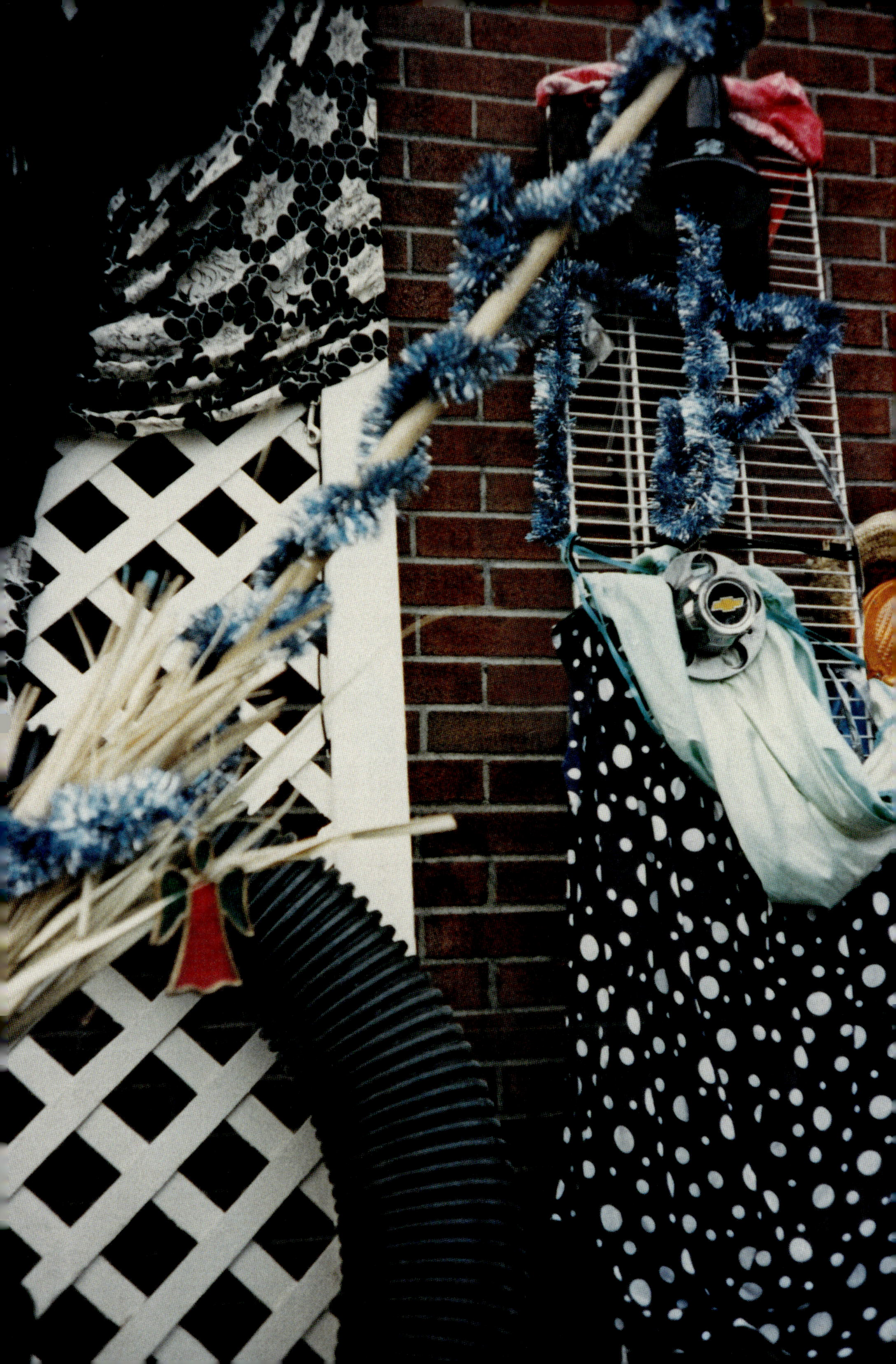

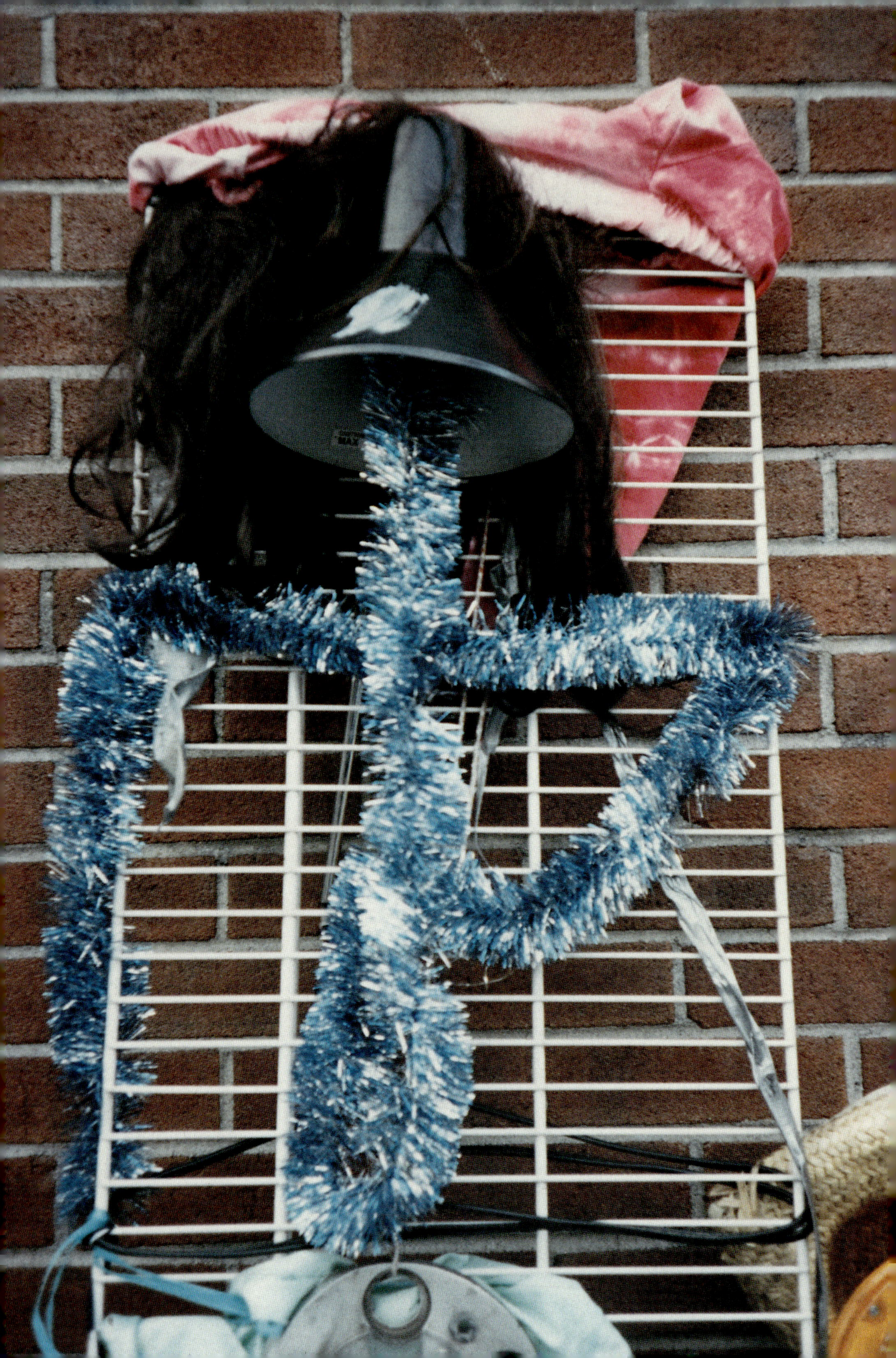

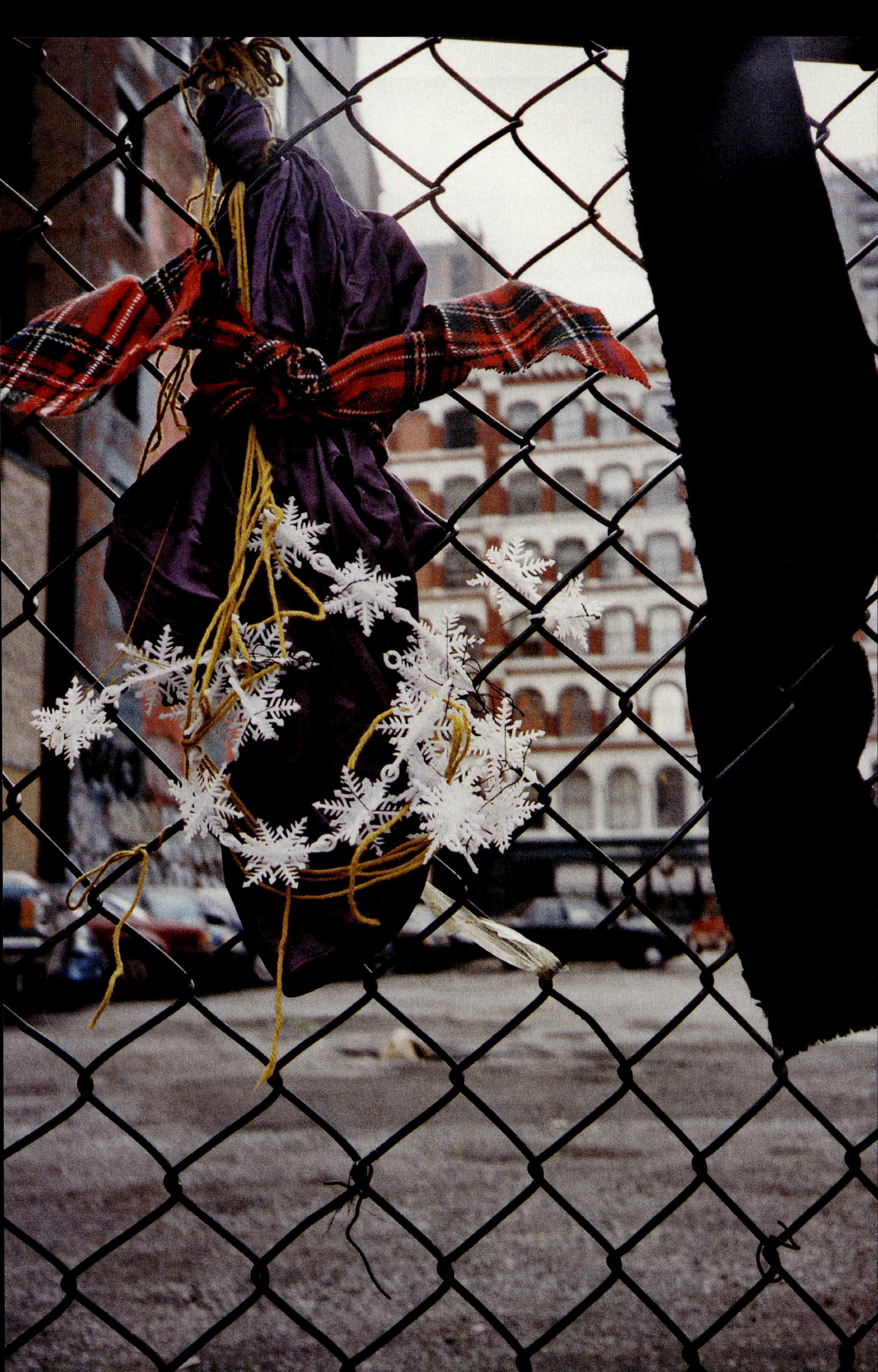

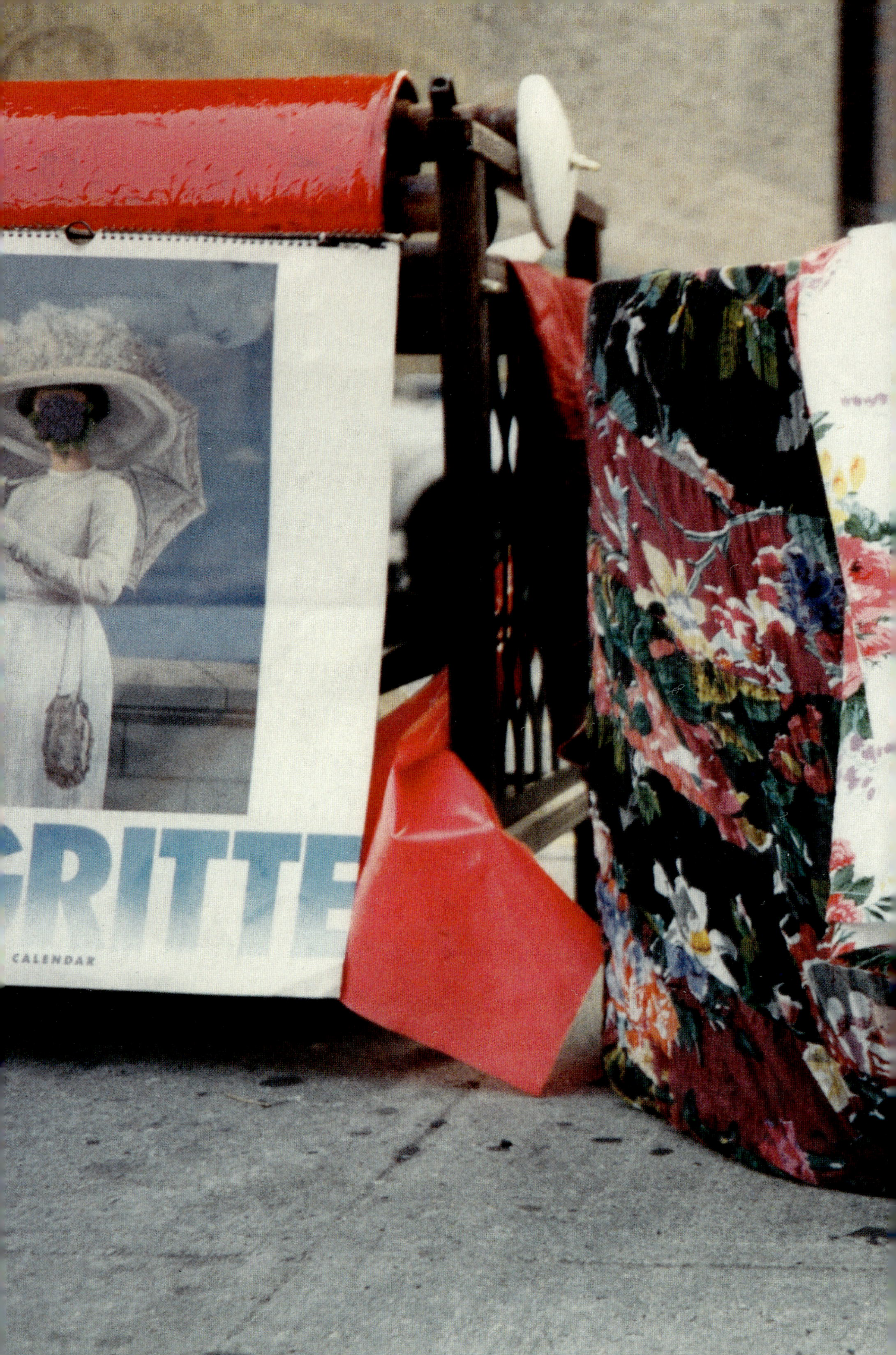
GRITTE
CALENDAR

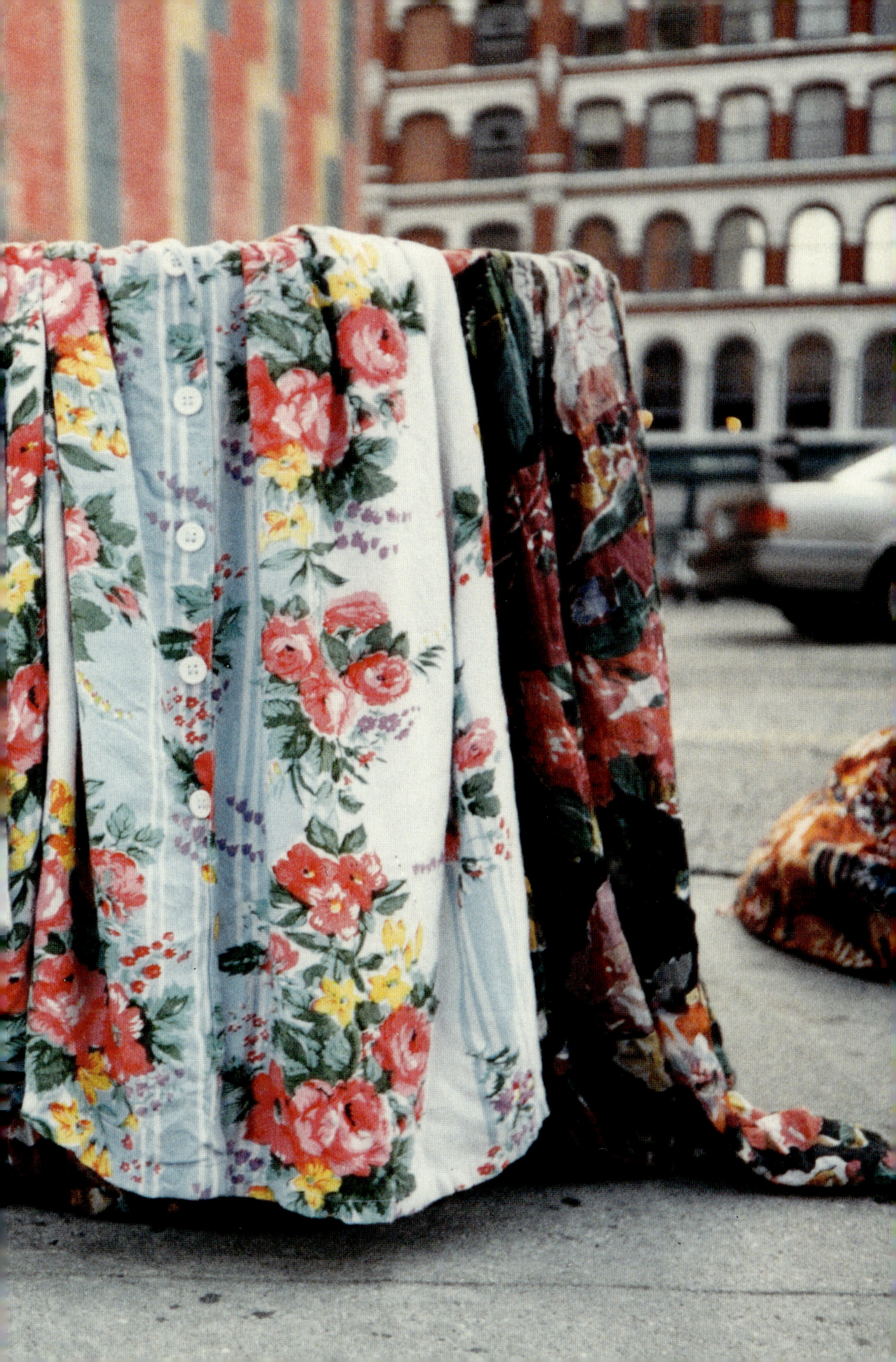

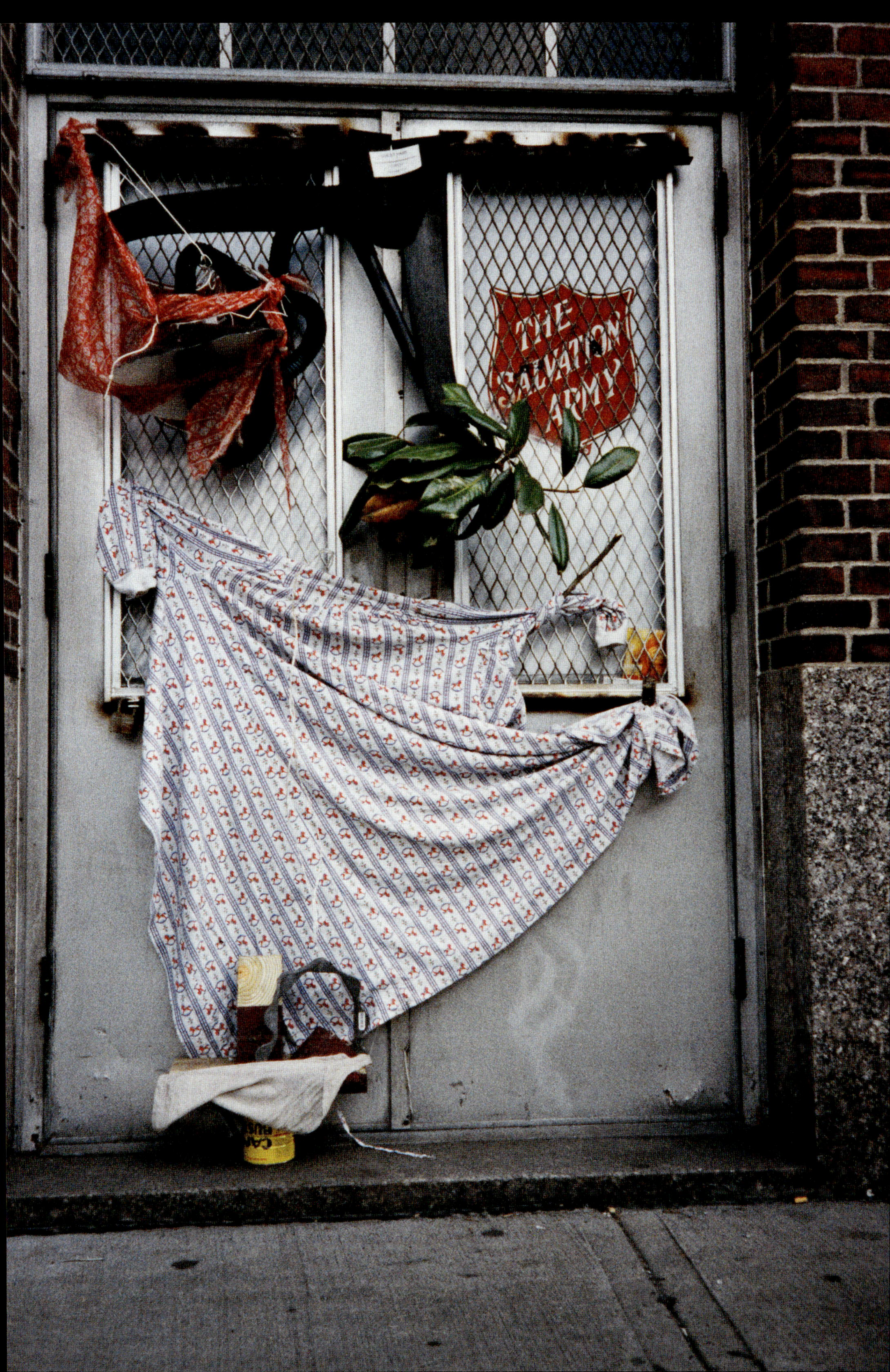
THE SALVATION ARMY

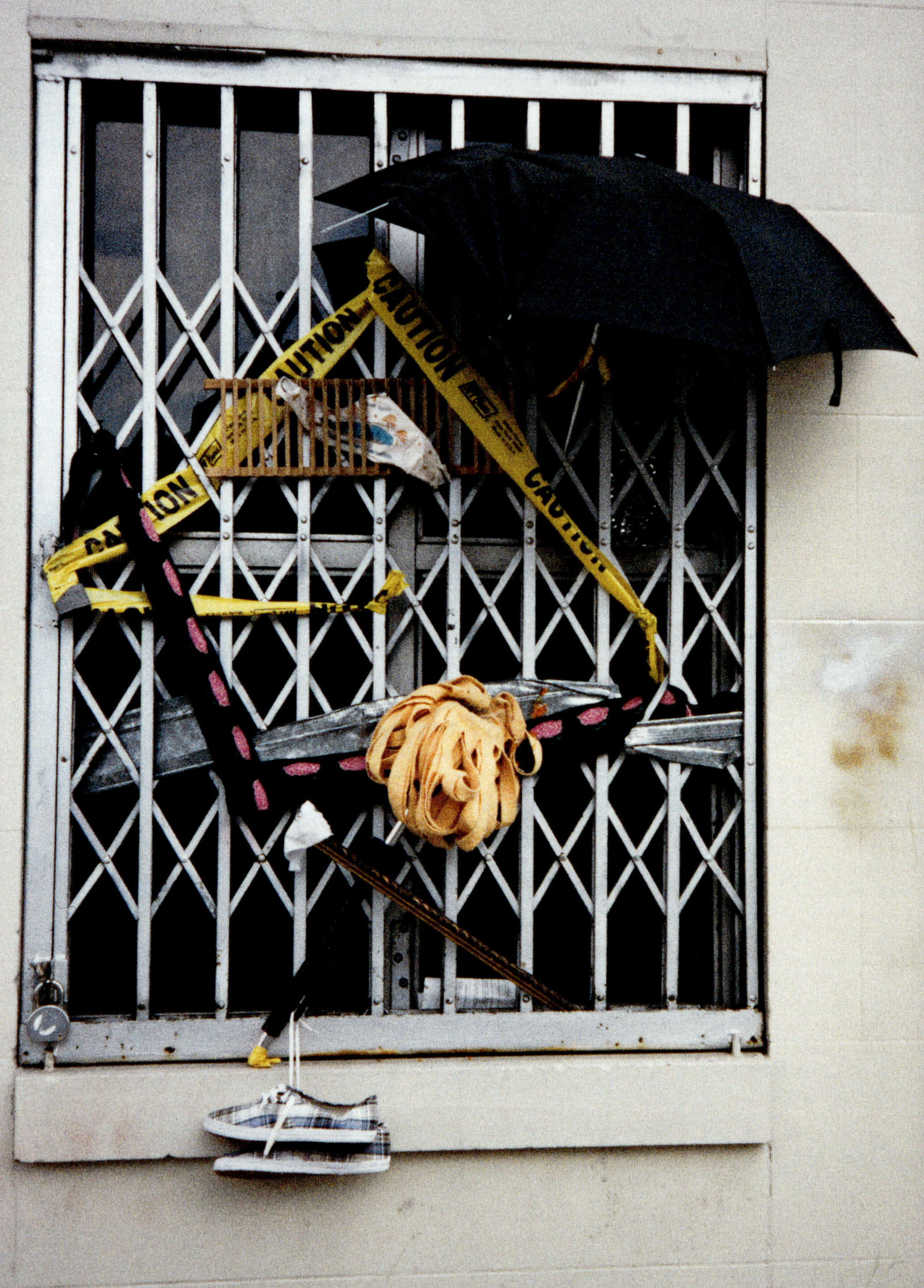
CAUTION
AUTION
CAUTION

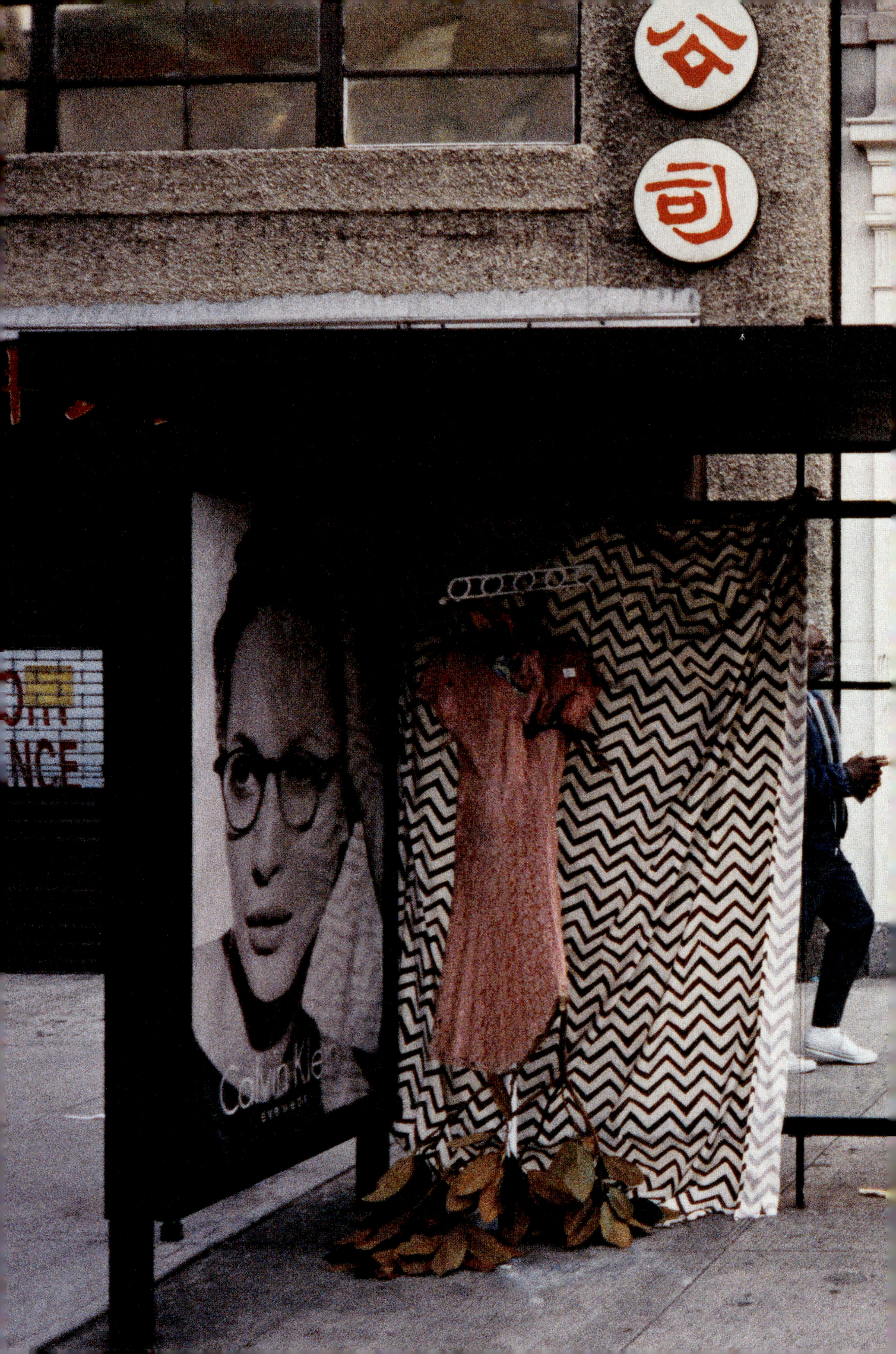
公
司

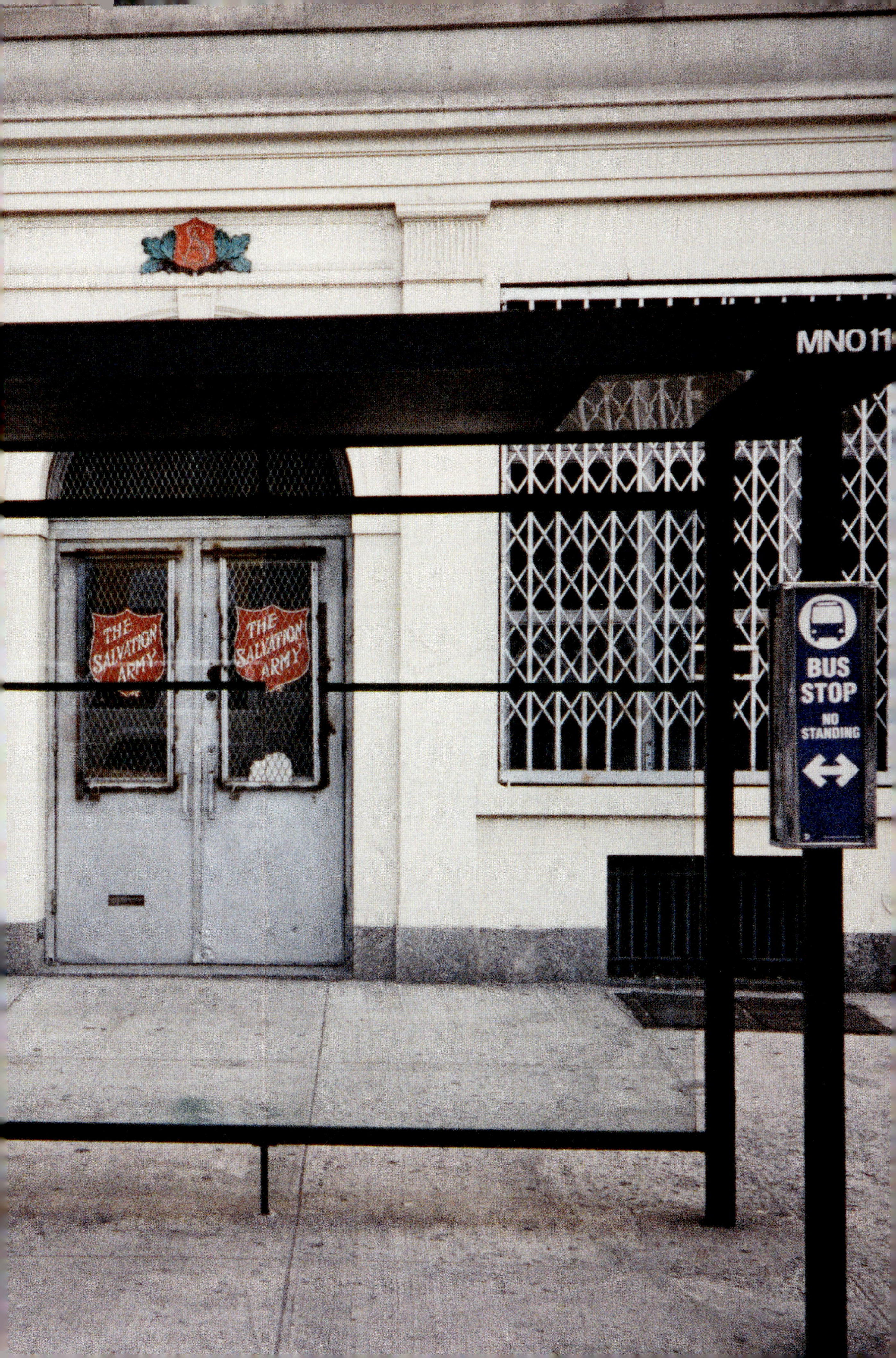
MNO11
THE SALVATION ARMY
THE SALVATION ARMY
BUS STOP
NO STANDING

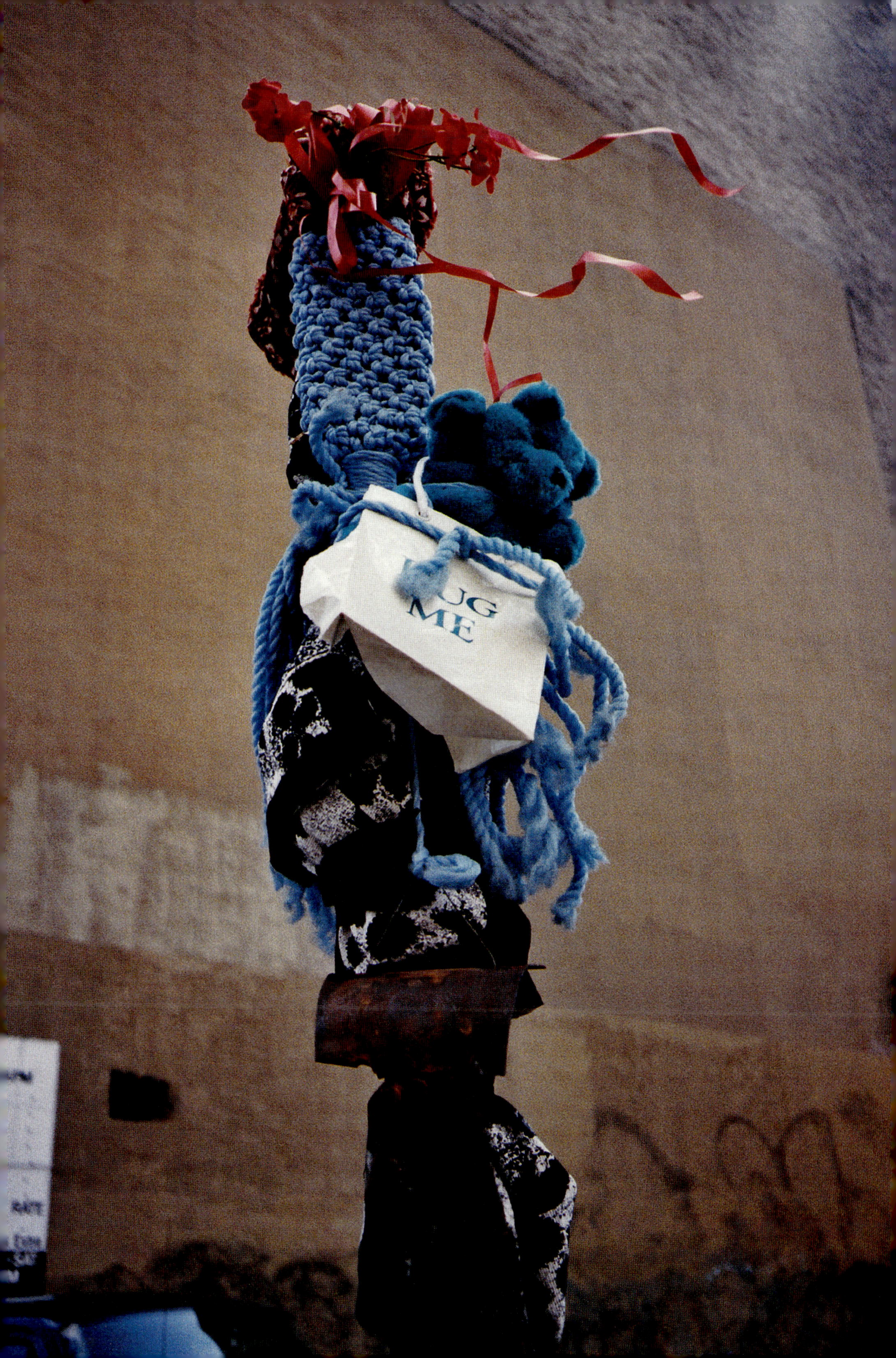
UG
ME

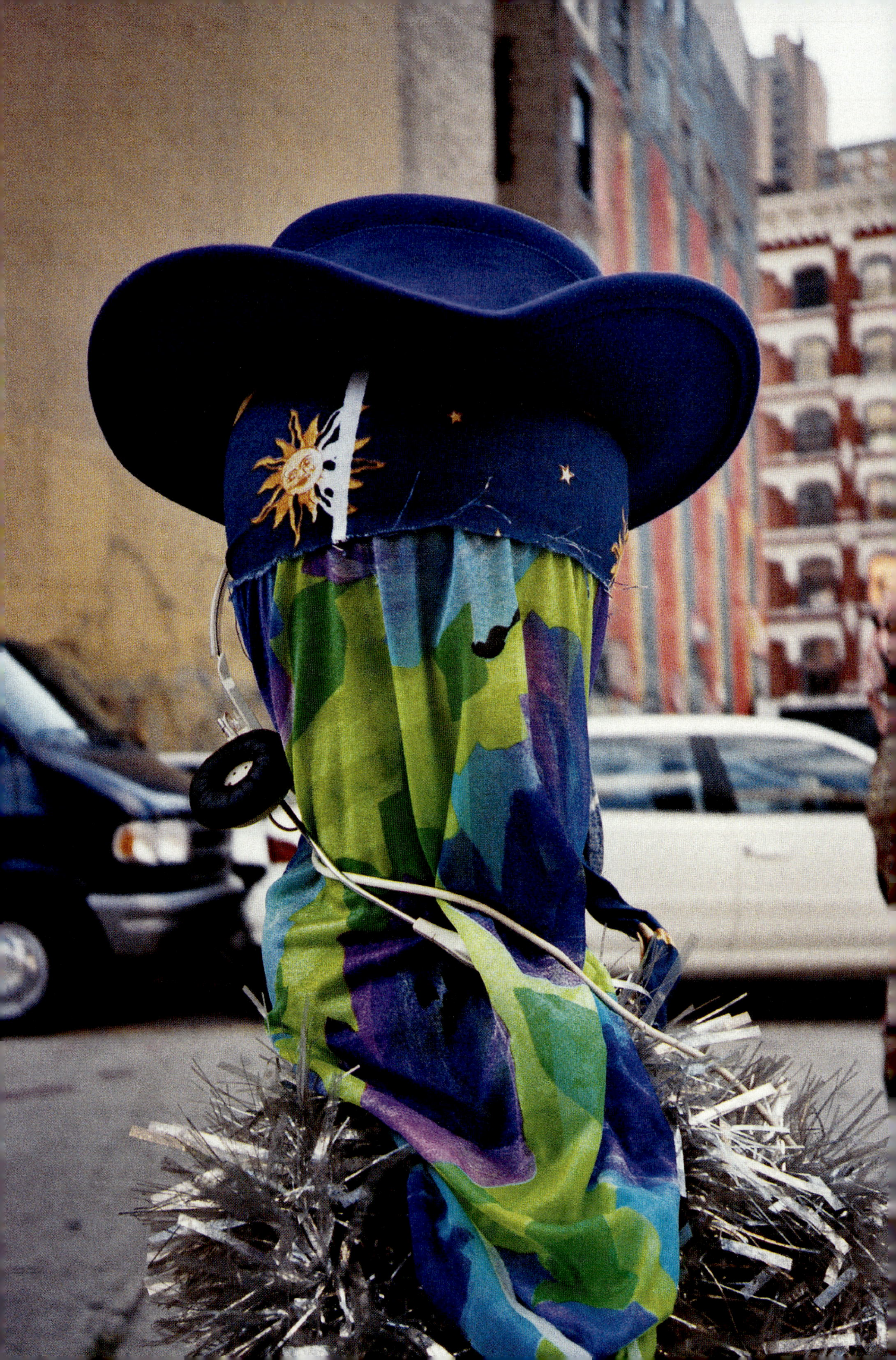

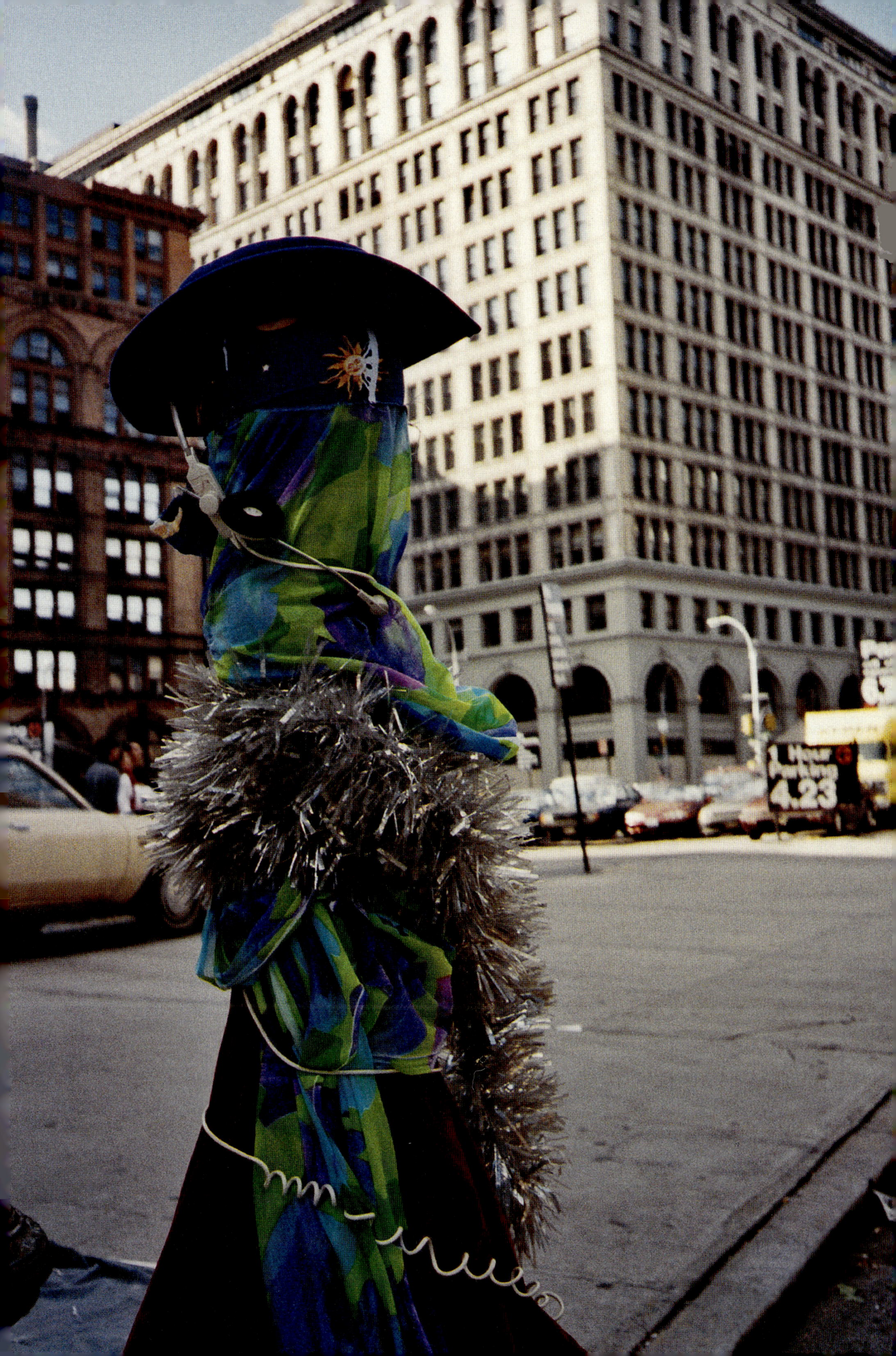
1 Hour
Parking
4.23

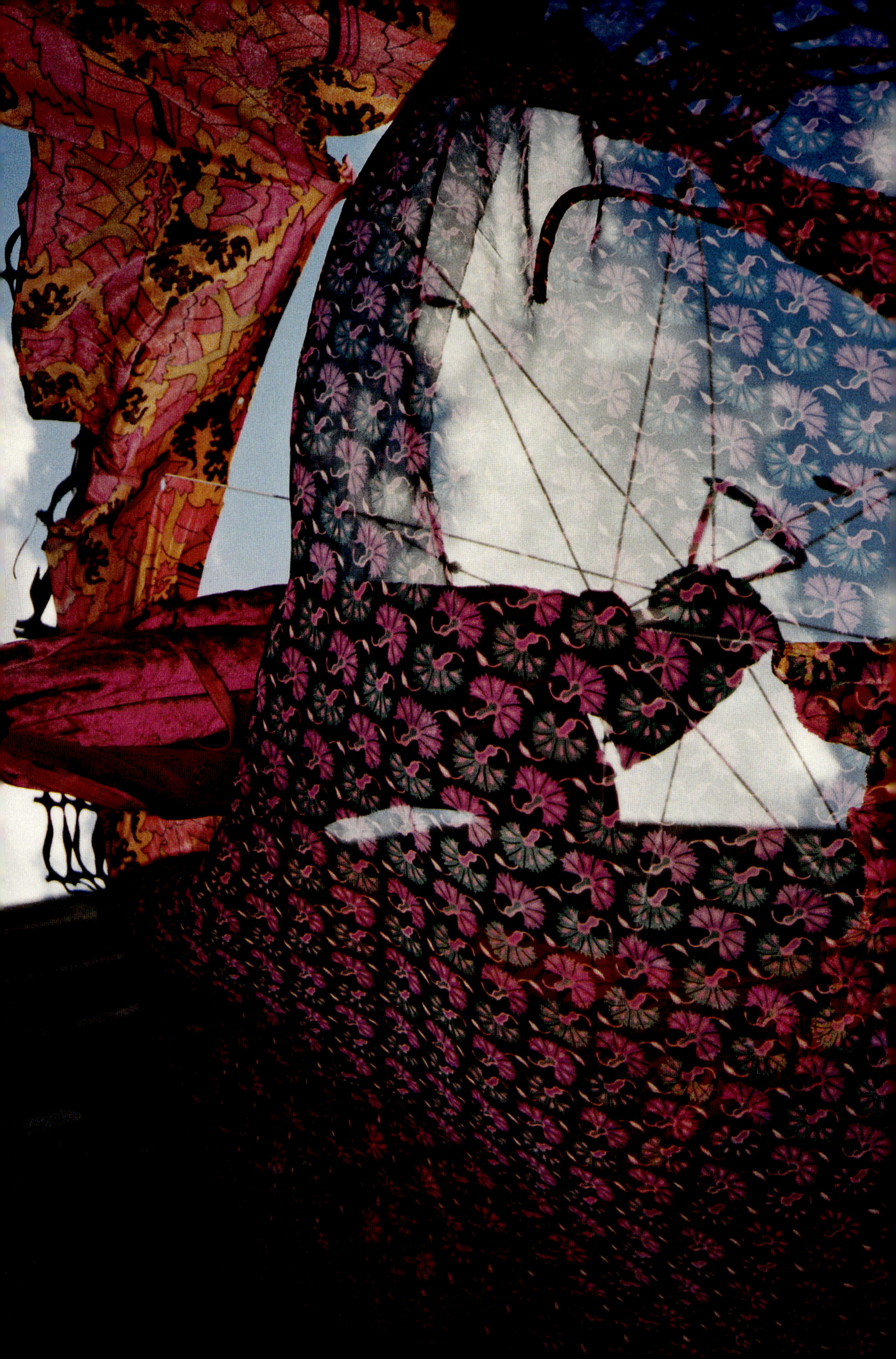

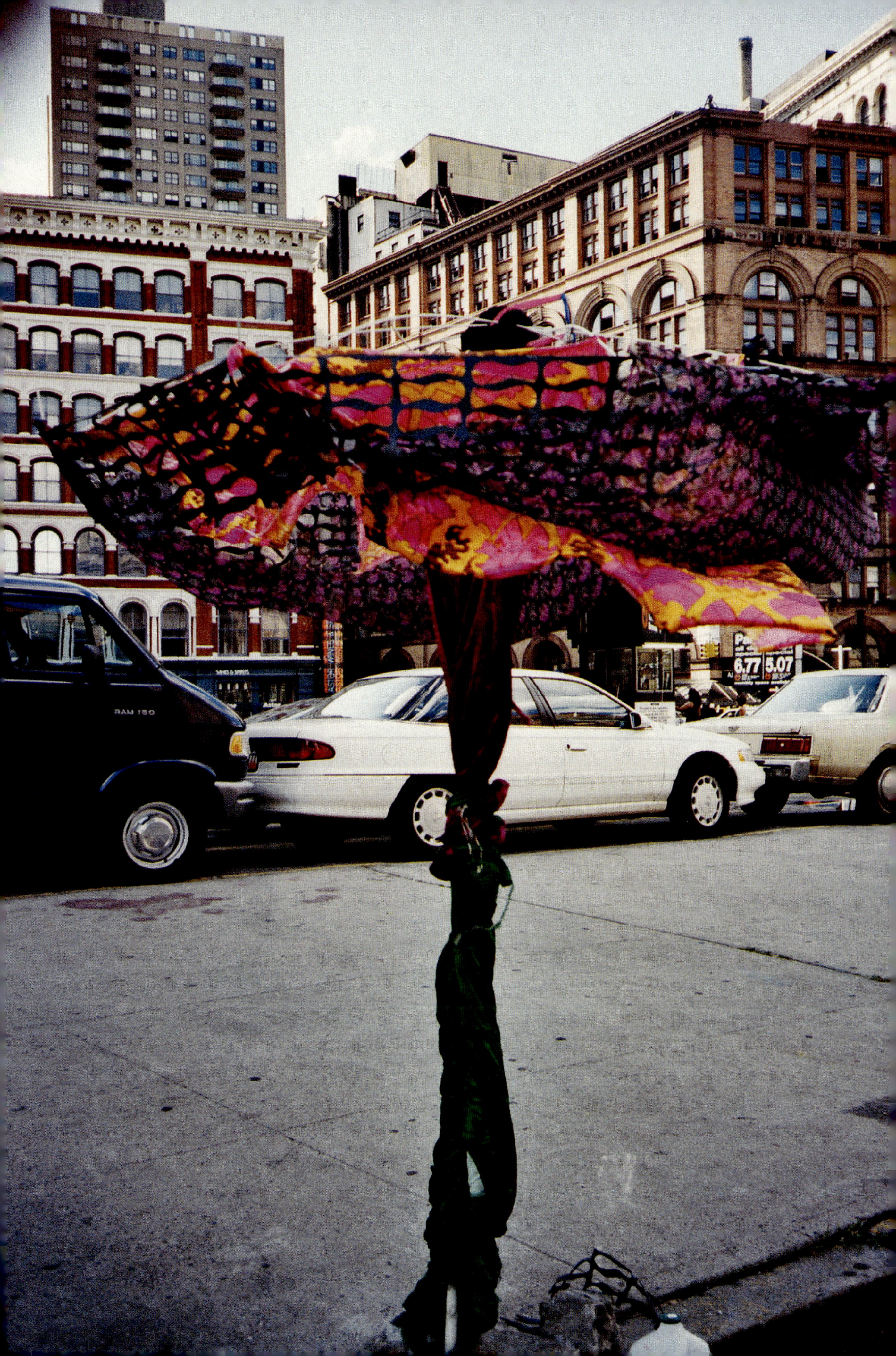
RAM 150
6.77
5.07

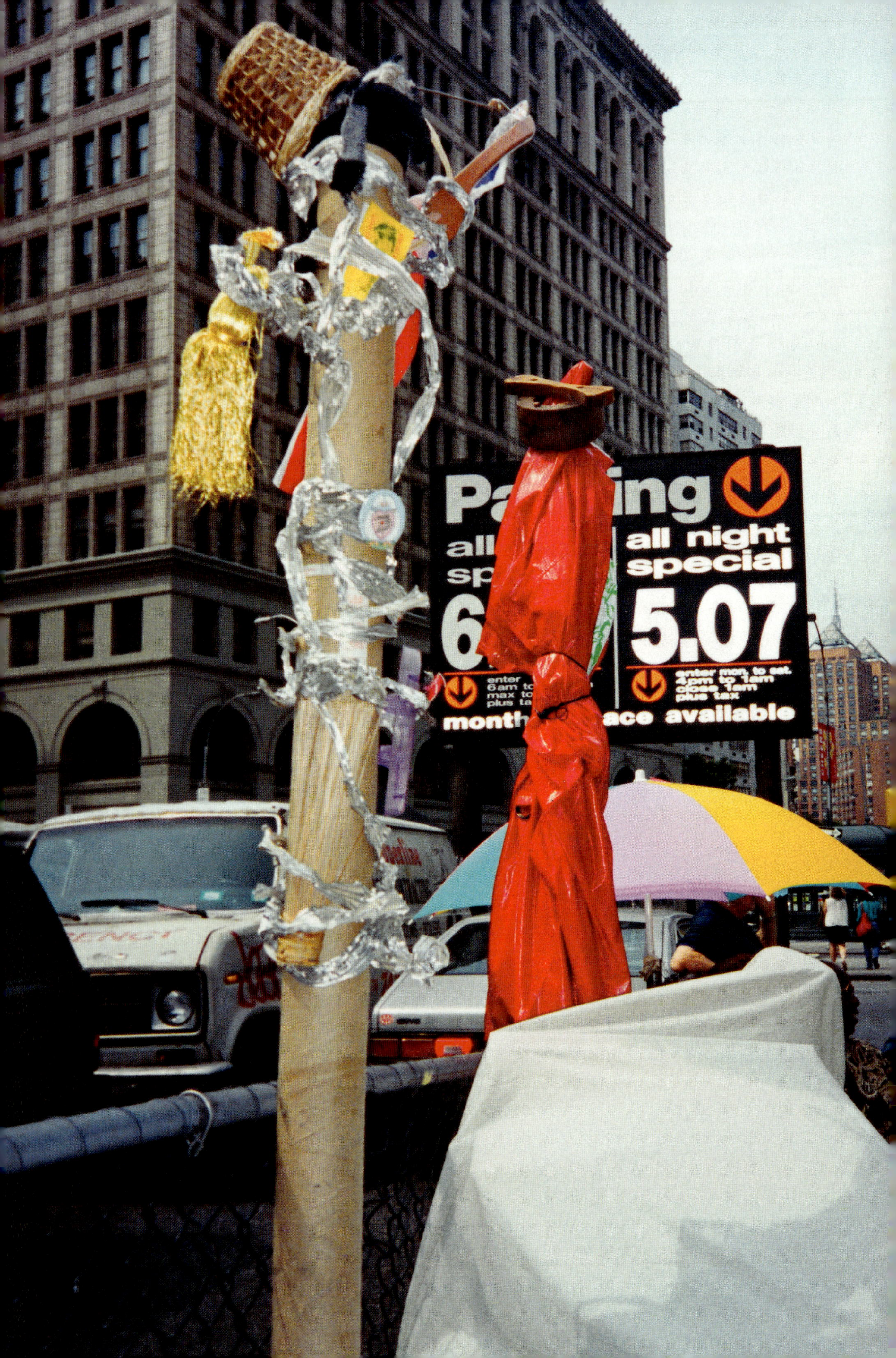
all night
special
5.07
enter mon. to sat.
4pm to 1am
close 1am
plus tax
available

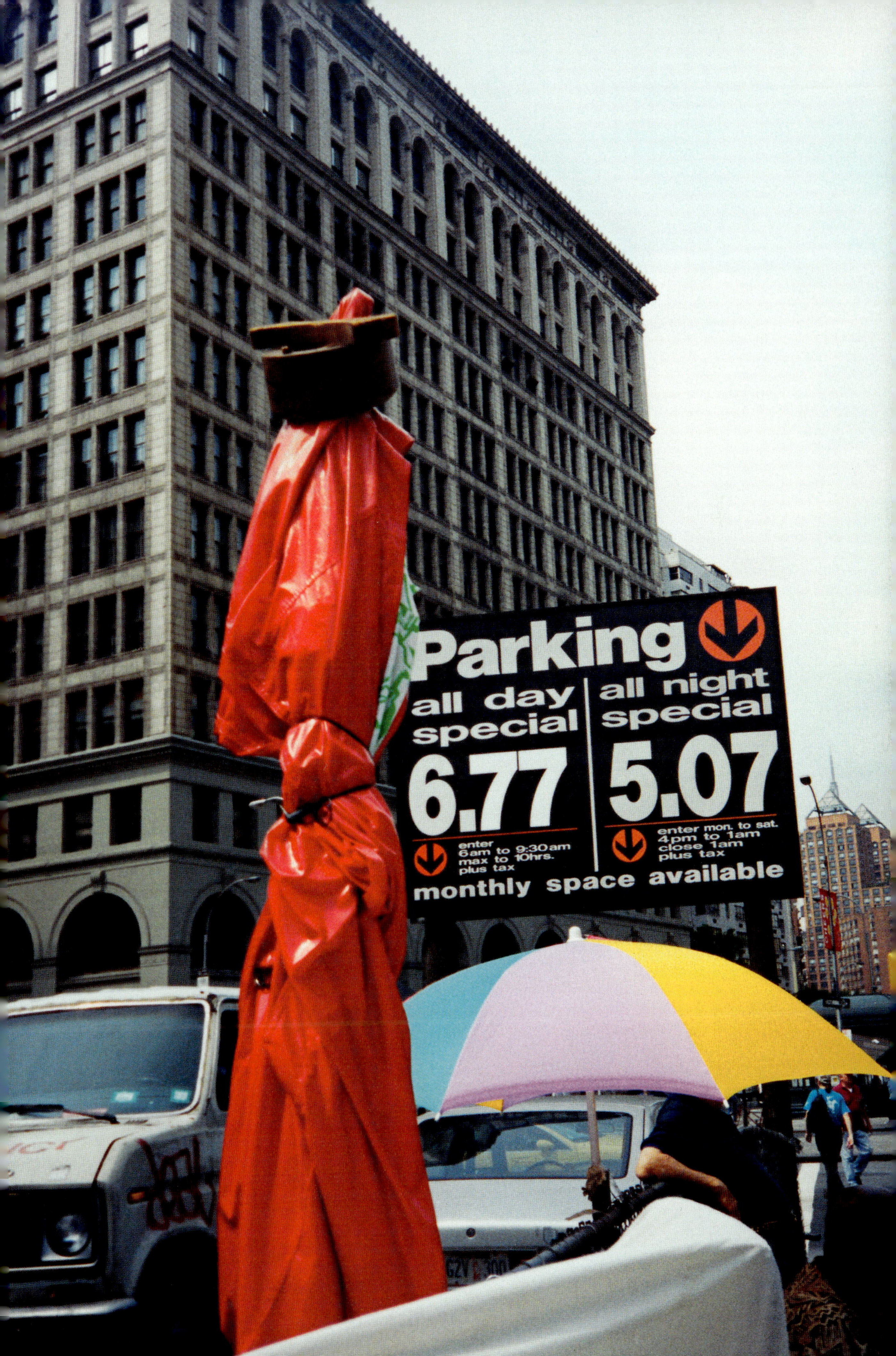
Parking
all day special
6.77
enter 6am to 9:30am max to 10hrs. plus tax
all night special
5.07
enter mon. to sat. 4pm to 1am close 1am plus tax
monthly space available

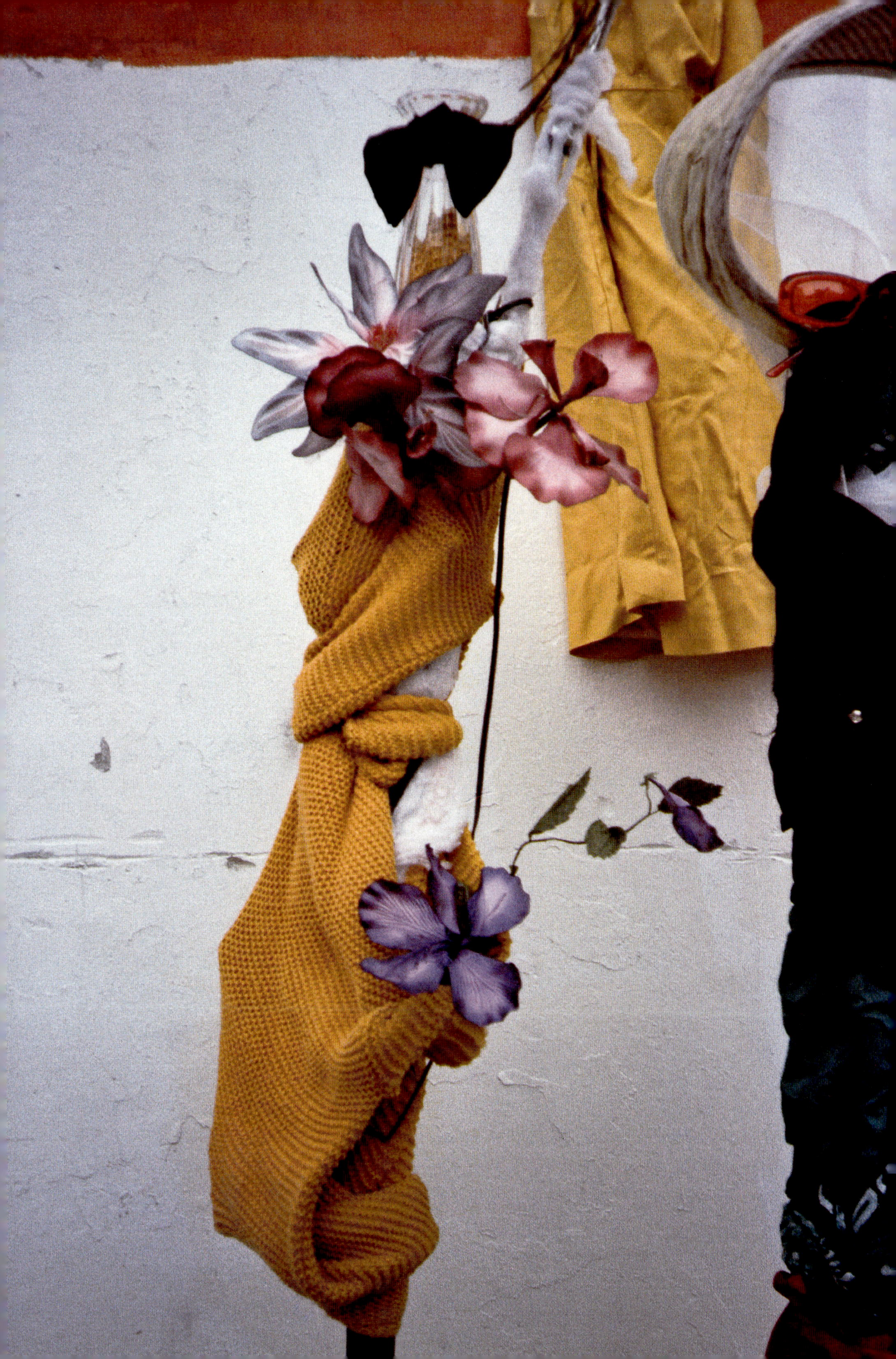

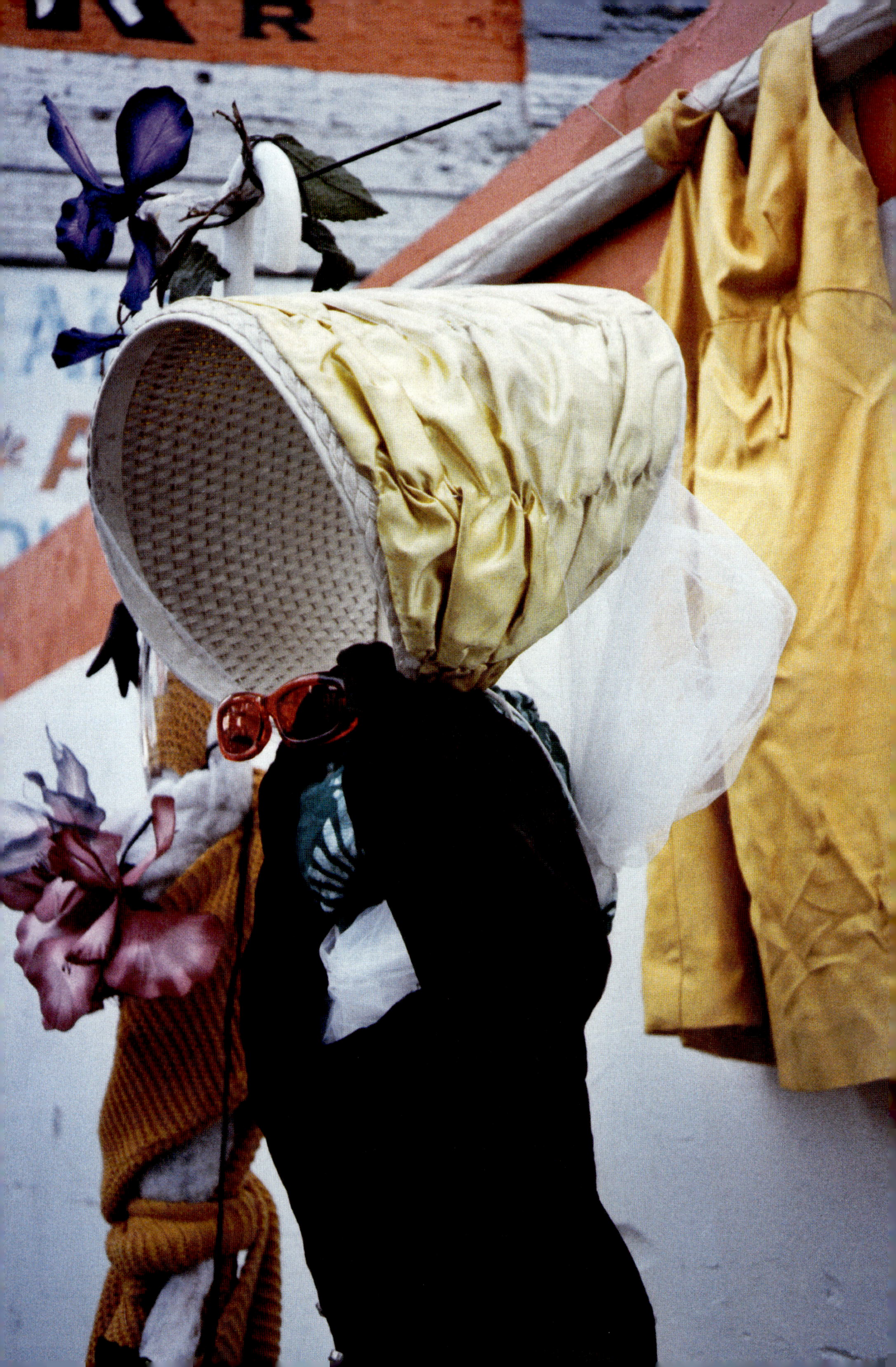

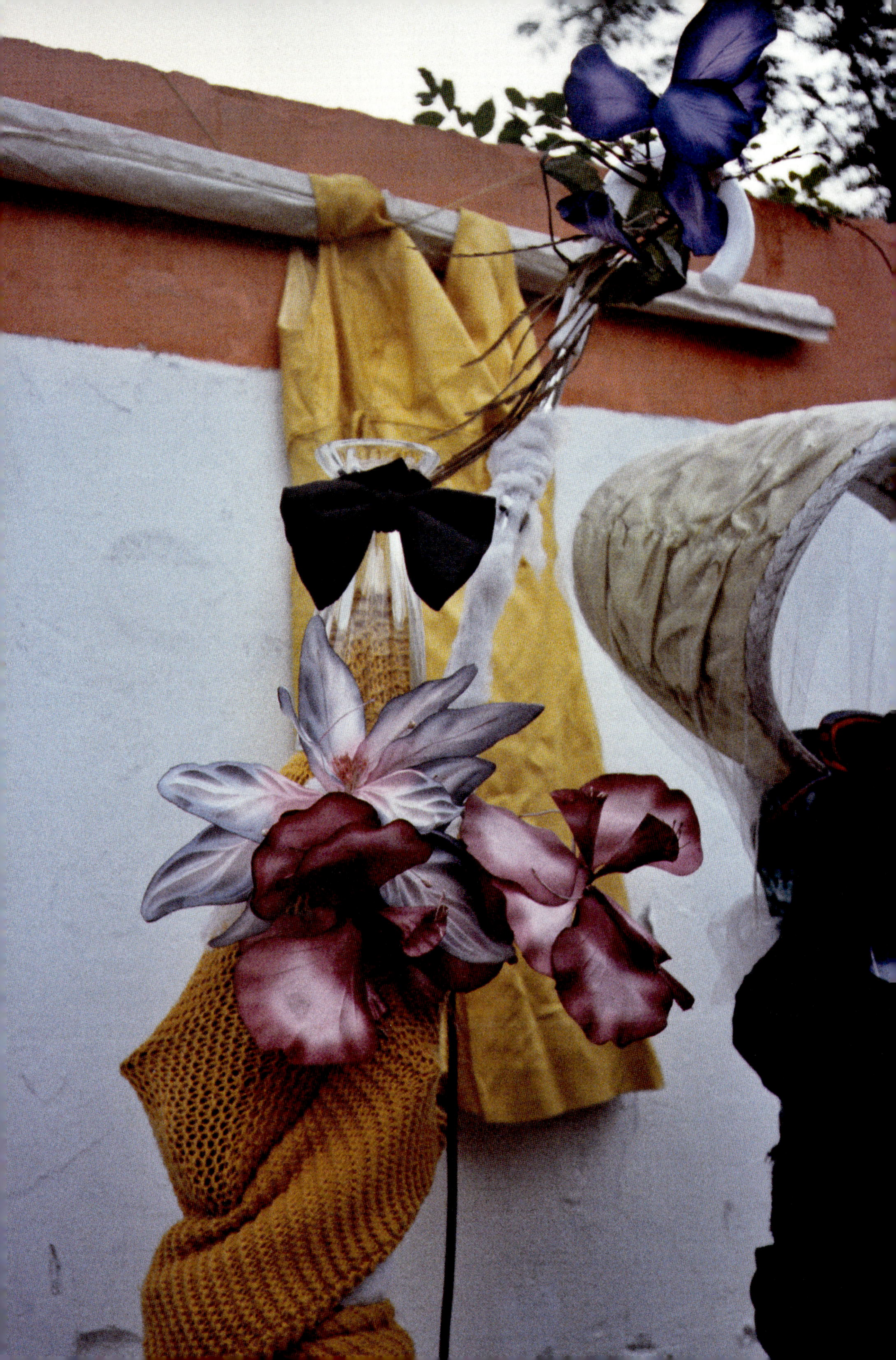

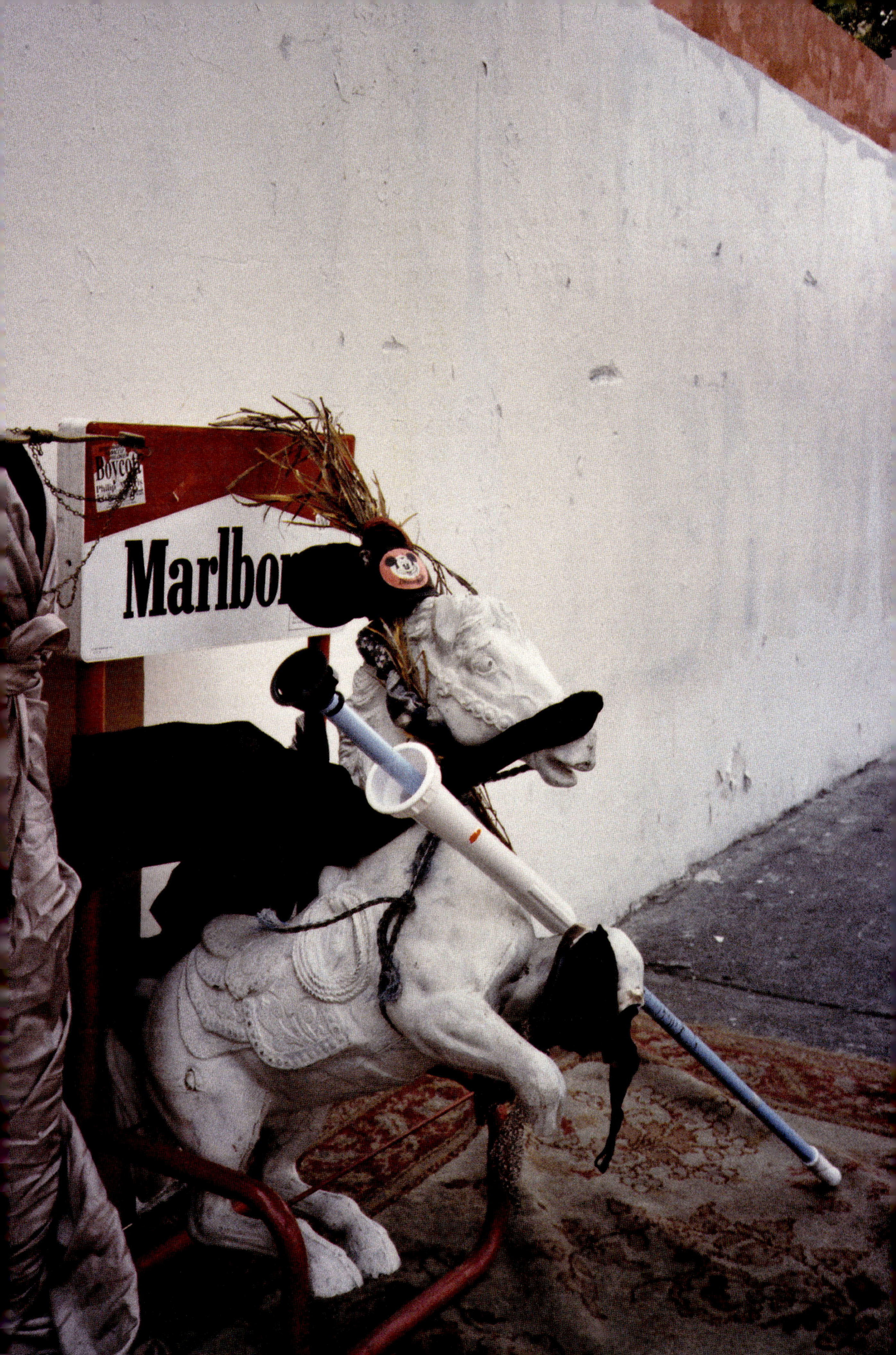
Boycott
Philip
Marlbor

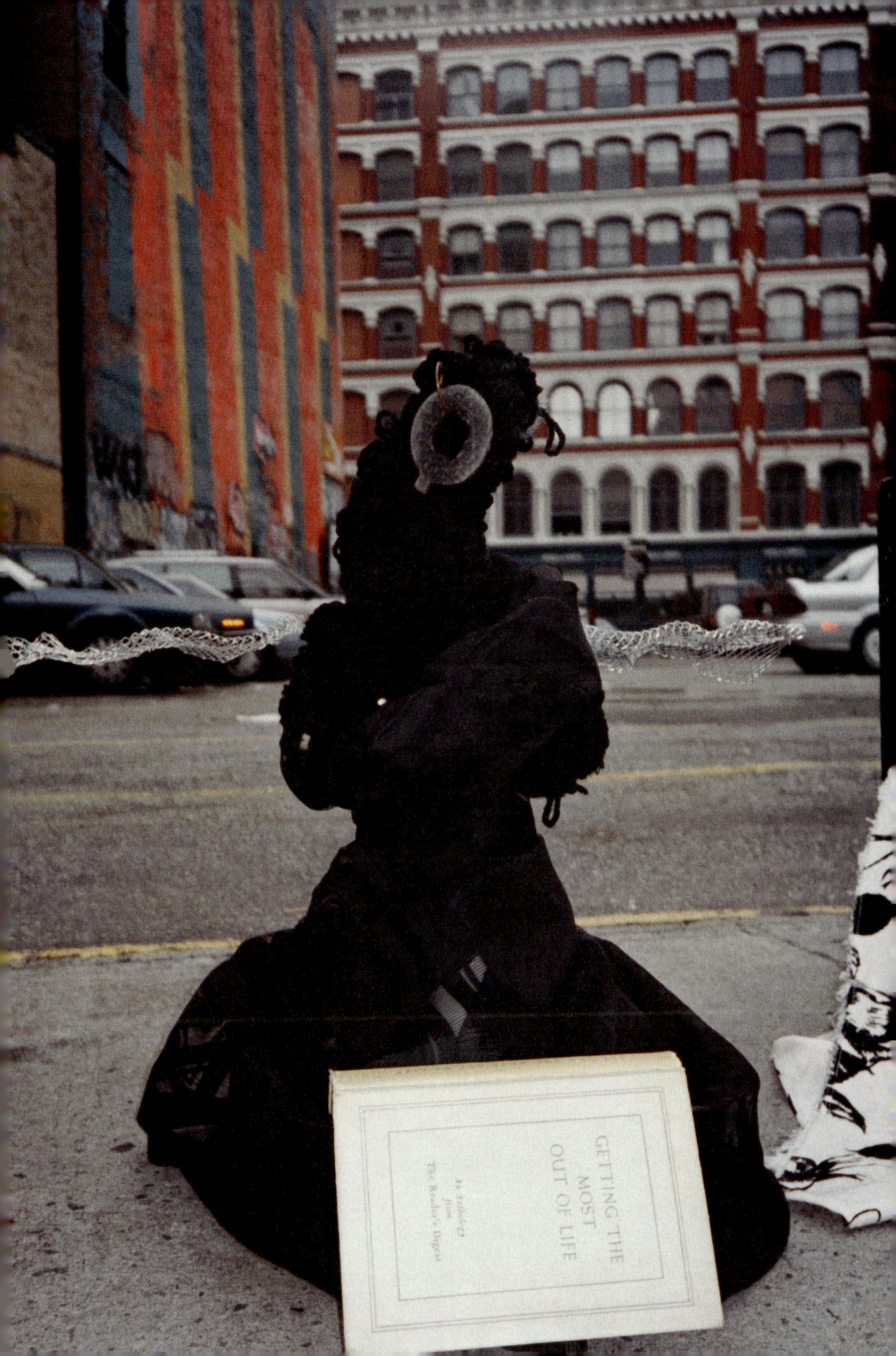
GETTING THE
MOST
OUT OF LIFE
An Anthology
from
The Reader's Digest

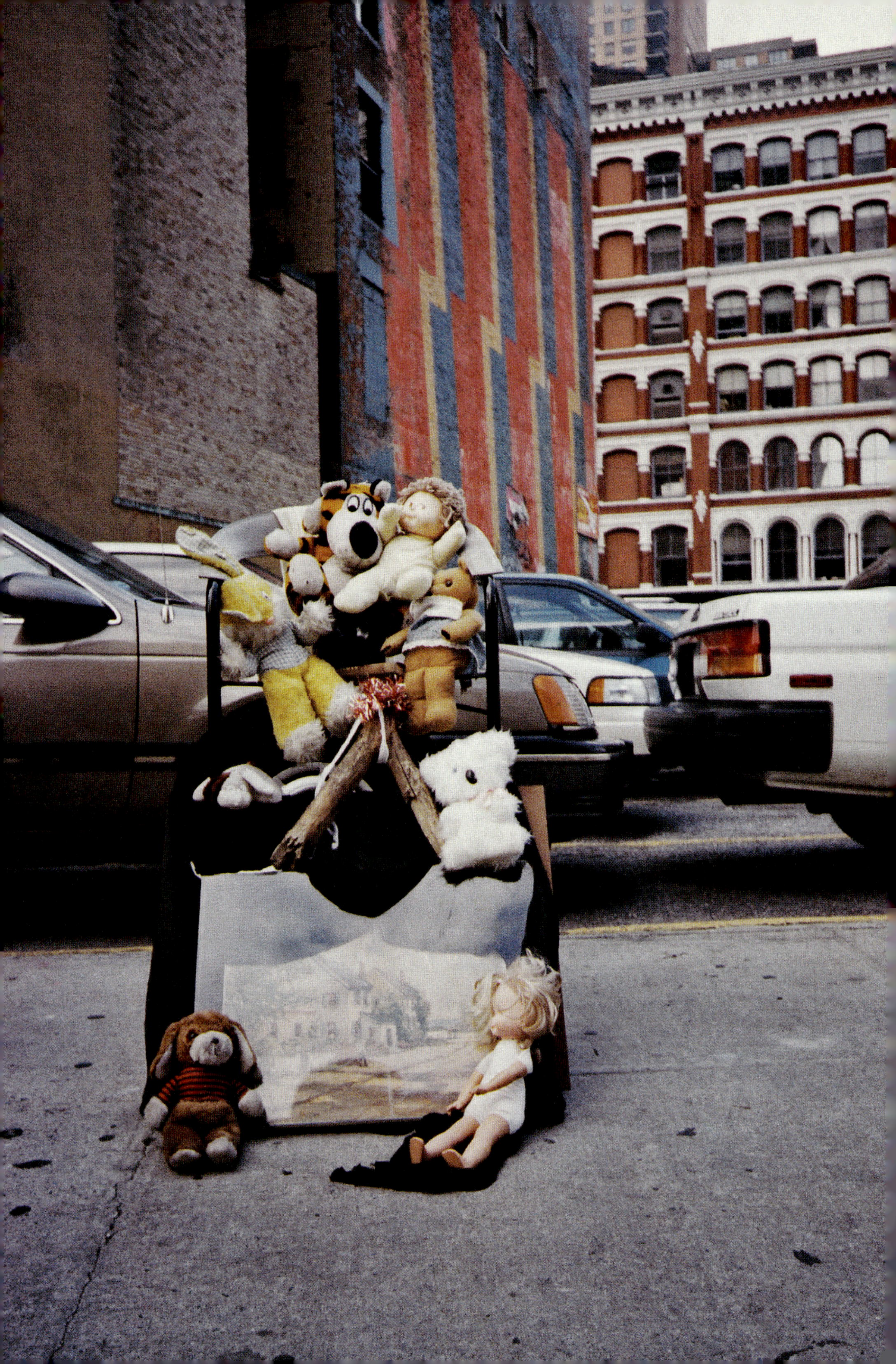

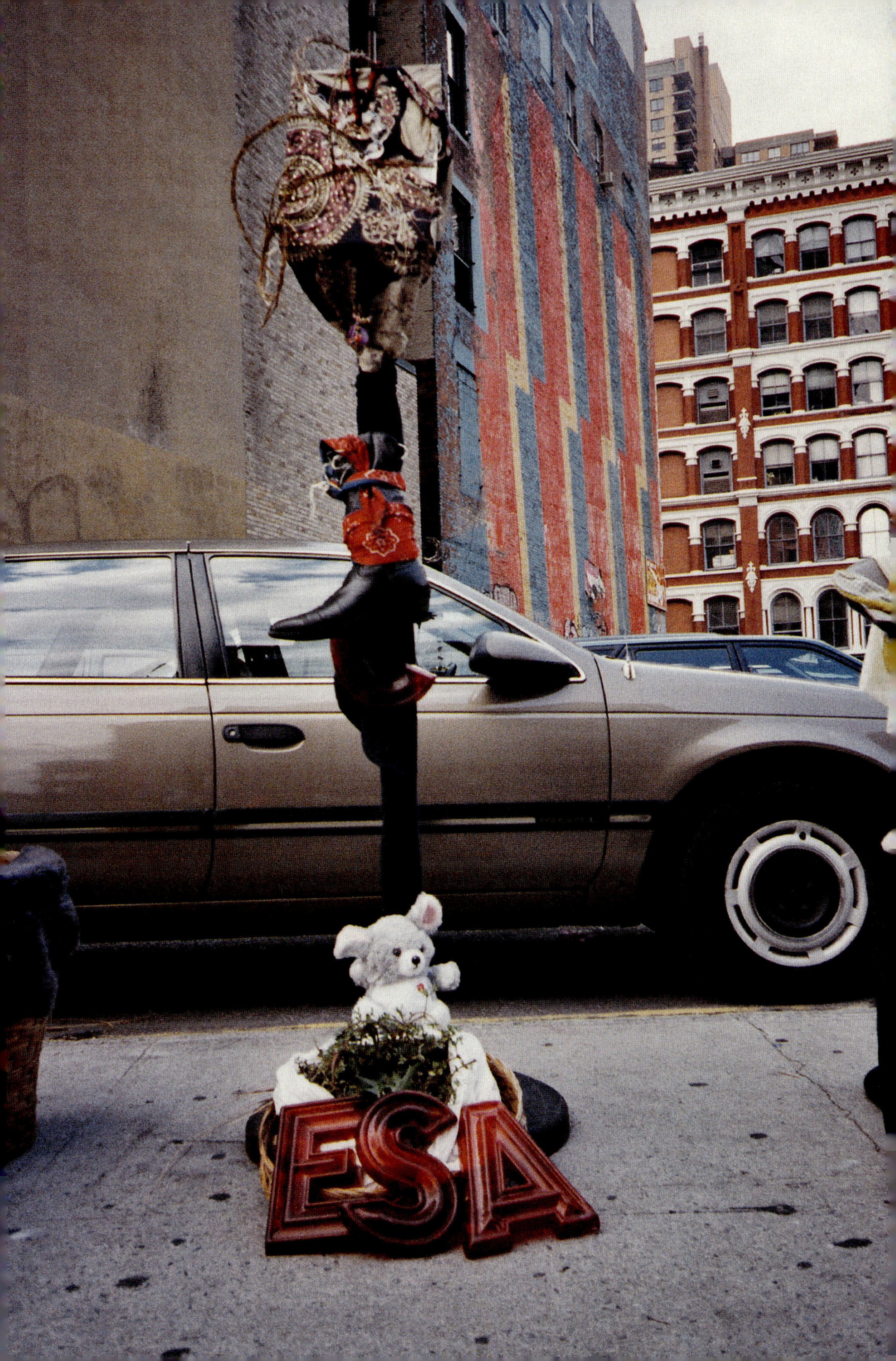
ESA

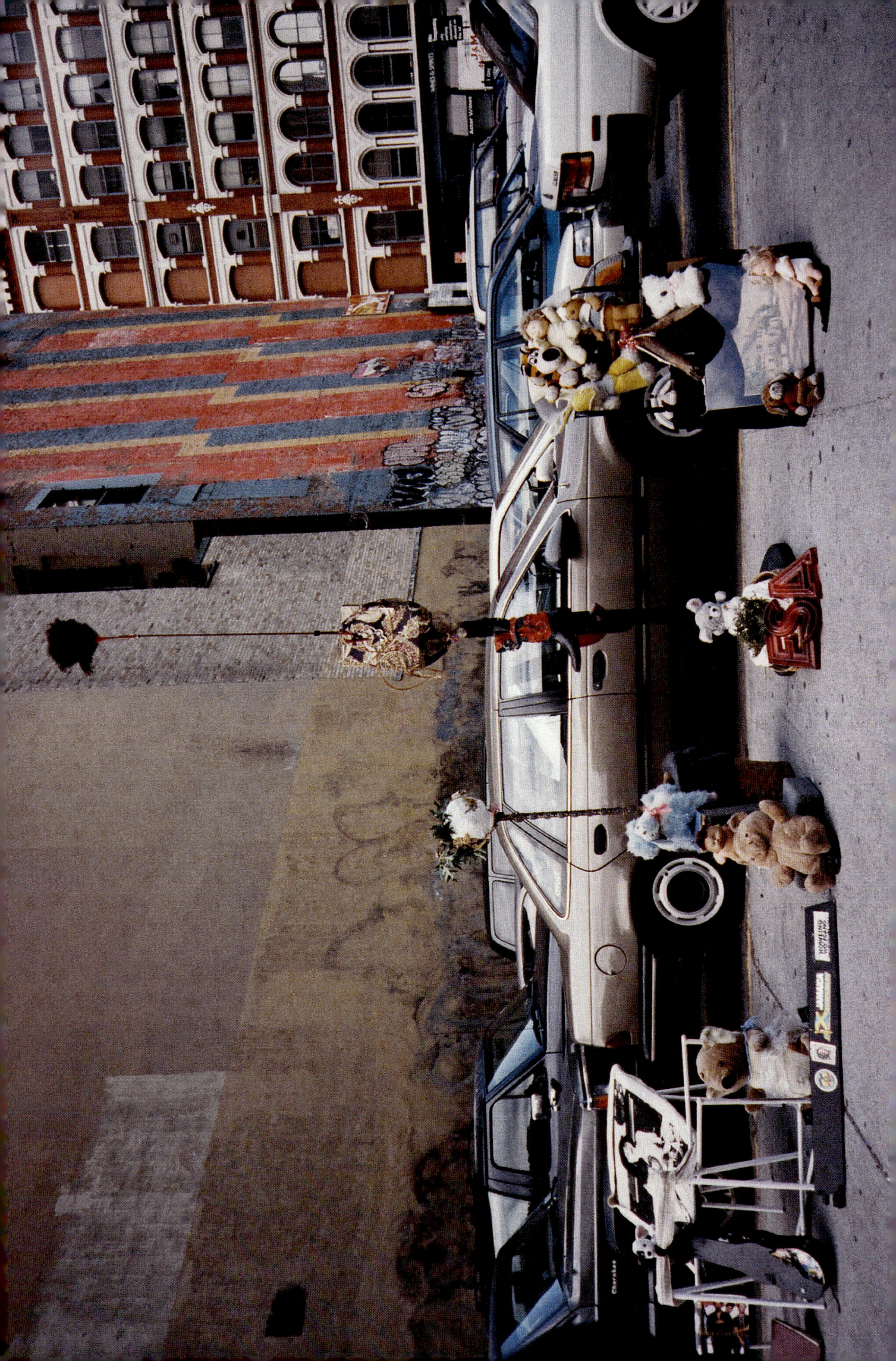

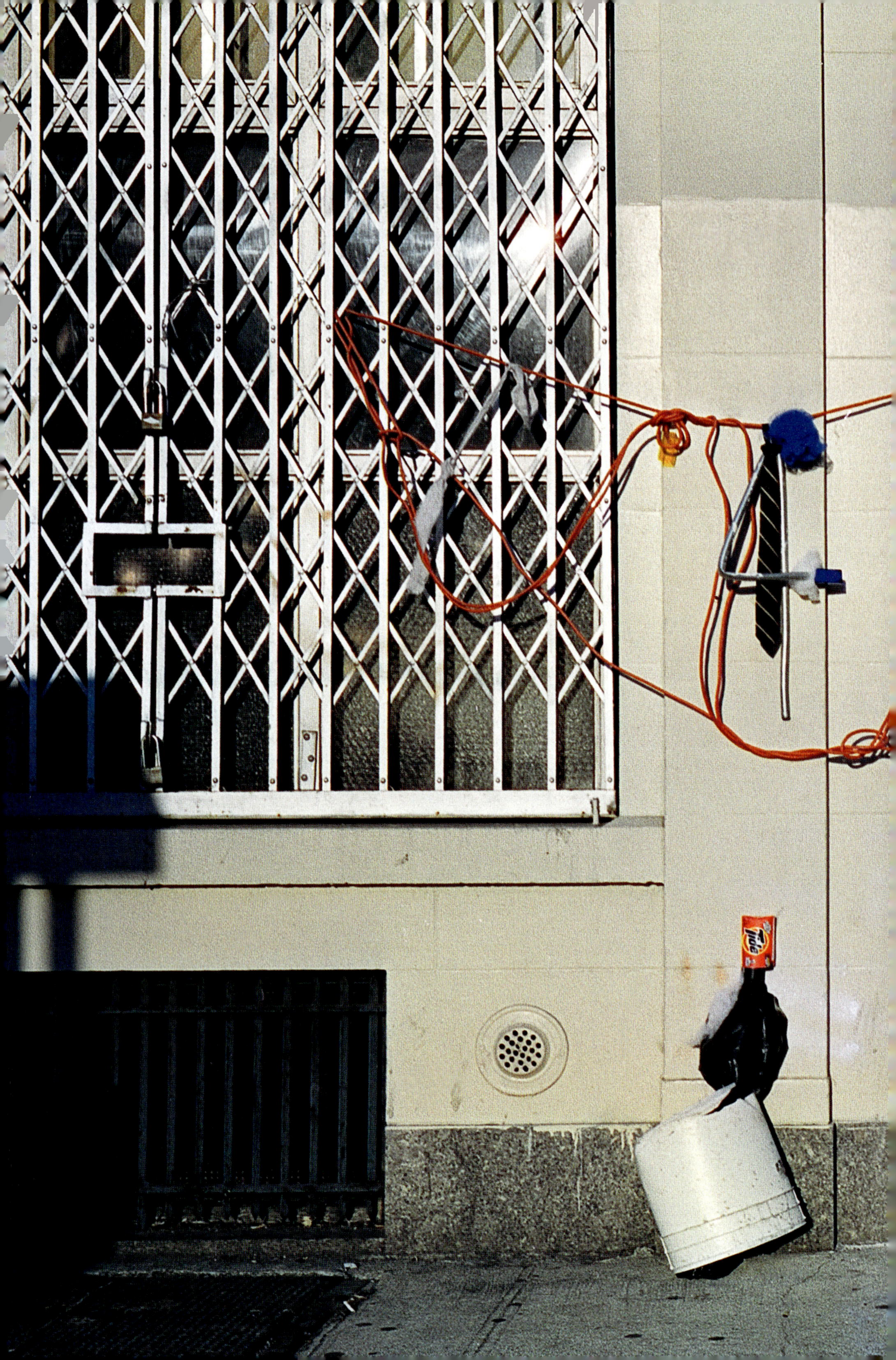
Tide

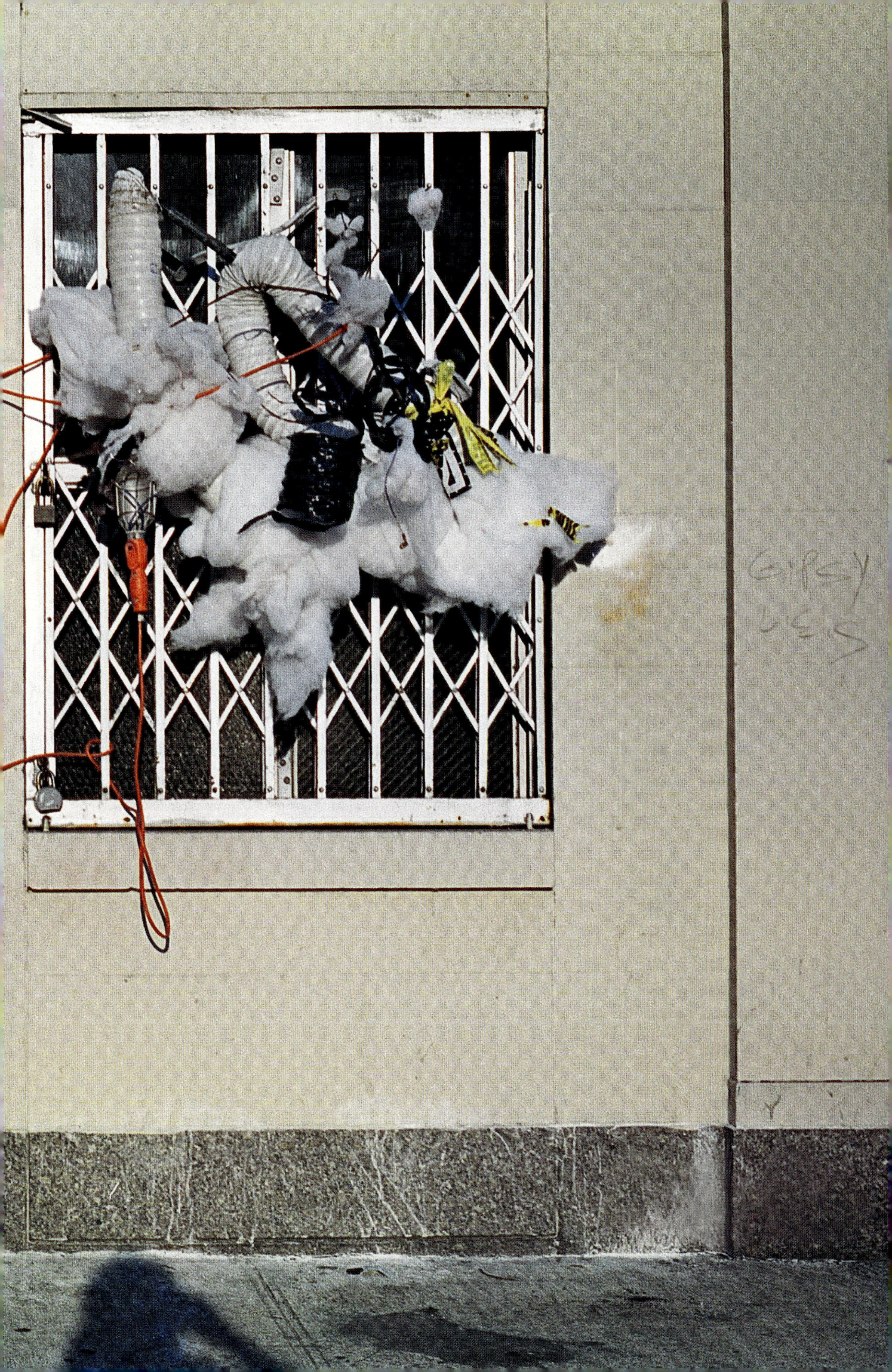

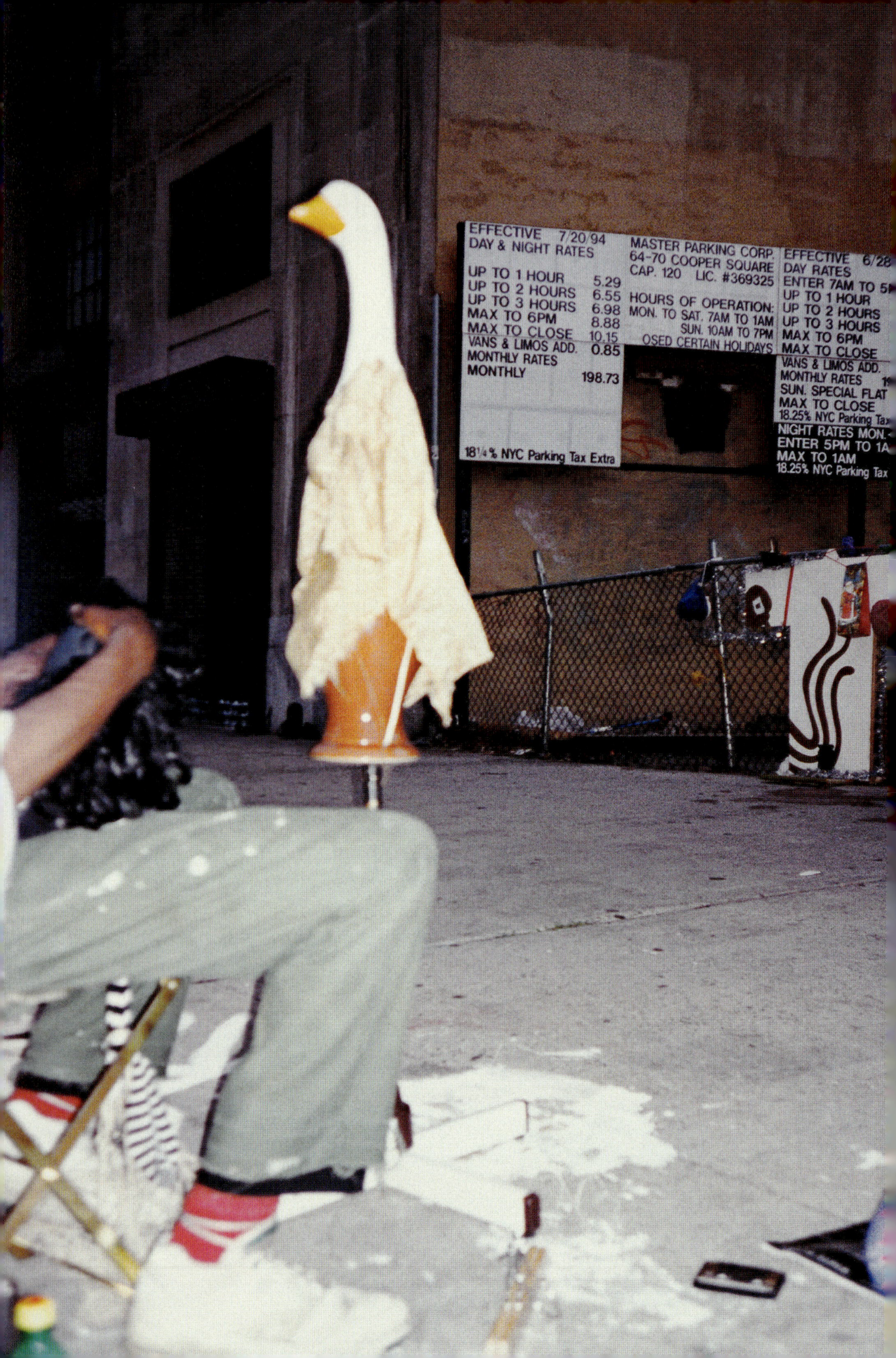
EFFECTIVE 7/20/94
DAY & NIGHT RATES
UP TO 1 HOUR 5.29
UP TO 2 HOURS 6.55
UP TO 3 HOURS 6.98
MAX TO 6PM 8.88
MAX TO CLOSE 10.15
VANS & LIMOS ADD. 0.85
MONTHLY RATES
MONTHLY 198.73
18¼ % NYC Parking Tax Extra
MASTER PARKING CORP.
64-70 COOPER SQUARE
CAP. 120 LIC. #369325
HOURS OF OPERATION:
MON. TO SAT. 7AM TO 1AM
SUN. 10AM TO 7PM
OSED CERTAIN HOLIDAYS
EFFECTIVE 6/28
DAY RATES
ENTER 7AM TO 5
UP TO 1 HOUR
UP TO 2 HOURS
UP TO 3 HOURS
MAX TO 6PM
MAX TO CLOSE
VANS & LIMOS ADD.
MONTHLY RATES
SUN. SPECIAL FLAT
MAX TO CLOSE
NIGHT RATES MON.
ENTER 5PM TO 1A
MAX TO 1AM
18.25% NYC Parking Tax

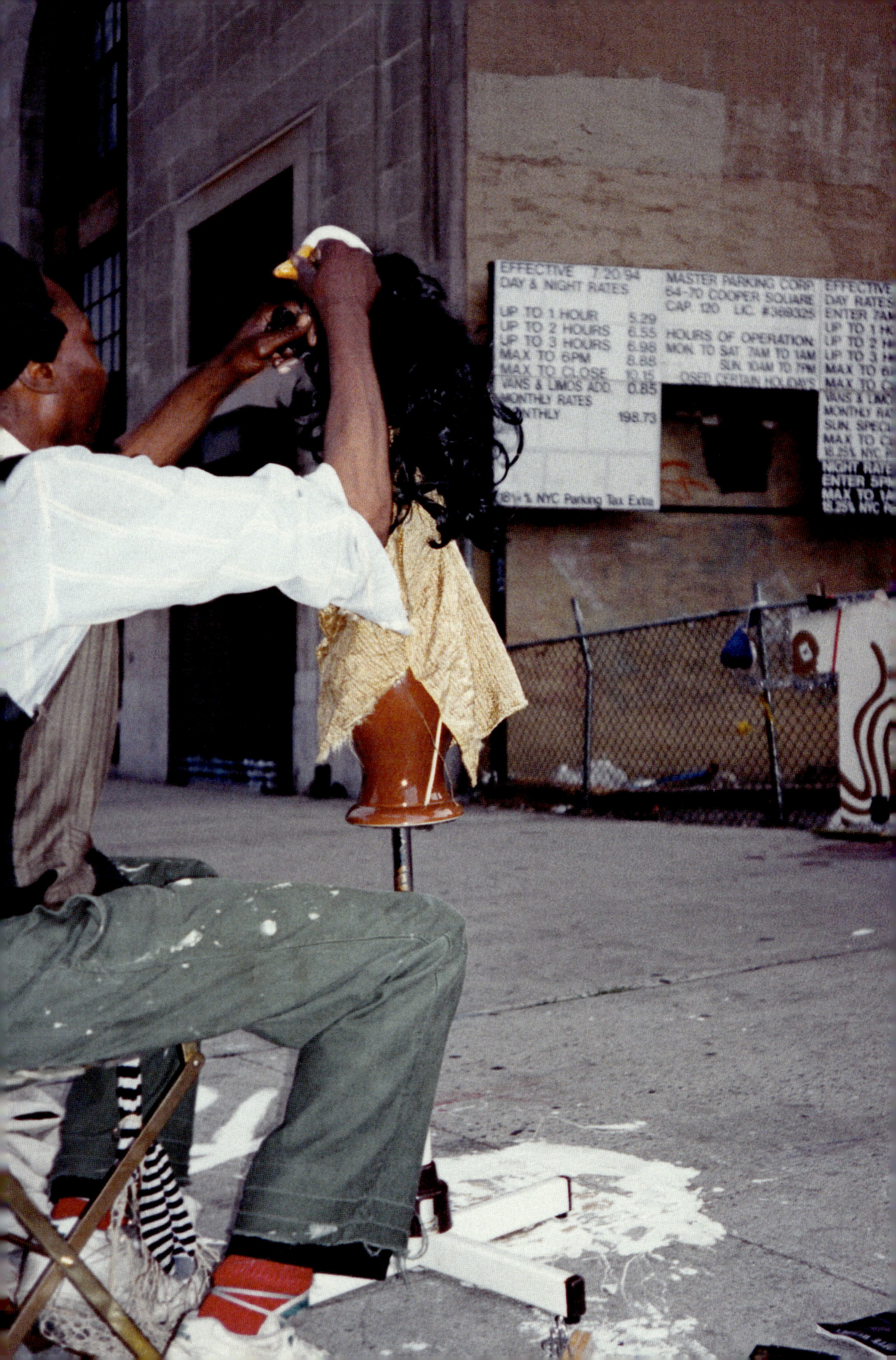
EFFECTIVE 7/20/94
DAY & NIGHT RATES
UP TO 1 HOUR 5.29
UP TO 2 HOURS 6.55
UP TO 3 HOURS 6.98
MAX TO 6PM 8.88
VANS & LIMOS ADD 0.85
MONTHLY RATES
198.73
NYC Parking Tax Extra
MASTER PARKING CORP
64-70 COOPER SQUARE
HOURS OF OPERATION
MON. TO SAT. 7AM TO 1AM
SUN. 10AM TO 7PM

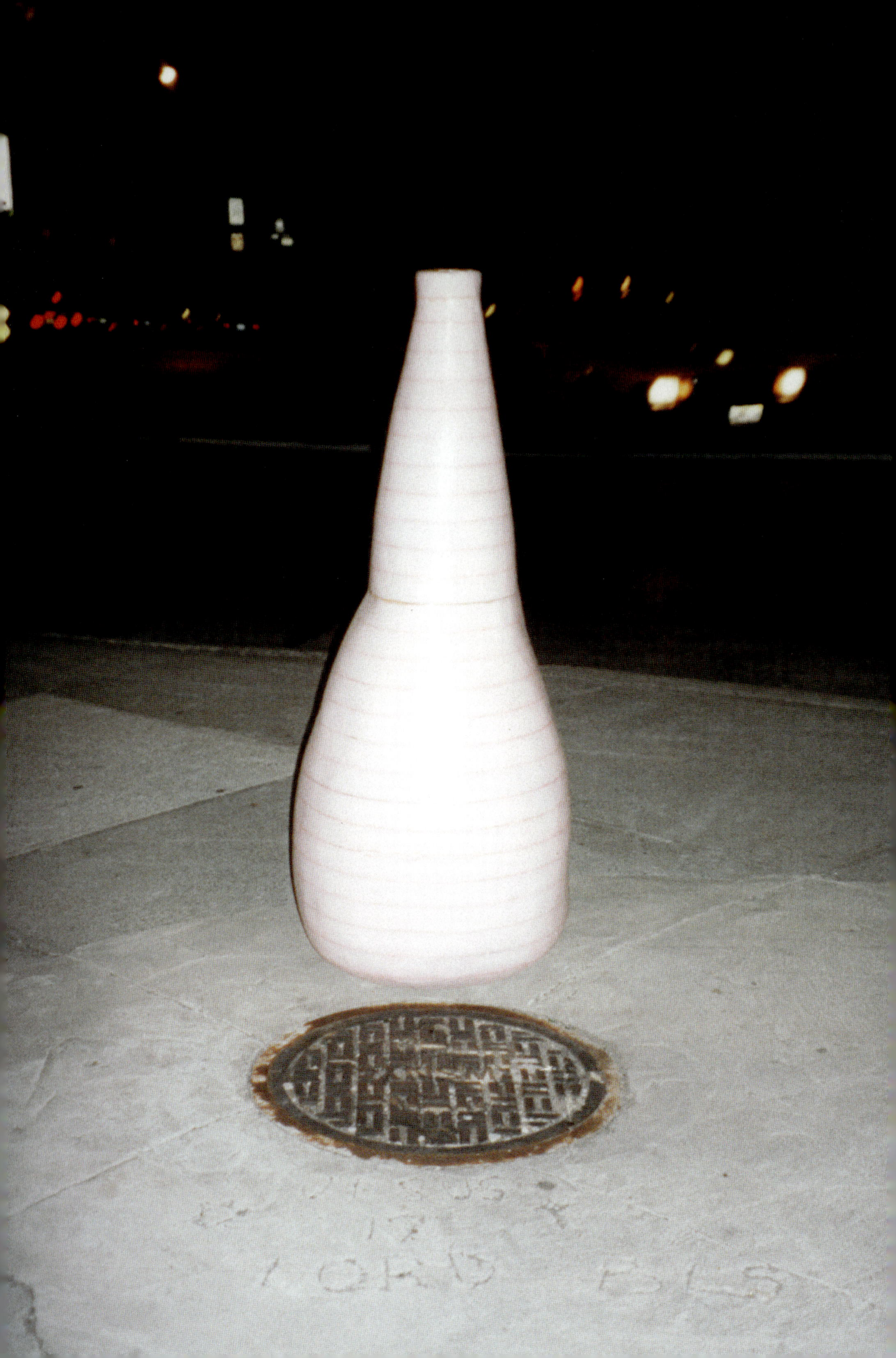

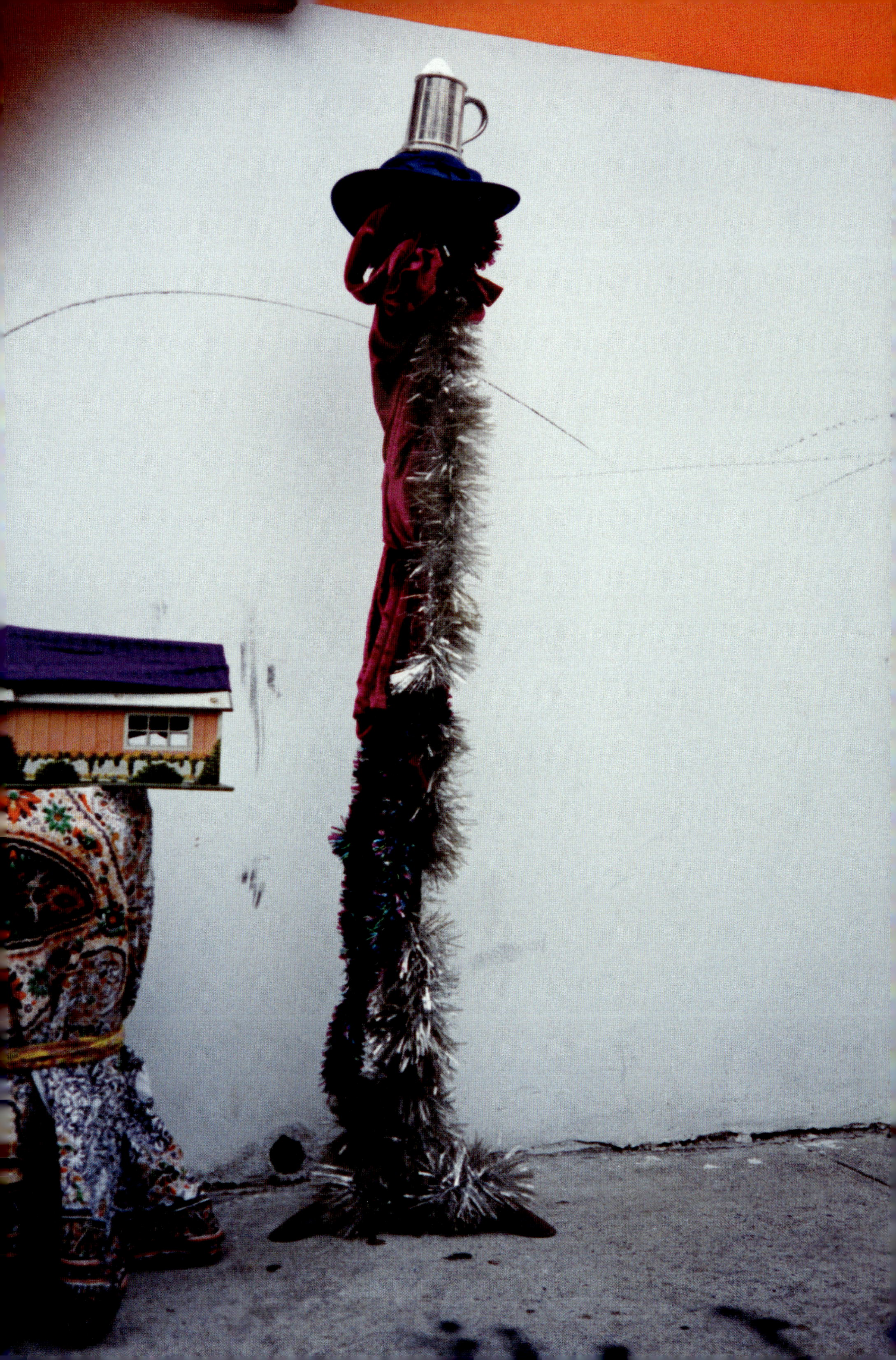

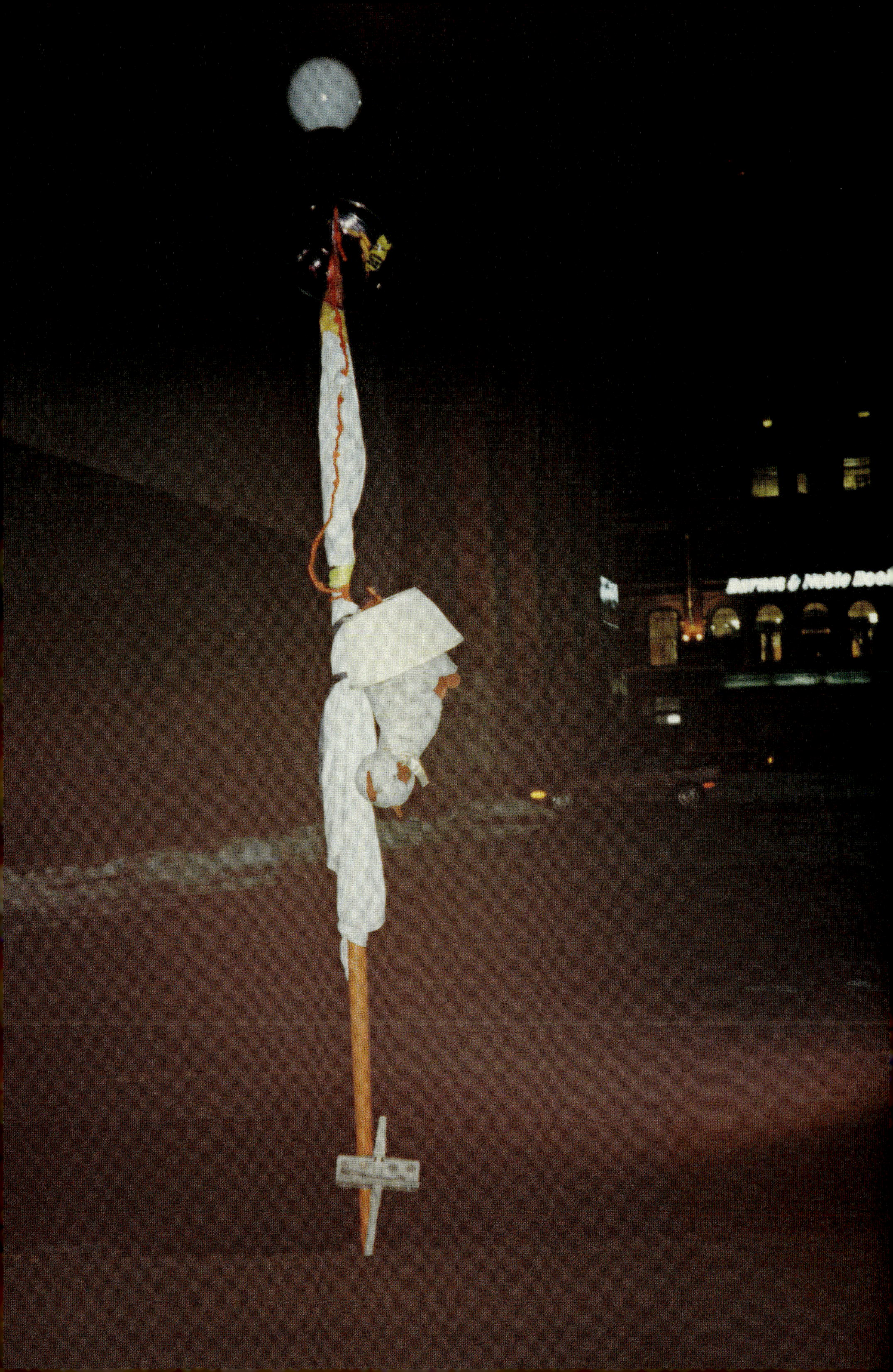

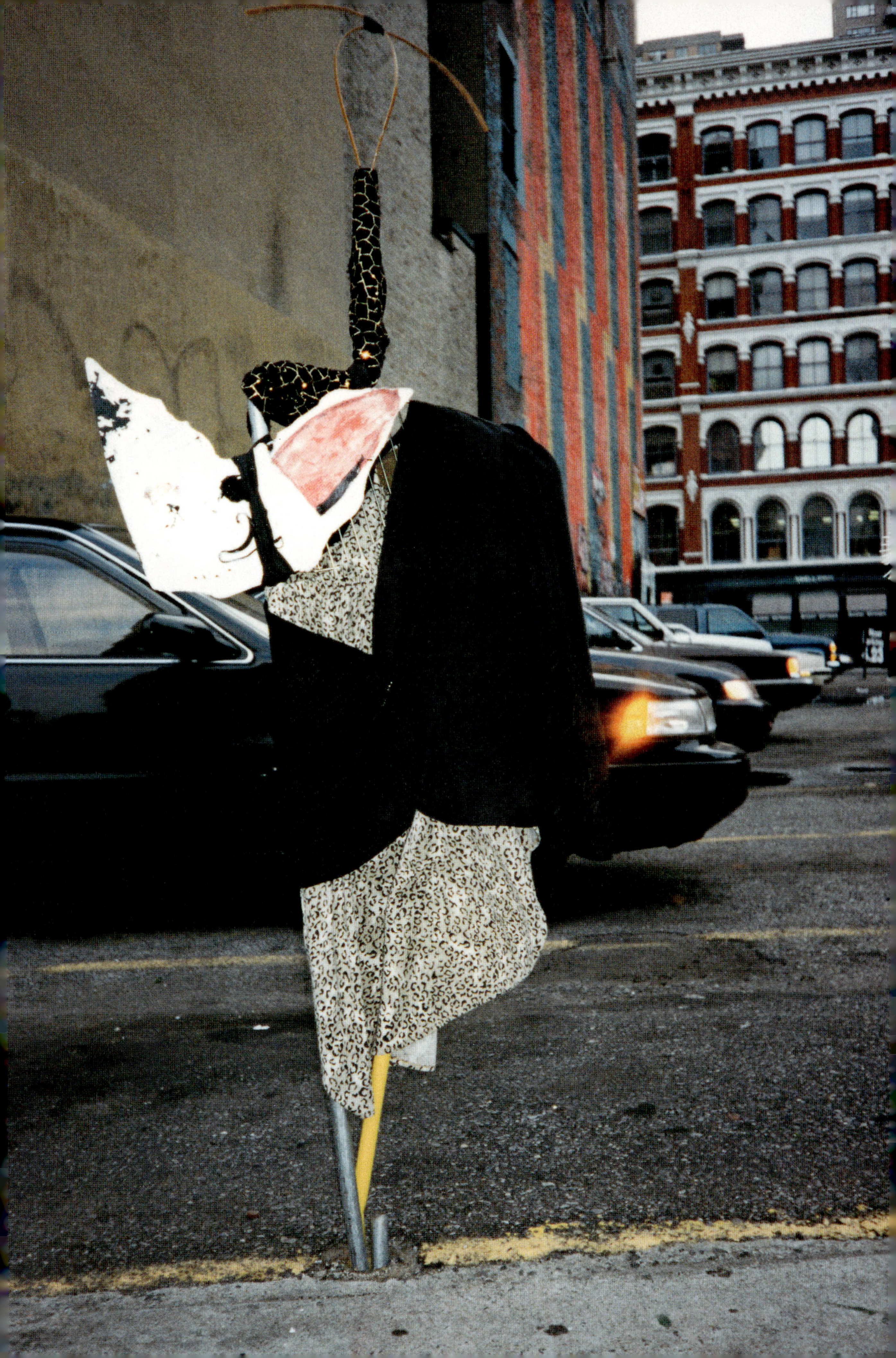

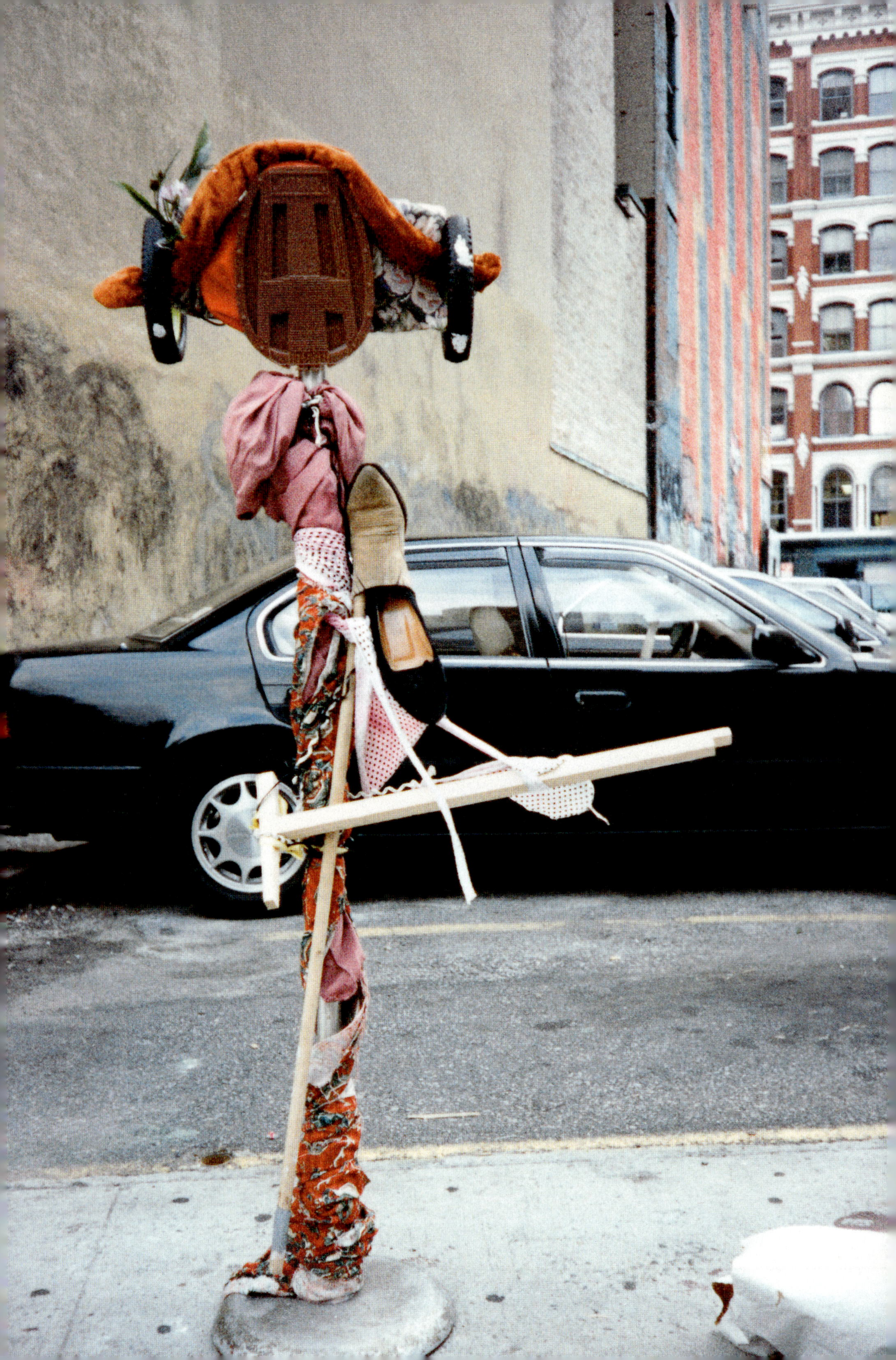

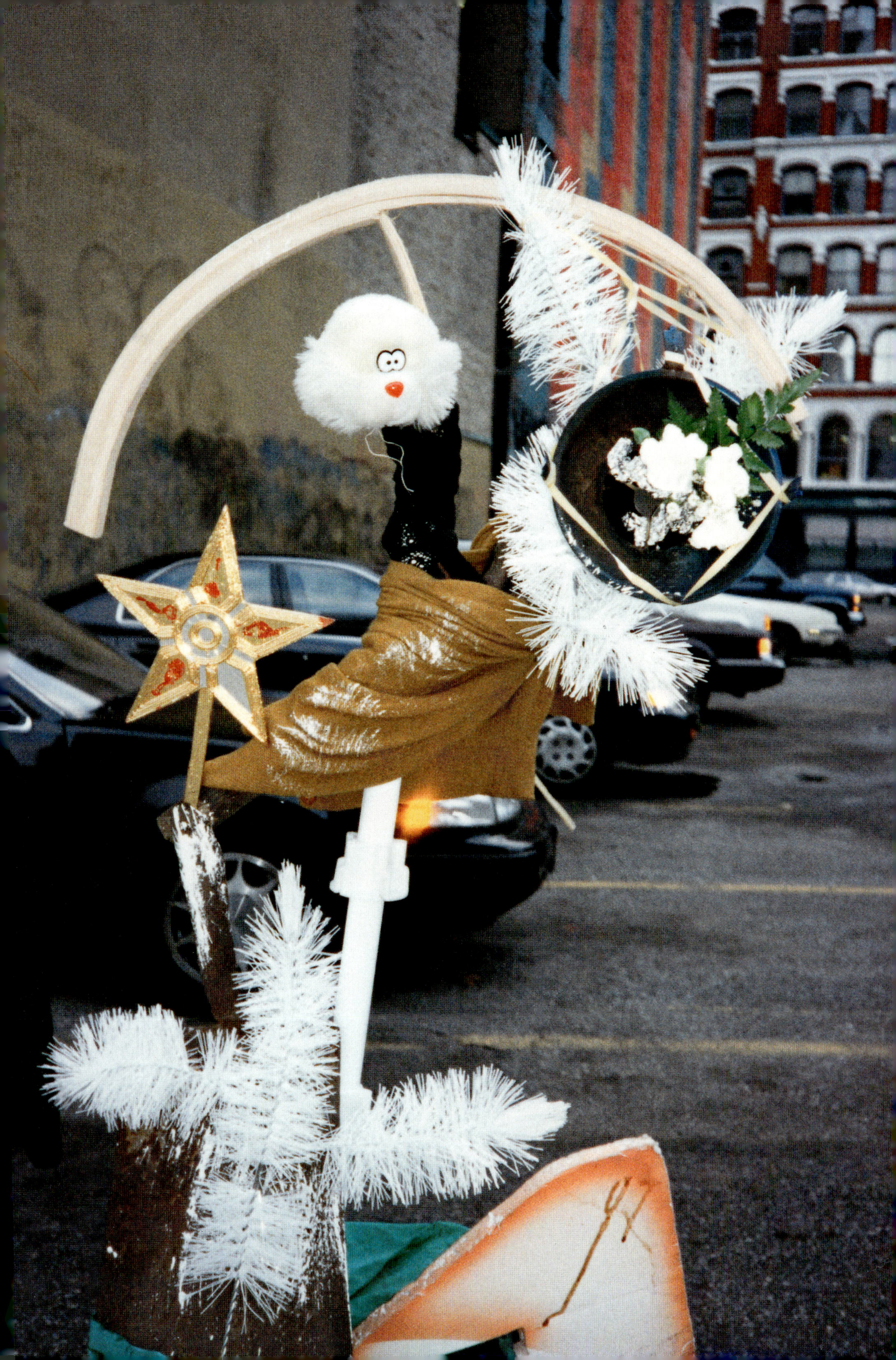

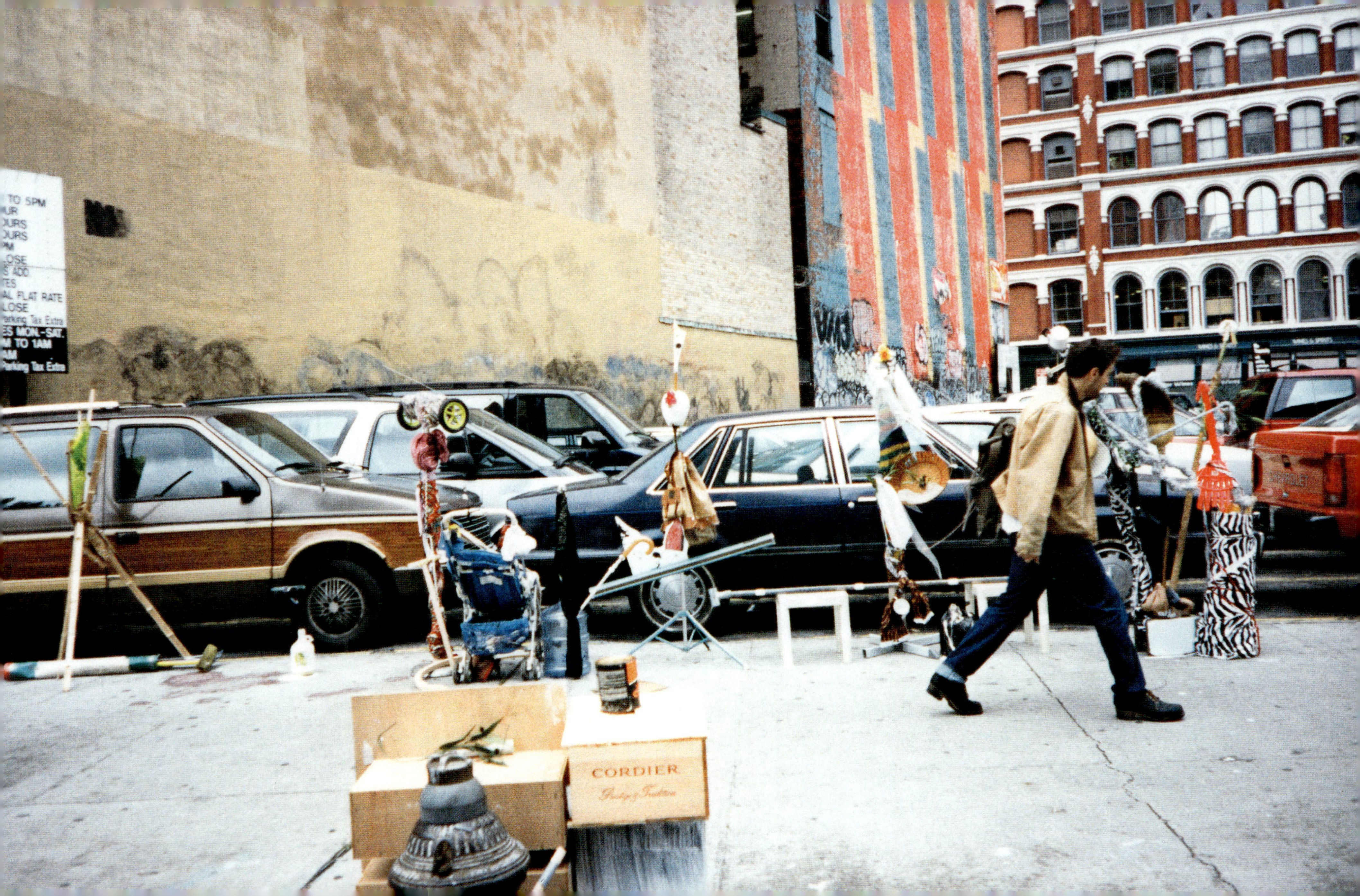
CORDIER

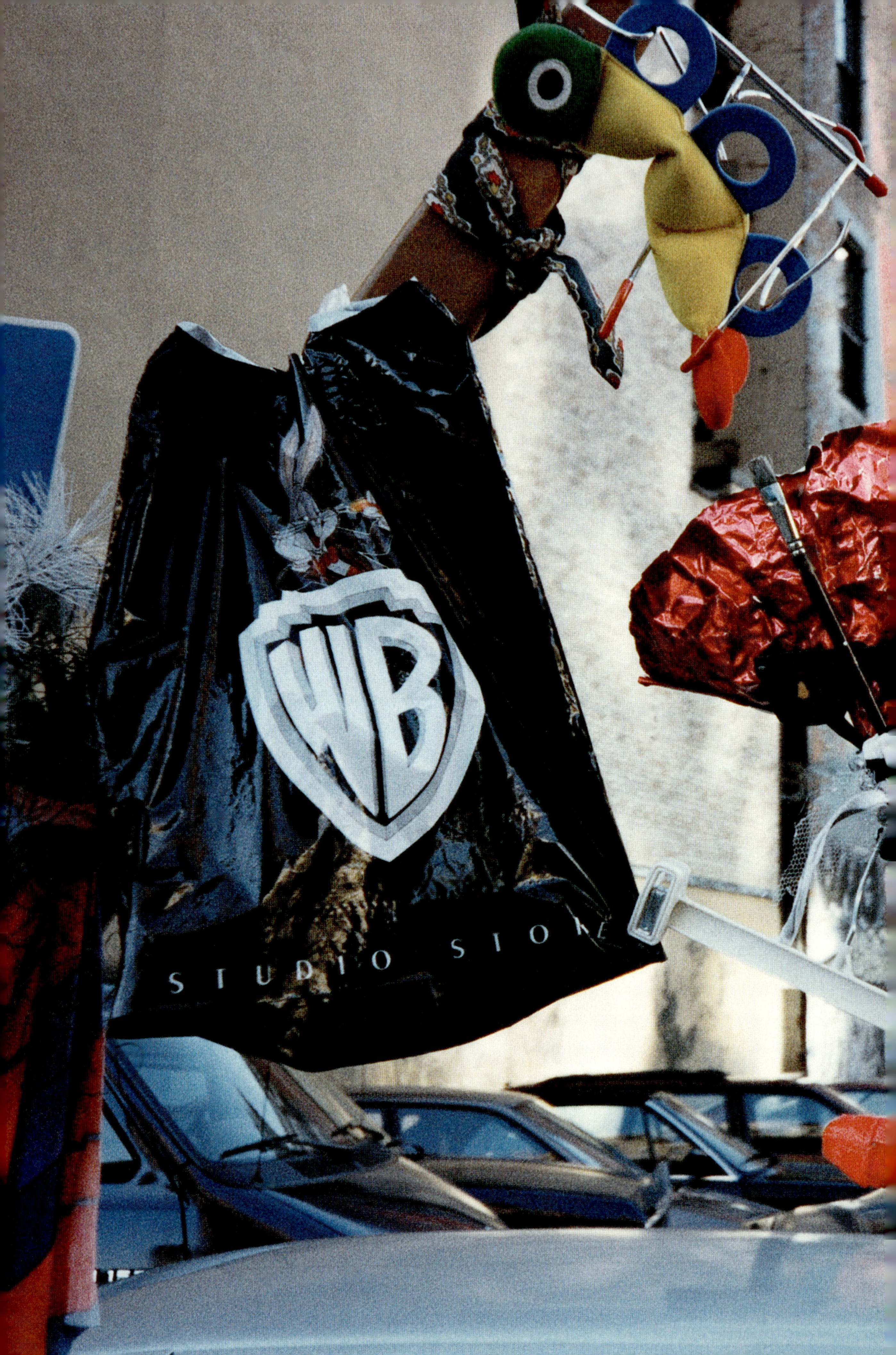
WB
STUDIO

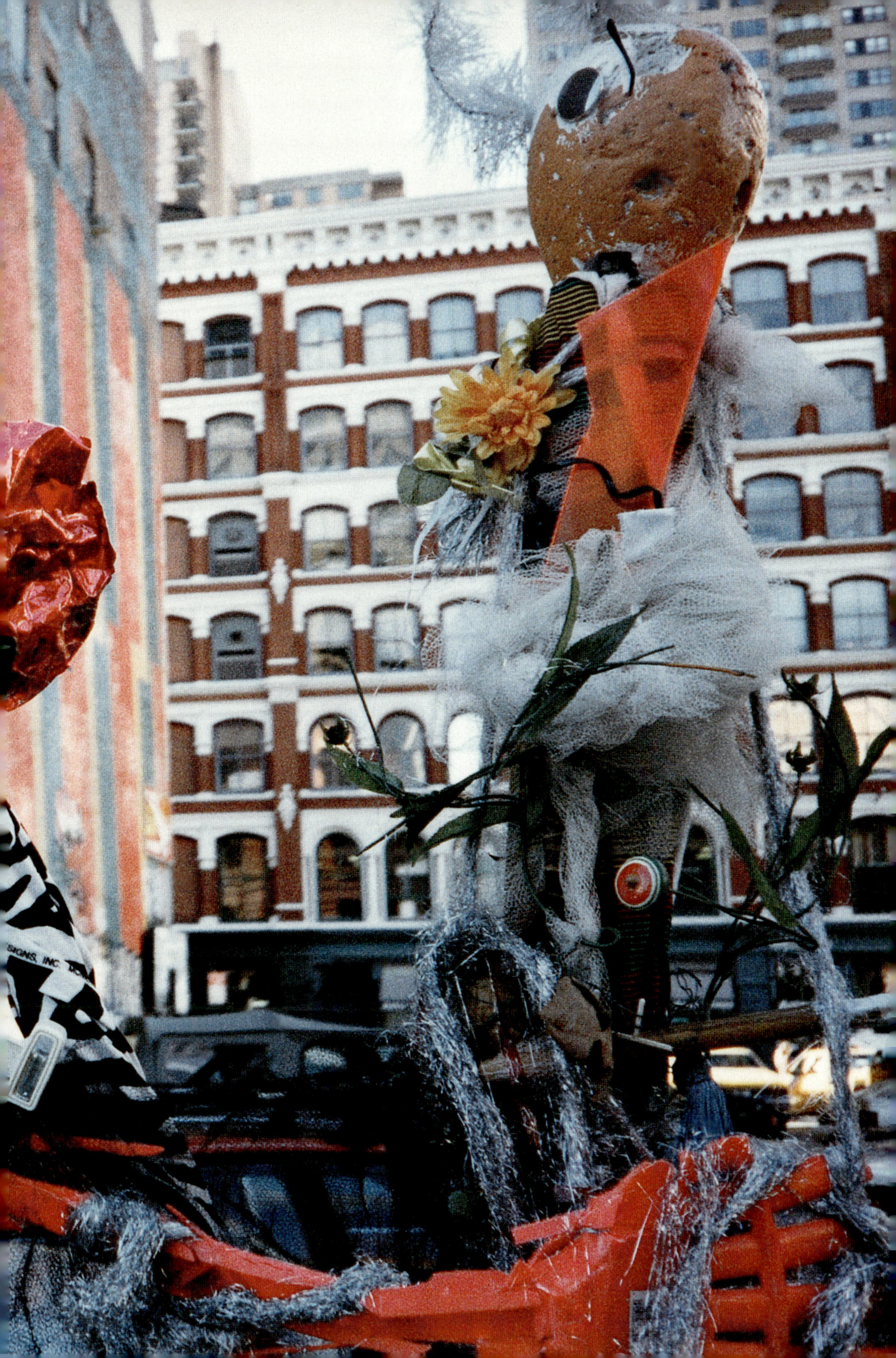
SIGNS, INC

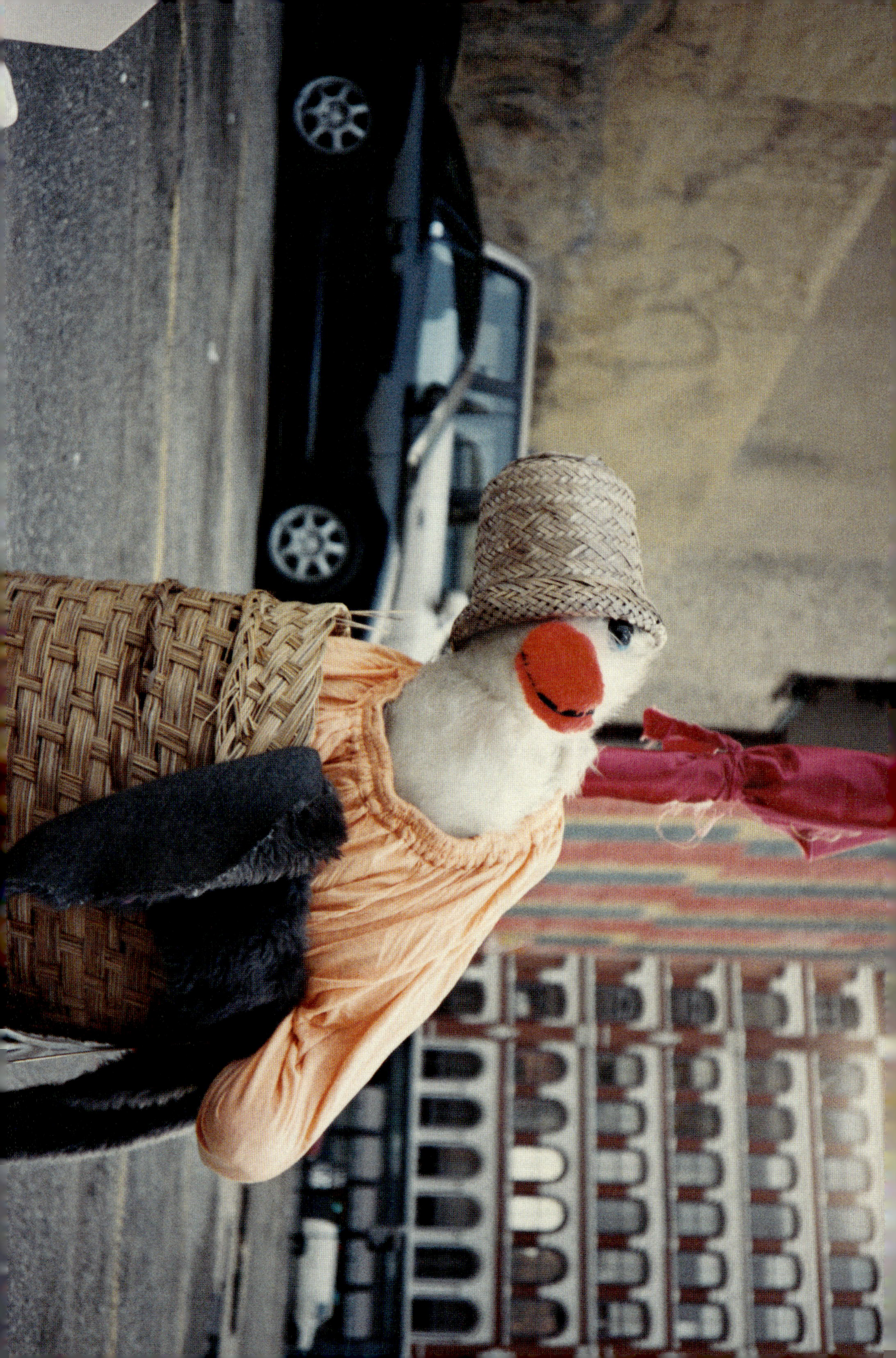

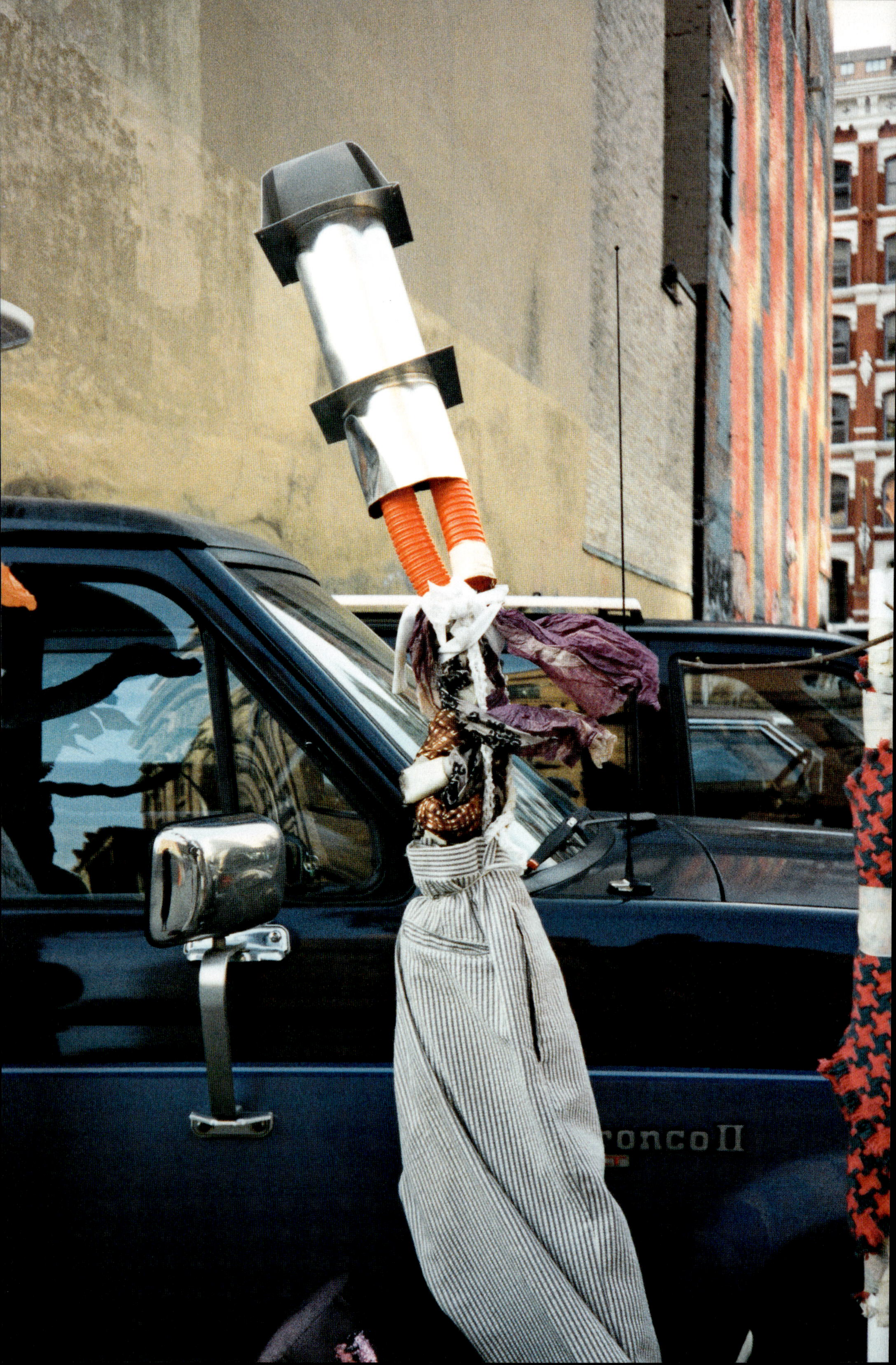
ronco II

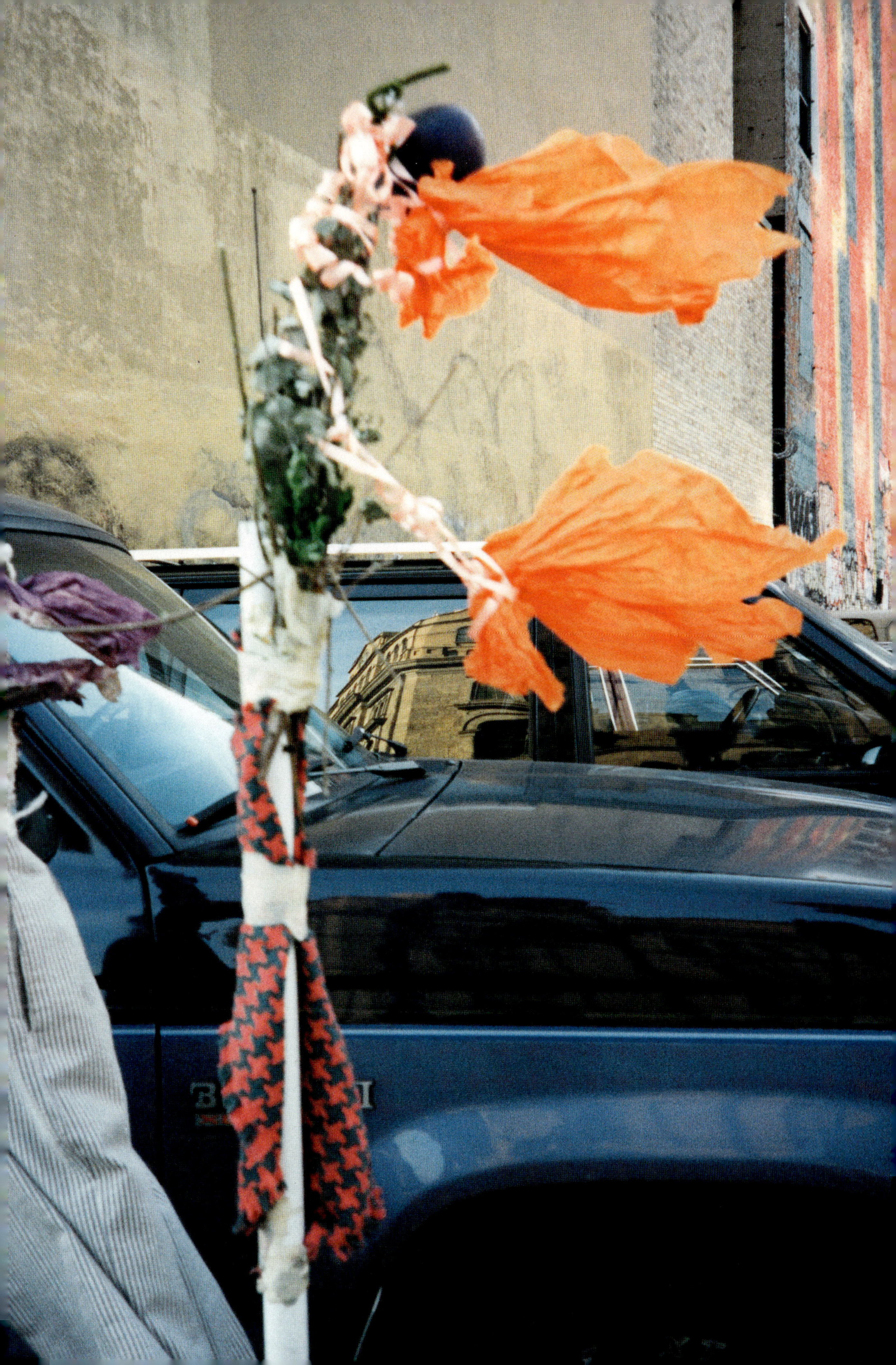

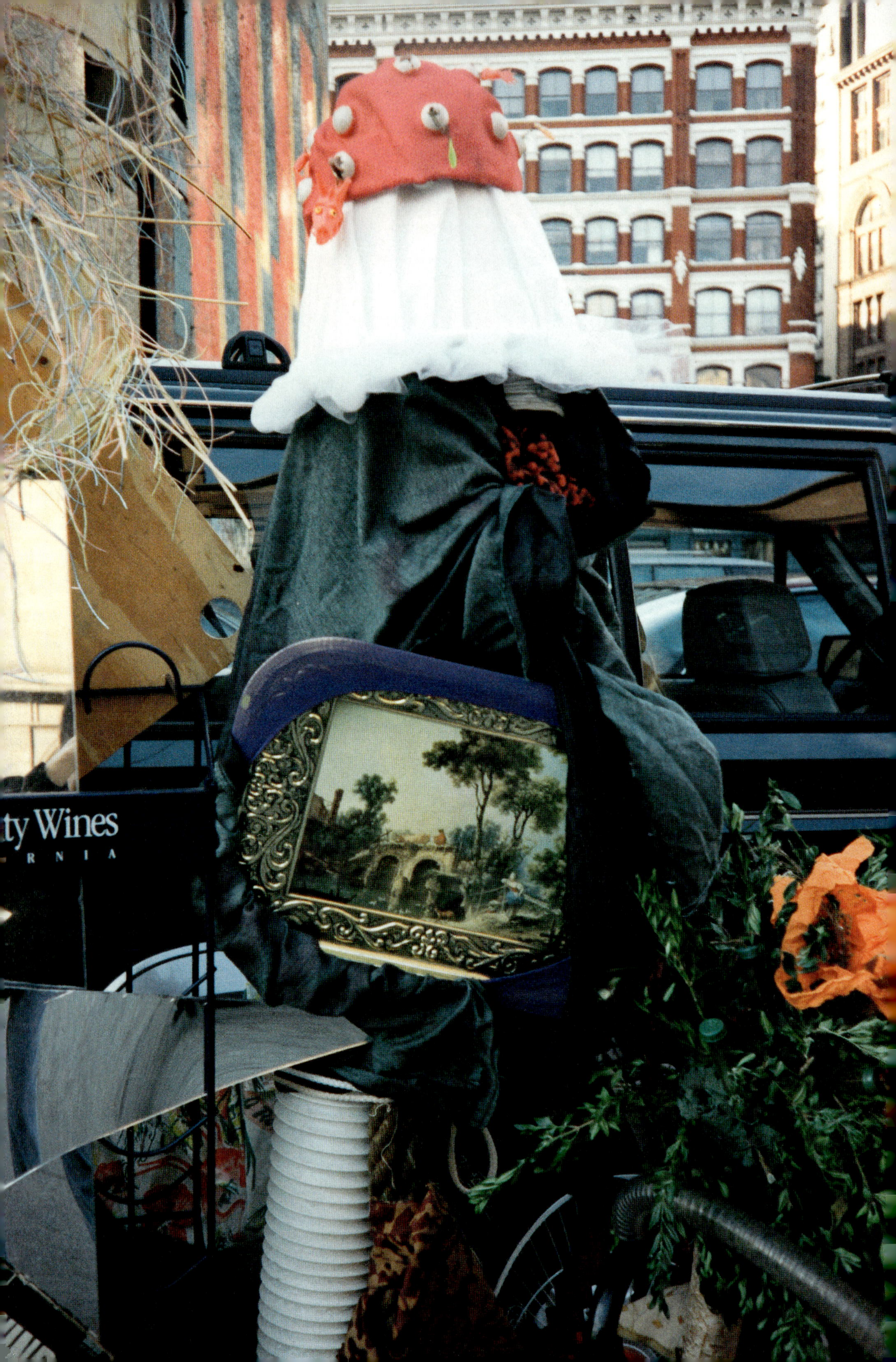
ty Wines
R N I A

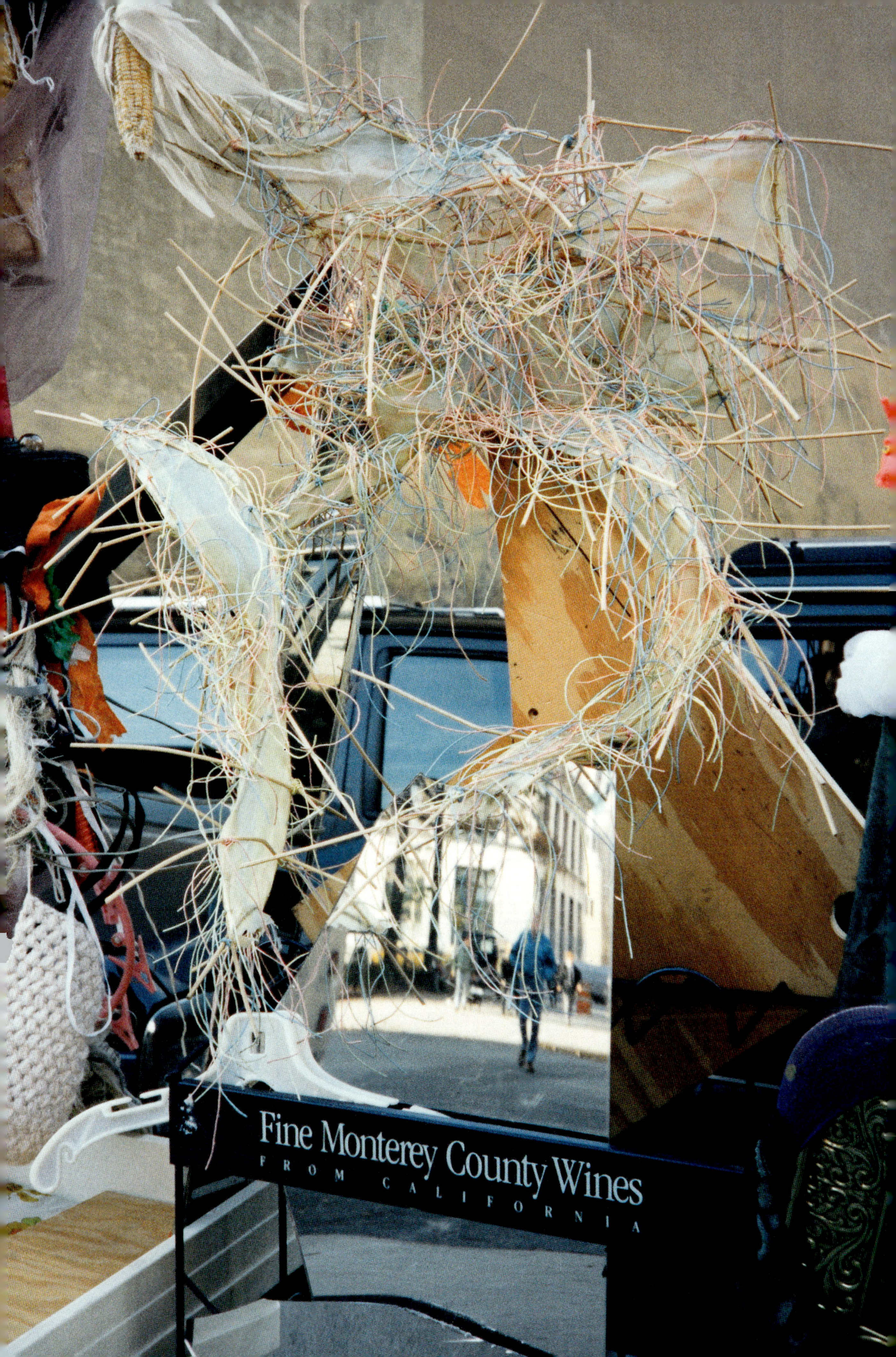
Fine Monterey County Wines
FROM CALIFORNIA

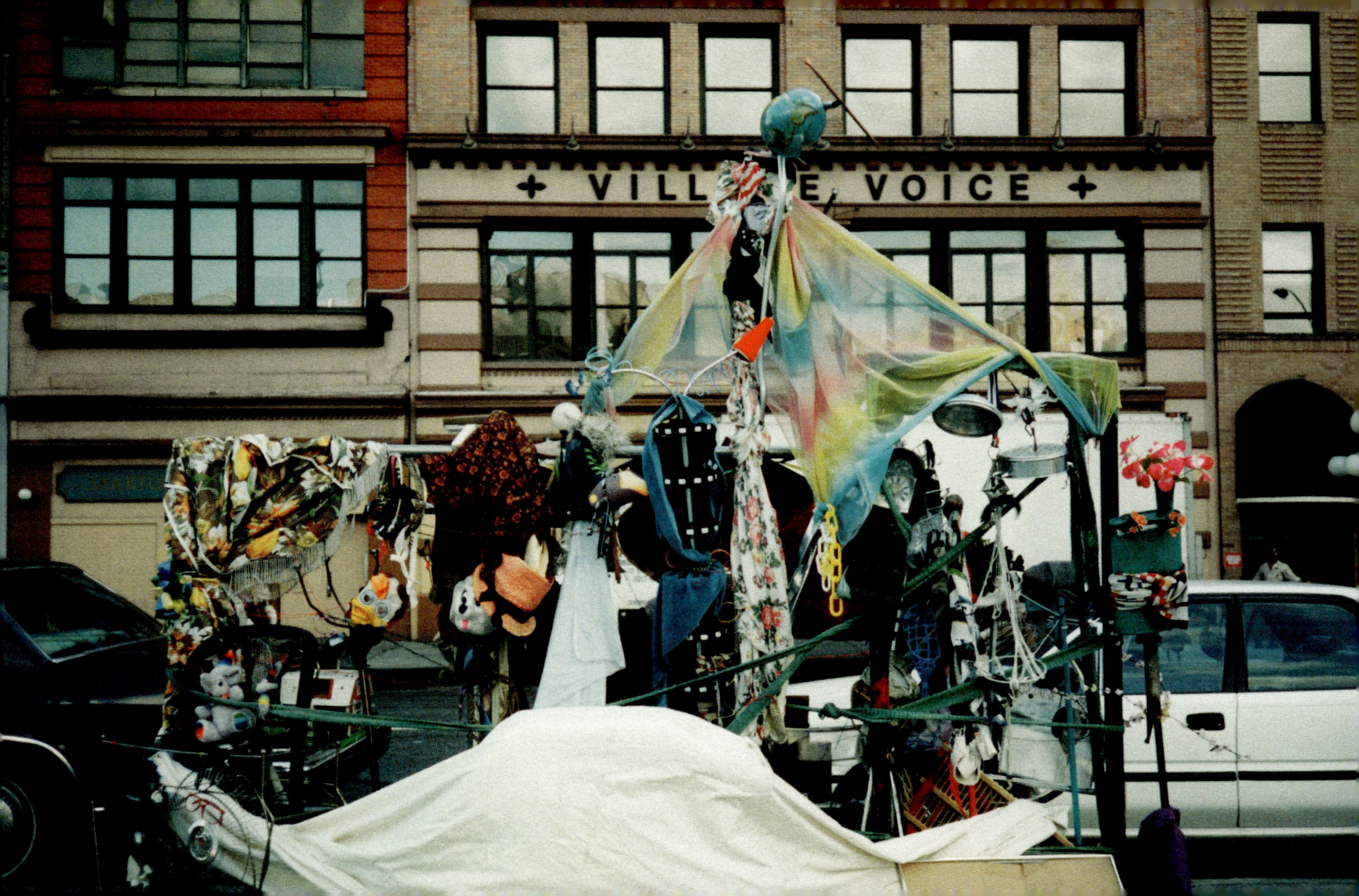
VILL E VOICE

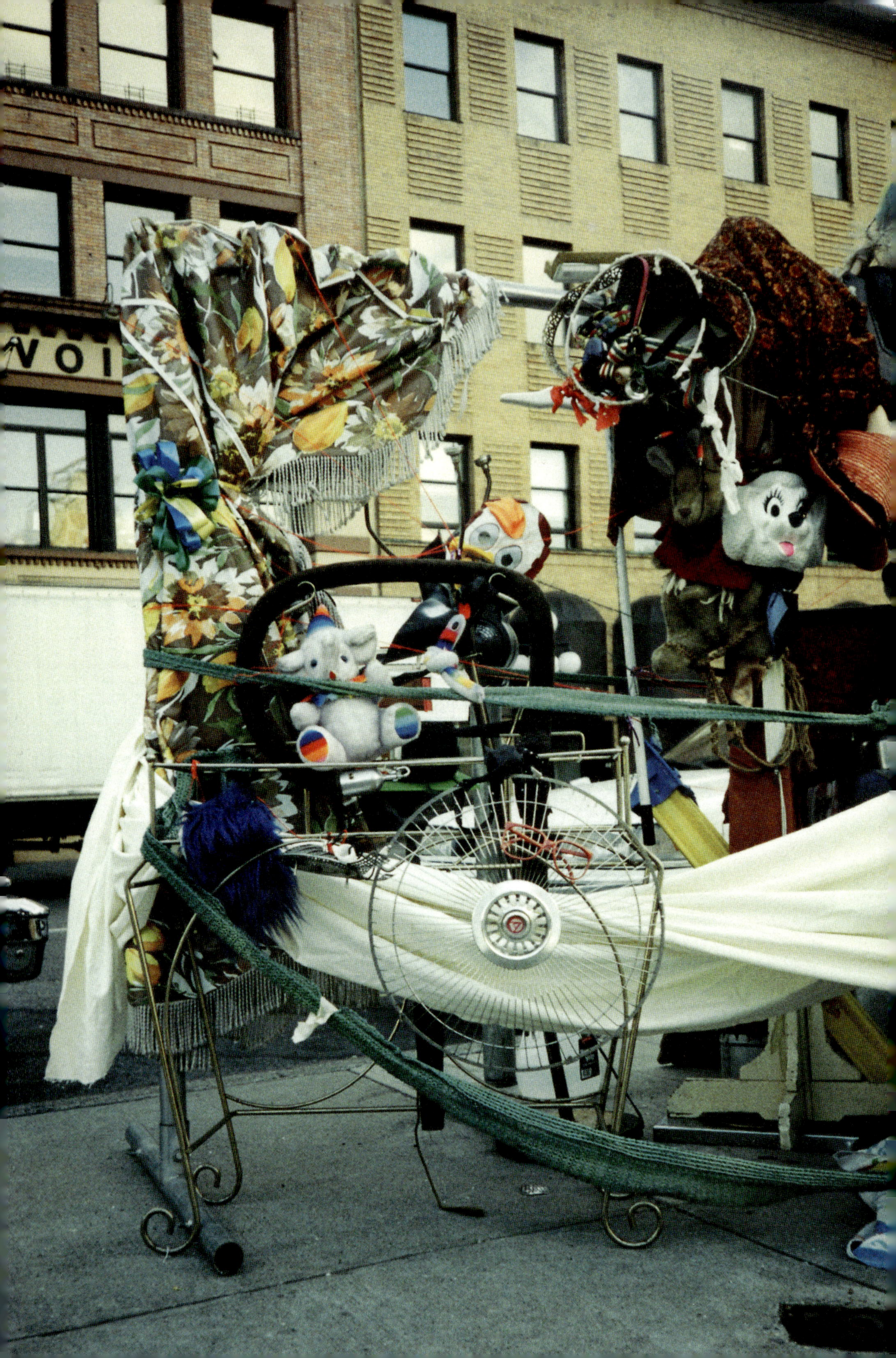

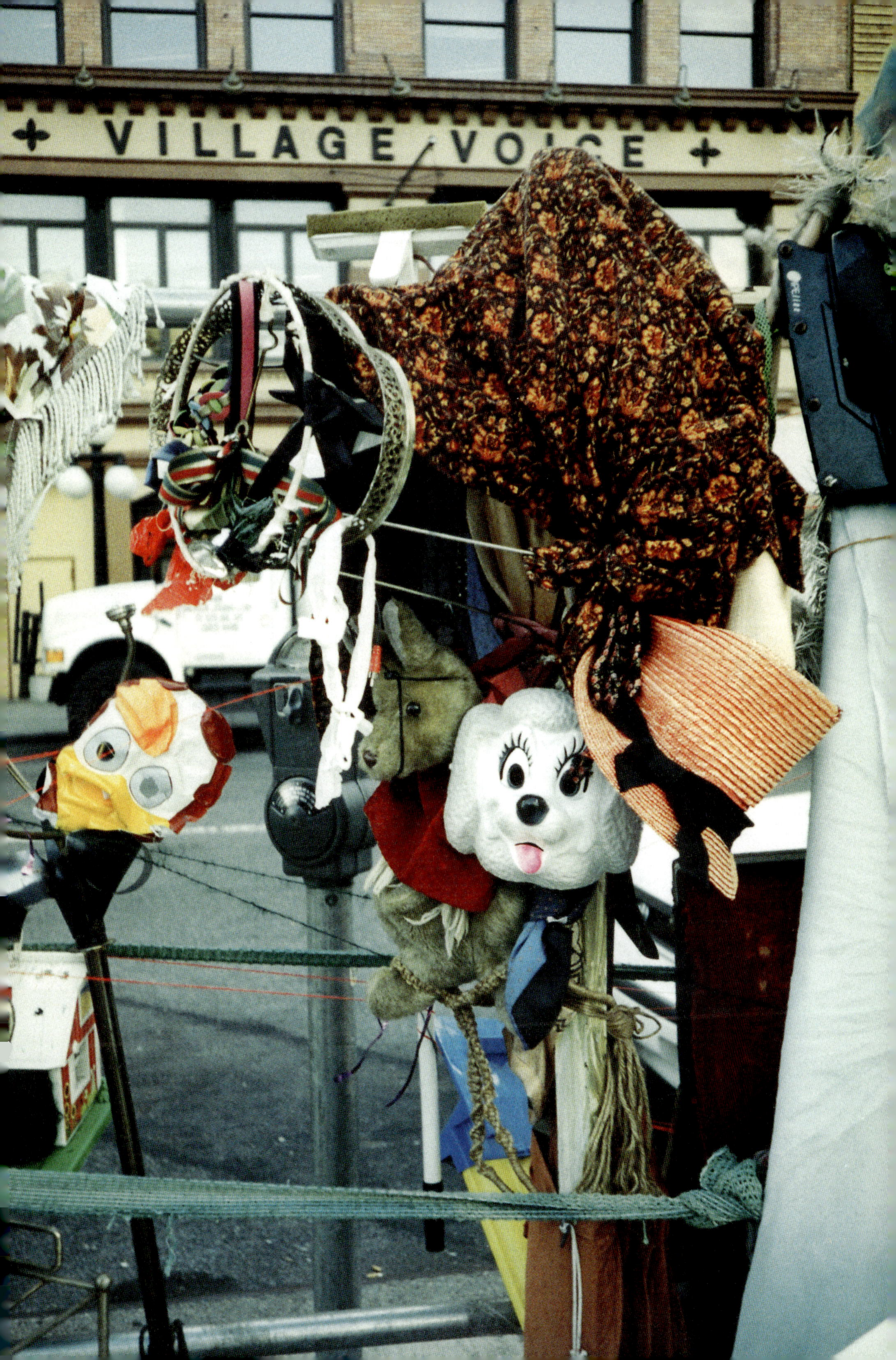
VILLAGE VOICE

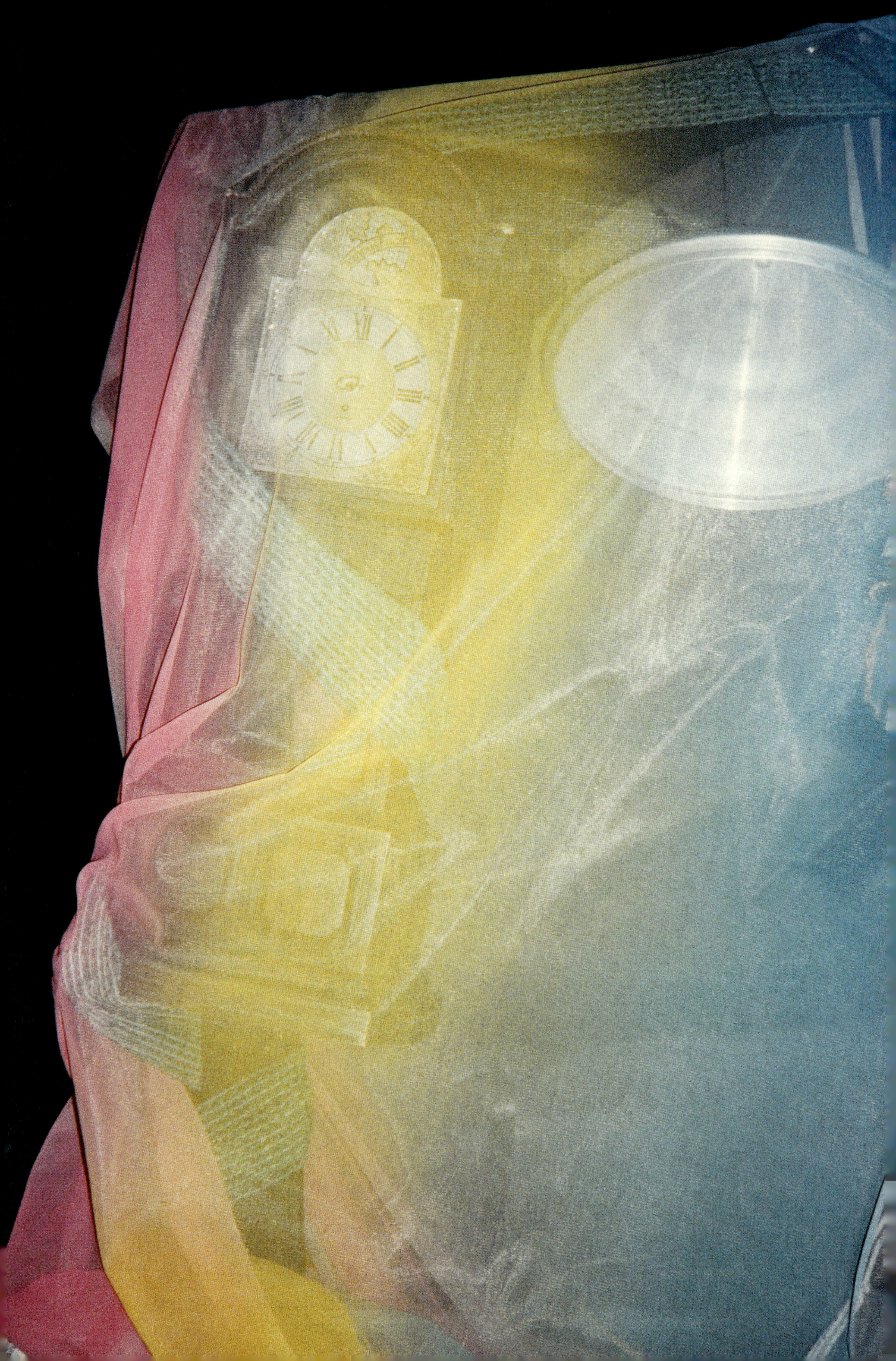

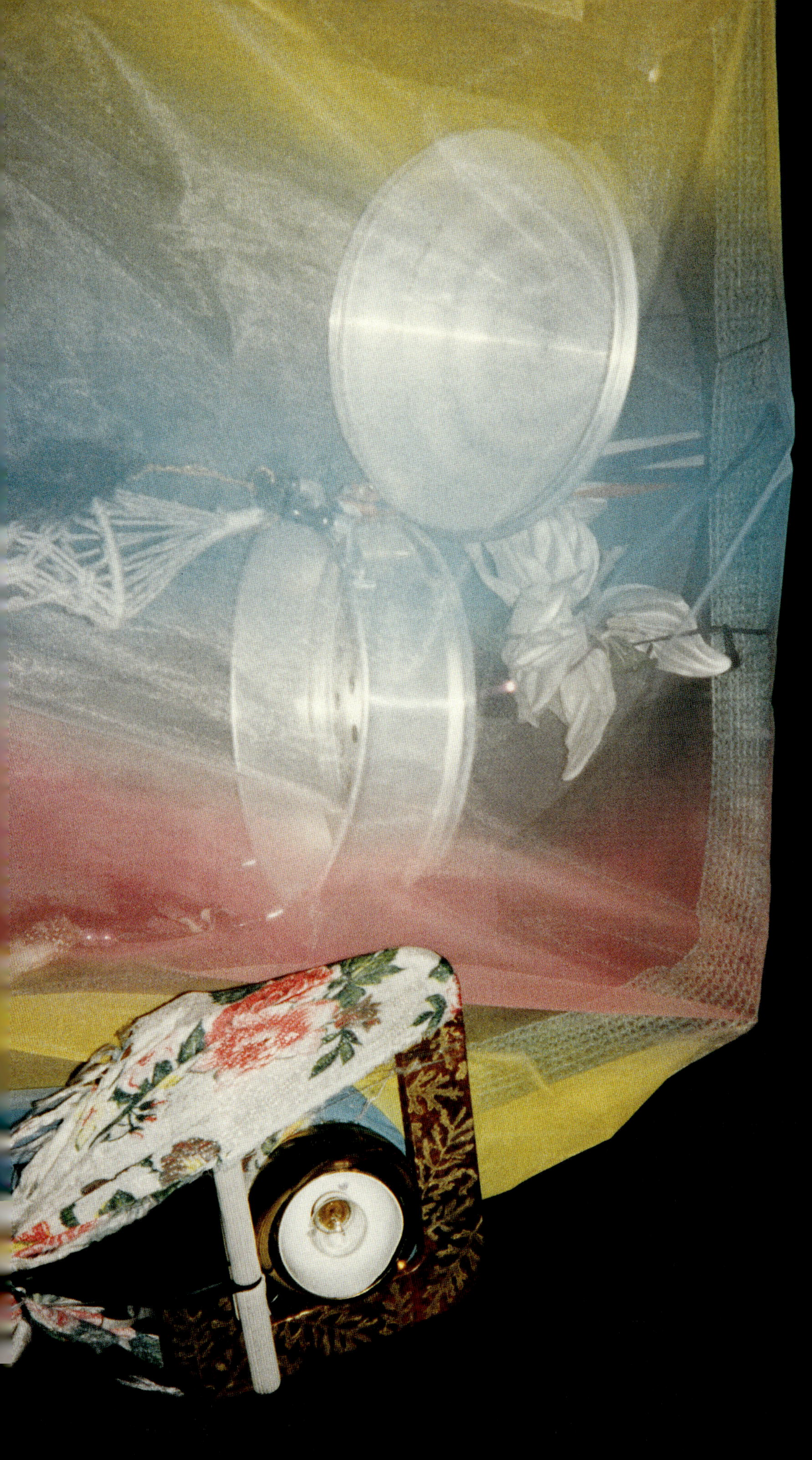

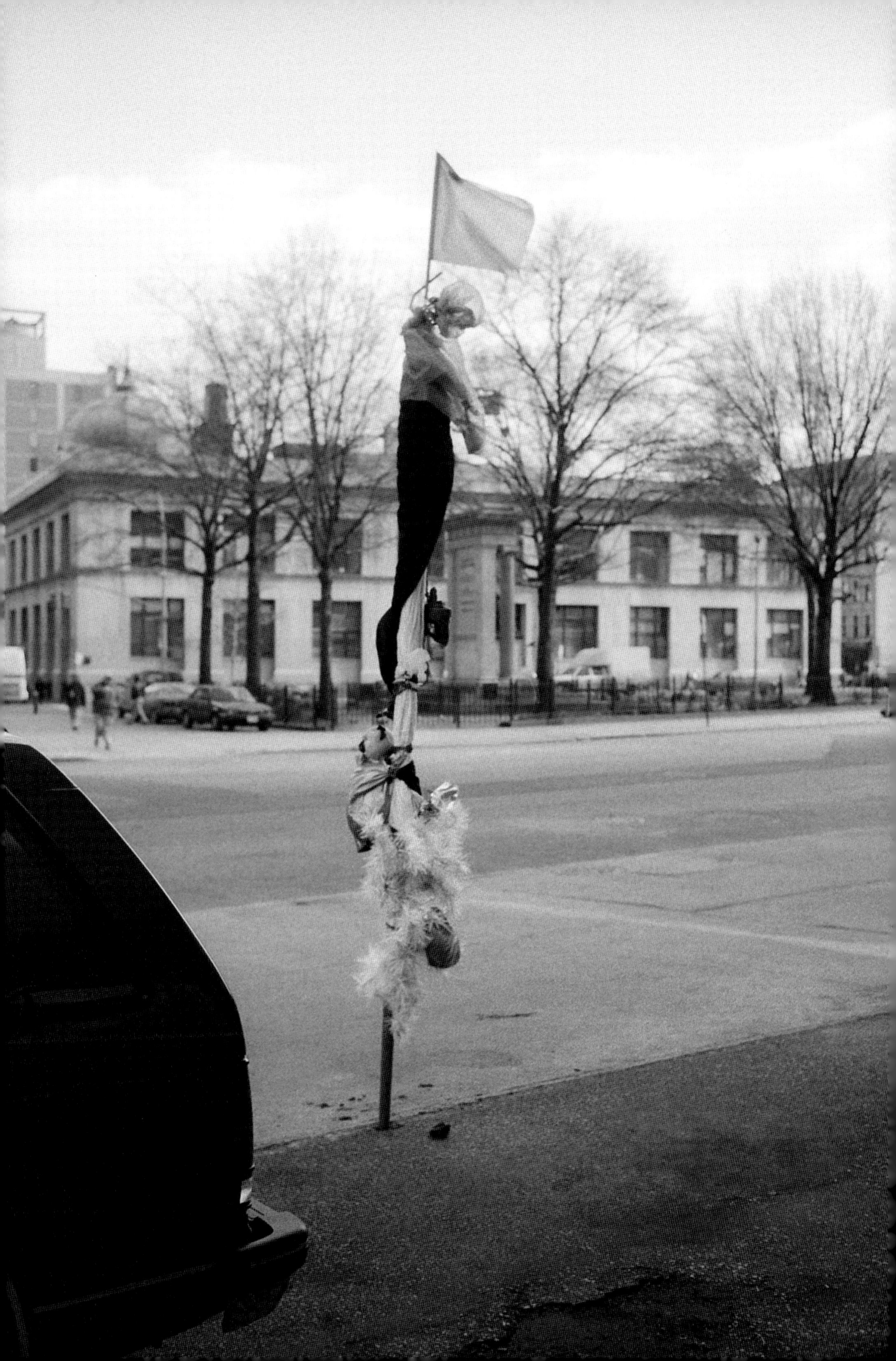

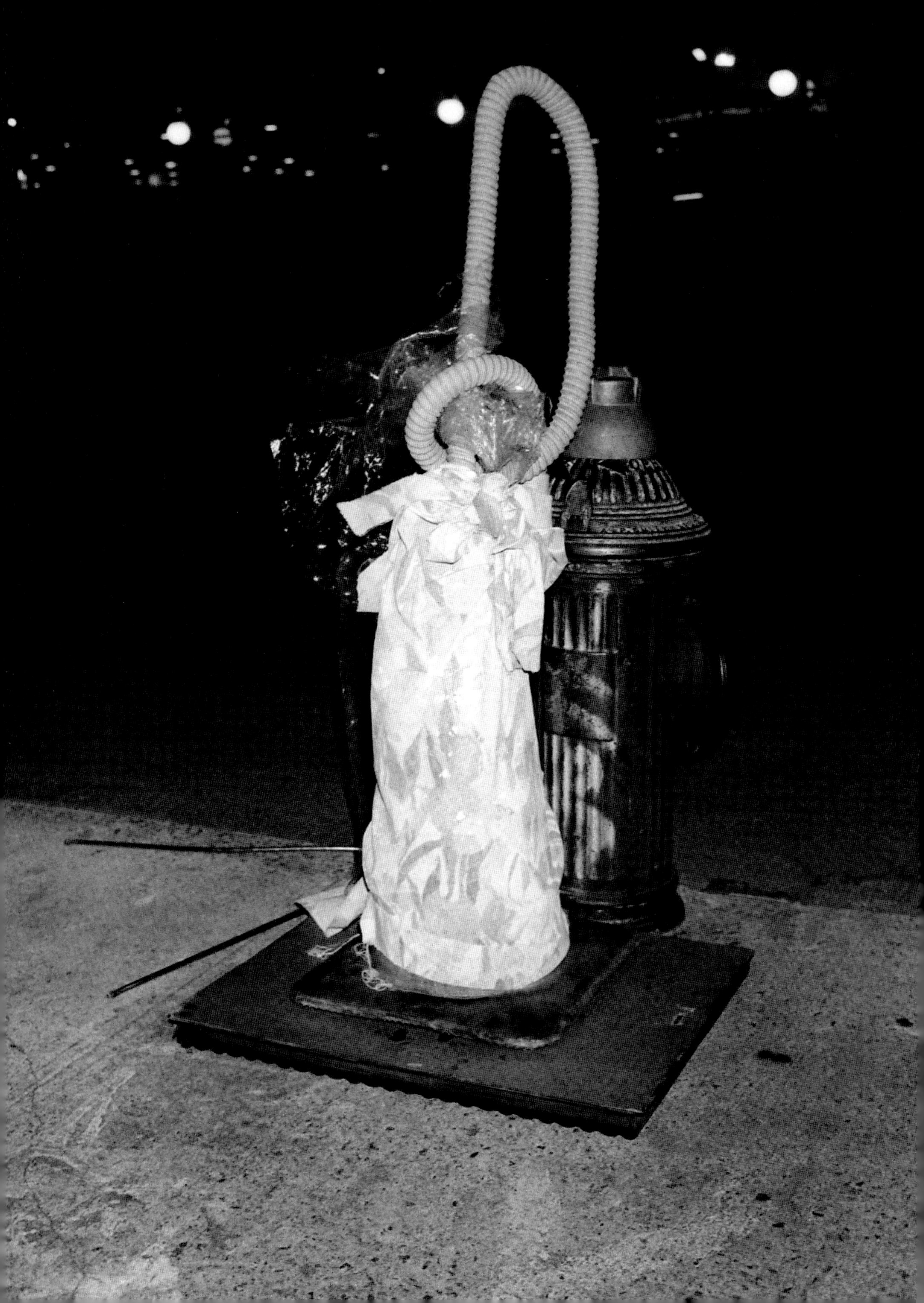

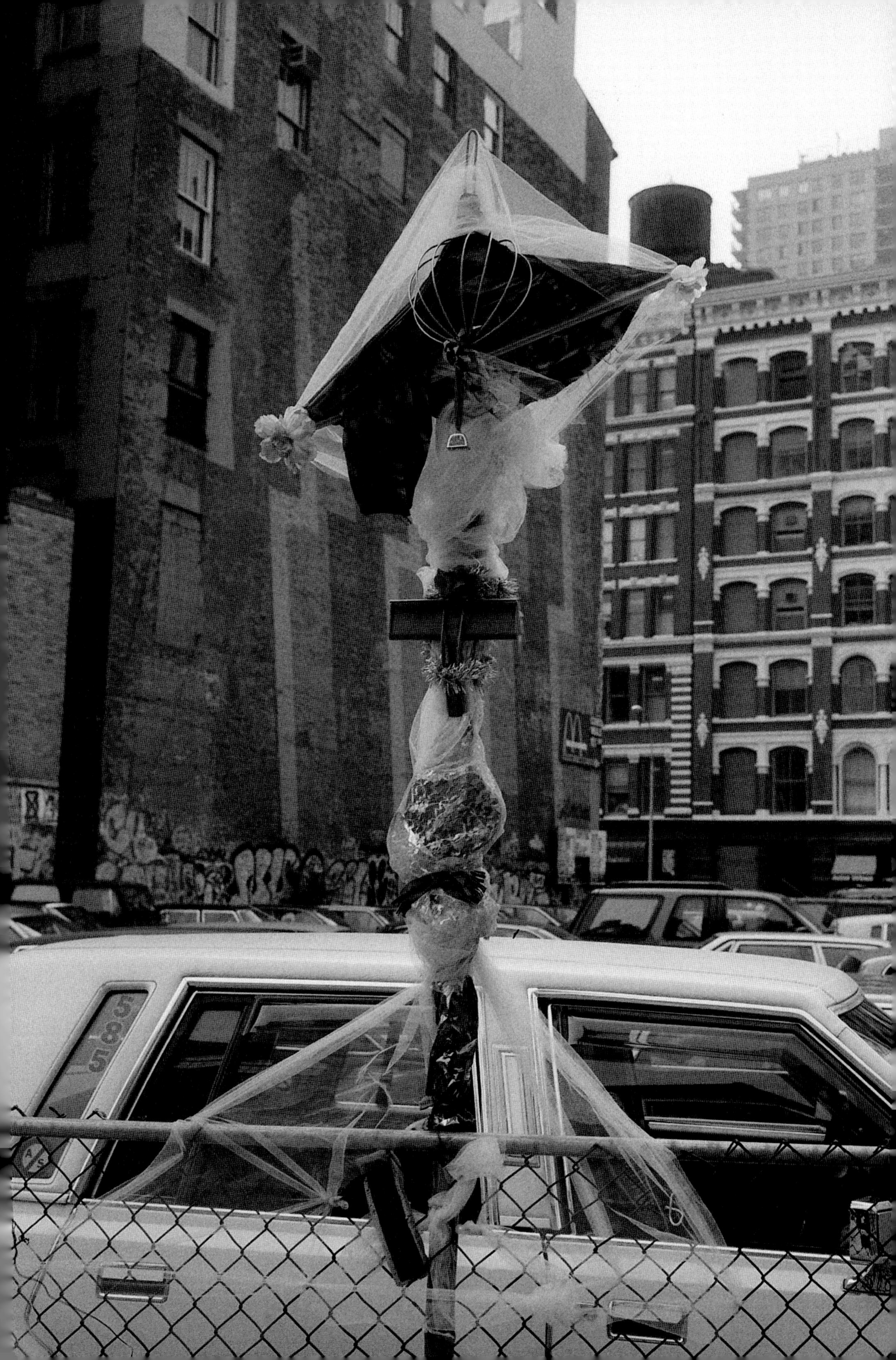
585

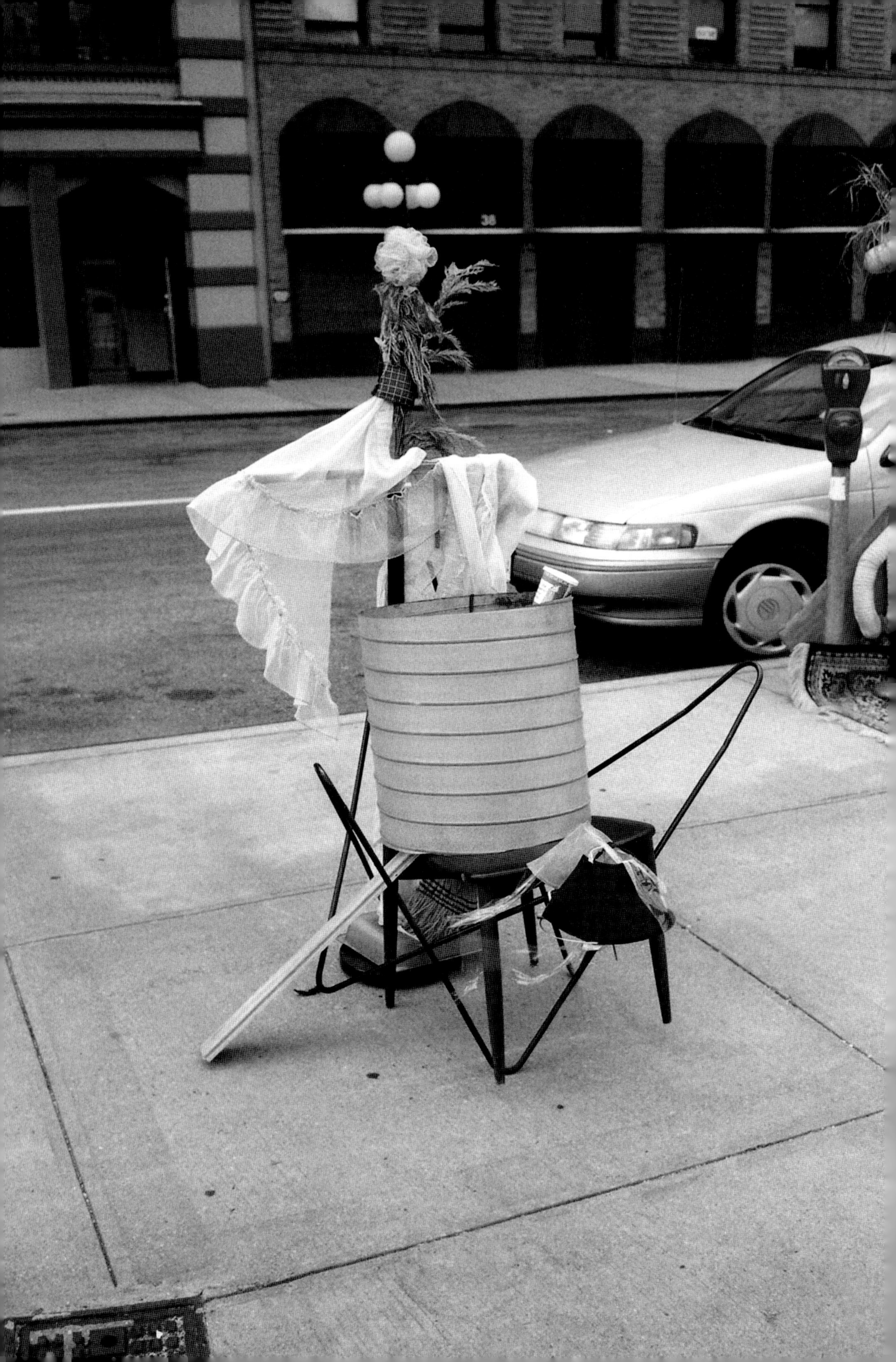
38

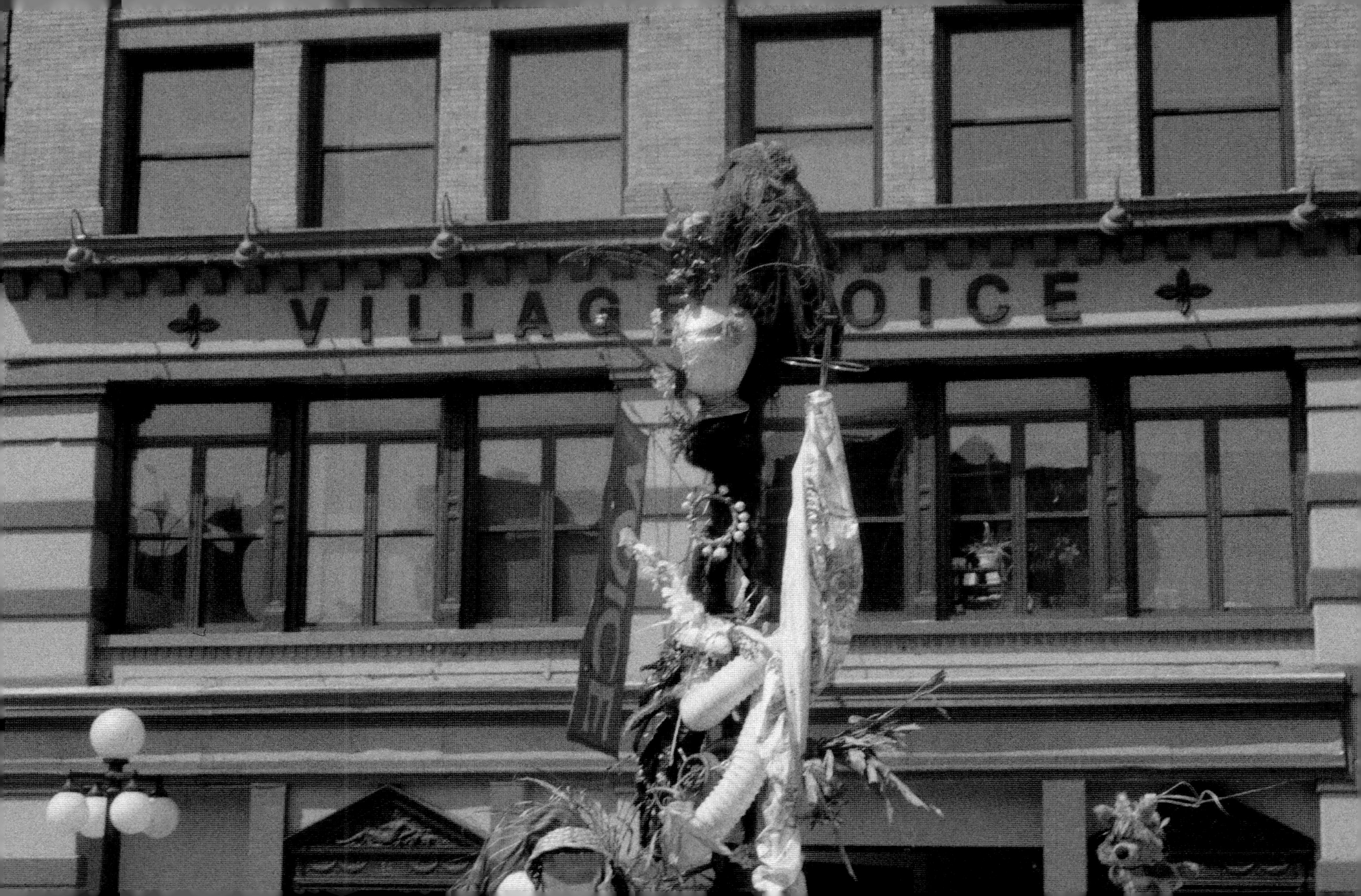
VILLAG
OICE

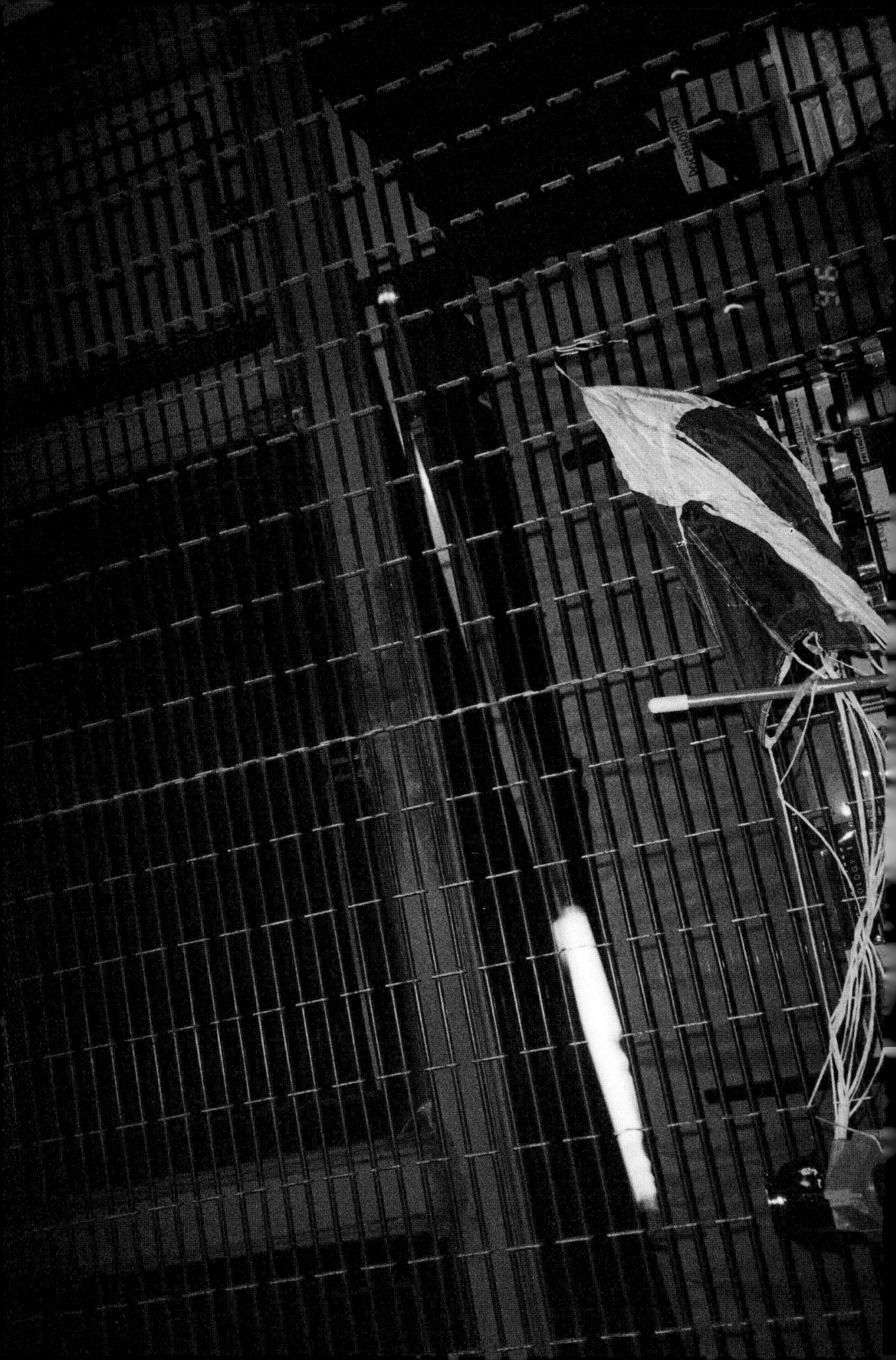

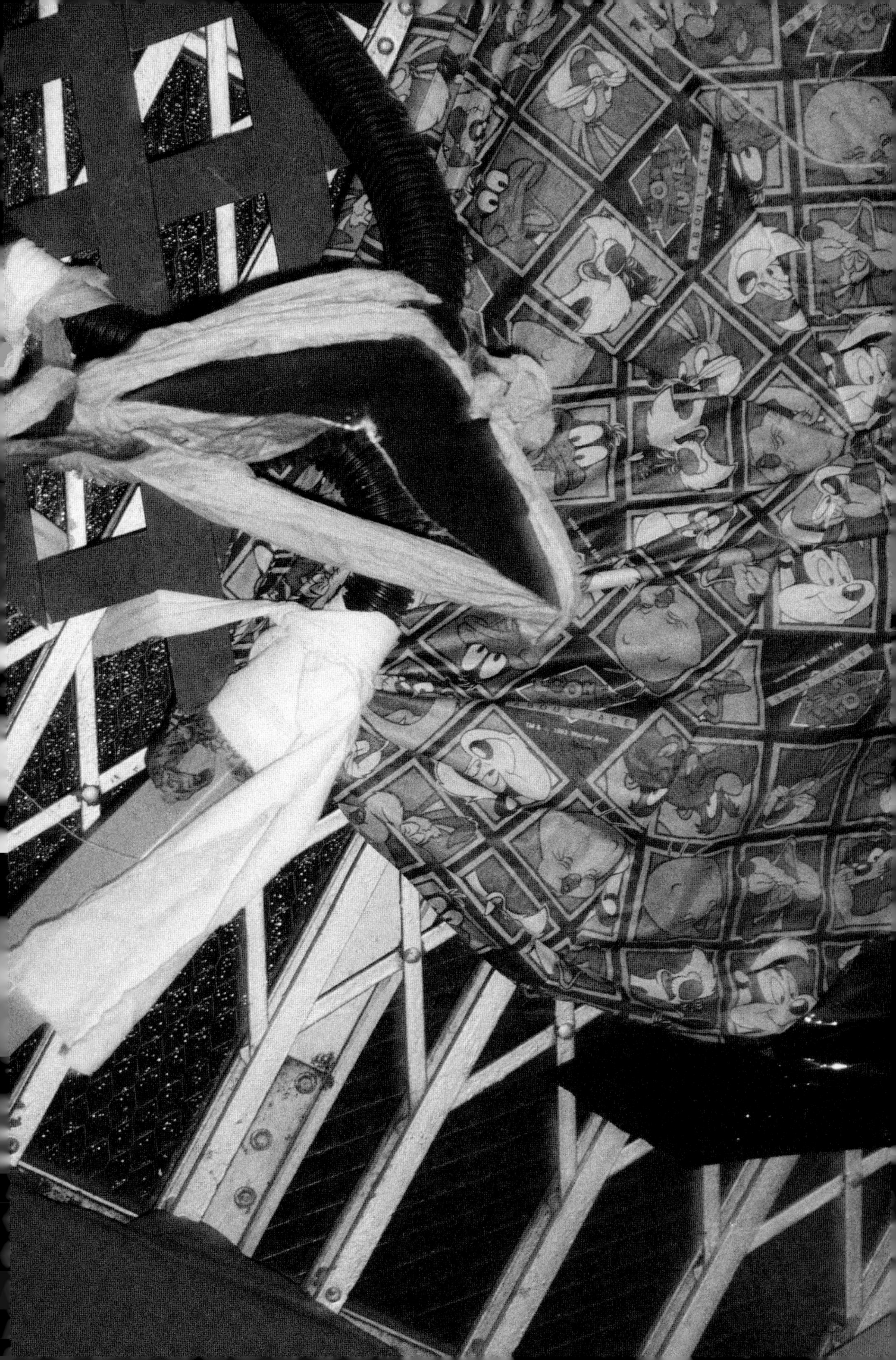

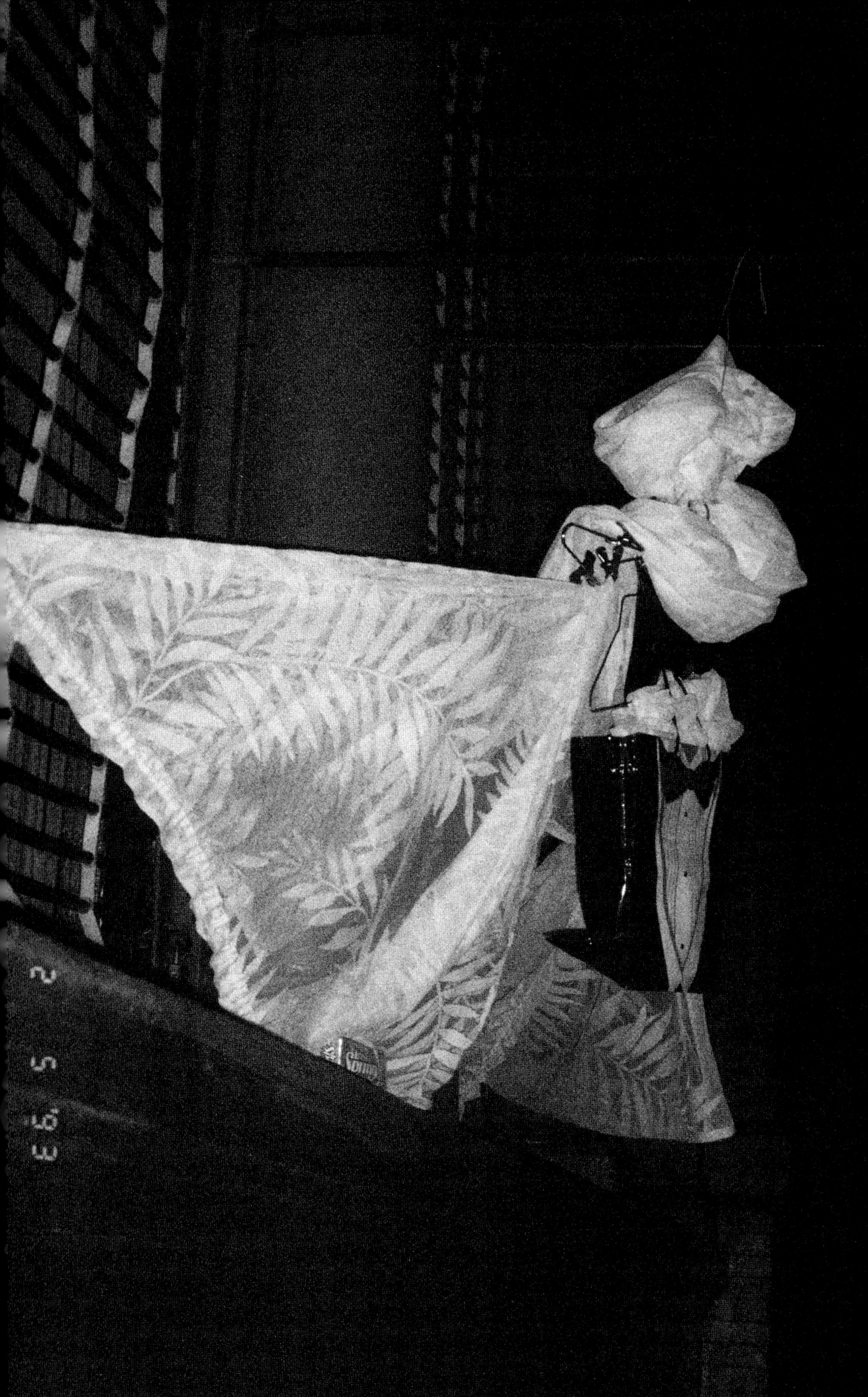

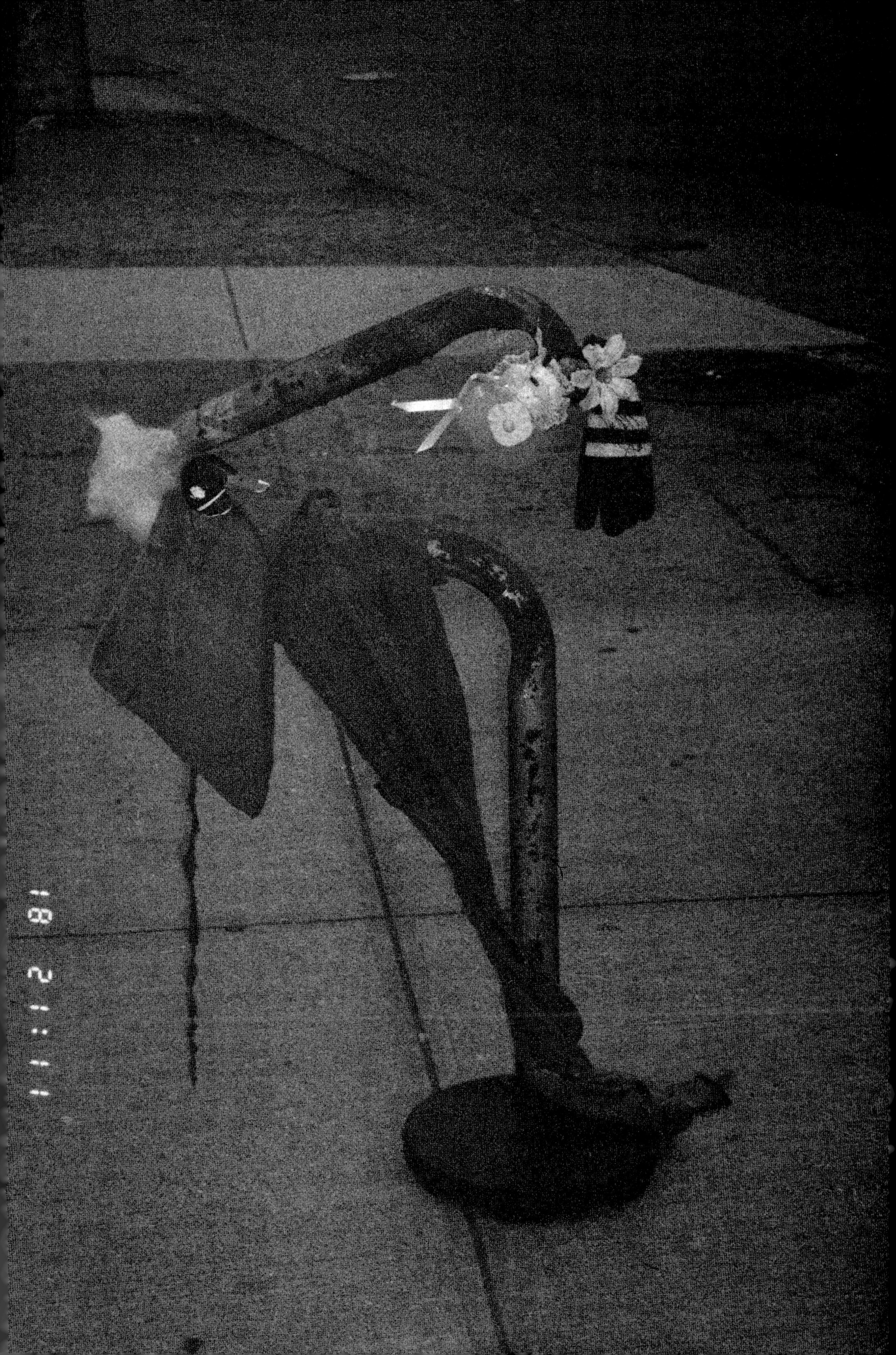

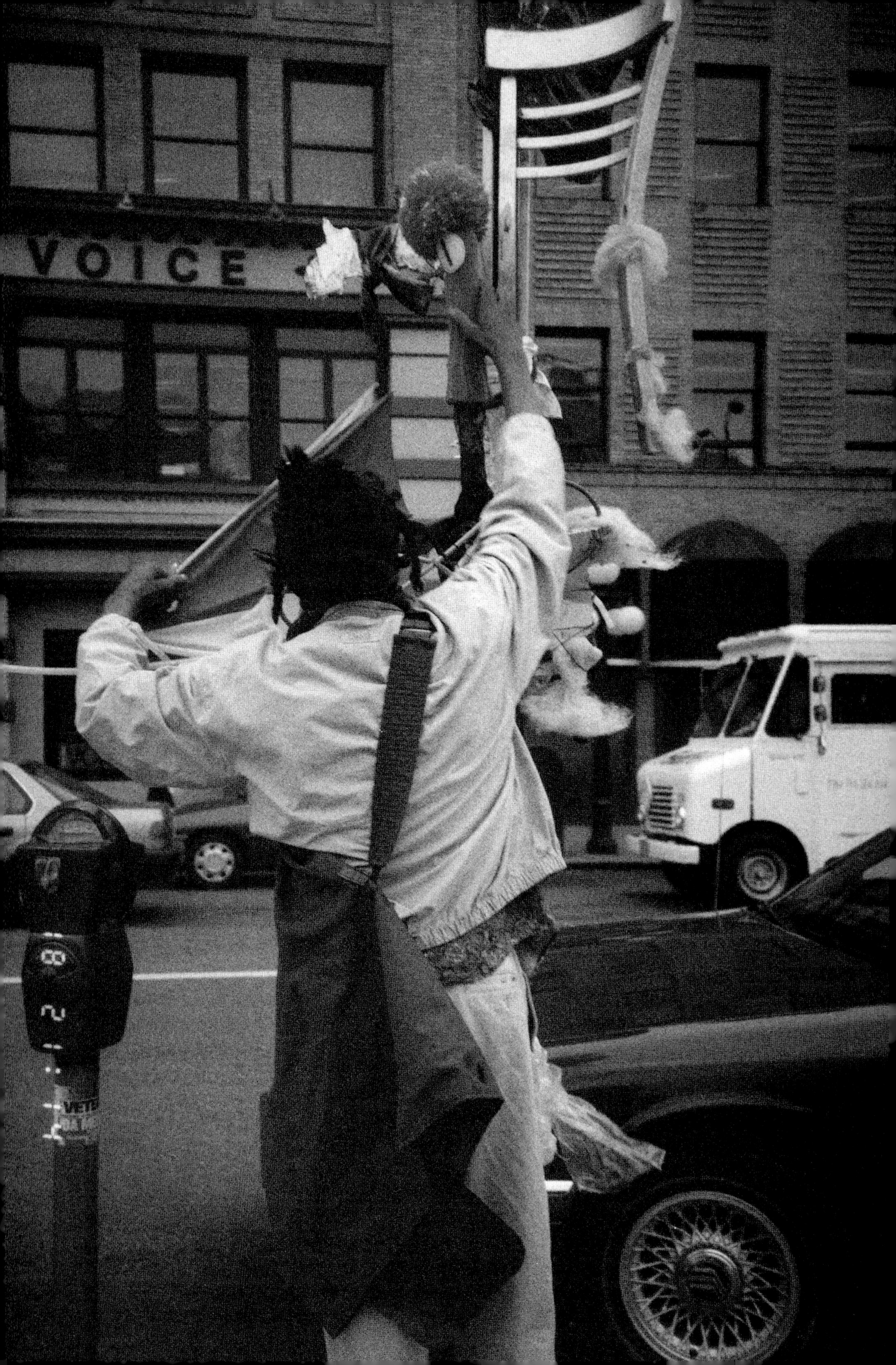
VOICE

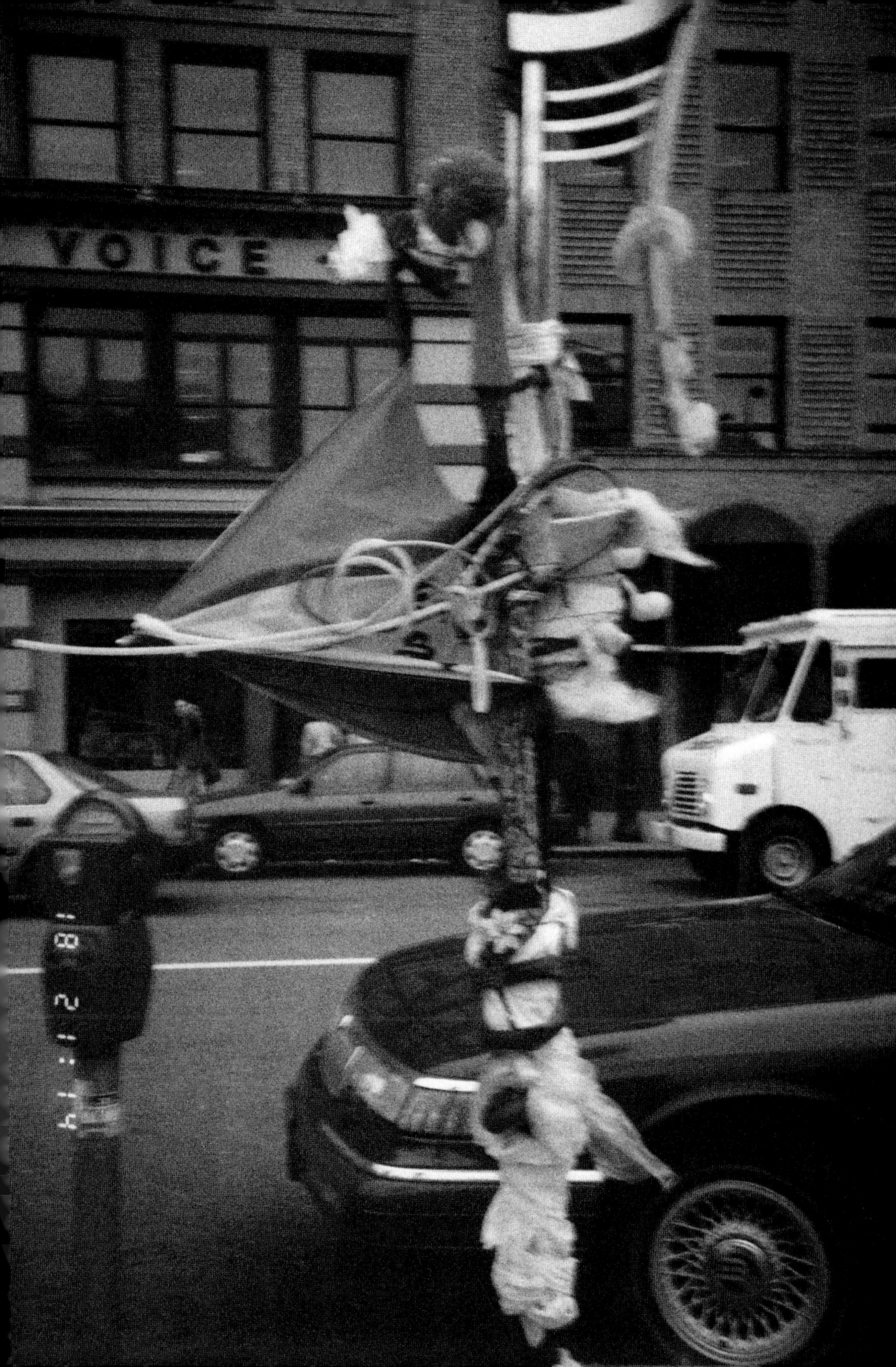
VOICE

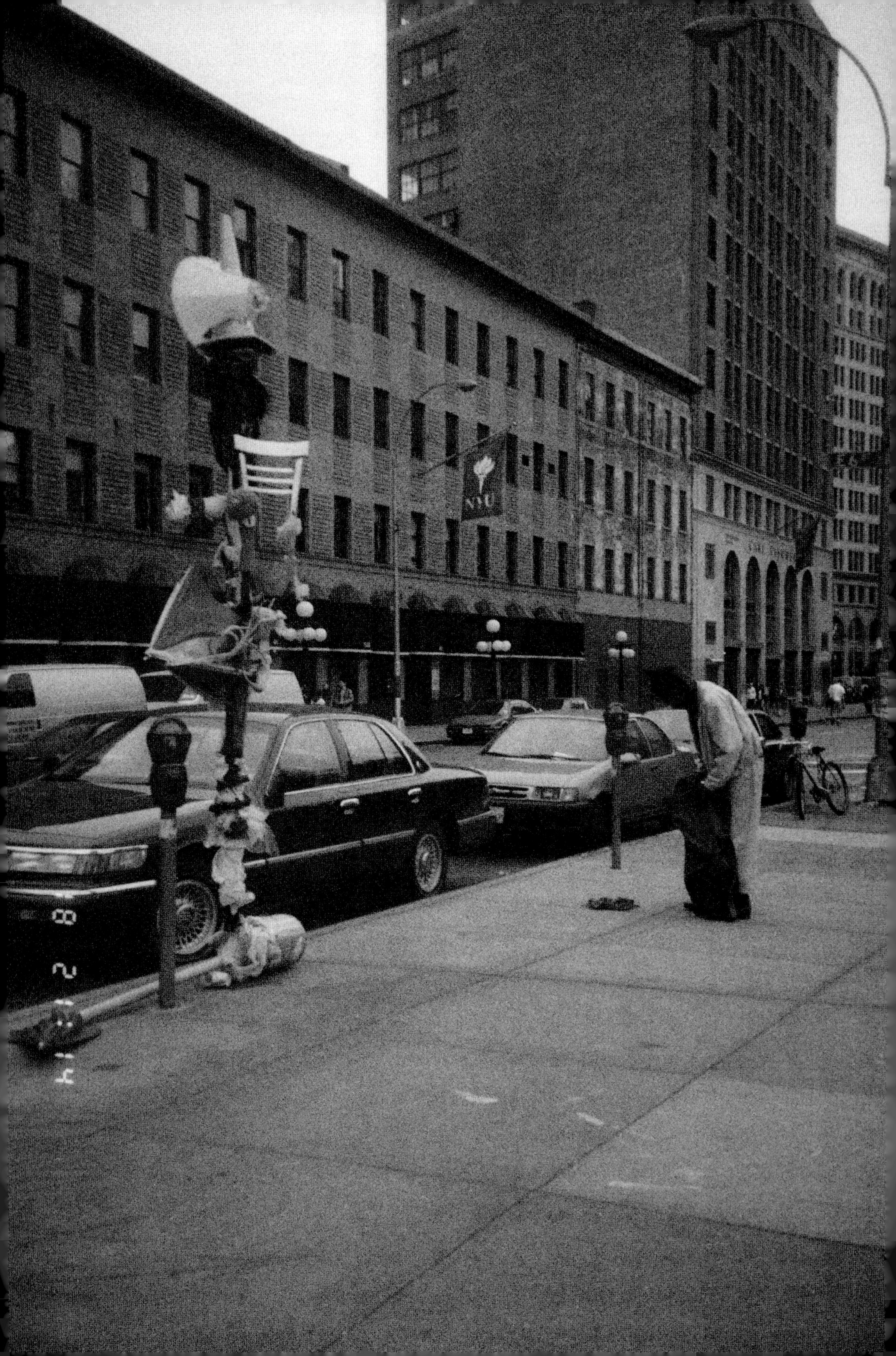
NYU

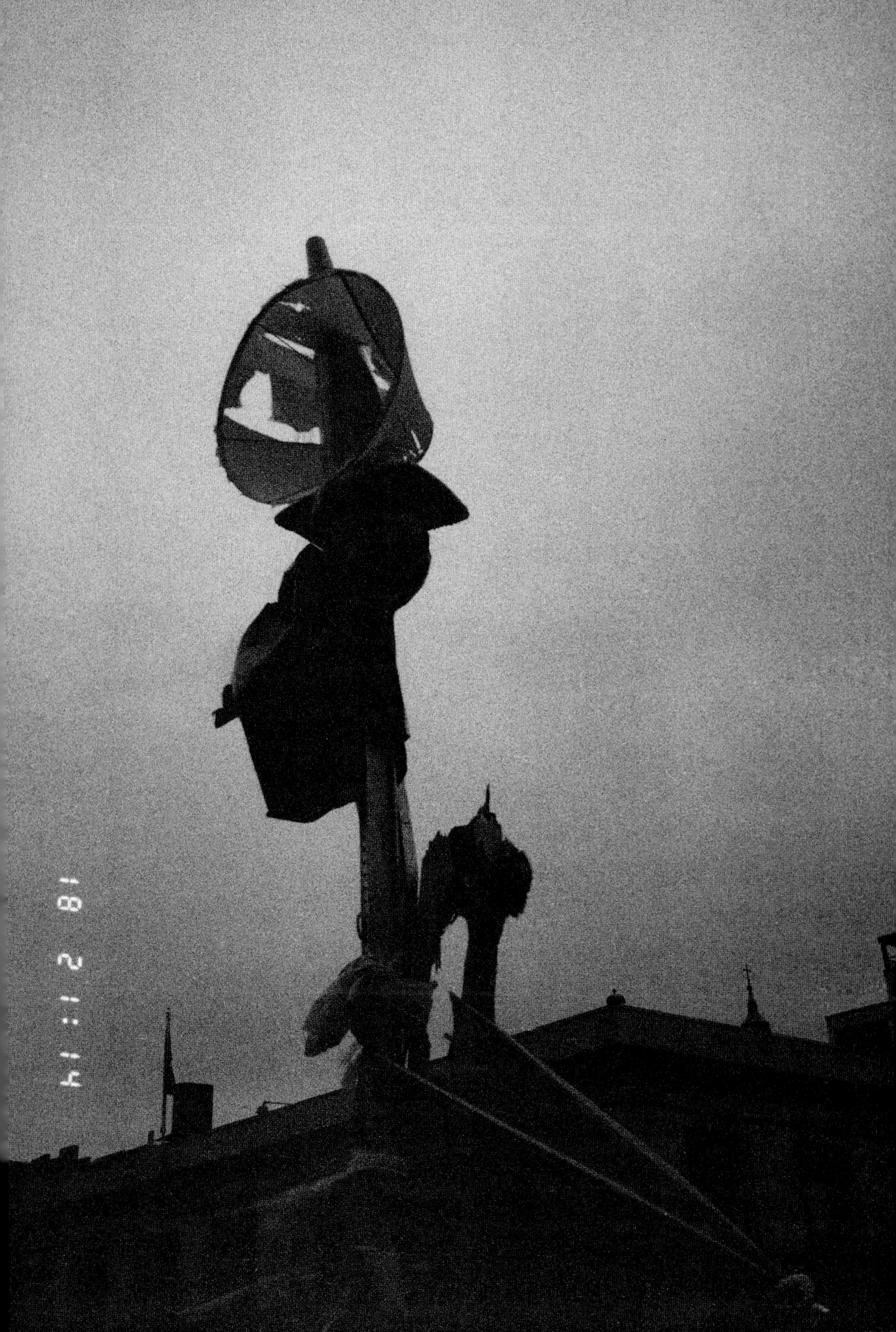

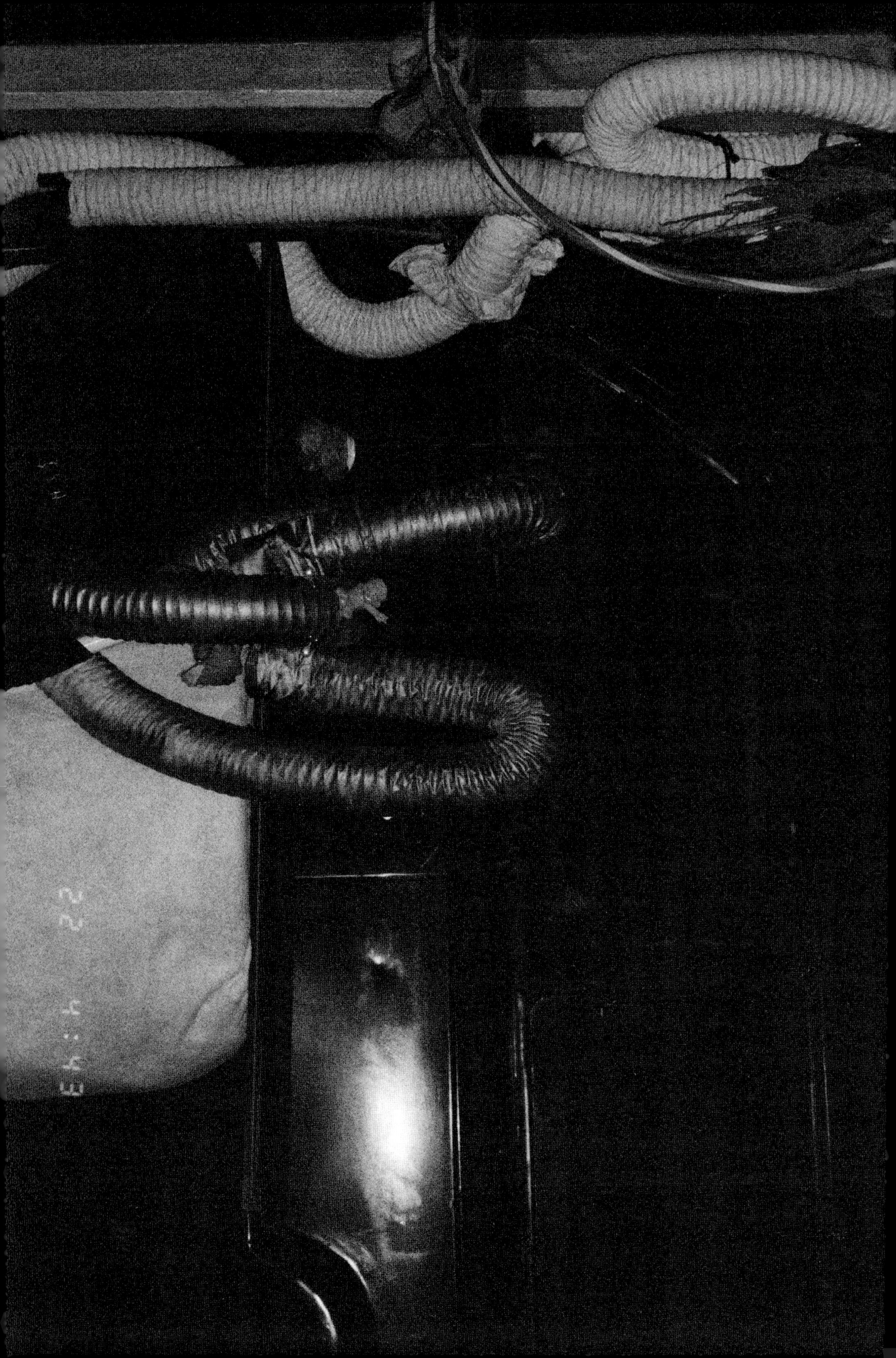

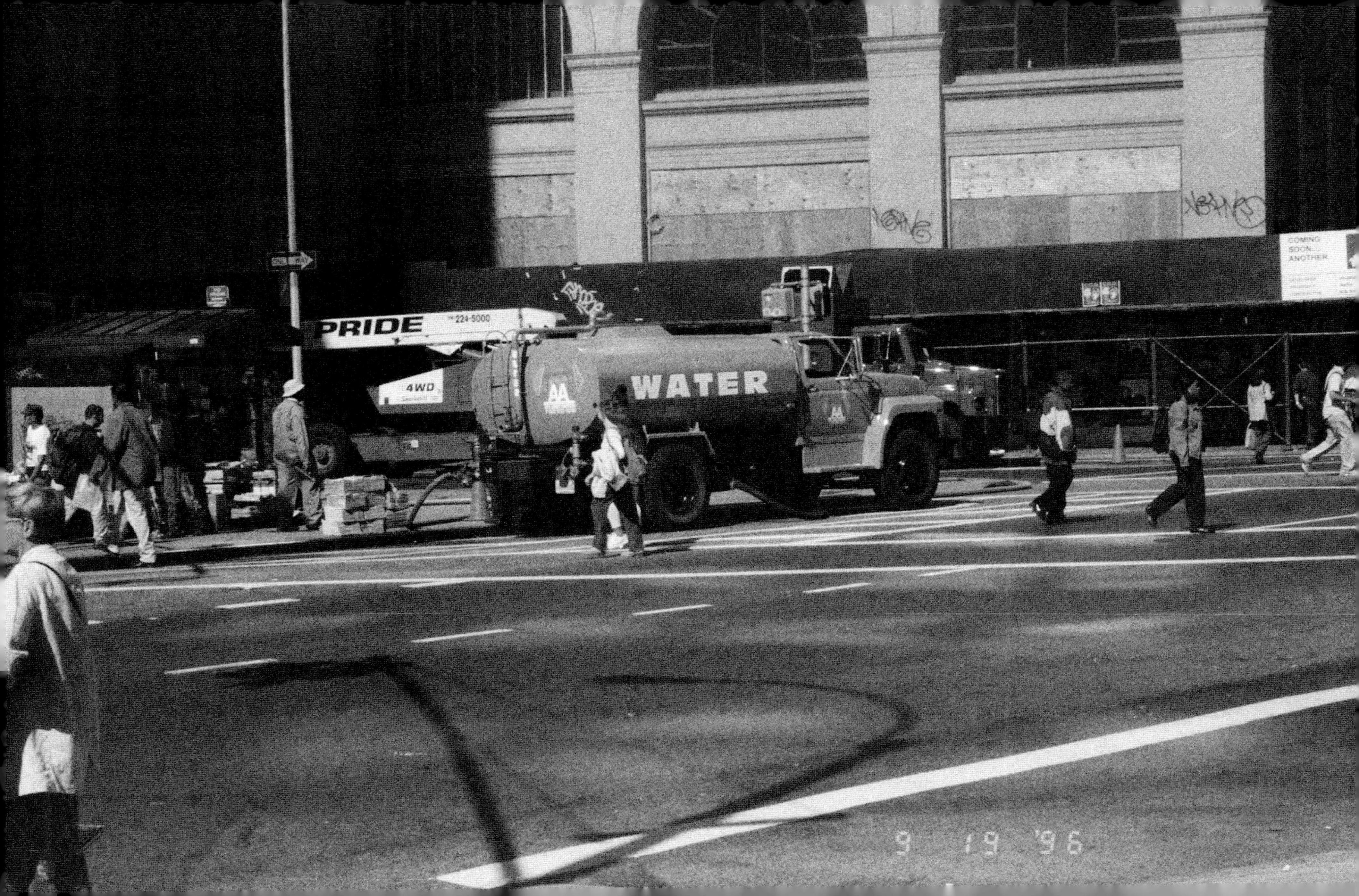
PRIDE
224-5000
4WD
WATER
COMING
SOON...
ANOTHER
9 19 '96

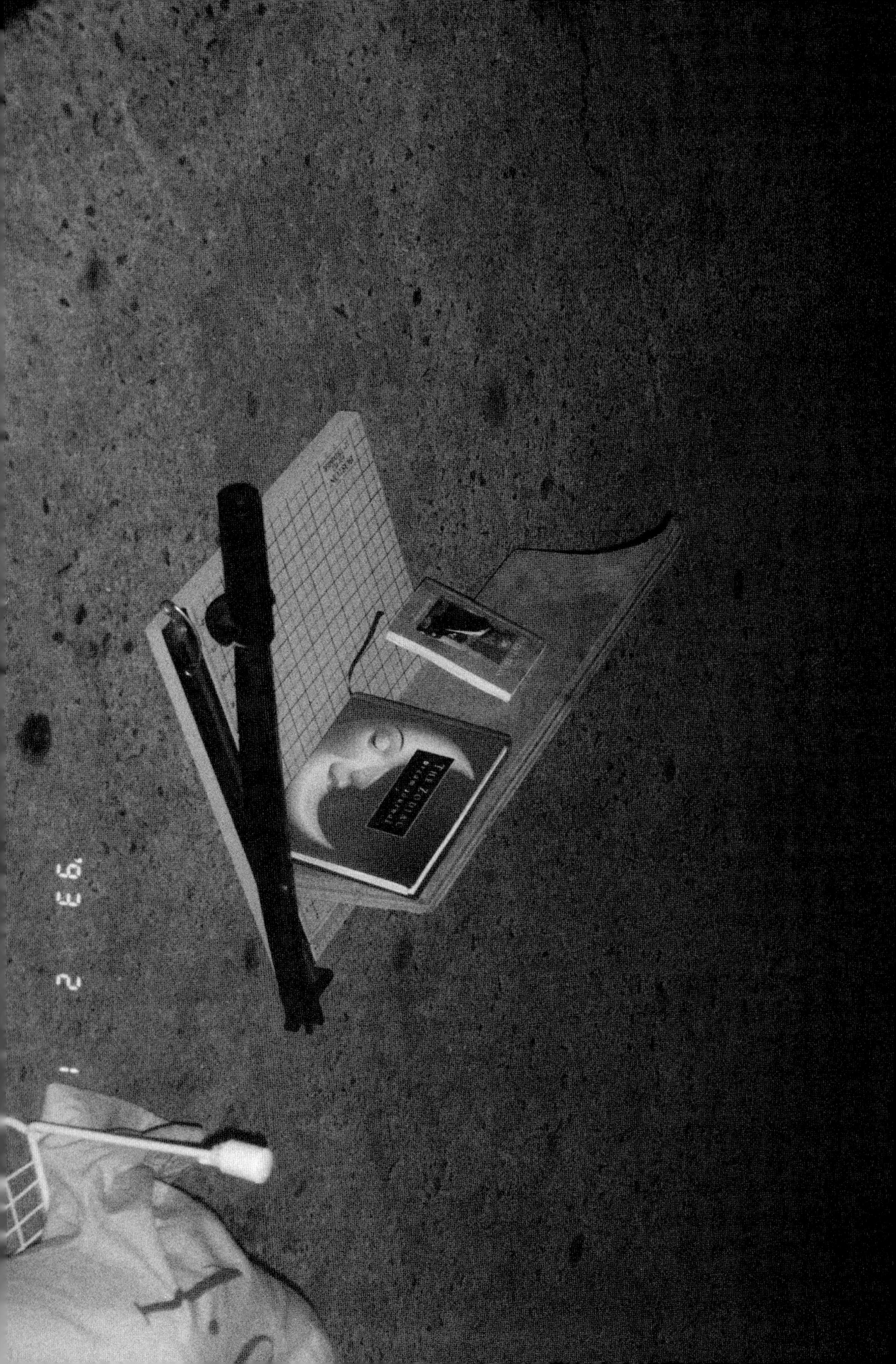

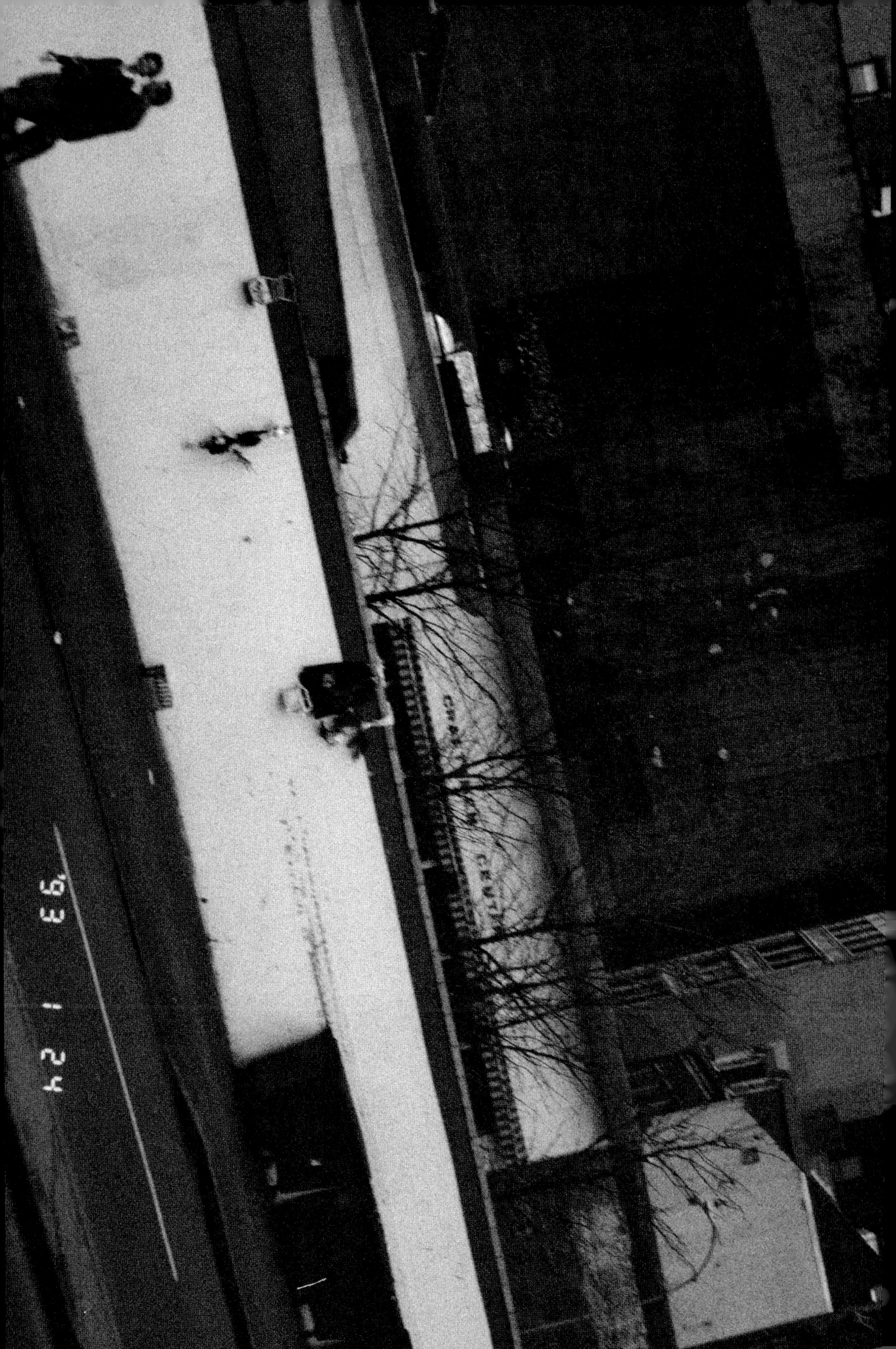

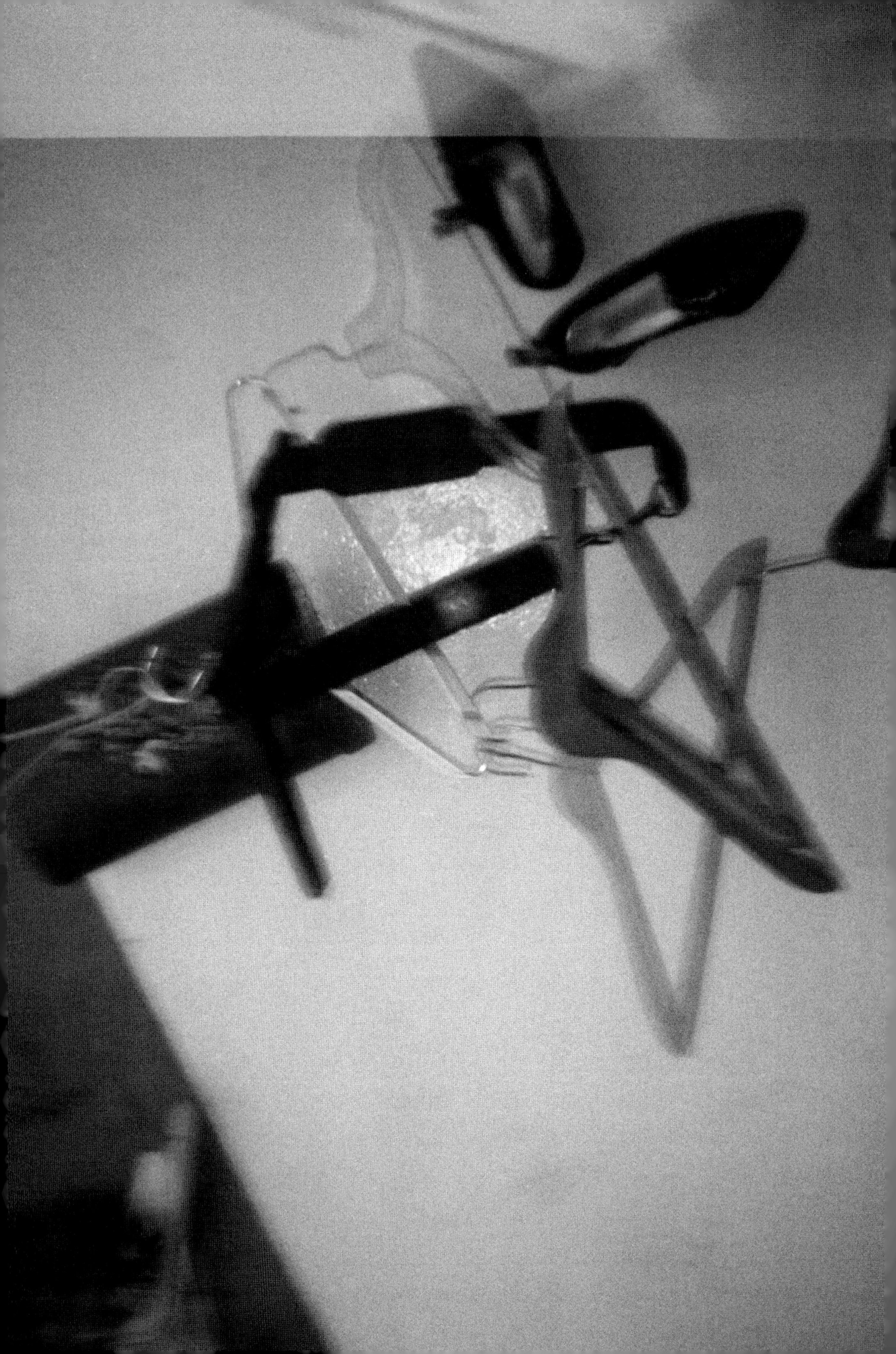

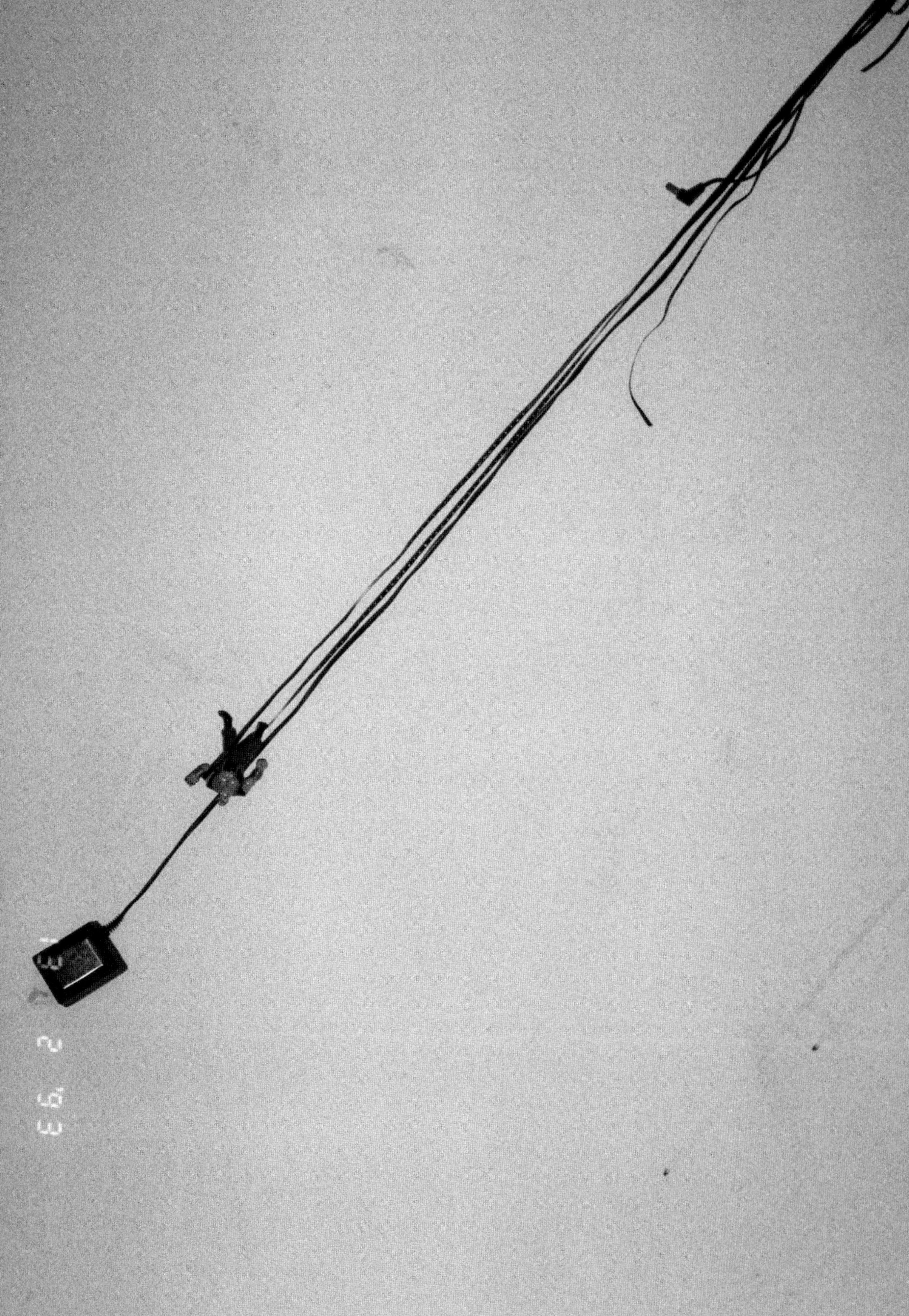

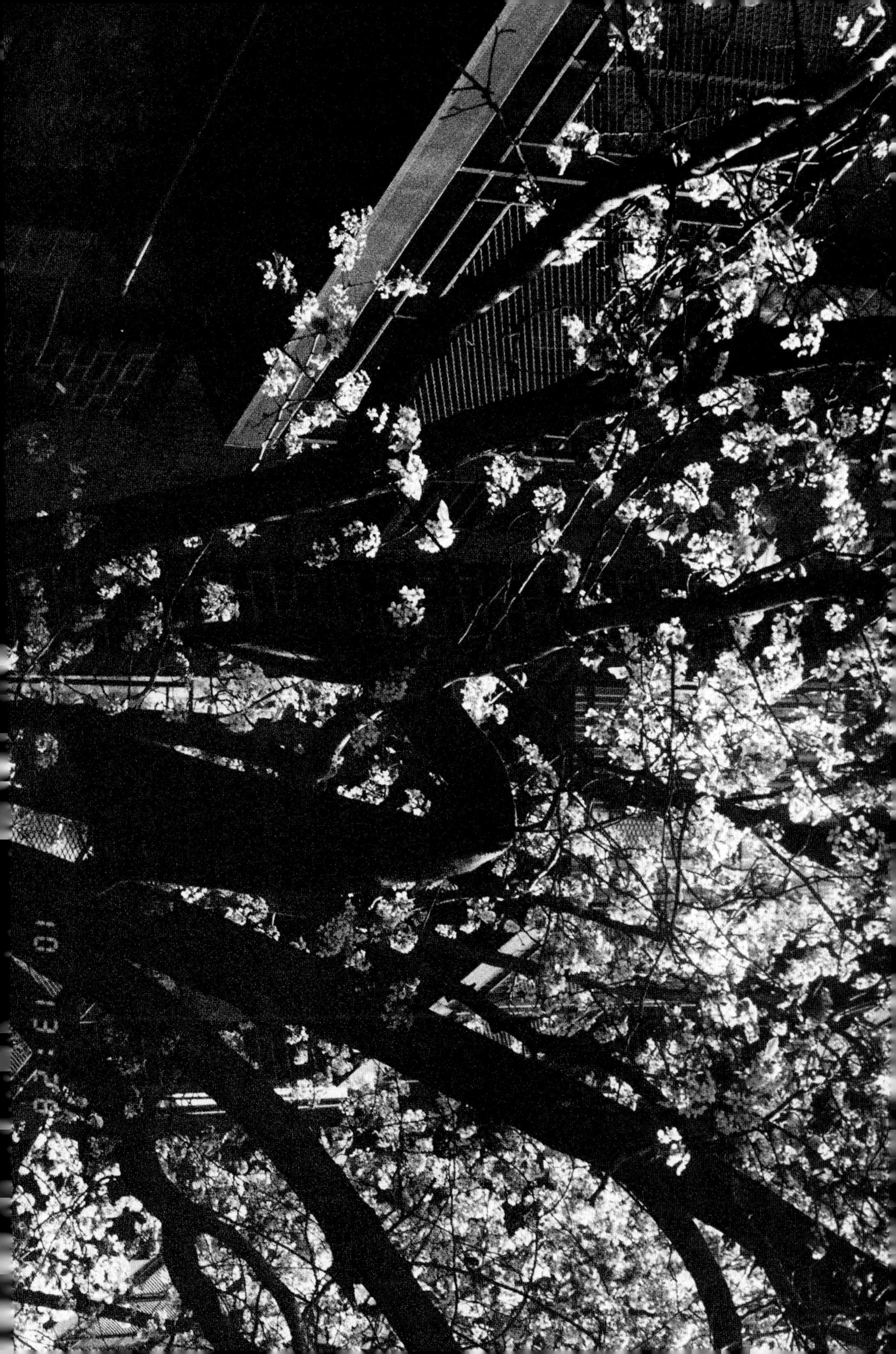

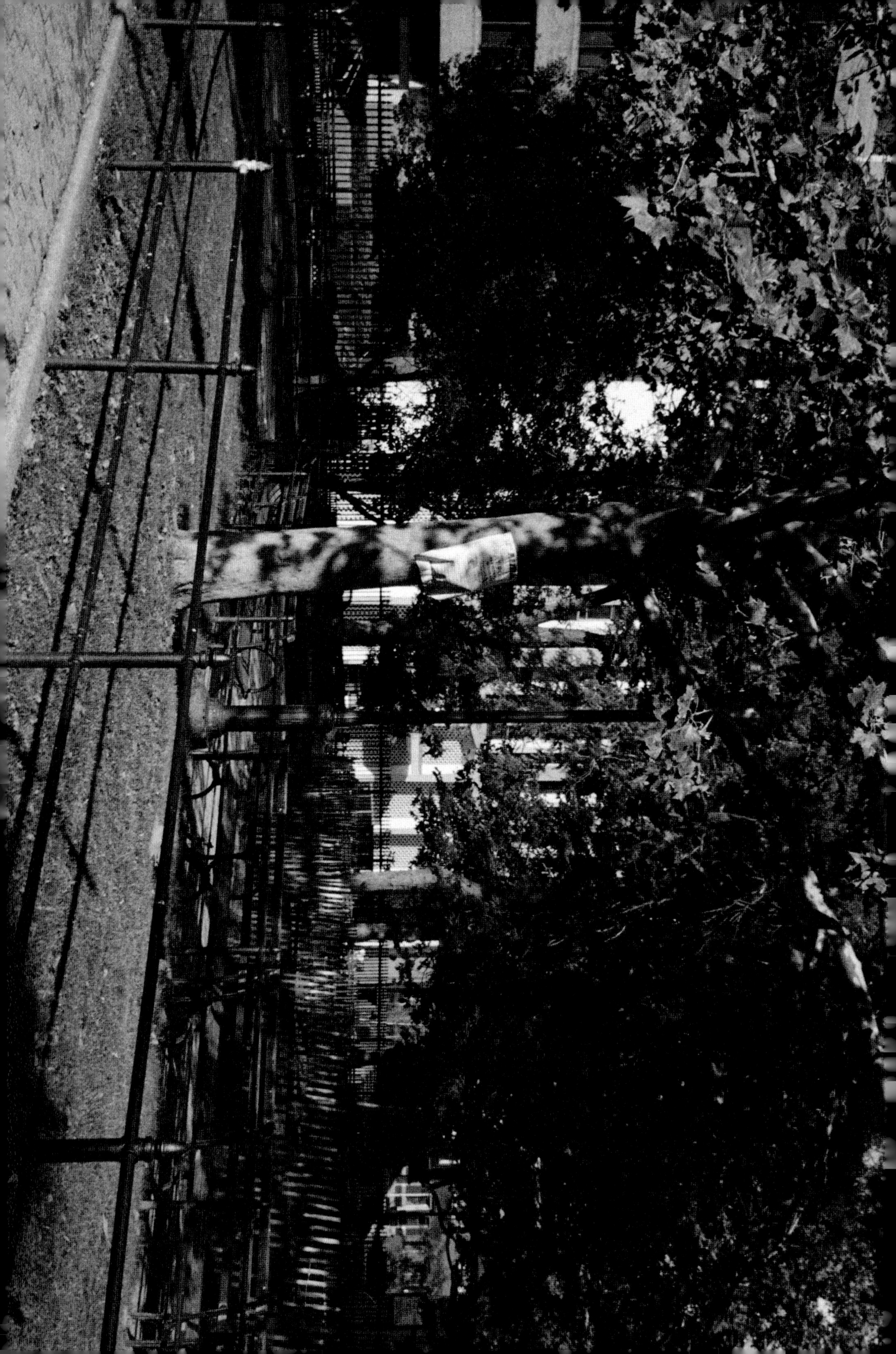

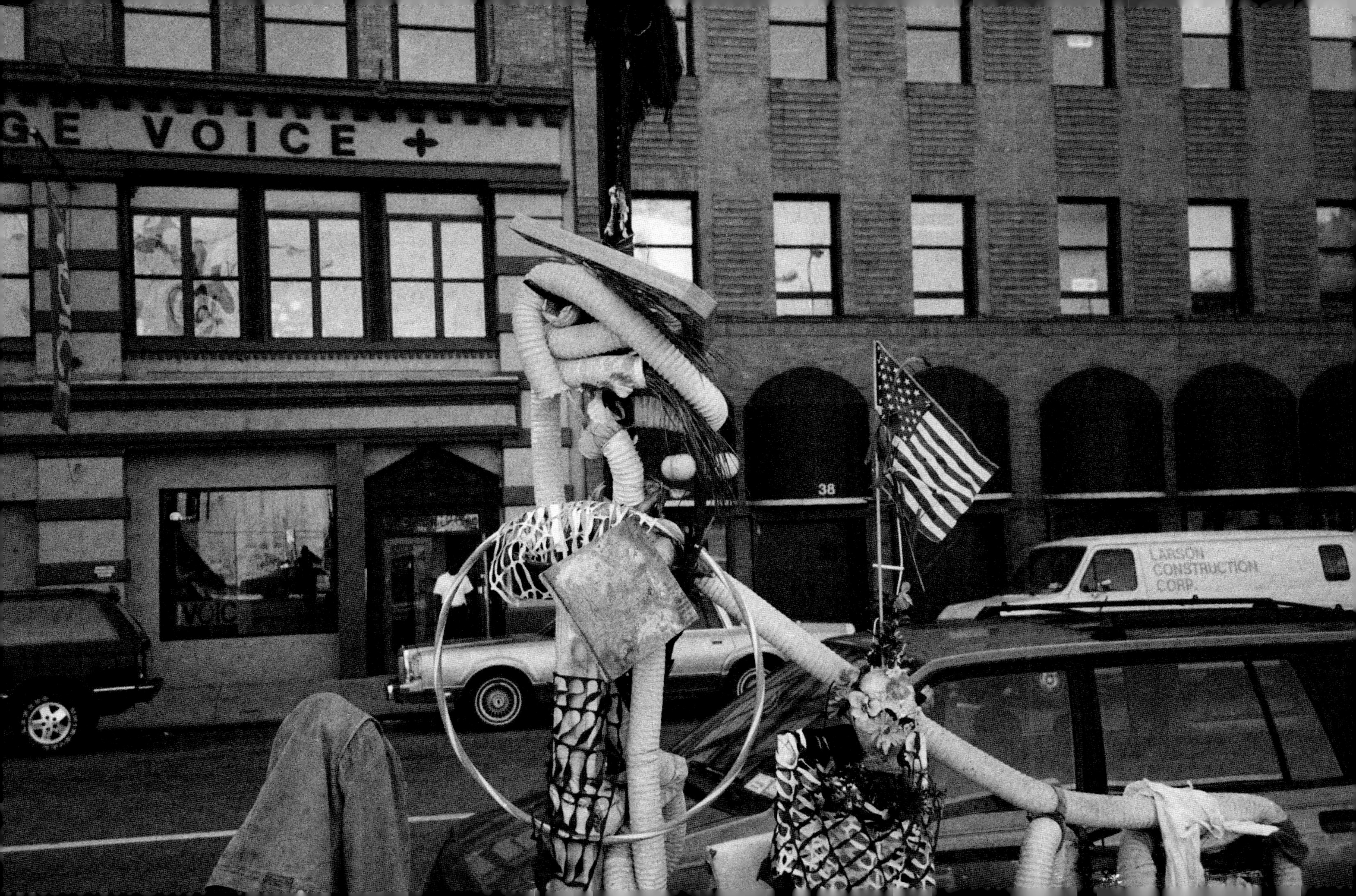
GE VOICE
38
LARSON
CONSTRUCTION
CORP.

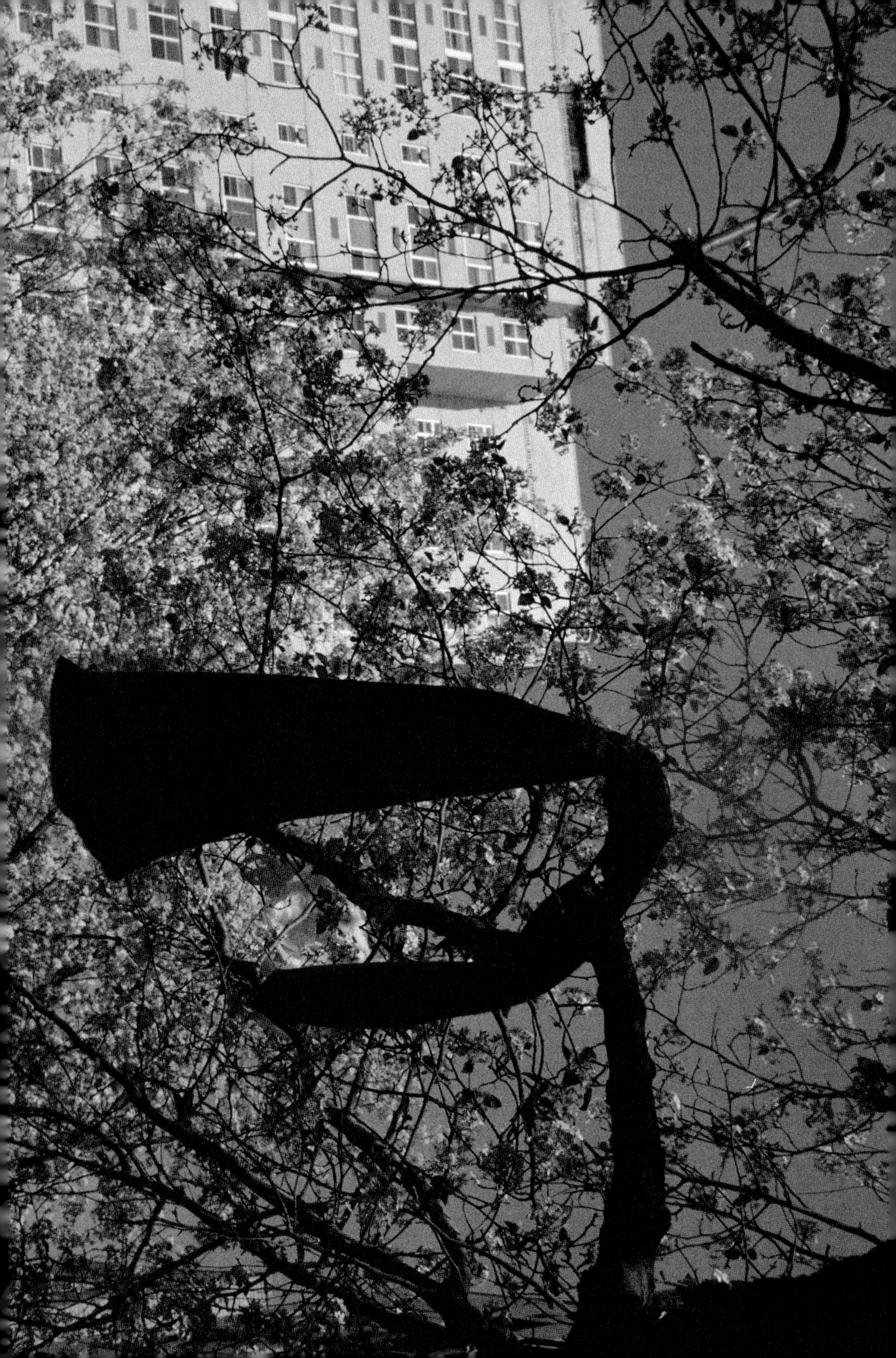

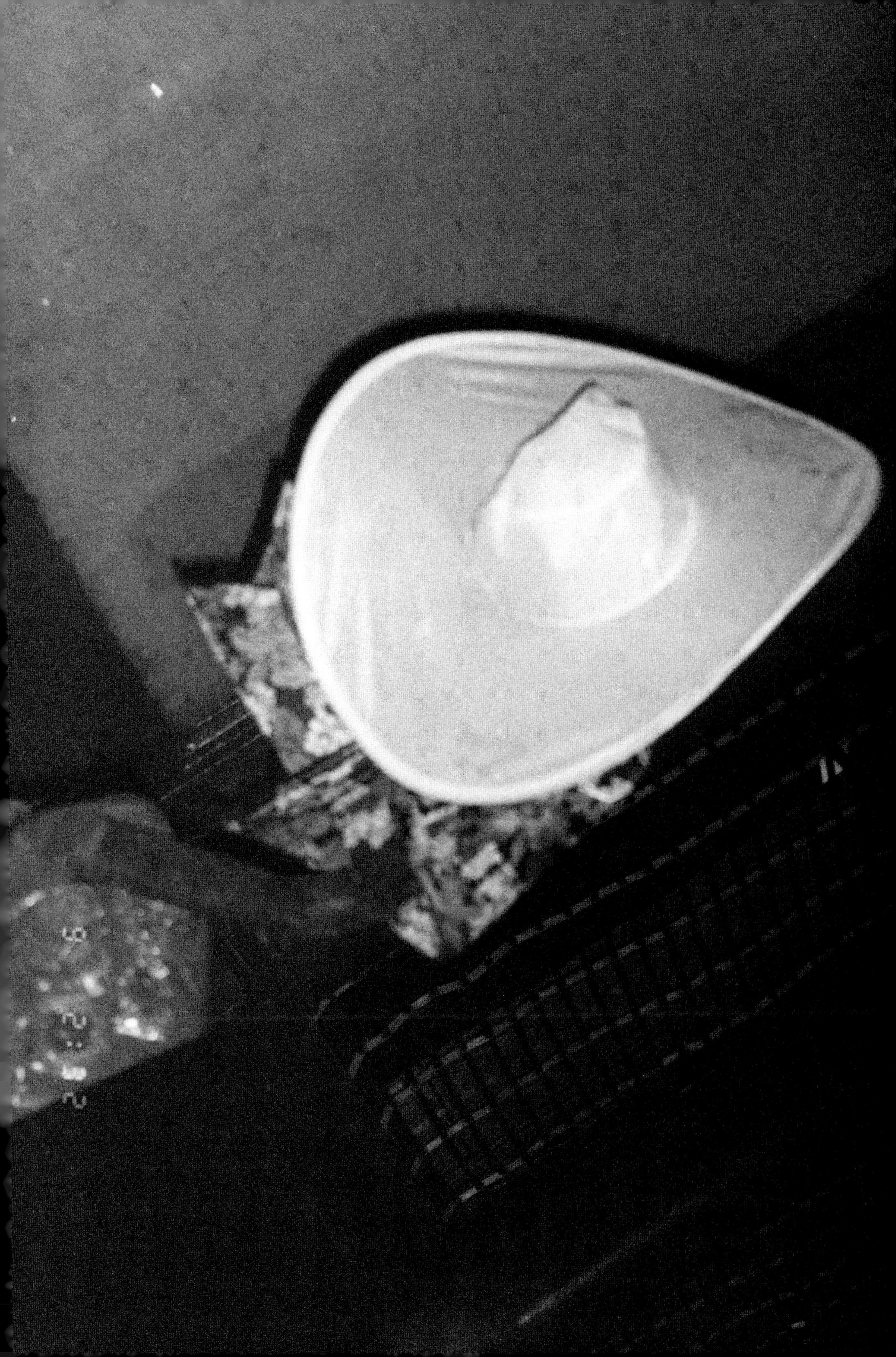

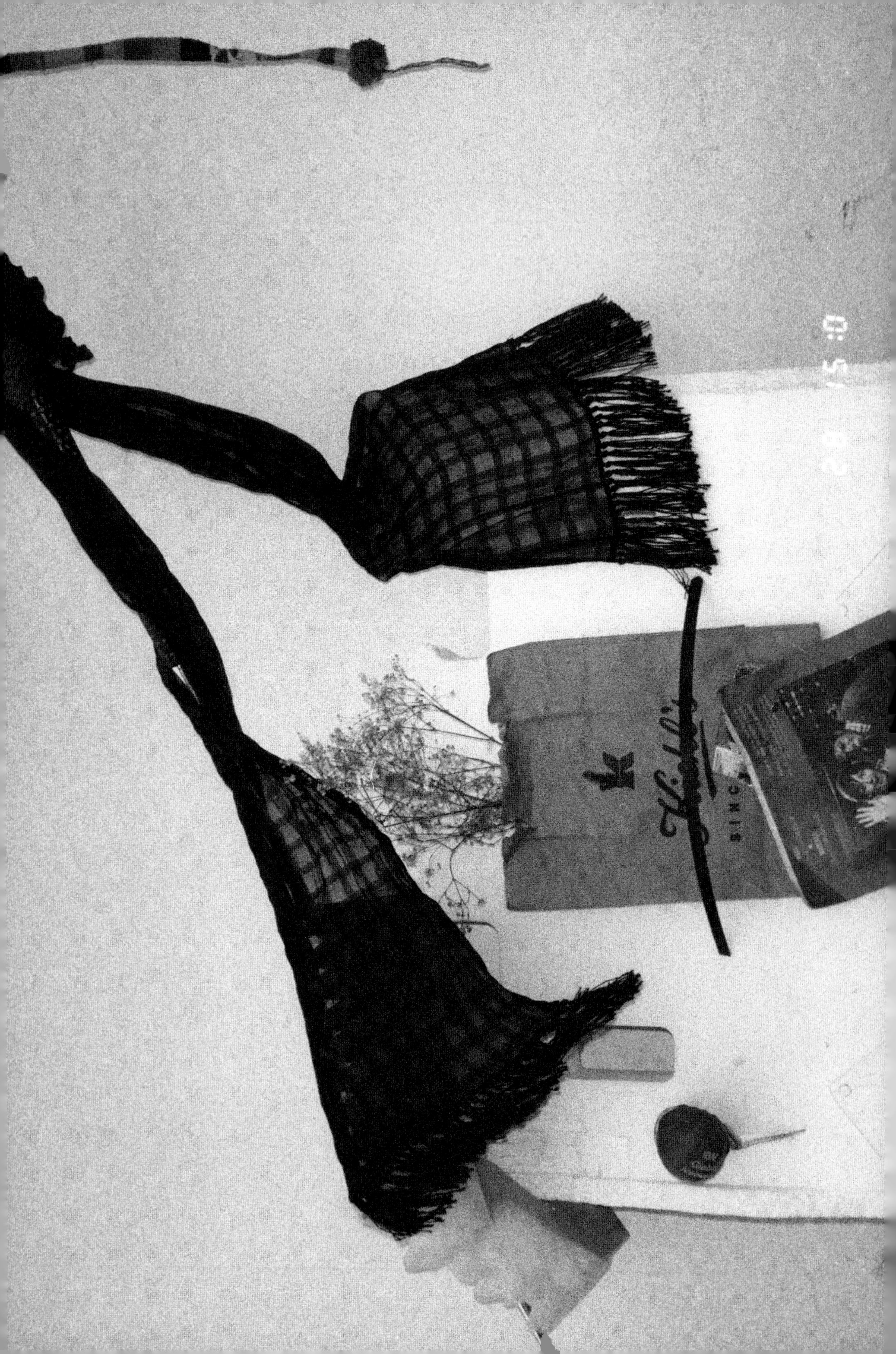

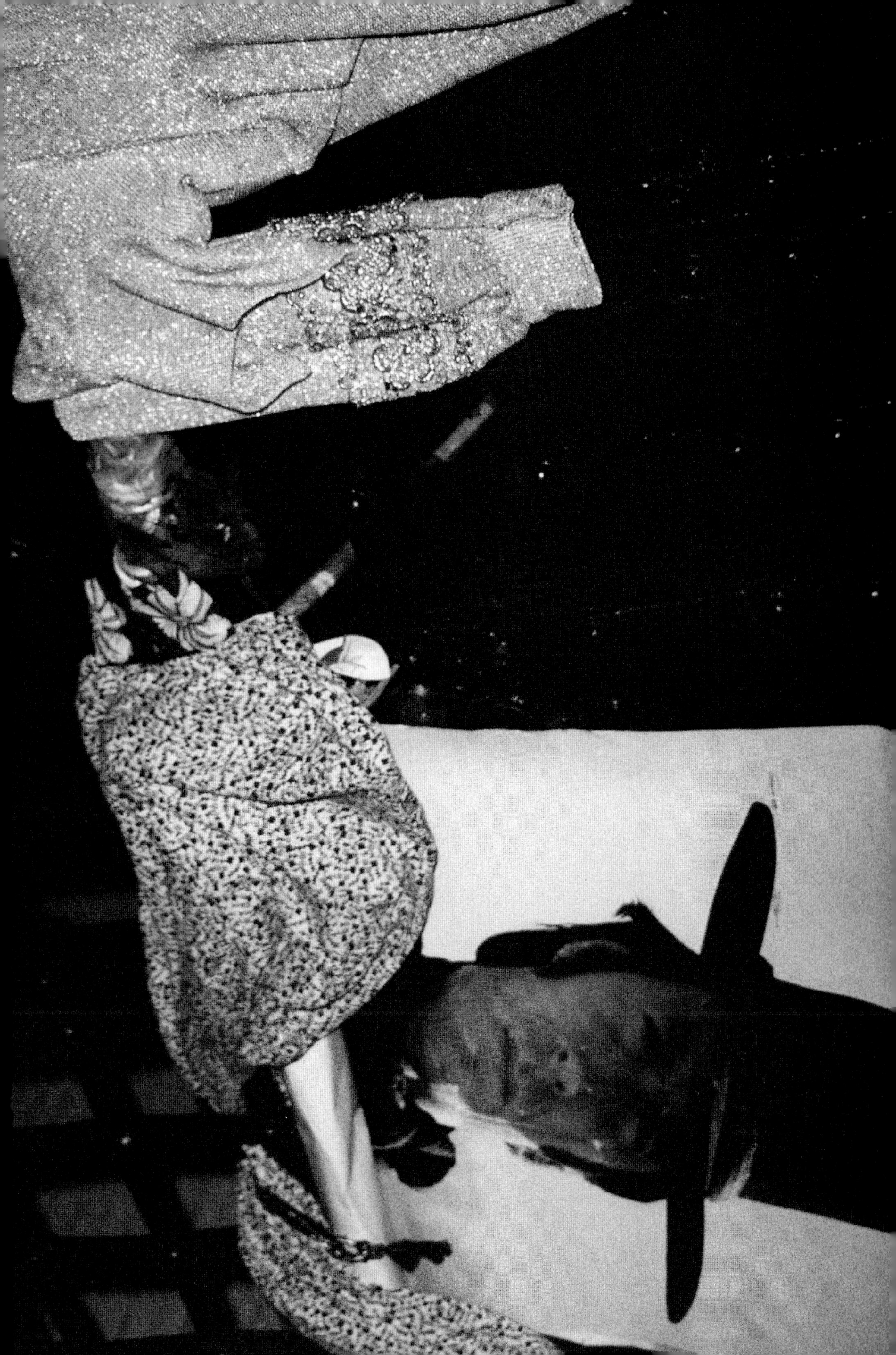

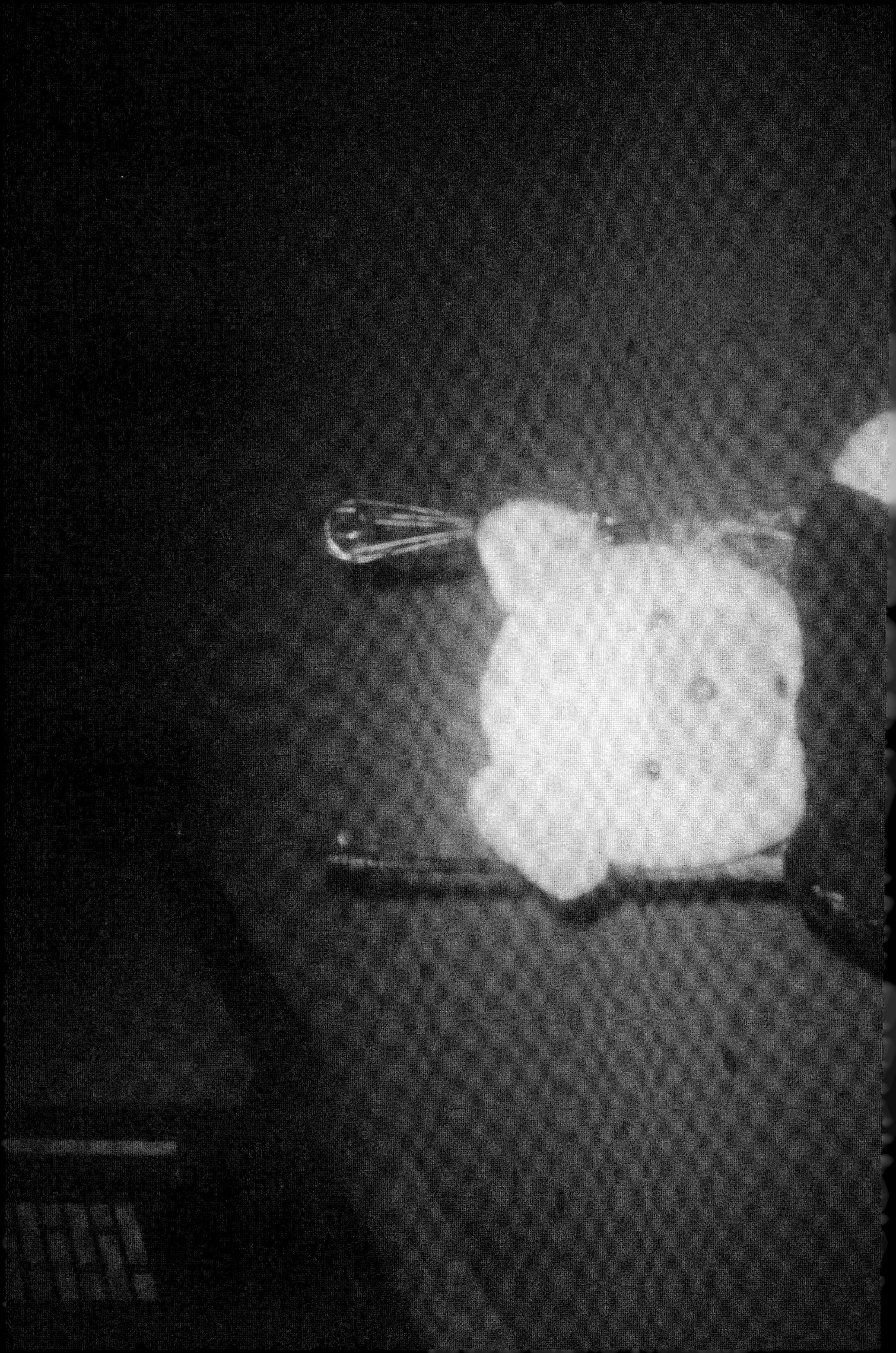

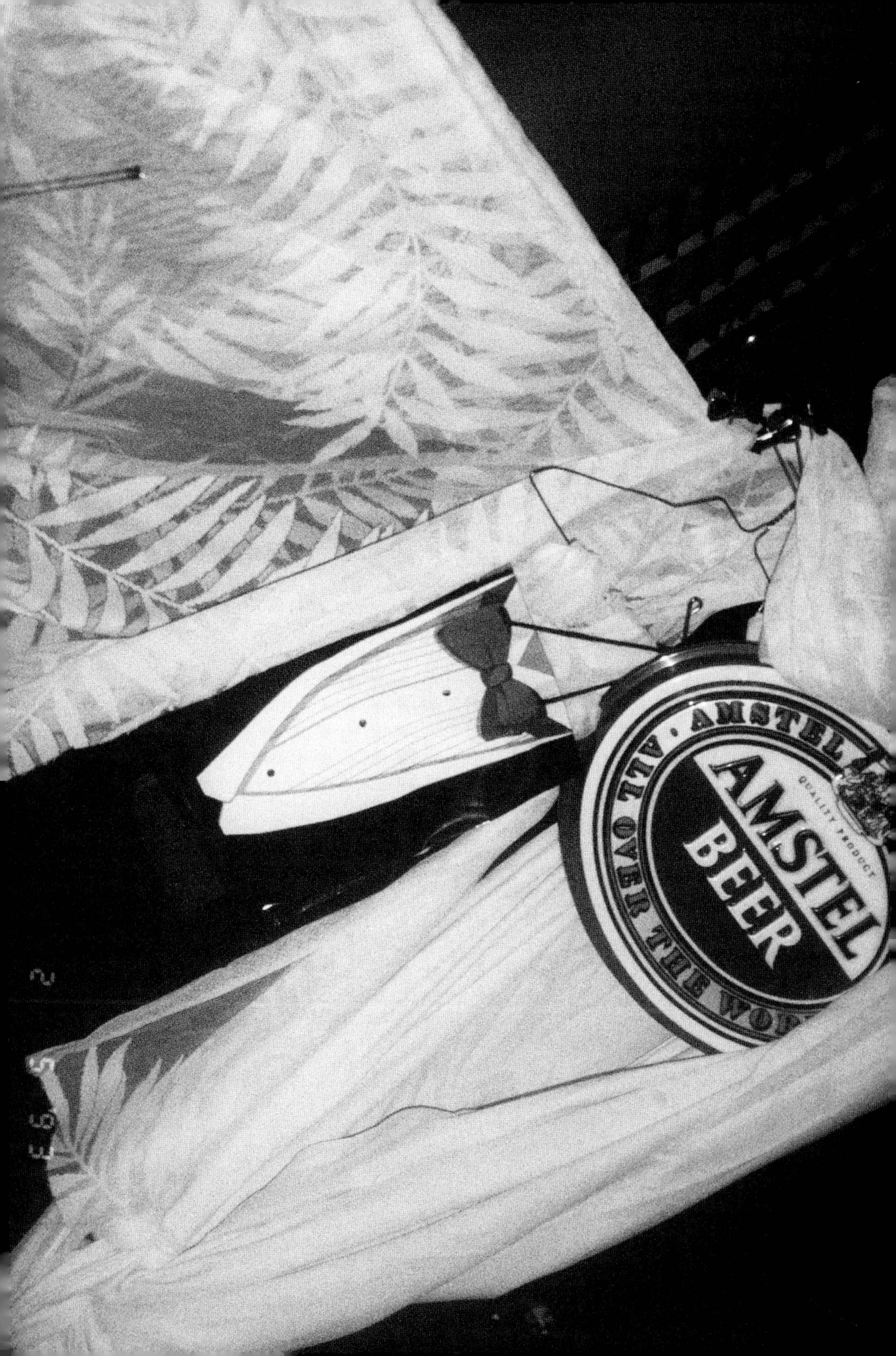
AMSTEL
ALL OVER THE
QUALITY PRODUCT
AMSTEL
BEER

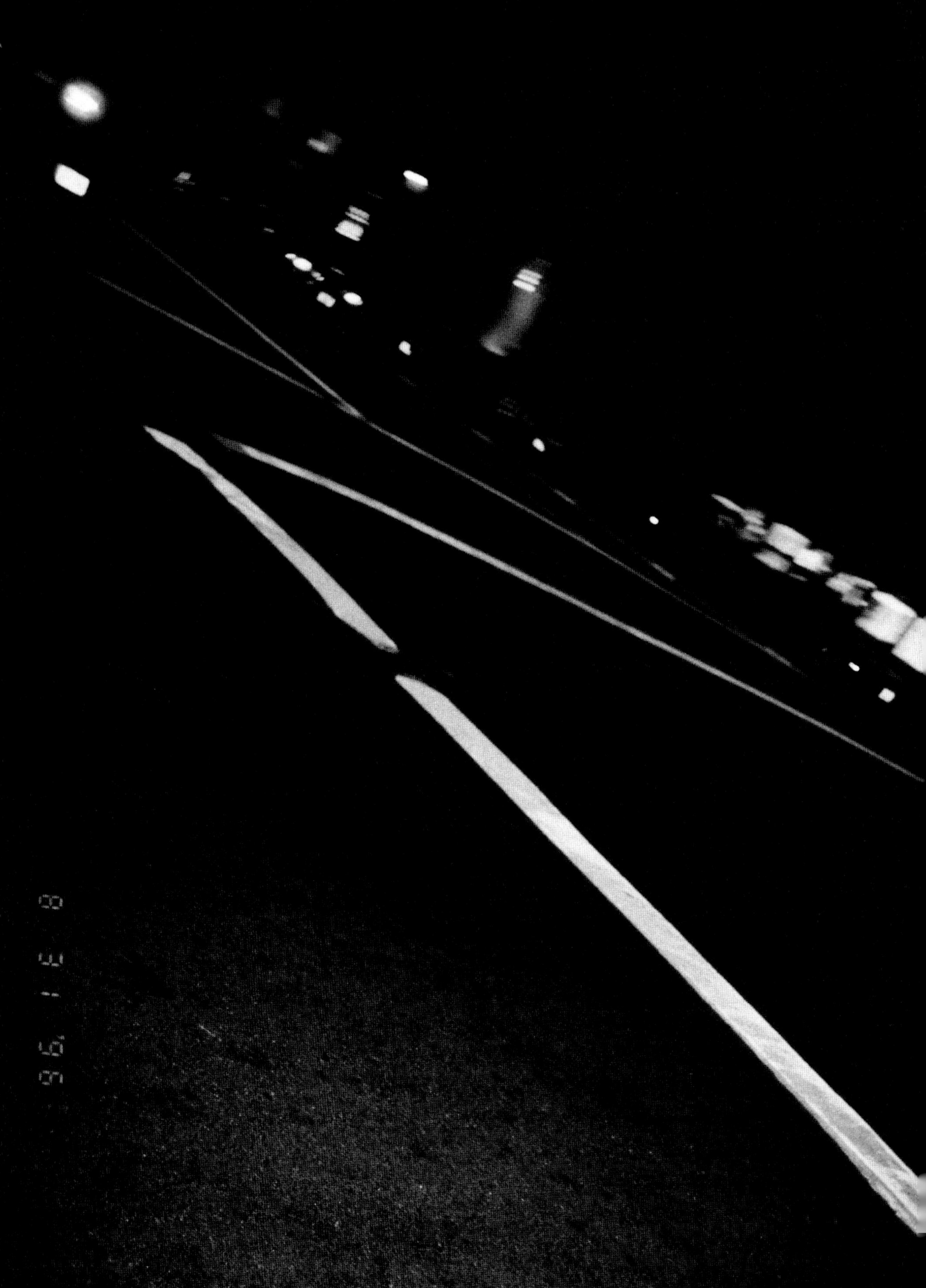

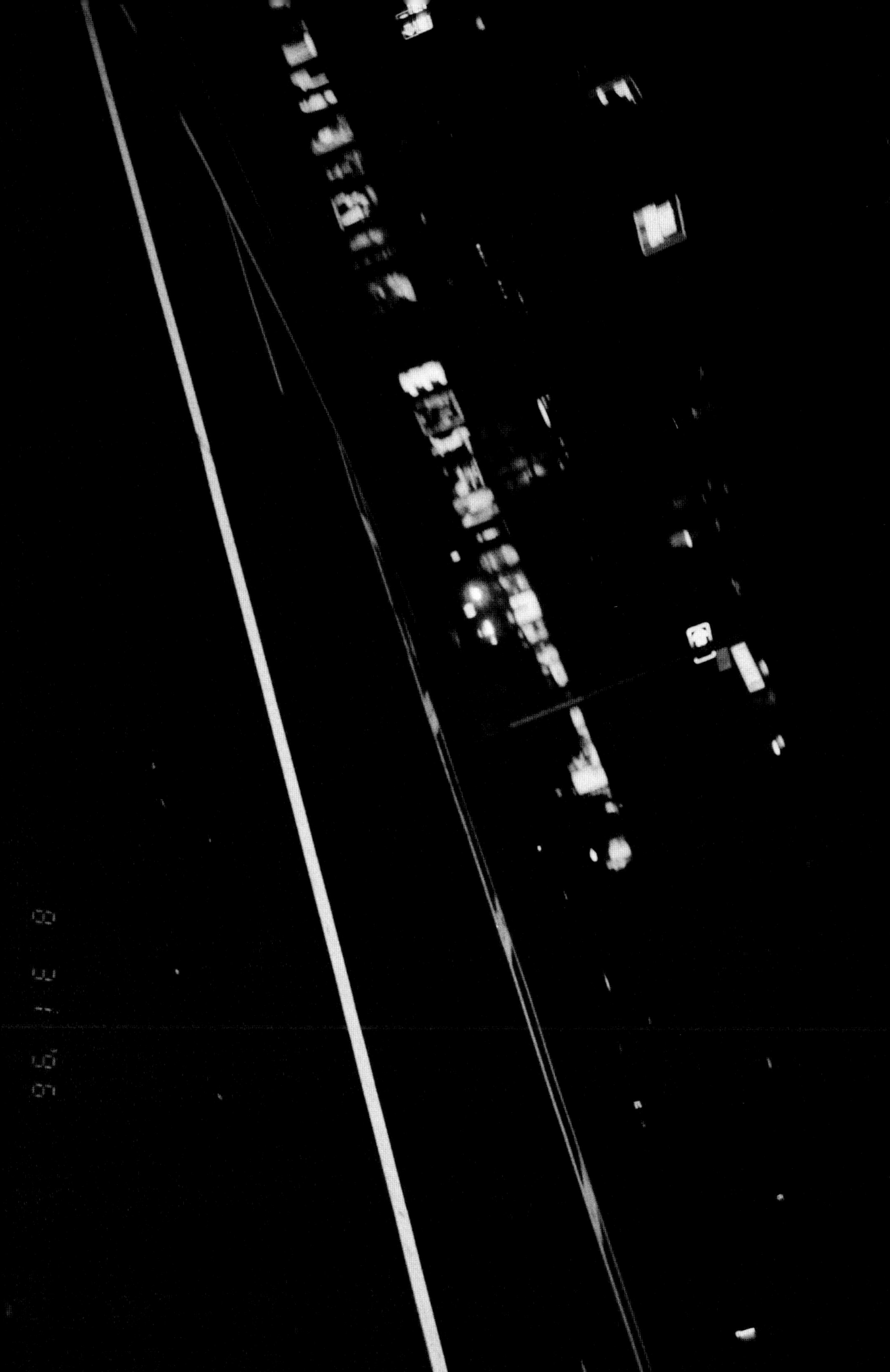

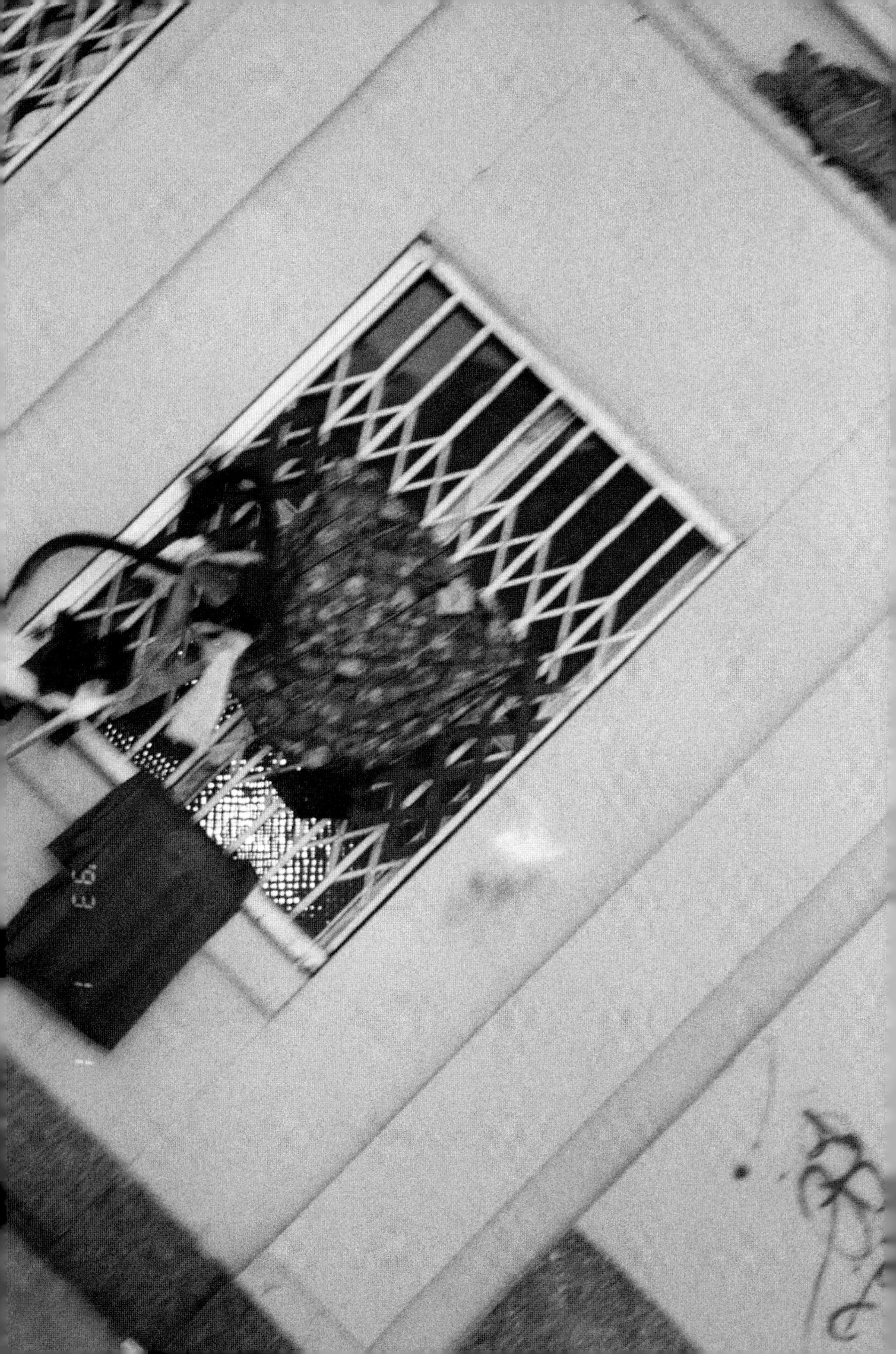

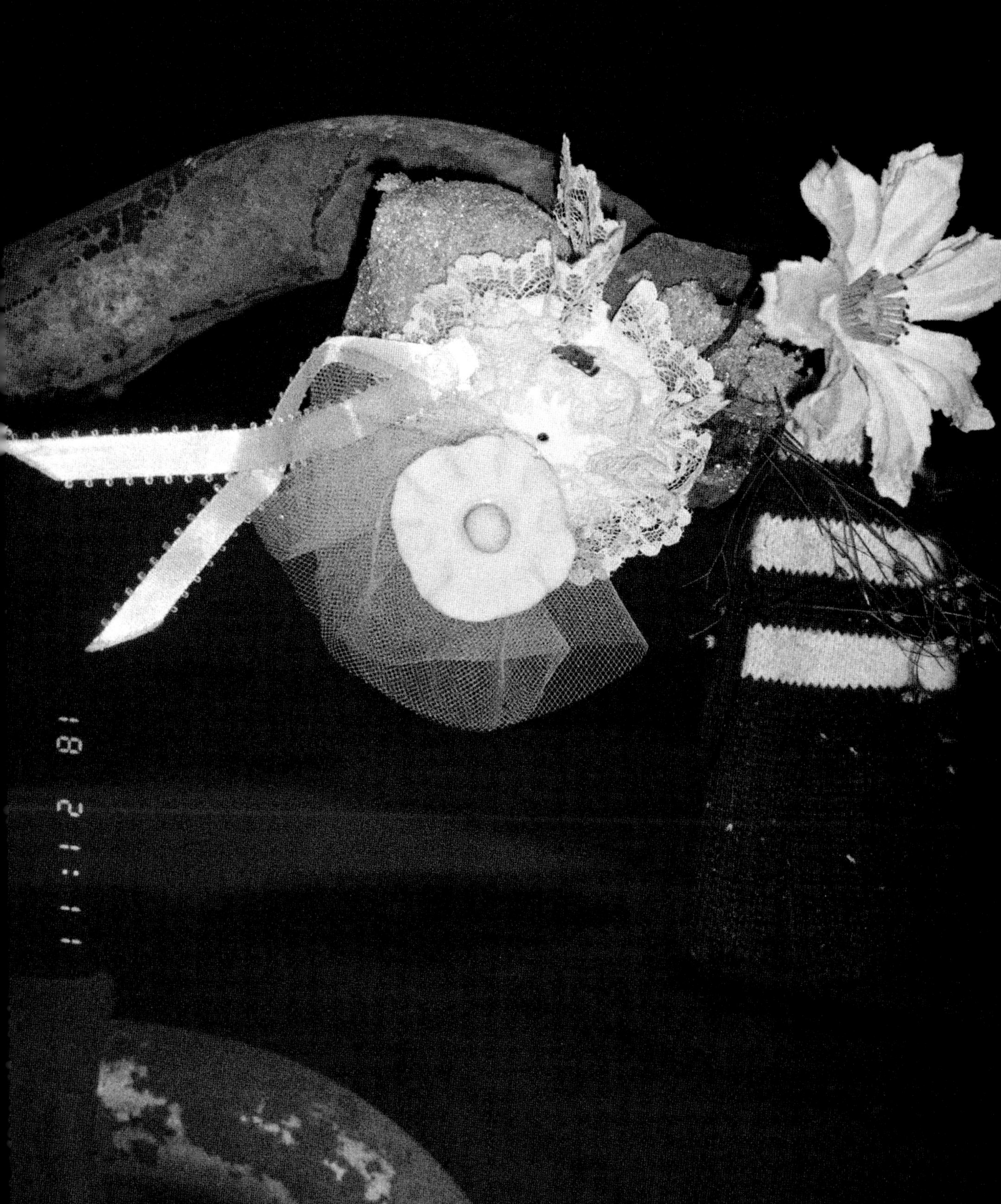

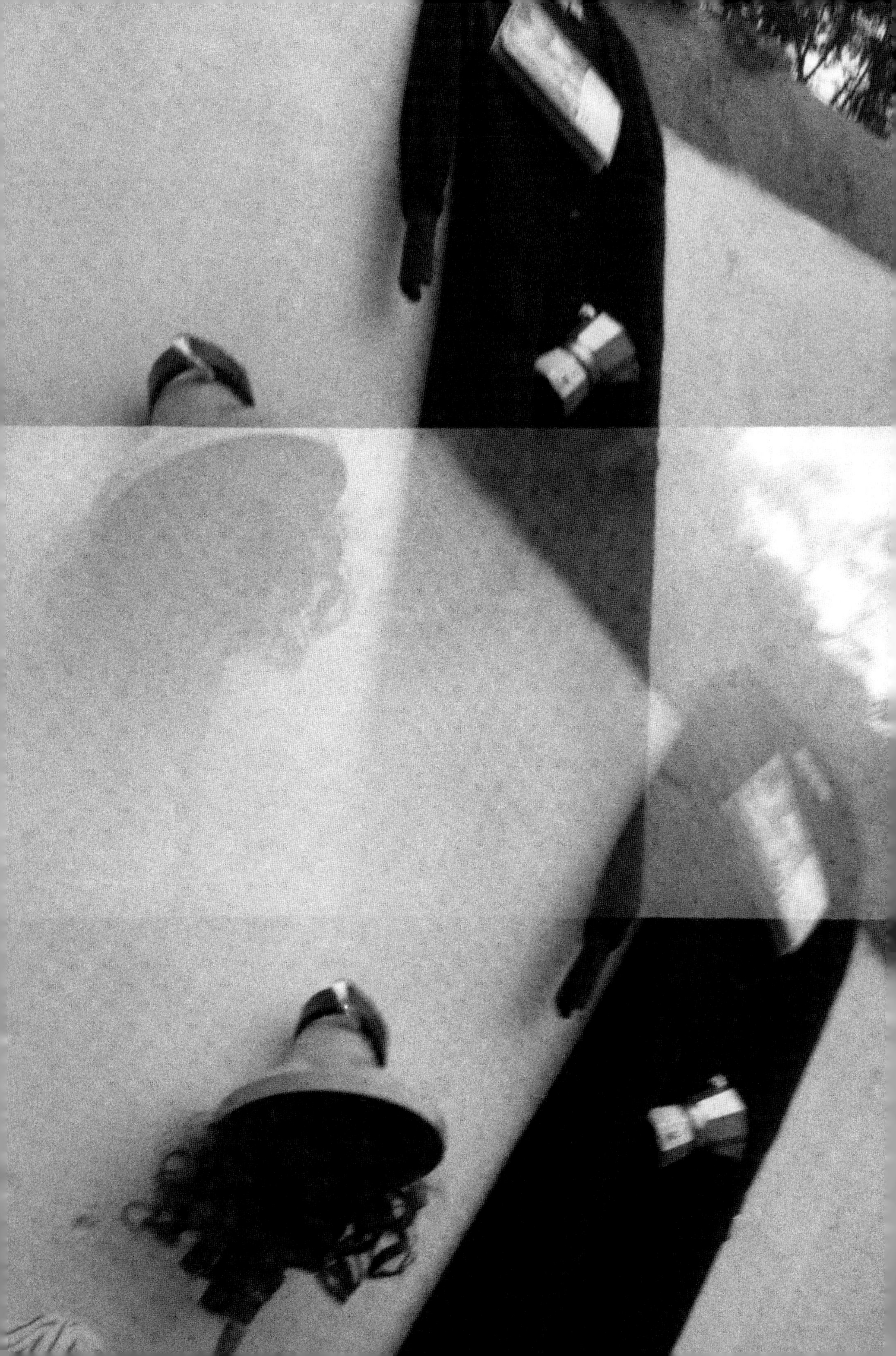

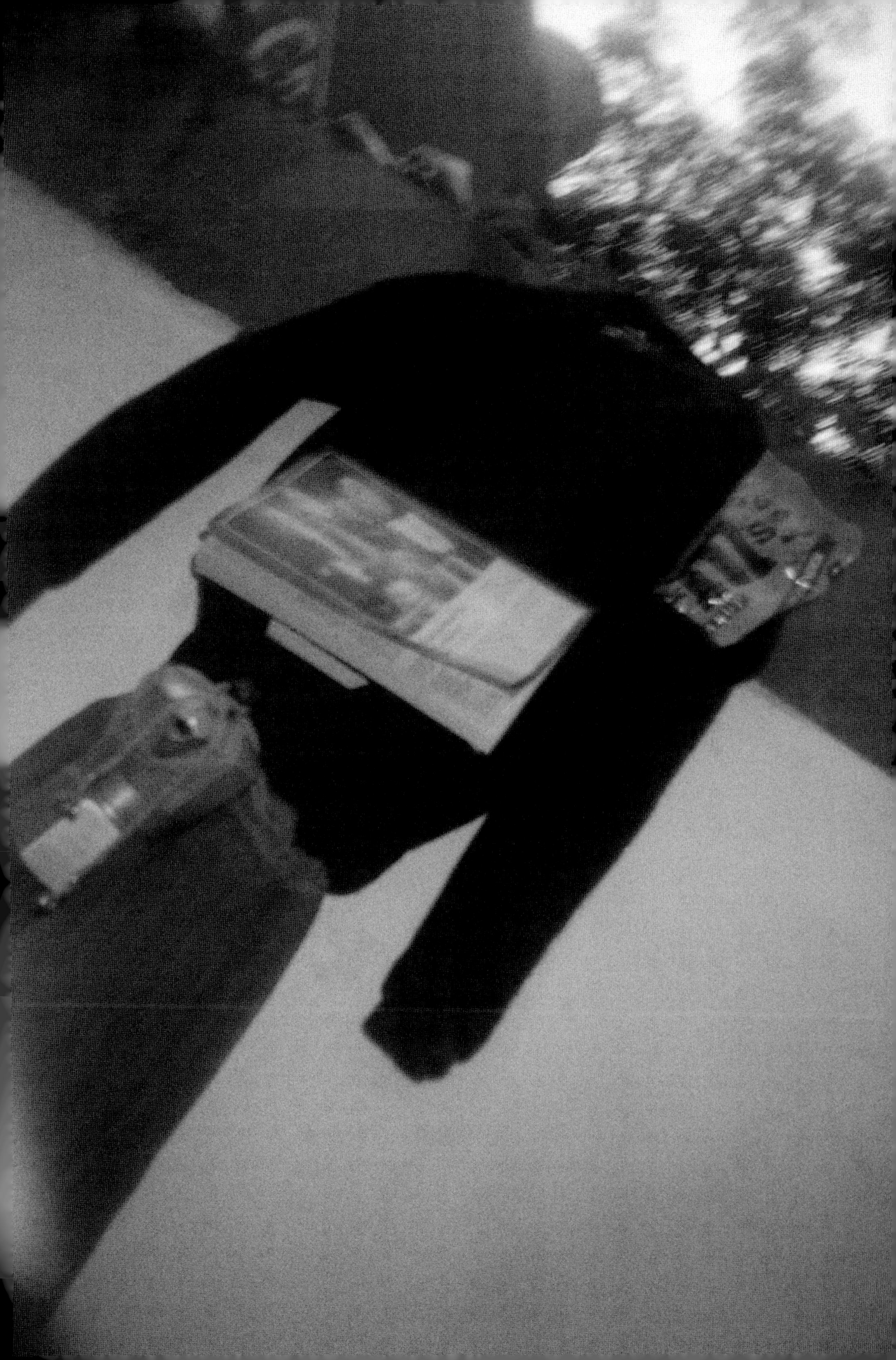

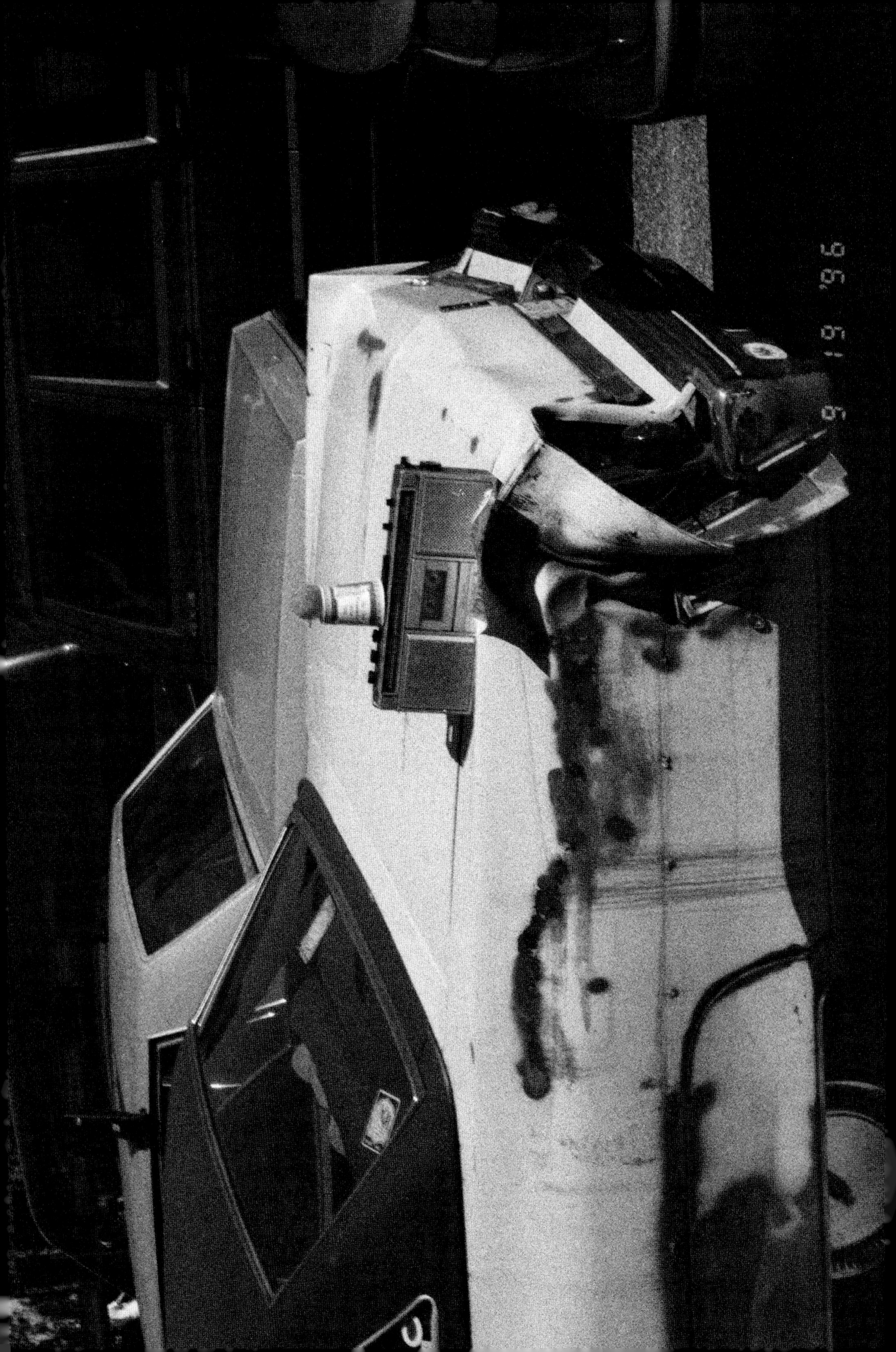

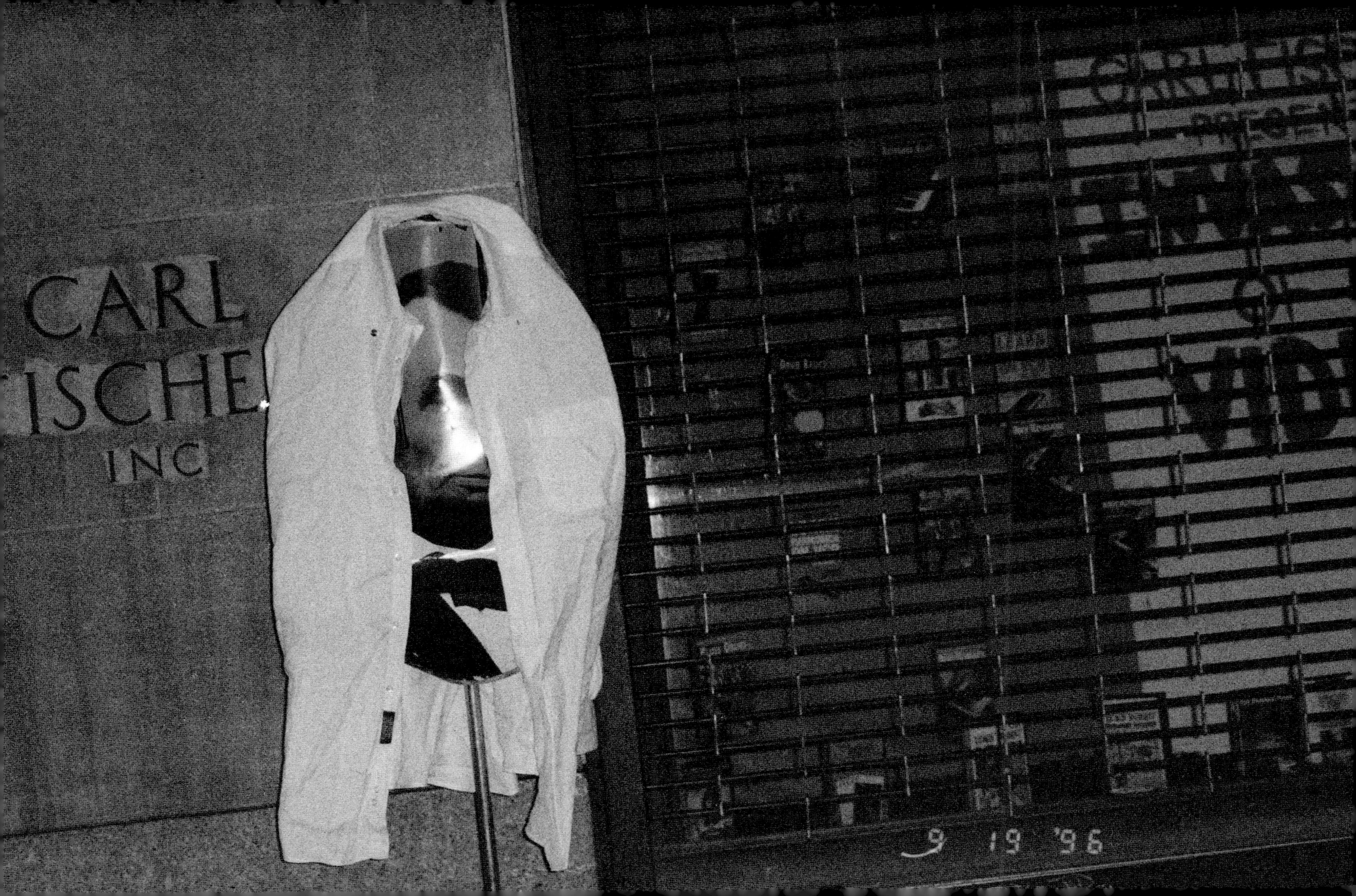
CARL
ISCHE
INC
9 19 '96

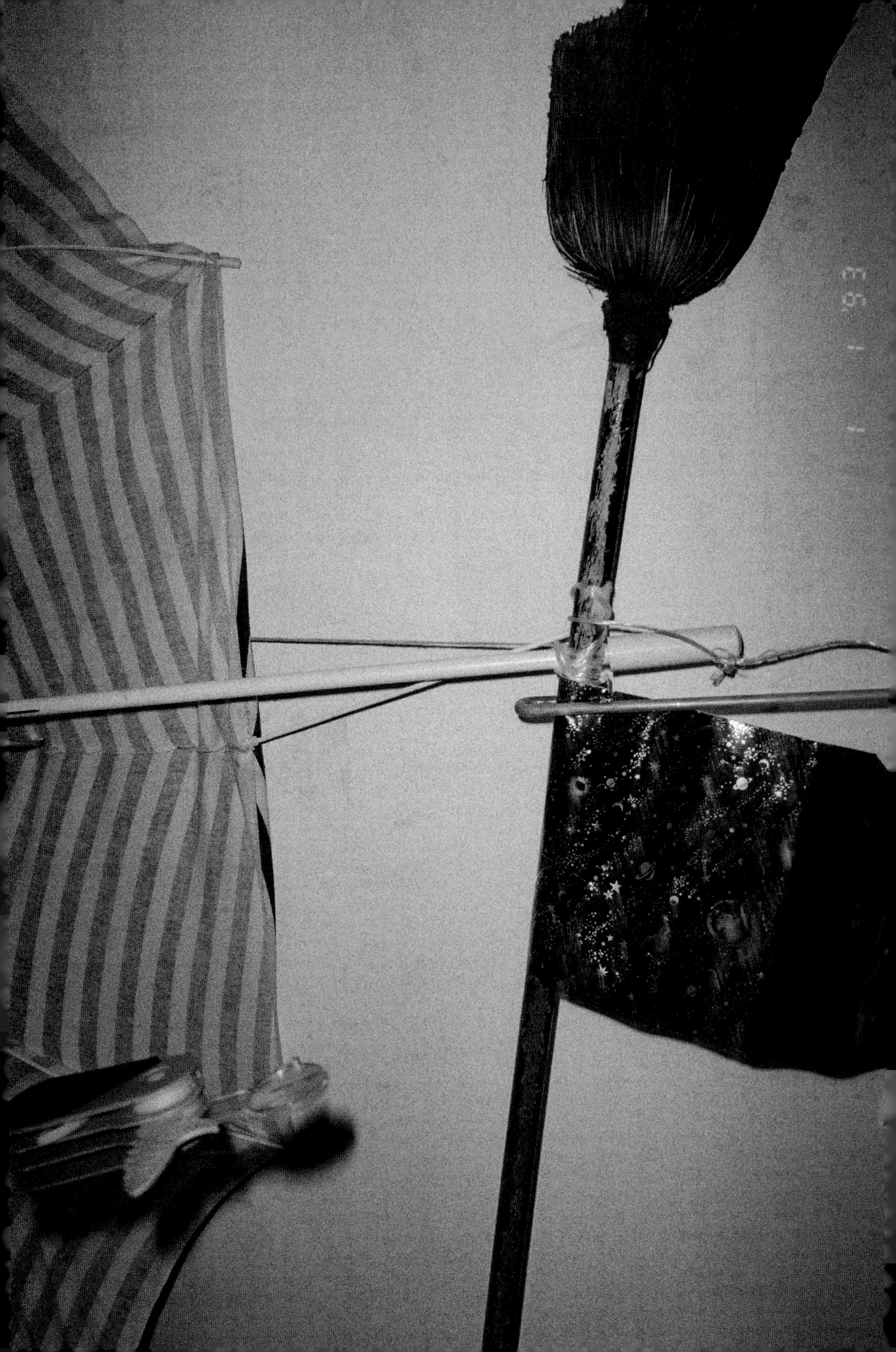
1 1 '93

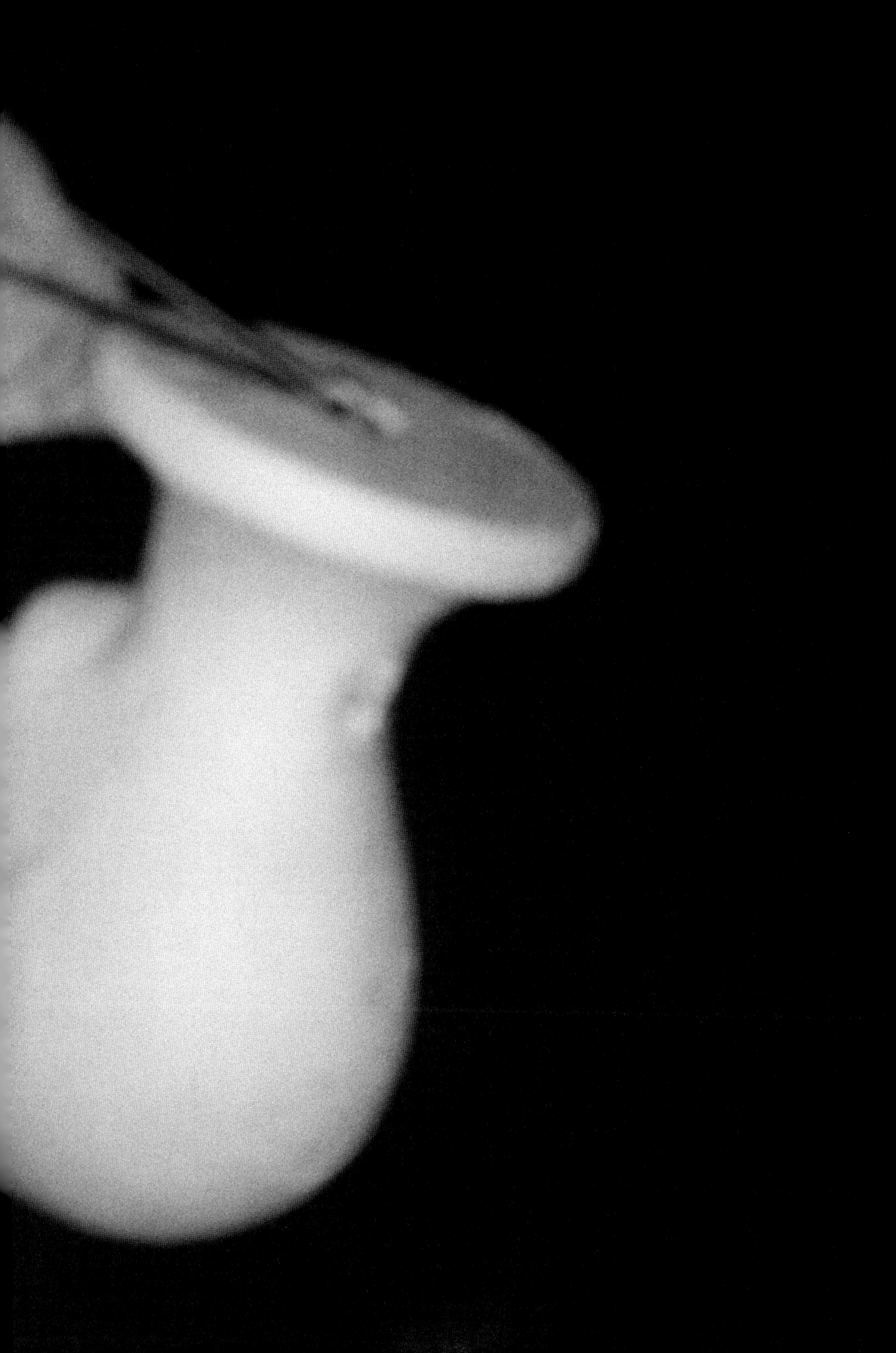

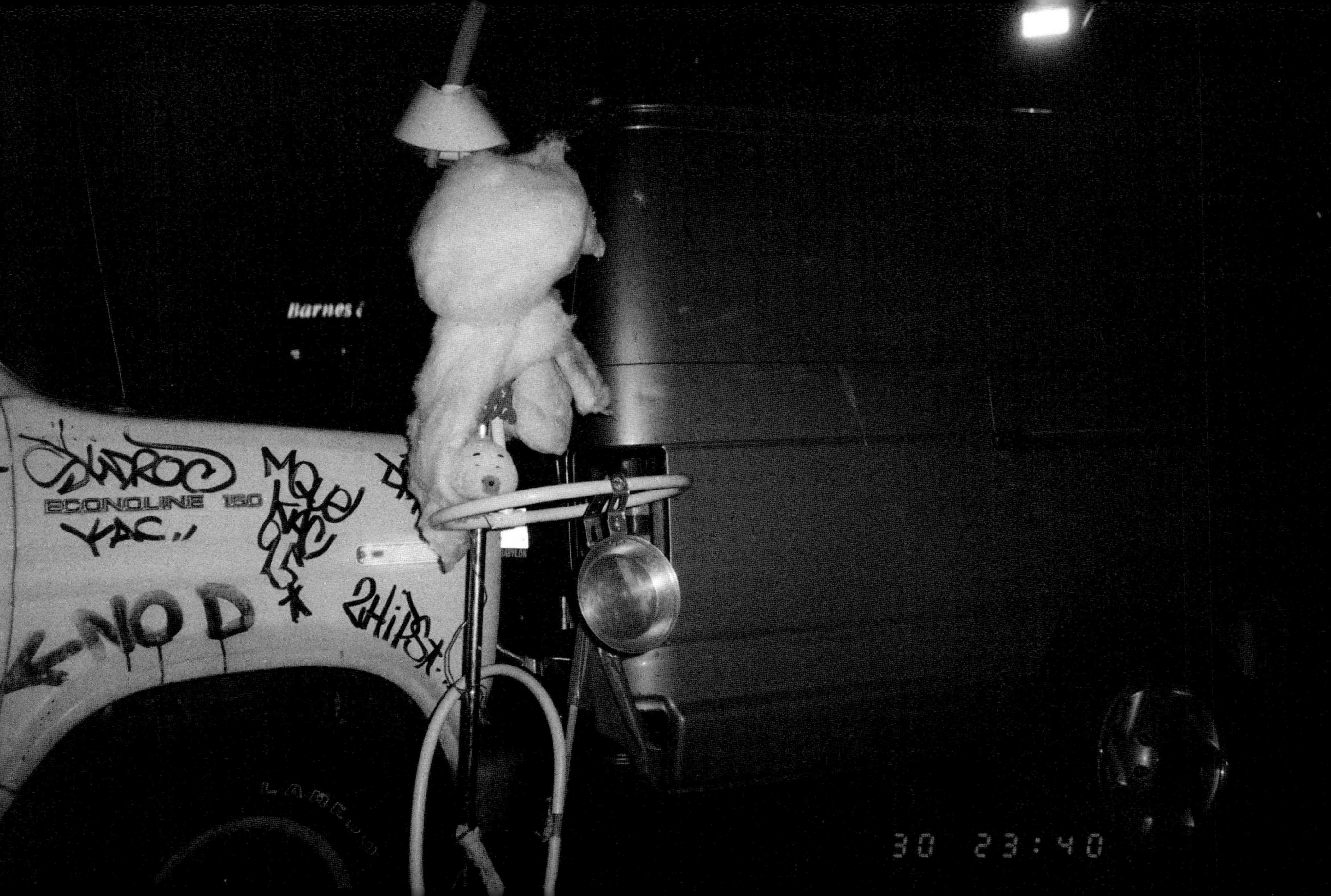
ECONOLINE 150
Barnes
30 23:40

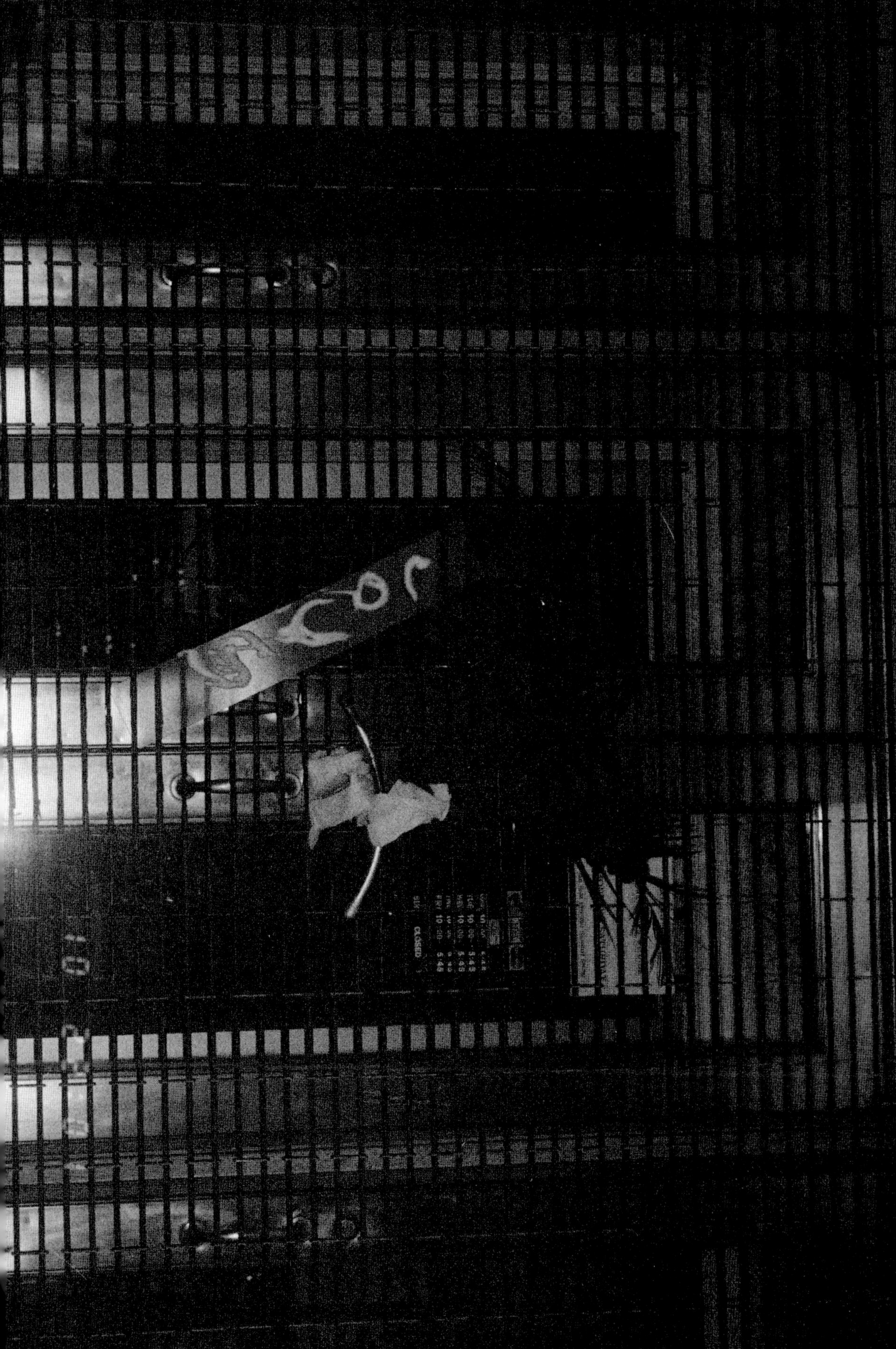

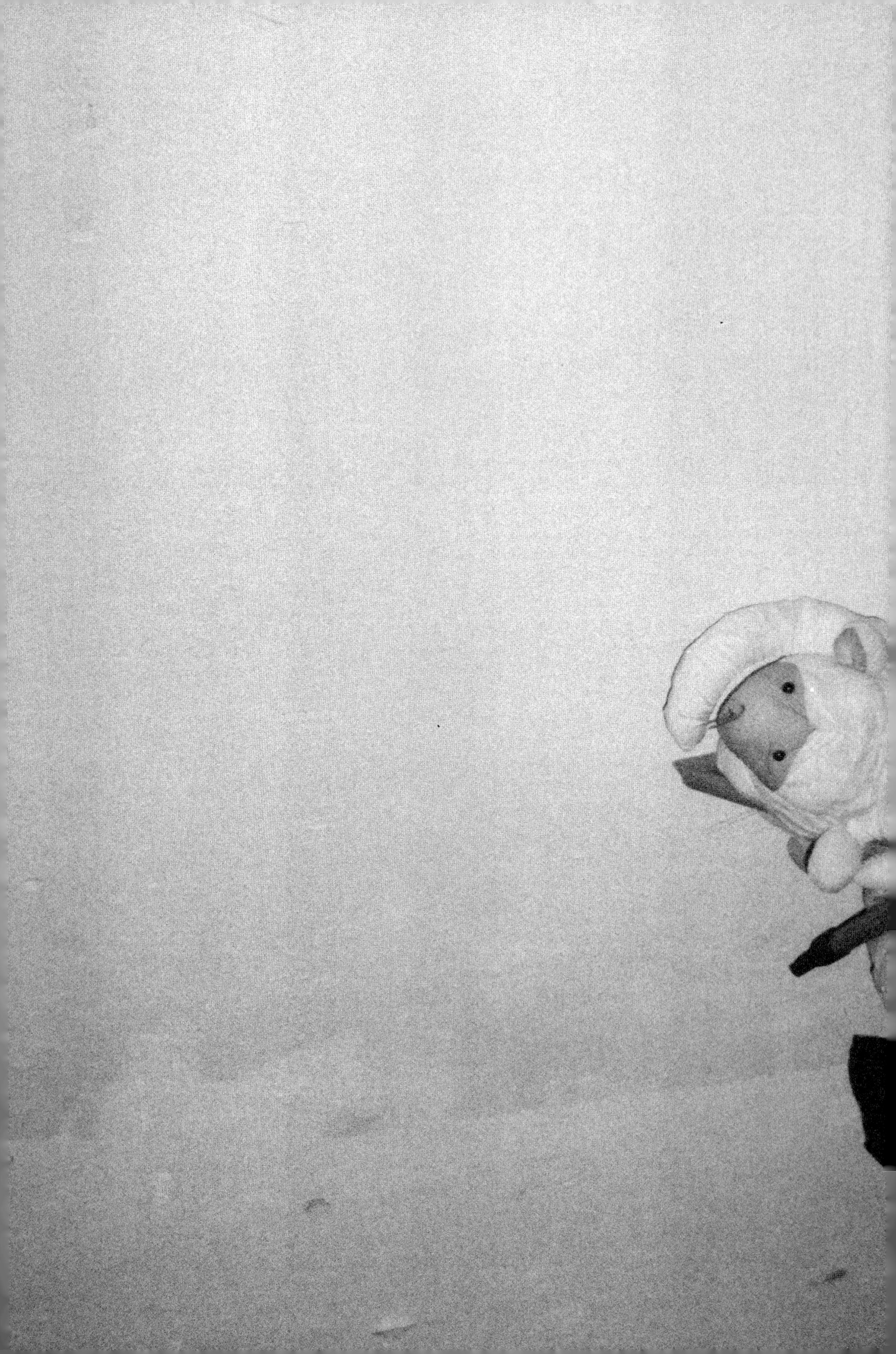

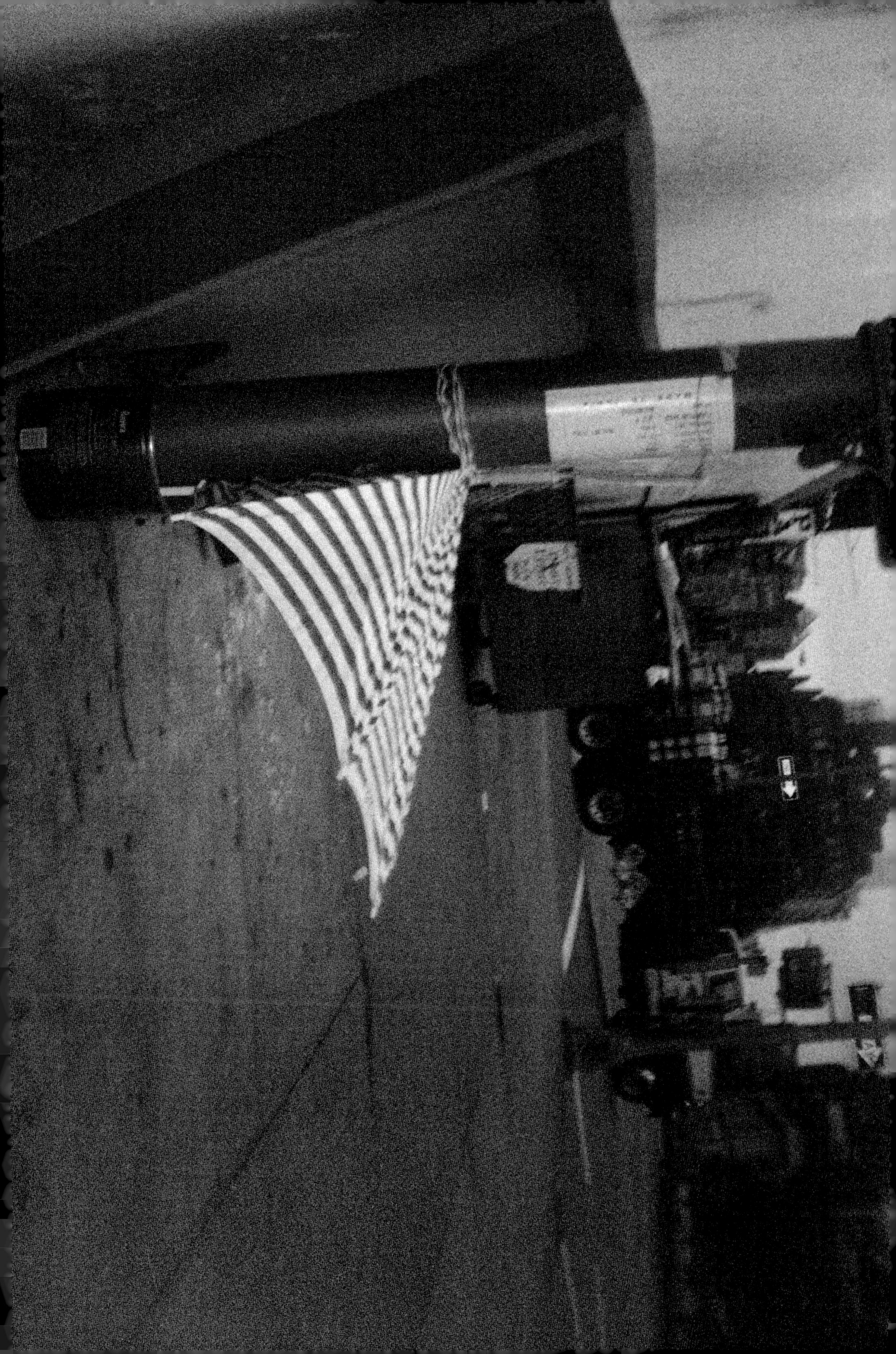

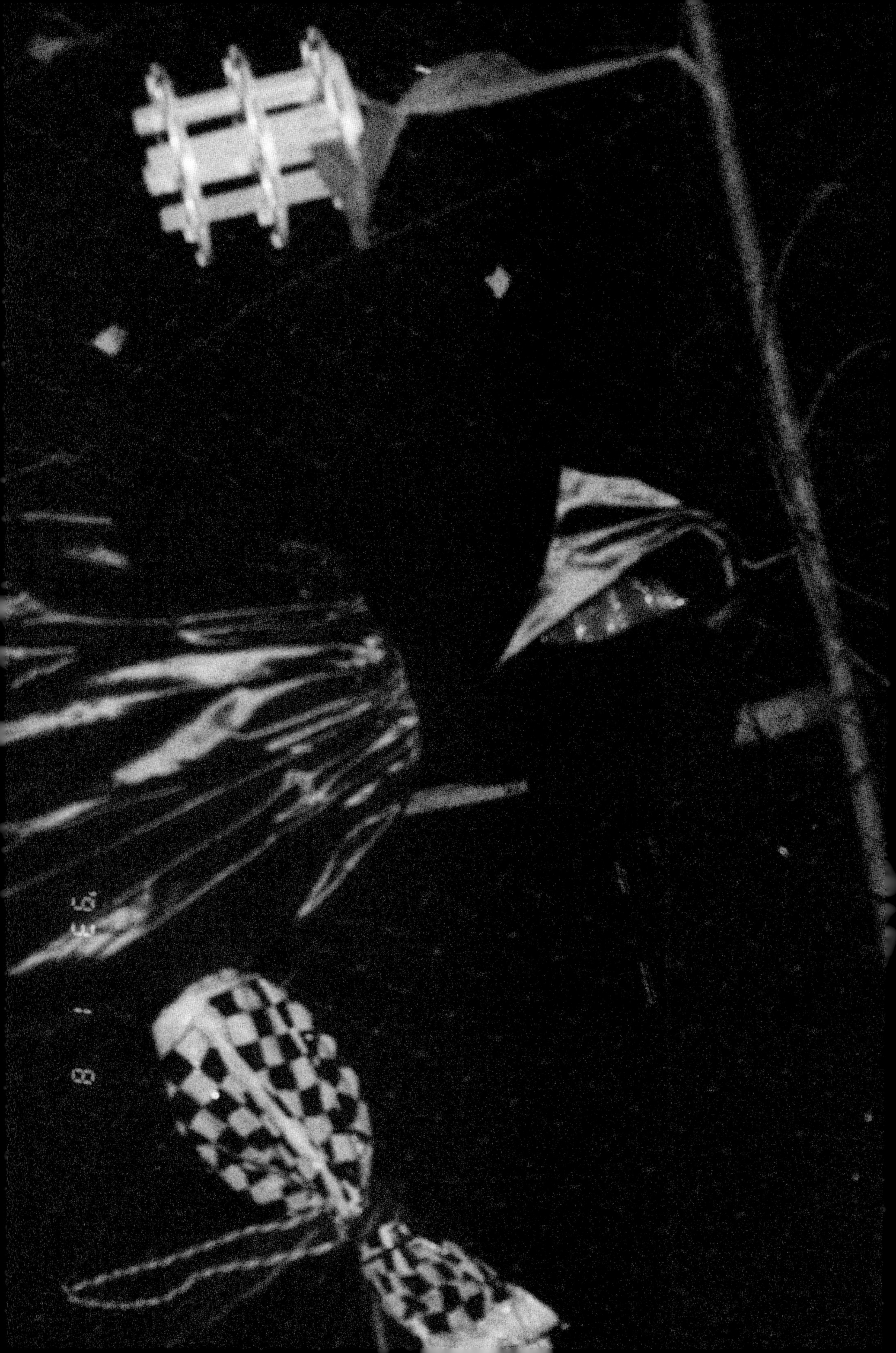

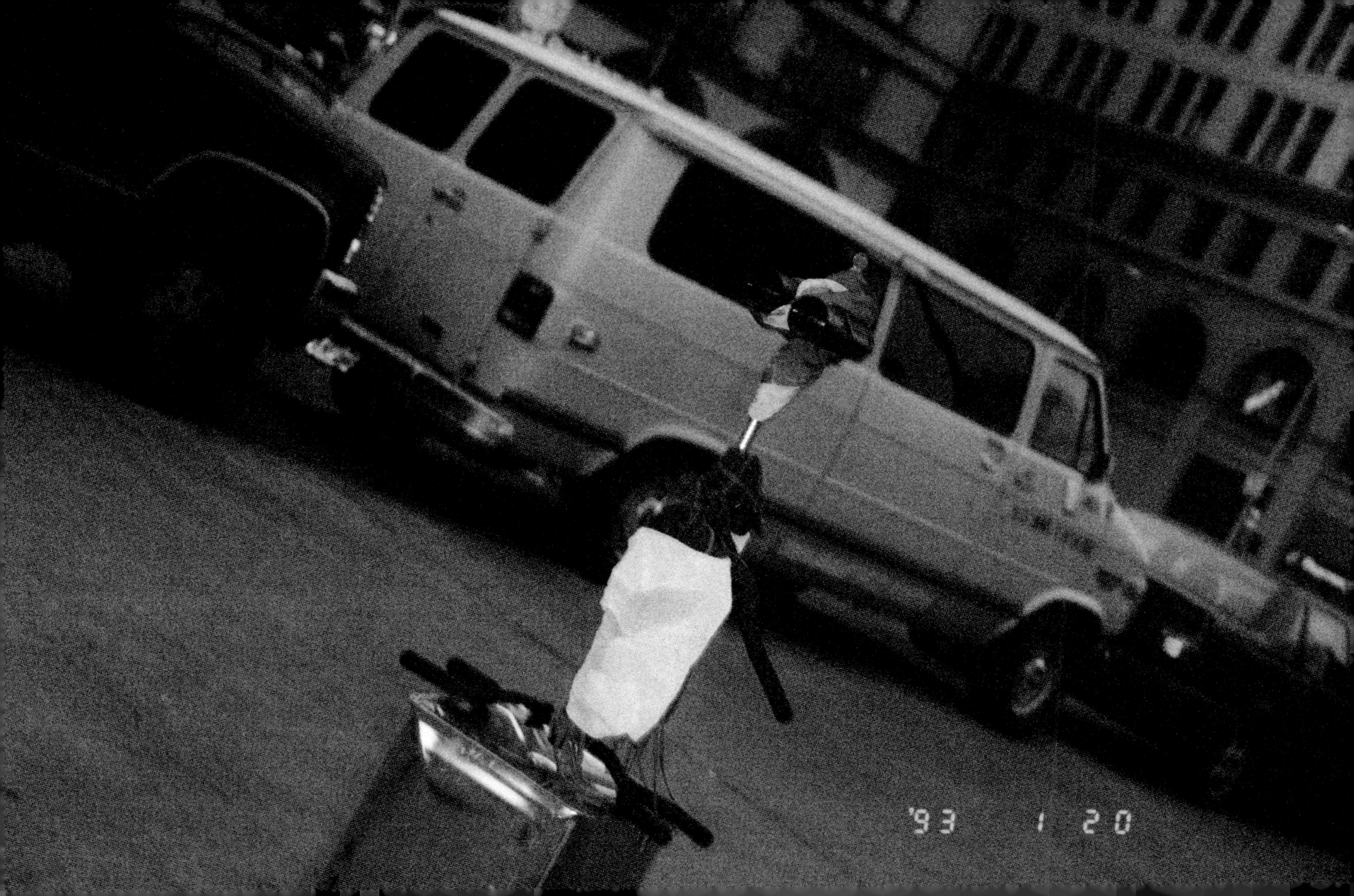
'93 1 20

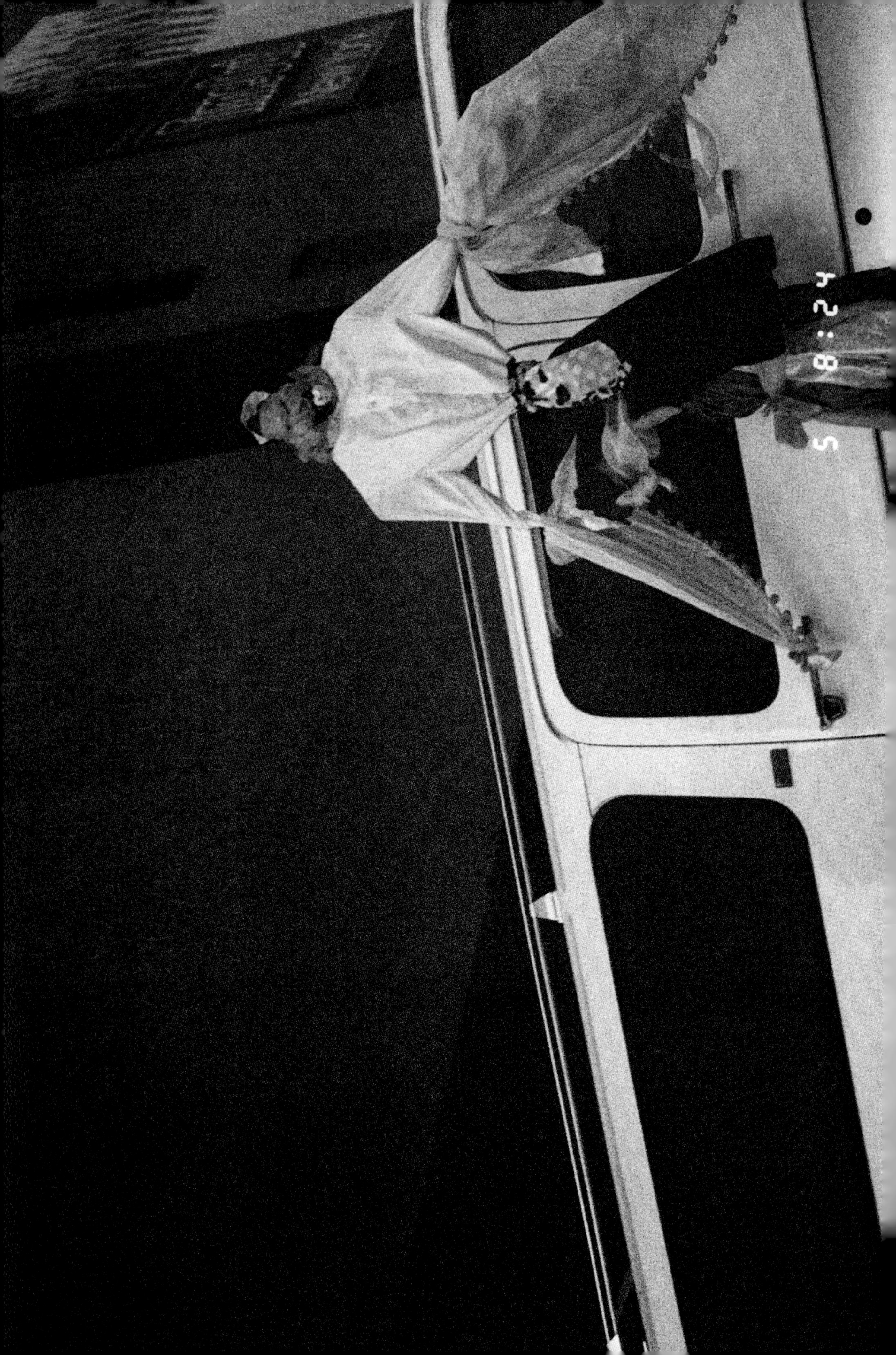

I make sculptures for spaces that need life. I put my art in public places for people to catch love, secrets, and respect. See, art to me is a dream, without being asleep. It comes to me in a puzzle. When I go to sleep it vanishes from me. When I awaken I go seek it in the most unlikely places. The first piece of art I ever made was of turning a mop upside-down. The first thing I noticed was my Grandma's head, face, and hair. So I started putting clothes on it and making a body under the head – the arms, the legs, and the feet. So behind that, it's shown me everything to proceed forward with my art. Little works of art, monuments, invisible art. My art goes in many dimensions. See, being an artist is a very risky profession. You've got to be very deeply concerned with your creation. Not just what you make of your art, but how it affects others. My art is medicine. I want my art to show people that we're all equal. To make the world more fair. I want my art to be like a prophet. Giving the world what it needs. My art gives people company, comforting everybody. It's a very good friend. That's what I hope for.

Curtis Cuffie, 1998

This Trash Should've Been Free
Ciarán Finlayson

"Much of the beauty of Curtis's work," wrote Carol Thompson in a 2002 eulogy, "was in seeing him create it and seeing it unfold from day to day."[1] This book, focusing on Curtis Cuffie's public sculptures, erected and inevitably torn down across the East Village in the 1980s and '90s, presents this beauty as it unfolded in the streets and in photographs taken by the artist himself, his romantic partners, and two professional photographers who lived in the neighborhood. Although Cuffie's artwork was exhibited in galleries, museums, alternative art spaces, and nightclubs, his major venues were the fences, sidewalks, and traffic medians of downtown Manhattan.

"Curtis made art as a daily devotion," Thompson continued, and though many captured his public performances on camera, none did so with the parallel devotion of Katy Abel, who took hundreds of snapshots of Cuffie at work in the mid-'90s.[2] Her intimate collection, which she arranged into dozens of albums for Cuffie's brother Alvin and sister-in-law Peggy after the artist passed, are at the very heart of this book. Abel, born in Greenwich Village, was living in a loft on Cooper Square that she had shared for many years with her former partner, the bassist and composer Sirone (Archie Shepp and Amiri Baraka were their neighbors). For twenty-seven years she worked at the Village Vanguard, in the cloakroom, as a waitress, and as a hostess. She was not, in her words, a photographer; before meeting Cuffie in her late forties, Abel had rarely used a camera in a concerted manner. In fact, the first time she saw his work she ran to grab a colleague to take pictures of it. Upon learning that its maker was a music lover she gifted him a radio. He asked her on a date for Independence Day. As Abel described it, the events of the Fourth were like something from a fairy tale. They met at a safe distance from the crowds, which Cuffie preferred to avoid, and watched the fireworks over the East River. When Abel left to get refreshments, Cuffie converted the shopping cart out of which he lived and worked into a festooned carriage, and upon her return, himself skirted up in an array of patterned fabrics, lifted her onto its mass of pillows and blankets and rushed her down the street, singing "Happy Holiday" to the revelers. Over the years, Cuffie stayed with Abel periodically and stored a number of sculptures in her loft. She would spend hours photographing him as he worked outdoors at different locations in the 1990s and early aughts, both in the city and at her house in Eastern Pennsylvania, where Cuffie once made a sculpture at the edge of her pond to scare off beavers. To her he professed a lack of interest in preserving his most ephemeral works, but he encouraged her photography and empathized with the desire to hold on to things in perpetuity, calling her "Katy the Keeper."[3]

These photographs, shot in and around Cooper Square, the Bowery, and Astor Place, where Cuffie would often erect works at the edge of an unsanctioned flea market subject to near daily police raids, illustrate how the art lived outdoors unprotected from the elements. When viewed in sequence, these images have a way of spoiling the idea of sculpture's fixity, permanence, and separability from the artist. Few of these works held place for very long; most were destroyed by law enforcement, the Department of Sanitation, or the grounds team at the Cooper Union for the Advancement of Art and Science – which would go on to hire Cuffie in 2001.

Cuffie moved to Brooklyn in 1970 at age fifteen, from his hometown Hartsville, South Carolina. He told several versions of this story. In one, he was sent up north after he'd turned into a goat and started eating clothes off his mother's laundry line. In another, he had sneaked into a local meeting of the Ku Klux Klan, seventy miles northeast of the state capital, dressed in a white robe. No harm came when he was discovered, but his family decided it was time for him to go stay with his brother Ernest, a social worker in Brooklyn. Cuffie attended John Jay High School in Park Slope before dropping out in the eleventh grade and working as a truck driver and hand laborer. He married and had three children. When his mother Jessie Bell Cuffie passed in 1983 he's said to have entered a deep and protracted depression, losing stable housing and living around Bryant Park.[4] He relocated to the East Village not long after, where he began to make works of art in public.

Homelessness is foregrounded in nearly all writing about Cuffie, though he was himself chary about discussing it. He told Sarah Ferguson at the *Village Voice* that he wasn't homeless but "holy," and to curator Tom Patterson he described himself as "holy and free."[5] Cuffie once remarked to Thompson on a drive home from Coney Island that the passing houses looked to him like coffins. Reportedly, he refused help accessing public assistance from his friend Darrell Maupin, owner of the East Village restaurant and club Flamingo East, where Cuffie's first solo exhibition was presented in 1992.[6] About his living conditions, he told the *Voice*, "I don't think of this – this street. There is no suffering, no misery, only love."[7]

This book's opening images were taken by Tom Warren, a countercultural photographer who participated in landmark exhibitions at ABC No Rio, capturing the early days of the East Village art scene through makeshift photo studios he set up in bohemian spaces around the city. In his images, mostly black and white and shot with a Contax T between 1992 and 1997, Cuffie's works stand resolutely on their own as objects. Self-contained, they take leave of the disinvested landscape, estranged from the pedestrian spheres of trash and commerce on Astor Place. His approach stands in contrast with that of Margaret Morton, a Cooper Union professor who spent the 1990s documenting the homes of New York City's homeless in the tradition of socially engaged photography. In Morton's lens the work emanates from its environment, and is inseparable from the teeming life of the city and realities of the artist's situation. Morton captured the way Cuffie's "intricate assemblages of used clothing, broken jewelry, discarded toys, ostrich feathers, and advertisements would mysteriously appear and disappear on the chain link fence" across from the school at Fourth Street and Bowery.[8] She was fascinated by the work's ironic qualities, how it made "wry commentary on the excesses of consumerism – even as it was clearly inspired by refuse and waste."[9] It has been said that every Cooper Union student from this period knew and learned from Cuffie, whose sprawling pieces were often installed around the school's premises. Years later Morton's photographs of Cuffie and his art were hung in the school's Great Hall at a memorial held three months after he suffered a fatal heart attack in his East Tenth Street apartment at age forty-seven.[10]

This publication closes with a selection of photos taken by Cuffie himself. Throughout the '90s, the artist used a point and shoot to record his art and environs on more than 100 rolls of film. These remained undeveloped in his lifetime and have been safeguarded, along with much of the rest of his archive, by Thompson, who in addition to being his partner was also the first art historian to produce scholarship on Cuffie's work. When Thompson began this academic writing in 1996, she had left her job as a curator at the Museum for African Art in SoHo to pursue a PhD in Performance Studies at New York University; Cuffie would sit in on classes she was taking, and ones she taught at colleges across the city. He had moved into her sixth-floor walk-up on East Tenth Street that January, shortly after a historic blizzard, alternating between their shared quarters and life out on the Bowery in the early years of their relationship. Forgoing the hazards of New York City's shelter system, he was known to set up camp downtown, above a hot air vent that he named the Sahara and would decorate with floral comforters and dried palm trees.

An artist biography Cuffie and Thompson drafted together describes his work as an urban variation on rural, Southern folk art. In this view, inspired by Robert Farris Thompson's Africanist readings of contemporary Black American art, Cuffie was a yard artist without a yard. Unlike Joe Minter or Lonnie Holley, Cuffie owned no property.[11] His work accumulated on public and disused land: the traffic medium south of Cooper Square, a boarded-up gas station on East Fourth Street, a hurricane fence on the corner of Bowery and Great Jones. After assembling a large piece, or a procession of smaller ones, Cuffie would sell the parts, give them away, or rearrange them until being forced to move along by the police. In 1993, writer Chippy Irvine spoke with him about working in such conditions. "Every now and then, the weather – or the sanitation department – removes all of Cuffie's works and his carts full of the beach towels, place mats, fake flowers, and menus that he uses as material. The last time it happened he was devastated, and went to church to cry. But then he started all over again."[12]

Cuffie's sidewalk sculptures and booming voice had been in Thompson's life since she moved to the East Village in 1988, but they became partof her daily commute when the Center for African Art relocated from the Upper East Side to SoHo five years later. They met when she heard him sing "Little Red Riding Hood" as she walked down the street in a red beret. Thompson helped Cuffie earn recognition within the East Village arts community, curating two solo exhibitions of his work at long-standing Black-owned galleries in the neighborhood. Of their working relationship Thompson wrote, "Curtis has asked meto write his words down, to tell his story, in order to help make his art, in his own words, 'fully respected.' He said, 'Don't paralyze my ego. Keep it plain and simple. I'm a country boy.'"[13] She helped write grants that won him awards and residencies from the New York Foundation for the Arts, the Pollock-Krasner foundation, and the Lower Manhattan Cultural Council.[14] They took regular trips out of town: to South Carolina and Minnesota to visit each other's families; to Maryland to see his work at the American Visionary Art Museum. A research trip to Burkina Faso, however, was blocked by a spiteful parole officer who refused to let Cuffie leave the country over a technicality.

The first solo exhibition Thompson organized with Cuffie took place in 1996 at A Gathering of the Tribes, a space run by writer Steve Cannon at an Alphabet City townhouse he bought in 1970 using money made from his infamous novel, *Groove, Bang, and Jive Around*.[15] Cannon was well known as a community builder and ran his home as a literary salon until his death in 2019. Tribes, remembered by friends and younger poets as "the last crash pad on the Lower East Side," formalized as a nonprofit organization in 1990.[16] Cannon set up a literary arts journal and a writing workshop on his stoop. "The people I knew down on the Lower East Side complained about not having any place to publish their work. . . . So I started *Tribes* magazine . . . Just to get them to shut up."[17] His house would become a venue too, hosting writers and musicians including Ishmael Reed, Bill Gunn, Butch Morris, and Sun Ra. It was funded in part by donations from friends such as David Hammons, who wrote the organization's second supporting check and gave a comment to the *Times* for Cuffie's obituary.

In the summer of 2000, Carol would curate another show of Cuffie's work, "Heaven is Under Your Feet," at 4th Street Photo Gallery, an unassuming storefront rented by South Carolina–born artist Alex Harsley on East Fourth Street and Bowery. Harsley opened the space in 1973, two years after starting the nonprofit organization Minority Photographers, Inc., as a place to congregate and exhibit. In a video Harsley made of the opening, a saxophonist plays amidst an overgrowth of sculpture; the word "LOVE" is written on the wall in shaving cream.[18] Harsley knew Cuffie from the neighborhood and took photos and footage of him making work near the gallery. In one recording made along the wall of the Bowery Bar, the artist spins quickly, tosses the lid of a coffee tin high into the air, spins again, and catches it. He would send these discs into traffic and dodge the oncoming cars. "The name of the top is flying medicine," Cuffie wrote in a note dated July 12, 1997:

> *First, I learned it releases me from being lonely and confused. Three more reasons for the top: confused, angry, bored. It cures my confusion, it entertains my boredom, it takes away my anger. Put it this way, it is like meditation but in action."*[19]

Cuffie's risky antics, loud singing, and Delphic interviews all shaped his public persona. When the pair moved in together Thompson sought professional help for him. Following a period of psychiatric assessment, a doctor suggested to her that he suffered not from schizophrenia, as many had assumed, but from addiction to crack cocaine. In the wake of this realization, Thompson's writing on Cuffie shifted. Unlike the art-historical and local-color profiles he had received in publications such as *Raw Vision* and *Art & Antiques*, she adopted a new, political approach rooted in cultural studies and anti-colonial history. His varied public personalities, relentless generosity, twisting moods, and nearly animistic conceptions of the objects he would find and rearrange, then, were defenses against the difficulties of life on the street, a kind of non-ceremonial spirit possession mediated by the narcotic – an Americanized version of the Hauka movement. His hardships, which manifested in his erratic comportment and ethereal work, were being compounded by the Ronald Reagan and Rudy Giuliani administrations' wars on drugs. Cuffie got sober the following year.

"Once when I walked by, Curtis was standing facing the wall with arms and legs splayed wide, all the while talking loudly to himself as though being arrested by an invisible policeman," Thompson writes.[20] Between the ages twenty-one and forty-two Cuffie was arrested thirty-one times, primarily for gambling (he played three-card monte) and drug possession. Though he rarely discussed this aspect of his life even with close friends, it's expressed in the titles of works such as *Flag with Handcuffs for the Fourth of July*, 1996.

Kenny Schachter, who organized the 1992 Flamingo East show with Maupin, and who from 1991 to 2000 included Cuffie in many buzzy group exhibitions alongside the likes of Sanford Biggers, Rachel Harrison, and Vito Acconci, once appeared in an issue of the Sunday *Times* holding a Cuffie sculpture beneath his arm. The caption, which identified the work as "untitled," upset the artist. "All my works have titles," he said to Thompson, though most often they were bestowed the moment he parted with a piece.[21] Absent titles to guide them, most visitors to his public installations would have been in the presence of the artist, who would, if he wished, lead them through a complex of allegorical narratives:

> *Soft-spoken, almost diffident, Cuffey [sic] offered explanations for his constructions only when pressed.... However, once launched into a description of a particular piece he would literally follow the thread (or ribbon, string or wire) of his thoughts from one three-D tableau to another.... He moved along the sidewalk—his creations stretched along a good 30 feet—and showed me "the kitchen of a reckless life." He banged a few of the cheap ruined sauce pans he'd hooked onto the fence and touched a tattered black negligee, which inspired him to comment "too much sex." Next to it, he said, was the "wife going off on her own." As he spoke, he pointed to the kind of shoulder bag that's given away at trade fairs and conventions. Blaring on its side in big white letters were the words: Service Business Success.... A foot or so away was "the president's phone," a partially disassembled touchstone desktop model neatly installed beneath a large photo of Reagan."*[22]

US presidents recur across Cuffie's interviews and imagery. In particular, Abraham Lincoln, whom Cuffie revered – he traveled with Abel to see the memorial in DC – and Ronald Reagan, ambiguously referred to by Cuffie as the "General."[23] Related to the latter, Cuffie often discussed his own work in salvific tones occasionally portraying himself as sort of '80s evangelist (he once told Sarah Ferguson that he traveled to New York "with Johnny Cash's ministry," which was aimed at those struggling with substance abuse, to run a spiritual recycling program under Reagan).[24] The former president figures not only as a symbol of contemporary faith but as the architect of modern homelessness. Under his administration, the department of Housing and Urban Development had its budget cut by nearly seventy percent. That same period saw the broad introduction of mandatory sobriety as a prerequisite for access to public housing.[25]

The social crisis these policies induced and its effects on the lives of artists are the subjects of much of Alan W. Moore's writing. A 1992 essay by Moore that Cuffie once commended as brilliant closes out this book. It details the successes and shortcomings of the downtown scene's efforts to support the artist's life and rise to the challenge of his work.[26] At this time, Moore had been writing for Tina Anton, whose nonprofit Art on the Edge distributed art supplies to homeless shelters and exhibited and sold the resulting work, and whose commercial gallery, co-run with her husband Aarne, focused on self-taught artists. Moore was also researching Hope Sandrow's Artist and Homeless Collaborative, an initiative at a women's shelter connecting well-known artists with residents to work on public projects; John-Ed Croft's squatted art gallery Chocolate Milk, which showed and sold art by the unhoused; and a theater troupe operating in an encampment beneath the Manhattan Bridge. Moore was himself a member of Collaborative Projects, a democratic artist group that squatted buildings for exhibition space and made polemical, collective work addressing the real estate industry.

In light of this historical interest in art by and about the homeless highlighted by Moore's work, Cuffie's sculptures should be understood not only in terms of their plastic inventiveness – their celebrated contributions to radical assemblage and found-object installation – but within a continuum of East Village contemporaries that includes its squatters, hardcore musicians, and art activists; the community of homeless artists that brought Cuffie to the attention of gallerists; an older generation of Black avant-gardists, and the heady post-conceptualists of lower Manhattan.[27] This confluence structured the downtown scene in which Cuffie's work was first received and provides the context in which it should be understood today. Inspired by the motto engraved in the cornerstone of the Salvation Army Bowery Corp., "Dedicated to the Service of God and Humanity," Cuffie regarded his work as his mission.[28] He was gathering lost souls on St. Mark's Place and offering them a chance at reincarnation; giving mistreated objects new life through elaborate tableaux of dissolution and salvation. But the work is equally concerned with history, intervening on that centuries-old byway of social murder known as the Bowery. In his expressive recasting, the street's disjecta membra become delicate, suspensive constructions "in which a car is no heavier than a straw hat" and no more precious.[29] Cuffie's art, surviving mostly in memory and in these photographs, transgressed the rule of property and transvaluated poverty, both the artist's and the world's, confronting Manhattan's deprivations through its own vagrant, transverberative life.

1
Carol Thompson, untitled speech manuscript, unpaginated. Collection of Carol Thompson.

2
Carol Thompson, untitled speech manuscript, unpaginated. Collection of Carol Thompson.

3
Katy Abel, in discussion with the author, Greenwich Village, New York, February 3, 2023.

4
"Obituaries: Curtis Cuffie, 47, Artist of Life on the Streets," *New York Times*, September 21, 2002.

5
Lynne Browne, "Uncommon Artists X: A Symposium," *Folk Art Messenger* (Spring 2002), 29.

6
Flamingo East on Second Avenue, between Thirteenth and Fourteenth Streets, had an artist's studio upstairs that doubled as a gallery. Cuffie's work appeared in several shows there, all organized by Kenny Schacter, where most of the art was for sale and a portion of the proceeds were set aside for a homeless organization. "At six the restaurant opened, at five we had a staff meal and Curtis came almost every day for eight years to eat with us at the restaurant," Maupin has said. "He was a dear friend, magical . . . the best dressed man in New York, a stylist of all proportions." Darrell Maupin in conversation with Carol Thompson, "Meet Me at the Margin: A Love Affair with Curtis Cuffie," February 14, 2020, for the exhibition "Souls Grown Diaspora" at Apex Art, New York, curated by Sam Gordon, https://youtu.be/mmKVrbUOyM8.

7
Sarah Ferguson, "Artful Dodger," *Village Voice*, June 1, 1993.

8
Margaret Morton, "Curtis Cuffie: An Artist in Public," in *At Cooper Union* (Winter 2003), 39.

9
Margaret Morton, "Curtis Cuffie: An Artist in Public," in *At Cooper Union* (Winter 2003), 39.

10
Three of the medium format photos from the memorial are reproduced on pages 74–75 and 78–80 of this volume.

11
Cuffie visited Holley in Georgia with Jerry Thomas, Jr., an art dealer and former lawyer to Bill Arnett, during one of several trips he took to Atlanta to see Thompson, who had relocated there for a job at the High Museum shortly after September 11, 2001.

12
Chippy Irvine, "Wings of Hope," *Art and Antiques*, December 1994, 70.

13
Carol Thompson, untitled paper for the class "Spirit Possession" with Barbara Browning at New York University, Performance Studies, March 13, 1997, unpaginated. Collection of Carol Thompson.

14
The Cuffie text preceding this essay is a "description of work" written as part of a grant application for Change, Inc., an organization formed by Robert Rauschenberg to help artists cope with financial emergencies.

15
Colin Moynihan, "Steve Cannon, Whose Townhouse was an East Village Salon, Dies at 84," *New York Times*, July 18, 2019.

16
Bob Holman, "Art In Conversation: Ishmael Reed," *The Brooklyn Rail* (March 2023), 33.

17
M. H. Miller, "A Blind Publisher, Poet – and Link to the Lower East Side's Cultural History," *T: The New York Times Style Magazine*, February 9, 2018.

18
A similar inscription graces a storefront gate in a photograph by Cuffie on page 229 of this volume.

19
Carol Thompson read this note aloud in conversation with Darrell Maupin for the event "Meet Me at the Margin: A Love Affair with Curtis Cuffie," February 14, 2020, at Apexart, New York.

20
Carol Thompson, untitled paper for the class "Possession" with Barbara Browning, New York University, Spring 1997, unpaginated. Collection of Carol Thompson.

21
Carol Thompson, in discussion with the author and Robert Snowden, Harlem, New York, August 9, 2022.

22
Phyllis Orrick, "Houston and About," *New York Press*, August 21–27, 1991.

23
Alan W. Moore, "Curtis Cuffie on the Bowery," in *Curtis Cuffie* (New York: Blank Forms Editions, 2023), 244.

24
Sarah Ferguson, "Artful Dodger," *Village Voice*, June 1, 1993.

25
On the legacy of these cuts and mandates today see Tracy Rosenthal, "Inside LA's Homeless Industrial Complex," *The New Republic*, May 19, 2022.

26
Transcribed discussion between Carol Thompson and Curtis Cuffie, November 23, 1997. Collection of Carol Thompson

27
Moore has contrasted the support and attention given to exhibitions such as Martha Rosler's "If You Lived Here" (1987–89) – a discursive, politicized show at Dia Art Foundation's SoHo gallery which brought together activists, politicians, nonprofits, and neighborhood residents – with the comparative neglect shown to contemporary exhibitions in the area's squatted galleries such as Bullet Space (which was itself a major community contributor to "If You Lived Here"). See Alan Moore, *Occupation Culture: Art and Squatting in the City from Below* (New York: Minor Compositions, 2015), 9.

28
Carol Thompson, untitled paper for the class "Museum Theater" with Barbara Kirshenblatt-Gimblett at New York University, Performance Studies, December 18, 1996, unpaginated. Collection of Carol Thompson.

29
Walter Benjamin, "Poverty and Experience," in *Selected Writings*, vol. 2 (Cambridge, Massachusetts: Harvard University Press, 2005), 733.

Curtis Cuffie on the Bowery
Alan W. Moore

I'm on my way up the Bowery last summer when I see this guy sleeping in front of an odd construction strung onto a fence at East Fourth Street. People sleeping on the street are no novelty, not with the recent explosion of homelessness, nor in the near twenty years I've lived on the Bowery, traditional mecca of bums. The impromptu shanty of cardboard, the pile of belongings, some heaped into canvas-sided post office carts are also common sights.

What struck me about this sleeping man's stuff, however, was the artfulness with which it had been arranged. Strung up on the fence, this detritus scavenged from the street was arranged syntactically. The more I looked at these bits of trash, the more layers of meaning were revealed, all created by juxtapositions. The composition was sound and simple, combining forms like barricades, flags, house shapes, and windows. By his feet lay a few rudely shaped pieces of glazed clay, like those made by children; a strange, old, and battered coppery-green vessel with a pipe stuck in it; and a few old books; a beaten aluminum pot stood on a wooden platform nearby. These several objects were placed as if strewn along the sidewalk with the sure touch of a Japanese flower arranger.

There was no question in my mind that what I was seeing was art. But of what kind? I lacked the nerve to wake this man. If he turned out to be a professional artist, say, a Yale MFA doing a street project for the Public Art Fund, I would not have been surprised. Seeing him sleeping like this presented a nearly classic instance of observer determination of meaning in art, indeed its very definition as art, hanging fire.

Art is about who makes it and where it is seen. That this work resembled a fine art–gallery installation of the kind now called "scatter art," sculptural collages made from found materials, "garbage" or "recycled" art is pure coincidence. This coincidence of the times, however, could represent something of a break for Curtis Cuffie, because art is also about who sees it – which is why I set out to write this essay.

I interviewed Curtis for Mitch Corber's poetry cable-TV show the day after I saw him asleep. My main impression was of a man with great charm and energy. Of course he was "on," and had been looking forward to the interview since I spoke with him the day before. He said he composed his work – which he quite definitely viewed as art – according to a sacred logic gleaned from the letters of signs on the street, including the partially intact sign on the abandoned gas station before which he'd made his construction. His rap was heavily larded with loose Christian references, as well as mentions of Kennedys and "General Reagan," the "antique."

Curtis transformed our meeting into a happy half hour of play, scampering about, setting up his couch, pulling his cart about. I was moved by the intensity of his delight in having a media audience of sorts. He's playful in the way he handles his objects and the connections he makes, and his work indeed refers insistently to childhood, to mother, to a regular home life long ago. While enthusiastic, he was also quite circumspect and elliptical, interspersing his talk with snatches of popular songs for emphasis. Curtis fished objects from one of his canvas-sided containers and performed combinations for Mitch's camera, turning a tennis ball, an old wicker basket, and a cup into an impromptu game. The things he produced from the can were both ordinary and remarkable: old food containers, children's ceramics, a fragment of a Chinese carved-ivory bowl. He said he kept nice items mixed in with trash so people wouldn't steal them. Nothing he puts out, he said, is for sale. He asks people to give him donations for the work he does as a whole. I gave him ten dollars for the interview.

That was the easy part. There are some very wide gulfs between us, however, which lie along the way of considering Curtis Cuffie's art. Curtis says he's from South Carolina, that he came here twenty years ago, and drove tractors and trucks. As a working-class African American homeless man, his speech is substantially unintelligible to me, a middle-class WASP. Only in playing the tape back again and again was I able to understand what he said. "The first thing I learned on the streets was caution." Although I have long hair, the people with whom Curtis has had the most contact who look like me are probably priests and cops, which has to have had a lot to do with how he reacted to me.

Cuffie's is the kind of art that is usually denominated as "folk," or more recently, "outsider" art. Recent writing has named a particular group of contemporary rural, mostly black American outsider artists (for example, Mose Tolliver, Jimmy Lee Sudduth, the white Reverend Howard Finster), yet the rubric of "folk" is still largely used to describe what is sold in antique shops, not art galleries. This is a commercial category of exhausted elasticity, encompassing handmade tools and carved portrait heads; amateur paintings, both laborious and slapdash; handicrafts reflecting the broad circulation of yesterday's popular crafts magazines; and, ultimately, much art that is simply anonymous. At its most degraded, "folk art" can mean simply "old, handmade, function unknown." This broad and fluid group of objects can be fascinating to consider, but usually only on a level of historical fantasy; because what links nearly all of them is an utter absence of context: they are by nobody and from nowhere. This is not only a failure of living memory. Antique dealers, even more than art dealers, are loath to deal with a live maker. They buy their wares primarily from the dead, or more properly, their uninterested heirs, and live for the unrecognized rarity that can be had on the cheap. Everything else is just "merch," and it comes by the box lot. There is every reason why vernacular culture is anonymous. Just as every effort is made to identify the makers of high art, salon paintings, bronzes, and the like, to identify a "listed artist" vaults your object into a realm of agreed-upon value, generally reflected in published auction lists. Anonymous and stripped of context, folk art and handicrafts become purely decorative objects, components of decor, with connotations mayhap remote from their original intention.

A living contemporary urban homeless street artist is not what dealers or collectors of folk art are looking for. So, despite what seemed to me the fascinating instance of a person of rural southern origins responding to the situation of homelessness with powerfully expressive collage artworks, i.e., what appears to be a remarkable bridging of rural traditions with urban realities, there was little interest from that quarter. Instead the response came from contemporary artists, particularly those involved in New York City's avant-garde. (Curiously it was the interest of advanced artists in vernacular expressions that revalued folk art early in this century.)

After I told the peripatetic artist Dan Asher about Curtis, a swirl of activity began around him. The art dealer Andrea Rosen photographed his work, although she did not include him in a fall exhibition of scatter-art installations. Independent curator Kenny Schachter put two of Cuffie's pieces in a show at the nightclub Flamingo East in July, and Asher placed one he owned in Dooley Le Cappellaine Gallery's large and well-attended September group exhibition, "Values." In late August, Curtis was profiled in the downtown weekly *New York Press*.

At the same time, the street was proving a problematic exhibition space for Curtis. He'd antagonized a resident next door, and she complained daily to officials of Cooper Union, the nearby school that owns the parking lot Curtis had decorated. Beat cops told him to move, and when he didn't they demolished his constructions. He relocated a block south to another fenced empty lot, but the police continued to pull his works apart, until the owners of that lot finally hired a crew to clean it and nearly all of Curtis's work was thrown into a dumpster. In early 1992 I saw Cuffie's single shopping cart moored alongside the huge parking lot opposite Cooper Union, an impossibly tenuous situation.

As I watched Curtis leaving the show at Flamingo East to take a ride back to his street corner in artist John LeKay's car, I had a simultaneous feeling of happiness that we were "doing something" for him, and a bald presentiment that it would not work. Some efforts have been made in tribute to Cuffie's genius, but artists, critics, and curators are not social workers, nor are any of us in a position to support him. The system of exhibition, promotion, and sale of artwork operates in the anteroom of wealth, "on the grounds," as it were, of the palace. Jackson Pollock may have pissed in Peggy Guggenheim's fireplace, but rowdiness as a rule is not allowed. Curtis is not always an easy person to be around. He can be relentless in demanding money on the street; one visitor to his display reported him avidly consuming a pipeful of crack (performed with typical Cuffie aplomb – he said, "I'm going to take your picture," then dodged under a black cloth from whence issued clouds of smoke). Curtis doesn't seem to have much of a chance at a real art career. What works in the street doesn't in the salon.

Cuffie surely has his share of human failings, yet he remains an artist of extraordinary plastic inventiveness whose work is consistently fresh, surprising, and winsome. To an extent he played well to the ideal of the pure artist, as described in the Bhagavad Gita 4:19–20, "He whose undertakings are free from anxious desire and fanciful thought . . . such a man in truth has peace: he expects nothing, he relies on nothing, and ever has fullness of joy." Dan Asher saw Cuffie's work as very nonmaterialistic, and certainly Curtis foregrounded its religious significance in his explanations. John LeKay said Curtis had "cut through all the bullshit we have to deal with." As we discussed how we might assist him, LeKay commented, "He's probably happier than we are."

When I met him Curtis told me beatifically, "Nothing is for sale, take whatever you want; people take things and that's all right." Later it became clear that he sold things all the time and aggressively cadged money, still I think what he first said to me was the way he felt a true artist should operate, that is, it was consonant with his own ideals. Regardless of his character, even those who'd have nothing to do with Cuffie continued to profess admiration for his work.

When I first saw it I experienced the rare phenomenon of new eyes: a sudden and prolonged understanding of the ravaged, trash-strewn Bowery and Houston Street neighborhood as beautiful. With its antique and second-hand stores and vendors of used kitchen fixtures, the area is a magnet for rubbish. Piles of it continually appear and vanish on streetcorners, changing as they are picked over by street vendors who carry things away to sell in better-trafficked locations.

In the accumulations of refuse peculiar to these streets are strong accidental contrasts of color and form, patterns of vacancy, the ruins of novelty. The dynamic of successive rejections is constantly in operation, certifying true valuelessness – the thing that is broken past repair, rejected by many.

This protean flux of refuse on New York City streets is one of the town's most salient features. Consistent and persistent waste is the byproduct of wealth, of tremendous consumption. Waste heat, waste food, and building materials, waste goods to sell – all this enables the homeless to make a life on the streets instead of inside shelters. The disposal of trash here is more a matter of public display as it is picked over by people looking for something to use or sell. Those who do this are plying an age-old trade; in the nineteenth century rag-pickers bid competitively for the right to pore through municipal wastes. Today it is the abjectly poor – the homeless – who sift the trash, and not all of them are good at it, which is to say not all can recognize what is appealing in what has been discarded.

It seems reasonable to assume that Curtis's displays have evolved out of the commercial displays of the Bowery trash pickers, those who spread their found "wares" on the sidewalk for passing crowds. But he has gone way beyond that since he chooses not only things of evident value but things that appeal to him, things that he can use in his constructions. Most of this waste of course is packaging, the rind of consumer desire, emptied shells with commercial appeals which Cuffie's contexts make amusing, funny, pathetic, or disturbing. In his art Cuffie makes his statements with a syntax of discarded items that is very clear, eloquent, and truthful concerning his homelessness and what a home and family are. As a homeless non-person he really has no past and no future. Instead, since there are no expectations of him, he has been free to reinvent himself as an artist, and a larger-than-life character while he is about it.

Curtis's expressions perform best in their street environment. His constructions are not easily disassembled into discrete objects without robbing them of their power (although this has never deterred commodifiers from disassembling artists' environments for sale). Just to consider how he might be fit into any existing programs for the homeless, even those run by artists, revealed how standalone and self-sufficient the work he's doing is.

Homelessness is a topic of concern to the art community. Exhibitions address the topic, art is made on the theme, and numerous artists have worked with the homeless. This work, however, is about the homeless not by them. In "dealing" with the topic, artists can try to make the problem better known, the victims appear more human, and themselves feel better – but they can't really ameliorate conditions. A manifestly talented and productive homeless artist producing large-scale sidewalk installations is a remarkable epiphenomenon, not part of this expressive agenda. A secret conflict, like the artists' jealous hold on the patent of artmaking, lies at the heart of my difficulty in writing this account and in all my dealings with Curtis. The ideology, practice, and apprehension of art to which I am devoted is only fitfully congruent with its system of exhibition and promotion, which is determined by the social and economic realities of American life. An artist like Curtis Cuffie is by any measure I have interesting and significant, yet he seems unassimilable by the present art system. Such an expectation of course is foolish, since a mercantile system rewards talent occasionally and cleaves to principle, be it moral or aesthetic, only tangentially.

Finally, Curtis Cuffie is a pure artist, indifferent to a system from which he is excluded by class and social position. Despite taking him on briefly as a "case," my inability to do anything much for him stripped bare not only the structural failings of the "artworld support system" – or perhaps only my lack of cleverness in manipulating it – it also exposed the close-drawn limits of my own response to art, a predilection for happy home and settled life with art on the walls, not on the streets.

I saw a man with inner tubes wrapped around his neck like a cravat, another pushing a shopping cart full of shiny trash and flashing traffic barrier lights, and heard about one who takes garbage out of street containers and then carefully replaces it in a kind of slow public performance. All of these homeless people might be said to emulate the high art of their times as it has been filtered through popular media for two decades, producing trauma-born folk art that validates the high by reflecting it from the lower depths. That is a self-serving explanation, since the reasons that folk or vernacular art is made do not easily take their place in panoramic art historical systems. The contemporary artist is like the coy maiden who maintains chastity (i.e., uncompromised integrity) until the advantageous match presents itself; these street artists are nuns. It really isn't difficult to make art of some kind, yet very few try it, make expressive arrangements, convey something about their experience. To be making art out of garbage on the street is a gift of ephemeral magic, and, like weaving a rope out of sand, a meditative action out of principle.

1992

Curtis Cuffie

ISBN 978-1-953691-15-6
First edition

Image Editors
Scott Portnoy and Robert Snowden
with Julie Peeters

Text Editor
Ciarán Finlayson

Designer
Julie Peeters

Copyeditors and Proofreaders
Lily Bartle, Max Fox

Photographers
Katy Abel, Curtis Cuffie, Margaret Morton,
Carol Thompson, Tom Warren

Lithographer
Daniel Samulevič

Printer
Benedict Press, Schwarzach am Main,
Germany

Blank Forms Editions is produced with support from the Robert Rauschenberg Foundation, the Andy Warhol Foundation for the Visual Arts, Agnes Gund, and the founding Blank Forms Publisher's Circle including Jane Hait and Justin Beal, Christian Nyampeta, Linden Renz, and Charline von Heyl and Christopher Wool. Additional support for *Curtis Cuffie* was generously provided by Galerie Buchholz.

Special thanks to Katy "Piggy" Abel, Tina White and Aarne Anton, Carol Thompson, and Tom Warren for sharing their time and collections. Additional thanks to Daniel Buchholz and Christopher Müller, Rhea Anastas, Peter Currie, Stella Cilman, John Drury, Fernanda Escalera, Robert Funk, Michael Galinksy, Jody Graf, Samuel Hindolo, Arthur Jafa, Ruba Katrib, Darrell Maupin, Alan W. Moore, Carter Seddon, Chloe Truong-Jones, the Margaret Morton Testamentary Trust, Kenny Schachter, Chavisa Woods, and Bonnie Yochelson.

Front cover: Katy Abel, color, ca. 1994–96
Rear cover: Carol Thompson, black and white, ca. 1990–90

Blank Forms Artistic Director
Lawrence Kumpf

Blank Forms Managing Editor
Ciarán Finlayson

Blank Forms Editions
468 Grand St. Unit 3D
Brooklyn, NY, 11238
www.blankforms.org

Photo credits by page

1–15, Tom Warren, black and white, 1992–97
17–19, Tom Warren, color, 1997
21–31, Tom Warren, black and white, 1992–96
33–70, Katy Abel, color, ca. 1994–96
73, Tom Warren, black and white, 1992
74–75, Margaret Morton, black and white, ca. 1992
77, Tom Warren, black and white, 1993
78–79, Margaret Morton, black and white, ca. 1992
80, Margaret Morton, black and white, ca. 1992, detail
82–103, Katy Abel, color, ca. 1994–96
105–111, Tom Warren, black and white, 1992–95
113–183, Katy Abel, color, ca. 1994–96
185–190, Tom Warren, black and white, 1994–96
193–197, Curtis Cuffie, black and white, ca. 1990–99
198–200, Carol Thompson with Curtis Cuffie's camera, ca. 1990–99
201–234, Curtis Cuffie, black and white, ca. 1990–99